# HYPNOANALYSIS

*By* **LEWIS R. WOLBERG, M.D.**
*Lecturer in Psychiatry, New York Medical College.*

*Foreword by* **A. KARDINER, M.D.,** *Assistant Clinical Professor of Psychiatry, Columbia University.*

GROVE PRESS, INC. · · · NEW YORK

*Grove Press Books and Evergreen Books*
*are published by Barney Rosset at Grove Press, Inc.*
*64 University Place, New York 3, N. Y.*

*Distributed in Canada by McClelland & Stewart Ltd.*
*25 Hollinger Road, Toronto 16*

*To my children*
*Barbara and Ellen*

# CONTENTS

# FOREWORD

IT IS to the enduring credit of Charcot that he compelled the learned men of Paris to admit that hypnosis deserved recognition as a natural phenomenon and not as a manifestation of diabolical possession. Up to that time it had been necessary to reconcile hypnosis with the theological rather than the scientific conception of man. The consequence was that the practice of hypnosis was limited to charlatans and tricksters. Charcot made hypnosis—and incidentally hysteria—respectable. In fact, Charcot at first used hypnosis to elucidate the nature of hysteria by demonstrating that by means of hypnosis he could create an artificial hysteria. The concept of suggestion was the distillate of hypnotic practice. In the wake of this recognition, hypnosis began to flourish as a therapeutic technic. Excellent schools, notably those of Liébault and Bernheim, grew up in pursuit of the aims of suggestive therapy. But they were occupied with problems of technic in the induction of hypnosis, believing that the reason for the unevenness of its results lay in this sphere. Since this was a practice that had no theoretic basis, no questions were necessary if it worked, and if it failed no questions could be asked.

It is often forgotten that Freud was a pupil of Charcot and learned much from Liébault and Bernheim. Psychoanalysis was an answer to the failures of hypnosis: it was an effort to circumvent these impasses arising during hypnotic treatment. The method that Breuer called catharsis was the direct consequence of the failures of hypnotic suggestion. What happened to the method of catharsis we now know. Hypnosis was wrecked on the reefs of resistance, and it was the investigation of this latter phenomenon that led to the method of dealing with resistance through the avenue of free association. This effort also led to the discovery that the dynamism of repression lies at the root of the peripheral manifestation of resistance, and specific technics had to be devised for coping with this factor in turn. It had long been known that hypnotic suggestion failed more often than not and at best was a blind implement, the operation of which could not be controlled. Later Ferenczi made a noteworthy contribution to our knowledge of hypnosis by showing that although it is a natural phenomenon, it has in itself a content—a regression to an infantile state of abject dependency on a parental object—and hence can be reconciled with the phenomenon of transference.

Meanwhile, psychoanalysis as a systematic therapy, apart from its function as systematic psychopathology, has had more than half a century of trial. During this time, under the initiative of Freud as well as of others, many attempts have been made to advance the knowledge of the pathology in the interest of therapeutic efficiency. In spite of all these attempts, psychoanalysis is still an uncertain weapon of therapy, even though as a general psychology and system of pathology it has no peer today.

It is under the lash of some of the therapeutic failures of psychoanalysis that there has been in recent years a revival of interest in hypnosis as an adjunct to psychoanalytic therapy. Recently there have been new, important discoveries concerning its usefulness in exploring the unconscious. Technical innovations designed to bring about specific age level regressions by means of hypnosis, have had intrinsic value, as well as the value of demonstrating points long ago established by Freud. While no reliable theory about hypnosis exists today, it has made giant strides in the domain of technic. It remains to be seen whether these technical devices can be put to some constructive use in systematic therapy. Without psychoanalysis, however, it would be impossible to interpret the new data revealed by modern hypnotic technics, or to direct these technics to the solution of pressing problems in scientific psychodynamics and psychotherapy.

In recent years there have appeared several reports on the subject of hypnoanalysis. Most of them were unfortunately written by authors whose knowledge of pathology was too limited to guide the process or to distil from the experience some instructive principles, without which any technic remains a hit-and-miss procedure.

The present book contains a report on a hypnoanalysis. It has many tangible advantages over its predecessors. It is possible to reconstruct, from the protocol, the dynamics of a definite change in the functional organization of the patient. Moreover, the record of this transition, and the dynamics for which it can be mined, correspond to well established principles in psychodynamics. In addition, it is possible to formulate from it a specific bill of particulars with regard to what hypnosis does or does not do, at what specific junctures it gives material help and where it fails. And, finally, it is possible to reconstruct the scaffolding of the pathologic structure with considerable precision and to follow this structure through the experimental conditions created by the treatment. The report presents a fairly complete picture of one specific schizophrenic personality. These features of the book render it highly worthy of attention and study. The technical aspects of the experiment show its author to be possessed of a fine therapeutic acumen and of an uncommon technical virtuosity.

A. KARDINER

*New York City*
*August 1945*

# PREFACE

THERE IS an urgent need in psychiatry for an abbreviated form of therapy applicable to patients who are unable to avail themselves of prolonged treatment. Existent therapies include suggestion, persuasion, guidance, confession and mental ventilation, reassurance, re-education, desensitization and the correction of remediable elements in the patient's environment that have a destructive effect on his adjustment.

Such therapies admittedly are superficial, but they are justified by the fact that they often eliminate sources of stress and put a halt to behavior that brings the individual into conflict with others. They provide furthermore a medium for the most effective operation of whatever spontaneous forces of mental health remain. A brief period of psychotherapeutic treatment in which the patient receives understanding and help from the therapist, in which he relieves himself of the burden of guilt that has tortured him, may establish the beginnings of more profound mental change. There are some patients who, on the basis of a few interviews, get sufficient strength to carry on with their daily routines and even to attain an understanding of some of their compulsive neurotic drives and disorganized interpersonal relationships.

Unfortunately, insights gained through brief psychotherapy —so far as most of the forms of it are concerned—are so shallow that they scarcely touch upon the deeper sources of maladjustment. Difficulties rooted in unconscious conflict or in inimical experiences in the past go untreated, and while the patient makes a more tolerable adjustment to his environment, his characterologic defects remain. His inordinate demands on people, his undermined self-esteem, and his fears of the world continue to generate tension and anxiety that necessitate the elaboration of neurotic defense mechanisms.

The chief fault of most current brief psychotherapeutic methods is that they accept the deeper personality strata that foster a neurosis as a "liability" that cannot be altered. Efforts are directed to dealing with environmental forces that stir up the individual's liabilities and produce conflict. Without question, neurotics get themselves enmeshed in situations that create anxiety. The therapist can often detect the situations that cause trouble and can show the patient how to pattern his life around his weaknesses. For instance, the individual may have a problem involving compulsive ambition, and may fail in his customary work to reach the level of his expectations. Advising the patient to seek an occupation sufficiently below his aptitudes to permit of success may remove sources of tension.

This type of therapy is of course merely palliative and does not tackle the real problem as to why it is necessary for the patient to function masterfully on all occasions. A more rational form of treatment would be directed to determining what function the patient's character strivings serve in his psychic economy. Neurosis has its origins in defects in human relationships. An approach that investigates how the individual operates as a psychobiologic unit in an interpersonal setting offers the best chance of understanding the meaning of his neurotic collapse.

Psychoanalysis is by far the most elaborate form of relationship therapy. Through interpretation of the patient's free associations, his dreams, and his transference to the analyst, an attempt is made to arrive at an understanding of how experiences and conditionings of his early life are determining his emotional reactions in the present. The ultimate aim of psychoanalysis is a reintegration of the individual in his relationships to the world, to people, and to himself.

Psychoanalysis unfortunately has many practical drawbacks. As a major psychotherapeutic procedure, it is not indicated in all forms of emotional illness. It is both time-consuming and expensive; and there are relatively so few analytically trained physicians that the vast numbers of emotionally ill people cannot avail themselves of its benefits.

In recognition of the urgent need for a briefer form of psychoanalysis, an increasing number of analysts are experimenting with modified analytic technics.[1] Some analysts are convinced that psychoanalytic therapy can be applied to patients seen at infrequent intervals and over a relatively short period of time. Unfortunately, in a great many cases brief therapy scarcely suffices to penetrate the resistances that keep the patient from interacting freely with the therapist.

In recent years work in hypnosis by Erickson,[2-8] Eisenbud,[9] Kubie,[10] Lindner,[11] Gill and Brenman,[12] and Fisher[13] has indicated that hypnosis has possibilities as a psychotherapeutic method and that it possesses certain advantages over other brief forms of therapy. Standardized technics have not yet been worked out, nor is it known to what extent hypnosis may be valuable in the various syndromes. Nevertheless, hypnosis is rapidly being recalled from the limbo of departed therapies and is achieving a stature such as it has not enjoyed since its eclipse at the turn of the century.

Much of the current use of hypnosis is still along palliative lines. There have been reports of many cases of functional illness apparently ameliorated by hypnotic suggestion. Consequently there has developed a wave of optimism concerning the therapeutic possibilities of suggestive hypnosis far out of proportion to its actual worth. This is not to say that hypnotic suggestion cannot effect important changes, particularly in hysterical disorders. In some instances, suggestion promotes a rapid and even miraculous disappearance of symptoms. These happy results are, however, rare.

Emphasis on the uncovering of traumatic memories is a more rational approach. The content of many hysterical, obsessional, and compulsive symptoms may be determined by experiences and conditionings in the patient's past. In such patients the recovery of forgotten memories either through direct recall in the hypnotic state, or through recall and reenactment in the hypnotically induced regressive state, or through hypnotically stimulated automatic writing, drawing, play therapy, crystal gazing, and dreams, may cause a symptom to vanish. Any individual who has witnessed the dramatic cessation of certain symptoms through the recall of a traumatic experience cannot help being impressed by this phenomenon. However, hypnotic recall of repressed memories is not always successful, because the repression often serves an important function in protecting the patient against anxiety. The resistance to recall will maintain the amnesia even in the deepest somnambulistic states. One can spend many frustrating hours in a vain attempt to enucleate experiences that the patient in desperation may finally manufacture. Furthermore, the enucleation of repressed memories and experiences, even when successful, will, in most neurotic conditions, not effect cure.

Recent experimental work[14-19] with hypnosis as a method of inducing artificial conflict and of investigating many complex aspects of behavior has demonstrated that hypnosis brings out transference phenomena rapidly and in relatively pure culture. The patient reacts to the hypnotic relationship with deep inner strivings and fears, with defenses and resistances such as occur in a psychoanalytic relationship. In addition to facilitating transference, hypnosis aids in removal of resistance and in absorption and assimilation of interpretations. Hypnosis thus becomes an interpersonal experience that can have more vitalizing values for the patient than any curative suggestions implanted in his susceptible mind.

Many questions arise concerning the utility, dangers, and limitations of hypnoanalysis. Can it actually shorten the psychoanalytic process? Are the results permanent? What types of cases are responsive to the method? May not hypnosis introduce into the transference a foreign element that will interfere with a therapeutic interpersonal relationship? Will hypnosis make the patient dependent upon the analyst and in this way tend to infantilize him? Is there not a danger of precipitating psychosis in schizoid persons? May not the therapist's preoccupation with the more unconscious aspects of cognition and feeling during the trance lead to neglect of conscious and rational aspects of the personality? Does not hypnosis overemphasize the enucleation of traumatic memories or experiences and restrict therapy to a superficial catharsis? Can hypnoanalysis deal with the character structure itself and can it influence favorably the way in which the individual relates himself to others? Is the ego itself involved in the therapy and can it be strengthened by hypnoanalysis?

A complete answer to all of these questions is not possible at the present time, because hypnoanalysis is a relatively new science. Nevertheless, this book attempts to answer them as thoroughly as experiences with the method up to this date warrant. Without doubt many additions to and revisions of the theoretic and practical aspects of hypnoanalysis will be made as more is learned about the method.

A word of caution may not be amiss. Hypnoanalysis is no cure-all. It has definite values, but it will not move mountains. Failures occur with hypnoanalysis as they do with any other psychotherapeutic method. It is essential to stress this repeatedly, because several observers in their enthusiasm over certain effects of hypnosis on the psyche have credited it with powers that it does not possess. Whether we like it or not, there are a number of emotional conditions so malignant that they cannot be influenced readily by any known form of therapy. Resistance to getting well, whether due to anxiety associated with a reorganization of interpersonal attitudes, or merely to a refusal to relinquish the secondary gains derived from the illness, may constitute an insurmountable block to recovery. Some persons respond to hypnoanalysis when they have failed to respond to other psychotherapies. This is a far cry from saying that all patients can be helped or cured.

An attitude of scientific conservatism is justifiable, because overvaluation of hypnoanalysis will consign the method to the same scrap heap of decadent therapies that engulfed hypnosis in past periods when its virtues were exalted to absurdity. Hypnoanalysis holds promise of becoming an invaluable adjunct to psychoanalysis, but it must be explored more thoroughly before its complete scientific worth can be fully evaluated. The present volume is presented as a contribution in that direction.

Acknowledgment is herewith made to Dr. Charles Fisher, Dr. Milton H. Erickson, Dr. Margaret Brenman, and Dr. Merton M. Gill for reading the original manuscript and offering many helpful suggestions.

*New York City* L. R. W.
*August 1945*

# REFERENCES

1. CHICAGO INSTITUTE FOR PSYCHOANALYSIS: Proceedings of the Brief Psychotherapy Council, Oct. 25-26, 1942.

2. ERICKSON, M. H.: The investigation of a specific amnesia. Brit. J. M. Psychol. *13:* 143-50, 1933.

3. IDEM: A study of experimental neurosis hypnotically induced in a case of ejaculatio praecox. Brit. J. M. Psychol. *15:* 34-50, 1935.

4. IDEM: Development of apparent unconsciousness during hypnotic reliving of a traumatic experience. Arch. Neurol. & Psychiat. *38:* 1282-88, 1937.

5. IDEM: Hypnotic investigation of psychosomatic phenomena: A controlled experimental use of hypnotic regression in the therapy of an acquired food intolerance. Psychosom. Med. *5:* 67-70, 1943.

6. IDEM AND HILL, L. B.: Unconscious mental activity in hypnosis—psychoanalytic implications. Psychoanalyt. Quart. *13:* 60-78, 1944.

7. IDEM AND KUBIE, L. S.: The permanent relief of an obsessional phobia by means of communications with an unsuspected dual personality. Ibid. *8:* 471-509, 1939.

8. IDEM: The successful treatment of a case of acute hysterical depression by a return under hypnosis to a critical phase of childhood. Ibid. *10:* 583-609, 1941.

9. EISENBUD, J.: Psychology of headache. Psychiatric Quart. *11:* 592-619, 1937.

10. KUBIE, L. S.: The use of hypnagogic reveries in the recovery of repressed amnesic data. Bull. Menninger Clin. *7:* 172-82, 1943.

11. LINDNER, R. M.: Rebel without a cause: The hypnoanalysis of a criminal psychopath. New York: Grune & Stratton, 1944.

12. GILL, M. M., AND BRENMAN, M.: Treatment of a case of anxiety hysteria by a hypnotic technique employing psychoanalytic principles. Bull. Menninger Clin. *7:* 163-71, 1943.

13. FISHER, C.: Hypnosis in treatment of neuroses due to war and to other causes. War Med. *4:* 565-76, 1943.

14. LURIA, A. R.: The nature of human conflict. New York: Liveright, 1932.

15. HUSTON, P. E., SHAKOW, D., AND ERICKSON, M. H.: A study of hypnotically induced complexes by means of the Luria technique. J. Gen. Psychol. *11:* 65-97, 1934.

16. BRICKNER, R. M., AND KUBIE, L. S.: A miniature psychic storm produced by super-ego conflict over simple posthypnotic suggestion. Psychoanalyt. Quart. *5:* 467-87, 1936.

17. ERICKSON, M. H.: Experimental demonstration of the psychopathology of everyday life. Psychoanalyt. Quart. *8:* 338-53, 1939.

18. FARBER, L. H., AND FISHER, C.: An experimental approach to dream psychology through the use of hypnosis. Psychoanalyt. Quart. *2:* 202-16, 1943.

19. WOLBERG, L. R.: The mechanism of a hysterical anesthesia revealed during hypnoanalysis. Psychoanalyt. Quart. In press.

# Part One
# THE HYPNOANALYSIS
# OF JOHAN R.

---

# I

THE CASE of Johan R. is presented as an example of how the various hypnoanalytic technics may be applied in therapy. The case is interesting for its symbolism and for the astuteness with which Johan was able to report in his diary his mental processes. Hypnotic treatments were carried on for a period of four months, following a long casual contact with the patient. Hypnoanalysis was instituted as soon as Johan expressed a desire for more active help with his problem.

When I first met Johan he was confined in one of the chronic wards of a mental institution. Although the diagnosis of his condition was that of hebephrenic schizophrenia, there were many elements in his reaction that pointed to a more benign psychosis. However, he had regressed in his interests and habits and was preoccupied with his own thoughts to the almost complete exclusion of external reality. Interviews revealed intense emotion, which he concealed beneath a lackadaisical, apathetic exterior. He parried all questions with the statement that there was no need to bother him because he was satisfied with things as they were. His humility, hopelessness, and self-abasement were the most prominent symptoms.

According to his case record, he was born in Norway in 1894, the eldest of three siblings. From childhood on he had been a seclusive, sensitive individual who had very few friends, confided in no one, and revealed little concerning his private hopes and aspirations. He had come to the United States with his family in 1914 and had obtained a job as a messenger boy by day, attending school at night.   He had always preferred living alone, despite the fact that he was attached to his mother.   He was interested in drawing and after taking an art course obtained a position as a commercial artist.   An industrious worker, he earned enough to contribute part of his salary toward support of his parents.   He showed no interest in the opposite sex and was so taken up with his work that he had little time for social recreations.

The onset of his psychosis occurred early in 1937, when he was 42 years of age.   At that time he became tense and fearful and repeatedly expressed the idea that his life was meaningless. He condemned himself for having been selfish and evil, although he was unable to provide examples of these failings. As time went on, he lost interest in his appearance and for some unknown reason refused to take food.   He turned to religion for solace and finally gave up his work in order to devote more time to prayer.   On one occasion he heard the voice of God chiding him for his sins.   He was so upset that his family decided to bring him to the observation ward of a general hospital, from which he was committed to a mental institution.

On admission to the state hospital, he was manifestly down-hearted, depressed, and self-condemnatory.   He insisted that he had ruined his life because of excesses of various sorts, of the nature of which he was uncertain.   He was very obliging, cooperative, and retiring in his manner.   He made a splendid adjustment to the ward routine, and three months after admission had improved sufficiently to warrant a trial in convalescent status.

Upon leaving the hospital, all his feelings of worthlessness and self-condemnation reappeared and he again lost interest in his surroundings.   He was returned to the hospital in January 1938.   Shortly after his readmission, he began to regress in his appearance, habits, and interests.   He became absorbed in his own ideas and often could be heard mumbling to himself about such vague matters as atoms, molecules, the iniquities of life, and the philosophic differences between goodness and badness. He acquiesced readily in performing any sort of duty assigned to him and offered no objection to working with the cleaning squad at scrubbing basement floors.

An attempt was made to transfer Johan to a better ward and to provide him with tasks of a nature more in line with his previous occupation, but he resisted this passively and even seemed to resent having to talk with the physician. It was as if he were striving to detach himself from anyone who sought his friendship.

Early in 1939, active treatment was attempted in the form of daily interviews. These were singularly sterile. The patient persisted in making himself as inoffensive as possible, adopting an ingratiating, obsequious attitude, incessantly lamenting his plight, and flagellating himself with the hopelessness of his situation. In spite of his apparent agitation, he displayed very little real affect, and one gained the impression that he was attempting to insulate himself from a closer and more friendly relationship. Nevertheless, the interviews seemed to stir up some sort of activity, for he gave up his habitual mumblings and spent much of his time scribbling notes, in a fine meticulous handwriting, on tiny scraps of paper. The notes at first were devoted to lengthy philosophic speculations concerning the nature of the world, the indestructibility of matter, the transmutation of elements, and the nature of cosmic rays. Interspersed were metaphysical speculations on the meaning of life, with quotations from Kant and Schopenhauer. Later, autobiographic subject matter appeared, in which he described certain events of his life, emphasizing the idea of his wasted and misspent existence.

It was not until a year had passed that an element of resentment could be sensed in his writings. Unlike his anemic conversational attitudes, his graphic productions reflected a strong emotional tone and were often quite poetic. An example from one of his notes is as follows:

If death is a departing to a greater and happier life, if it is a period of rest before entering a greater field of endeavor where other work may be performed, why is it not the cause of joy and happiness? Why is it not the lying down to sleep with a happy smile and a whispered *Auf Wiedersehen*? If death is the admission to the "kingdom," why are the most arduous of the servants of the Lord filled with fear when life everlasting looms in sight? If death is a birth in spirit and in truth, why is the departure left in the cave of the most unworthy of all the children of men? When the sun is brightly shining from the summer sky, when life's great wave of warmth is against us, why do we search with shy and worried glances? Why do we pry and prowl for every thorn that stings us hard and sharp? Why should I keep holiday when other men have none? Why, when they are gay, do I sit and mourn alone, and why, when mirth unseals the tongues, should mine alone be dumb?

Of late I spoke to silent throngs and now their turn has come. Once I stood with an open book, each page was my life. "Write, write," I begged of the world, and my eyes saw dreamland unrolling. "Write what you will, evil or good, great or small. I give myself to fight or to suffer, but leave not one single white page."

And life wrote courage—wrote in blood. It came and tore all the empty white pages to shreds. There were days that flew like lightning—strong, warm, sunny days. There were others of terror, written of sorrow and suffering, but all a gift from life. How strange the runes that still may stand carved into my trembling soul. Still I pray: "Write, write, wonderful life. Write what you will. I beg of you still. I give myself to fight or to suffer, but I leave not one single empty white page."

Coincident with the querulous plaints that permeated his writings was an attitude of hopelessness about ever gaining those things that make life worth while. Inevitably, he asserted, one is punished for wrongdoing, whether one does right or wrong. The world must consequently be a place in which right does not exist. Pleasures are created by man in disobedience. Life is meant for suffering. Punishment is meted out in relation to simple pleasures of routine existence as well as for debauching the senses in riotous living. One is taught that one has rights, yet one is held to account for every tiny act in life itself. How intensely interesting life might be if one were permitted to express his yearnings, his desire to see things, to have things, to experience things, his desire for adventure—all those things that one was taught in childhood to regard as good. How unjust that he who abides by these teachings is punished—even though he confesses his faults and begs forgiveness, absolution is not forthcoming. Perhaps it is better not to strive at all. This is the torment of a lonely soul who pays for a moment of happiness with groans of unutterable anguish. Why was not life something glorious? He wrote,

I felt I had done wrong. Whether I did a thing in one way or whether I did a thing the opposite way. To starve or subsist, to remain or to go away, were equally wrong. Everything I have done in life has been utterly wrong, but had I done the exact opposite to what I did, it would still have been utterly wrong. My aim throughout life was to avoid wrongdoing, to do that which was worth while. I succeeded only in doing wrong. I have come to understand now that wrong is all there is. Right does not exist.

It was apparent from Johan's productions that from earliest childhood he had been motivated by an overwhelming compulsion to accumulate and to catalogue miscellaneous facts and knowledge. This, it developed, had been his major preoccupation.

Science in all its branches to me was absolute and eternal. My greatest sorrow was that there were so many things to find out about that it was impossible to absorb everything. I spent thousands of hours in libraries making numberless notes, and I kept complete lists of all the books I read, bibliographies, references, and so forth. I had shelves full of notes. Everything done in the sincere belief that I was doing no wrong. Only by knowing could I become complete. Knowledge is truth; it is something that cannot possibly be taken away from anyone. By gaining an immense store of knowledge, I could get something that no one could rob me of. Life is a quest for truth and knowledge. Truth is eternal. It is the same for ever and ever. It is like the sun. It remains eternal. Truth is truth in itself, not man-made truth, but a light that is unblinking—a light that persists like the sun itself. Without truth I am incomplete. I tried to familiarize myself with all the founts of knowledge, astronomy, philosophy, the sciences and the arts, with men of letters, scientists, inventors, and philosophers—all those who were endowed with highest of intellect as expressed in the universe.

Johan's thirst for knowledge had apparently led him to the pursuit of erudition to almost complete exclusion of other interests. To him learning in all its branches was absolute and eternal and without doubt. Those were happy years indeed when the story of mankind unrolled before his eyes. He often took children to museums, libraries, zoos, the aquarium, and the planetarium, trying to explain and to help.

I did not realize that study and knowledge and truth were forbidden. I did not appreciate that truth was as dangerous as the sun. A few thousand miles closer to it or further away and one would be burned to death or frozen to death. As God punished Adam for eating of the tree of knowledge, so I was punished for wrongdoing, not only toward myself, but toward those whom

I tried to help and serve. Especially does it hurt to think that these young ones, who through my efforts acquired a thirst for knowledge, will be despised and punished because of my mistaken endeavors. How can knowledge be a good and desirable thing and at the same time an evil and punishable thing? What good is fame or success or happiness or learning or ease or comfort or freedom or liberty if each of these has to be paid for with an eternity of unbearable anguish? There is no advancement except toward evil. All people have come down to their destruction when truth has become known to them.

And so for almost eight months Johan's relationship to me consisted of a desire to make himself as innocuous as possible, while at the same time he wrote incessantly, with an emotional fervor scarcely revealed by his outer detachment. Whatever drives remained within him, the overt expression of aggression and the ability to demand and to ask for things were not among them. It was of little avail to remind him of his past accomplishments, and he remained absorbed in nihilistic thoughts and ideas of wrongdoing. He wrote:

No one is supposed to have anything. No one is supposed to own anything. No one can own anything. Nothing belongs to anyone. Those who have set themselves at the head of things have taken many things to themselves. They are honored. The ones that have tried to take a few things to themselves are punished for doing so by those who have taken all. Everything I have done is wrong. By doing nothing one can avoid wrong, but even then one is despised.

Along with the desire to abstain from creative activities there lurked in him a strong preoccupation with his own unworthiness and contemptibility. He disputed any suggestion that one has a right to do some of the things that it pleases him to do, and he scoffed at the idea that it was possible for him to take advantage of his interests and aptitudes. In answer to such suggestions he would say: "I came here to repent and to do penance, but even this is denied me. There is no hope. God forsook me long ago, before I ever became part of life." When an effort was made to get him to take interest in his personal appearance, he cooperated very poorly. He refused to permit expenditure of any of his money for clothing. He had ample funds for the purchase of needed apparel, but he would not sanction use of them for himself. Finally, I personally escorted him to one of the local clothing stores and bought him a complete outfit, in spite of his protestation that the clothes he was wearing were good enough for him, even though they were threadbare and shabby. However, he refused to wear any of this new clothing and attempted stealthily to distribute it among other patients.

At about this period he became preoccupied with the notion that he was exuding bad odors that were offensive to those around him. Whenever he addressed anyone he kept his mouth covered and gazed down at the floor. He complained that his teeth were rotting: this to him was an indication of physical corruption and decay. A dental consultation revealed the presence of several teeth that needed extraction. Their removal precipitated an acute anxiety attack. He was convinced that he had in some way done irreparable injury to himself and as evidence pointed to his decaying teeth. His whole physical structure had a hereditary blemish, he insisted, for his father's people too had had bad teeth and pyorrhea, probably because they had led immoral and decadent lives.

I was never meant to have been at all. There was something wrong always from the very first. I did not know this. There is scarcely one human being that is perfect any more. Something has gone wrong in some way. To live a life like that of the Middle Ages—to have nothing, to know nothing, to experience nothing—has been my destiny. Inwardly I weep without ceasing because I am the one I am. Day or night there is not a moment's rest, since I find that I cannot have the truth. To rest, to sleep, to be part of nothingness forever. What blessing! Rest, sleep, do not exist in all eternity. Life is everlasting. Only by being perfect can one live in peace, and to be perfect is to gain knowledge. The truth makes one complete, but I have been forced to suffer suffering beyond endurance for trying to get the truth, for trying to get that which would have made me complete.

Following this, there appeared in his writings expressions of profound indignation directed against society, for leading people to believe that the most worthy things in life are to advance, to enjoy oneself, and to gain knowledge. Although his emotion was intense, it did not seep through into his interpersonal conduct, which continued to be of an apathetic, listless nature. He

manifested strong submissiveness and was never known to refuse
a single demand made of him.   When the matter of his compliance was gone into, he brought up the fact that he had always
had to subordinate his own interests in favor of those of his
parents and of his younger brother and sister.

The conditions in his home were very chaotic.   The father
drank heavily and when he was intoxicated he quarreled and
raged around the house.   As a drunkard, his father was a fearful figure.   On the other hand, when he was sober he was a
kindly man, who took a keen interest in books and in music.
Johan had always been attached to his mother and was out-
raged and chagrined at the treatment accorded her by his father.
Toward his brother and sister he was more or less indifferent,
but he always felt a certain amount of resentment based on the
feeling that they were treated more considerately by his parents
than he was.

# II

IN ORDER to awaken Johan's interest in art I purchased a supply of art materials and assigned to him an empty desk in an adjoining office, which was also occupied by a stenographer. Johan spent all his time reading art books, but made no effort to do any creative work. He sat quietly, scarcely daring to shift his position. The only sign that he was aware of what was going on was the change in the color of his ears, which became blood red whenever any person spoke to him or made a remark to the stenographer that could in any way be construed as applying to himself.

After several weeks of this behavior, he began scribbling letters in pen and ink, and soon he started to print various signs and notices that were needed in the wards. He was an excellent penman and his services were very much in demand. He was given more and more work, and one could almost visibly note a change going on within him as he realized that his efforts were appreciated. Nevertheless, he continued to minimize his accomplishments.

The first indication that he was beginning to regain an active interest in art was the appearance of small sketches in the form of marginal scribblings that adorned his various writings. A repetitive quality was noted in these drawings, and the objects most frequently delineated were the sun, various animals, insects, flowers, knives, daggers, axes, snakes; there were also peculiar wavy and jagged lines that, he declared, had no particular meaning. After that he started spontaneously to work in water colors, then in pastels, and, finally, after much procrastination, he began to paint in oils. His work had no originality, but displayed great meticulousness and fine detail. He confined himself almost exclusively to copying photographs, which he reproduced perfectly, including the spots and blemishes.

A slight change for the better occurred at this time in his relationships with people, but he still remained very shy and never spoke unless he was spoken to. He never spontaneously joined in a conversation, nor would he do a thing without first asking permission, and then he would hesitate to ask because he thought that he had no right to speak in the first place. As the stenographer expressed it: "He would sit there like a bump on a log with his ears glowing like a red-hot furnace."

It was, to a considerable extent, the interest in his work displayed by the stenographer that gradually led to his warming up to her. At first he would hesitate to walk past her desk and always asked permission to do so. Gradually he gained more and more confidence in himself, and after a while he would utter the words "Good morning" or "Good evening" instead of mumbling them to himself. The stenographer, a very intelligent young woman, intuitively sensed his devaluation of his self-esteem and his lack of self-confidence. She entered actively into the therapeutic situation by assigning to him various tasks that called for a greater and greater exercise of initiative.

While Johan retained his humble and obsequious attitude, his behavior gradually became somewhat more aggressive. For example, he stopped asking permission to leave his chair. He would even on occasion turn around and make a spontaneous comment or two to the stenographer. At this stage he was doing portrait work, copying photographs in water colors and oils. On one occasion he volunteered to make a freehand sketch of the stenographer, and when this was completed he signed his name to the drawing, something that he had avoided doing up to that time. His improved condition warranted a ground parole, which he utilized to meander around various parts of the hospital grounds, particularly near the water.

The character of his writings changed abruptly; a sense of humor crept into his productions. He made a collection of caricatures of his fellow patients and incorporated them into a book that he called "Nitwits." The book was very cleverly conceived, and the illustrations were excellent in that with a few brief sweeps of his pencil he had captured the mannerisms and idiosyncrasies of his ward companions.

One month later, as if he had been working on his personal problems in the meantime, he presented me with a small booklet of his writings entitled "To Do or Not to Do." In this he reiterated his belief that all human beings are given life for a definite purpose and that the meaning of life itself is to learn and to experience things. He had tried to fashion his life around this goal.

Then came the experience of finding that all my doings, all of my interests of life seemed wrong. I renounced all things that previously had meant life to me, and I accused myself of wrongdoing in all that I had done. Later, when I was told that I must learn obedience, and that the proper way of life was to sit still, I sincerely believed that that was so. I believed that all my previous experiences of life had been necessary, but that these later experiences served the purpose of showing that such interests one must not have. It seemed that all of life was just one lesson that I had learned. To strive for knowledge, is this evil? The early Hebrew writings say that evil came into the world through man's desire for knowledge. All knowledge, research, science has been persecuted.

He revealed that prior to his becoming ill he had been very much interested in the sun. This was part of his study of astronomy. He had even on several occasions tried unsuccessfully to photograph the sun. It was almost as if this experience had climaxed his failure to gain what he wanted most from life, for shortly thereafter he was filled with a sense of hopelessness and a conviction that his quest for knowledge had failed. Subsequently he was overwhelmed with shame and guilt and believed that he had done wrong. The only way to obtain absolution was to destroy what he had created. He burned his books, his treasured notes and possessions gathered over his entire lifetime. "In turning against science," he wrote, "I was also turning against myself, for I was a part of it all." The remainder of the booklet was devoted to ideas that showed considerable progress in his thinking and development, as illustrated by the following conclusion:

The question arises in my mind as to whether it matters what others think of one's doing, so long as one feels in one's own heart that one has done right.

Up to this time Johan had never indicated that he felt any resentment or hostility toward me. His attitude during our discussions was at all times polite, and he listened attentively to any comments made, nodding his head as if he accepted them without question.   The problem of his inability to assert himself and to express resentment was taken up in detail in our conversations, but no change in his behavior pattern was demonstrable.   Because of the pressure of my other duties, interviews were temporarily suspended, but Johan was invited to come into my office whenever he had the inclination.   He had merely to present himself to me at any time, and he would be granted opportunity to talk about any matter that he desired to discuss.   Johan failed to take advantage of this invitation, and, whenever he was asked whether there was anything that he would like to talk about, he shrugged his shoulders and stated that he would think the matter over and write more notes.   The content of his writings showed no particular change; it was concerned with his wasted life and with an interminable list of questions as to why science and society are constituted as they are.

Several months later the stenographer was obliged to absent herself for a short time for extensive dental work.   Johan began to show considerable concern and interest in her health. He wrote notes to her in a facetious vein, addressing her as "Ho Hum."   In one of these notes he expressed the idea that he knew that he had been charged with all kinds of misconduct and misbehavior.   He charged her not to believe everything that she heard, particularly not to believe those people who thought that mind and body are a unity.   These people were "the Freudians."

The Freudians are an unscrupulous lot when it comes to their pet hypotheses, and the Freudians are in power.  I may be as intelligent as they. I may know as much, have studied as much, learned as much, experienced as much.   Still they are in power.— —I was deprived of everything that gave meaning to life.   I was shut off from the people that were mine and that had depended on me.   I was deprived of my rights to think and to act or to do a thing about matters.   Everything I had done in life was ridiculed, and I was a play ball for the whims of those who were said to do my thinking for me.   All of these things are supposed to be helpful.   "Psychology," it is called.   Anyone who does not feel happy or satisfied under such circumstances, anyone who does not adjust himself, is considered perverse or abnormal. But to my way of looking at things, it is rather the one who does feel happy and satisfied under such circumstances that is abnormal. To hate and despise, to revolt against such conditions, seems to me normal, but the Freudians say otherwise.

This was the first indication of an open resentment toward psychiatrists. His accusation that he had not been allowed to express himself was particularly interesting, because he had so often been encouraged to voice his resentment and his indignation.

Several weeks later he brought me a little booklet of his writings entitled "A Letter to Myself." He prefaced the collection with an apology for what he had to say, and confided that he had finally come to the realization that to be seen and heard as little as possible was not all that was expected of him. He also expressed, for the first time, the idea that his convictions and opinions might not be irrefutable:

I would nothing rather than that they be proven false. Your world is the world that used to be my world. I would much have preferred had it remained my world.

In the booklet he stated that now when he started to write he was suddenly overwhelmed with sarcasm and hatred, which he attributed to the sham and pretense of civilization. He was particularly indignant over the fact that he had been unjustifiably hospitalized and deprived of his privileges as a human being, deprived of his freedom, of his ability to move about as he pleased.

I had tried to find answers to the questions as to why I was deprived of my rights to think and to act. Was I actually less capable than others to think and to reason and to behave in a logical and rational manner? — —It was only when I became aware of the fact that I had been part of a society that had been corrupt in its dealings that I accused myself of wrongdoing. I had been truthful always, and I thought I owed it to myself to speak the truth even though it caused my own undoing. Perhaps this is held against me. Perhaps it is worthy of punishment. Perhaps to be honest and truthful in a world that is founded upon falsehood and dishonesty is abnormal. Perhaps this is why I was deprived of my rights to think and to act for myself.

He then went on to voice his anger at the ward attendants, whom he accused of having little consideration for patients who sometimes lost their tempers. More interestingly, he began to express open resentment toward me:

The circumstances that shaped my life were totally different from the circumstances that shaped your life. That one set of circumstances is more correct or more worthy or more in conformity with the external purposes of things, no one can dare to say. Your kind of work may be more important than my kind of work, but everyone cannot do the same important kind of work. If your interests and my interests do not coincide, and if your reasoning and my reasoning do not agree, this does not prove my inability to reason, to think and act for myself, any more than it proves your inability to think and to reason and to act for yourself. Independent thought and independent reasoning should not be considered abnormal. Is this a sign I have a deranged mind? Is this a justification that I be deprived of my rights to think and to act for myself for ever after? Should this be the law? Then the law is corrupt. Then the law is evil.

In this place I was deprived of all my interests. Everything that meant life to me was ridiculed. Here I was put among those who never had any interests and those whose worthless interests I was told were the worthy mode of life that I had missed. I was looked down upon by those who were far lower than I. Here I had to sit, just sit for years, and I was despised for doing nothing, though I had no choice in the matter. What kept me going under the circumstances I don't know. I had come into a world utterly strange to me, a world in which all values were distorted or reversed, where stupidity and ignorance were at a premium, where I was a baseball for the whim of those who knew not one whit what it was all about, and I was deprived of my rights to think and to act. I was as helpless as though I had been shut off from the world and thrown upon the void.

No one should be deprived of their rights to think and to act for themselves. — — I have seldom met a doctor who has believed in taking his own medicine. Their system of make-believe is for others. They are different. — — I have seen doctors who are most loath to submit to treatment on the value of which, where others are concerned, they write lengthy and learned treatises. — — And here comes the great contradiction, namely, that doctors who do not admire coddling, who despise seekers of sympathy, ascribe my behavior in these matters to a perverse intellect or a stubborn stupidity. I ought to have done that which they would have despised me for had I done it.

If the whole of materia medica could be sunk to the bottom of the sea, it would be so much the better for man and so much the worse for the fish. — — The sciences do not deal with truth. They corrupt the individual.

They feed him untruth in regard to himself, that he may be kept unaware of his own corruption. — — Were one to abide by the requirements or laws laid down by the Freudians, one would not dare to think at all. Especially would one not dare to wonder about things or to philosophize about things. That which formerly was known as a rich, inner life they would term daydreaming or fantasy, the escape from reality or compensatory devices or some such thing. Everything that goes on beneath the surface will have to have some kind of label attached to it. It is all some sort of corruption or foul business, except, of course, in the case of themselves. — — The Freudians class religion, daydreaming, and drunkenness as compensatory devices, defense mechanisms. In fact, there is scarcely a thing that humans do that the Freudians would not classify as defense or escape mechanisms or compensatory devices— except psychology, of course.

Johan then terminated his diatribe with an apology for the evil things he had said about the Freudians, among whom there were some perfectly delightful people.

At one time I had acquainted myself with Adler and with Jung and even with Freud through their writings, and I was convinced of the worth-whileness and the greatness of their doings. That was when I was on the experimental end of things, before I was punished.

When Johan was asked whether he would like to discuss his booklets with me, he seemed eager for the opportunity. For a time thereafter an attempt was made to analyze certain aspects of his character structure, such as his need for compliance, his inner strivings, and, finally, his defensive devices of detachment and isolation from people.

Shortly after that he spontaneously asked for interviews and even expressed in writing an interest in having his teeth treated.

It seems to me that I am able to express myself more easily in writing than in speaking. In trying to understand myself and the reason for my faultfinding, is it not possible that frustrations in early life, together with a lifetime of suppressed emotions, may have resulted in a state of tension, that the dammed-up feelings of a lifetime finally had to burst through in some way? Is it not possible that the present faultfinding and antagonism toward people and conditions has some such explanation as this? I remember having heard you say at an earlier time that if one is going to hate, then hate. This presumably means that hatred toward people and things and conditions is perfectly normal or natural and perfectly legitimate. A few days ago you expressed the conviction that one had a perfect right to look out for one's own interests in conformity with one's likes and desires, and even to disregard the disapproval of others. This leads me to believe that faultfinding is not unconditionally bad or evil. Of course I realize that I am fortunate in being able to express myself to someone who does not take what I say as a personal offense. I have noticed that when I first started writing, my mode of expression was violent and crude. It seems that the worst edges have been worn off by this time. I have come to wonder if it could not be possible to turn my tearing-down tendencies into constructive channels.

What I would really like to ask you is whether you think I am mentally and physically able to rehabilitate myself? Do you think my make-up is such that it merits a try in the direction of your world? Suppose a craftsman is given materials with which to construct something beautiful or useful. On examining the materials he may find faults and flaws, and he may find them entirely unsuitable for his purposes, or he may find them unsuitable for any purpose. The materials may be thrown into the scrap heap, or he may construct something quite useless that may be unsuitable for anything but the scrap heap. Then of course it may also be possible that out of his materials he may create something which, although faulty and imperfect, still may be useful and serviceable. Now, if you would consider yourself the craftsman and me the materials, what would you do? Perhaps you are wondering what caused my change of attitude toward myself and toward life in general. A short while ago, when you expressed your opinion that my teeth ought to be taken care of, it seemed an indication to me that there might be something in me that was still worthy of consideration. My failure previously to do anything in this matter myself was not due to contrariness. It was simply a feeling on my part that things did not matter one way or the other.

There was little doubt that Johan had gained a considerable amount of intellectual insight. However, there was little material change in his actual behavior. He continued to slink about with his head down, gazing at the ground as if he feared to look people in the face. He bowed constantly when spoken to, ingratiating himself with the attendants and subordinating his interests to those of others around him. Furthermore, in spite of the eloquence of his written statements, there was considerable blocking in his conversation, and he continued to hold his hand over his mouth while he talked.

For several months the matter of his intense self-devaluation was explored in detail, with an inquiry into the reasons why he had always felt that he had no rights and had to lead a life of compliance and subordination. The possibility that he might be harboring strong resentments against those with whom he complied was presented to him. Also, it was suggested that for some reason he found it necessary to repress his hostility by withdrawing from active contacts with people and by living a life of detachment and semi-isolation. Because his interpersonal relationships were so unsatisfactory, it had perhaps been necessary for him to inhibit his impulses pertaining to certain vital needs and satisfactions that ordinarily were gratified in the relationship of one human being with another.

As in the past, Johan sat obediently in a chair and nodded his head in agreement with practically everything that was said. An attempt was made to analyze his hesitancy in expressing himself verbally, thus necessitating his recourse to writing. Johan defended himself by stating that he could never speak very freely and that he could be much more eloquent in writing. He verbalized no particular feelings toward me at this time, except for the fact that he now believed that I was interested in him and wanted to help him. He denied having any dreams and added that he did not remember a single dream that he had during the entire period of his hospitalization.

# III

Because of Johan's inability to associate freely, I decided to experiment with hypnosis, to see whether hypnotic suggestion could break through his detachment. Hypnosis was undertaken with some trepidation, because the intimacy of the hypnotic relationship was completely opposed to Johan's character defenses and his compulsive need for isolation and independence. On the other hand, I felt that if Johan could permit himself to go into a hypnotic state, he might benefit by the experience of getting close to another person without being injured.

As had been anticipated, the first few attempts at hypnosis were a complete failure. Johan showed very little response to the suggestions that he go to sleep. The only change that occurred in him was that he was restless during the night and had a feeling that he was dreaming, although he did not remember the content of his dreams. After a week of unsuccessful attempts at inducing hypnosis, Johan brought in a fragment of a dream: "I was sitting in a chair, and as I looked ahead of me, out of the wall an opening appeared. A hand started coming toward me and I was filled with vague forebodings and a sense of horror." The next evening he reported the same dream and was given the interpretation that the hand represented me, extending a helping hand to him in a therapeutic attempt, but that his need for isolation and detachment, his fear of entering into a close relationship with another person, filled him with horror and made it impossible for him to accept this help. Whether or not the interpretation was valid, it was noted that he gradually became able to sink into a light hypnosis, which became more and more profound with successive trances, until he finally entered deep somnambulistic states, with complete posthypnotic amnesia.

During the first few weeks, time was spent while he was under hypnosis in creating a happy emotional state free of tension, with extension of these tensionless states into his waking life through posthypnotic suggestions. The theory behind this was that if the patient could experience intense pleasure in a close relationship, it might lead him to yield a few of his defenses and to regard closeness as having some positive virtues. While under hypnosis Johan was told: "As you sit here your mind becomes occupied with a pleasurable scene. The most intense happiness comes over you. It is as though all of your cares are over. With each passing second you grow happier and happier. You recapture all of the joyous moments of your life in one. Your pleasure is greater than any you have ever experienced, and it grows greater and greater. Do you notice how happy you feel? Now listen carefully. When you wake up you will continue to feel this pleasurable emotion, which will embrace every fiber of your being. Everything will be rosy and beautiful. All of your worries will be forgotten. You will bubble with sheer joy. All the unhappiness you have known will have vanished. You will feel happiness growing inside of you. You will feel like the happiest person alive. Happiness will well up inside of you until it overflows, and the world will be a bountiful and joyous place."

Upon termination of the hypnosis, Johan was seen looking around him with a confused, joyous expression on his face.

"It is a funny thing," he said, "but I feel very happy, like singing. I feel like I did before I got sick, like I would like to do things."

He smiled broadly and finally brought his hand to his face because he was laughing, apologizing profusely for this undignified performance. Johan soon began to look forward to hypnotic sessions with a great deal of expectancy, and his conscious productions were concerned with how strange the emotion of happiness was to him.

These experiences did not seem to alter his unconscious fear, as revealed by a dream he had in response to a posthypnotic suggestion that he dream regarding his real feelings toward me. The dream he presented was the following:

I went into a store to buy something. At first it did not seem to be any particular store, or any particular thing that I wanted to buy. I spoke to the man in the store and told him what I wanted to buy. "We do not have any of this," he told me.

I laughed and thought: "This is like going into a bookstore and asking for a book and being told that they have no more books."

As I looked around I found that the place was a bookstore. I repeated my request, thinking that I had been misunderstood. "We have not got it," said the man, and he gave me an evil look as if he wanted to get rid of me.

The man seemed not to want to have anything to do with me. I then started to walk toward the door in order to leave the store. The man came running after me, took hold of my coat, and dragged me back into the store. He seemed to have changed. He was dressed in a way that reminded me of a longshoreman, trousers and shirt without sleeves. He was a rather belligerent, crude, evil person. I noticed that his arms were heavy and muscular. He turned to me with a wry smile and said, "You're next."

From the few associations that could be obtained, it was apparent that Johan had experienced no fear in the first part of the dream, when he had a definite feeling of distance from the man; but when he came close to the man, the latter's entire attitude seemed to change to one of belligerency. It happened that on the day before Johan had the dream I was interviewing a number of other patients while Johan was working in his customary place in the adjoining office.

Because the office was somewhat stuffy, I had removed my coat. After these interviews I had called out to Johan: "You're next." Despite the interpretation that I might be the man of the dream, Johan insisted that he felt no conscious fear of me. He was aware of a difficulty in expressing resentment, which he rationalized by saying that the expression of one's true feelings does not always pay.

Because inability to express aggression appeared to be such an important character trait in him, it was decided to experiment with hypnotically induced situations in which Johan would be able to express his aggression openly. Under hypnosis he was given the following suggestion: "You are going to remember an incident that occurred a few days ago and that you have completely forgotten. This incident is extremely important, so listen carefully. You were walking along a corridor when all of a sudden G——, the attendant, came walking out of the bathroom and bumped into you, almost knocking you off your feet. You felt very resentful but expected that he would apologize. Instead of apologizing, he suddenly launched into a violent stream of abuse, accusing you of being a fool and an idiot, warning you to watch yourself better. You became greatly irritated. For a moment you had an impulse to bow and to retire to a distance. However, the more you thought about the matter, the more definitely you decided that you had rights and were going to stand up for your rights. You were going to express yourself; you had the right to express yourself. G—— was in the wrong and there was no reason why you should not say what was on your mind. So you talked back to G—— and told him exactly how you felt about him, about his bad manners, and about other incidents in which he had treated you unjustly. As you began to express yourself, you felt that you had a perfect right to say what you did, and you noticed that G—— became apologetic and more friendly. You felt wonderful because you had been able to stand up for your rights and express your resentment. You are experiencing that wonderful feeling now. Don't you feel better?"

Johan nodded and stated somewhat hesitatingly: "Yes, I am glad that I told him how I felt."

A posthypnotic suggestion was then made to the effect that he would have a dream that evening: in it he would be in a situation in which someone did something to him that he resented, but he would be capable in the dream of standing up for his own rights.

Next day Johan walked into my office holding his head higher than he had ever held it before. He suddenly began talking spontaneously about such subjects as baseball and remarked that for some peculiar reason he seemed to be more at ease than he had been previously. For the first time he did not place his fingers over his mouth. He remarked that he had had a very peaceful night and that he did not remember having any dreams.

Under hypnosis, he was asked to remember the incident in which he had bumped into G—— and had stood up for his rights. He recalled this in detail and also recaptured the feeling that he had been absolutely right in doing what he did about expressing his resentment. This offered opportunity to talk about the inalienable right of every human being to express his righteous indignation and resentment and to stand up for things in which he believed. It was suggested that sometimes an individual, because of his relationships with his parents, has to submit and ingratiate himself so frequently that this behavior becomes a character pattern that later on interferes with his best interests.

In a deeper state of hypnosis, Johan was told that if he had had a dream the night before that he had forgotten, he would be able to recall this dream. He would then awaken and remember the dream upon awakening. As he slumped into his chair, his whole body suddenly became rigid, his muscles started twitching, and he had a fixed, stern expression on his face. This continued for about three minutes, after which he suddenly awakened, rubbed his eyes, and started smiling. He remarked that he had had a thought that was so strong it had awakened him. He said: "I was thinking of something. I remember now. It was the dream I had last night that I had forgotten. I was over in the dining room. I was late for dinner. They didn't want to serve me anything. I insisted upon it. I said I had been working for you. It appeared to me that I was there and that the whole incident was real. I insisted upon their giving me my food and they did. I asked them for my food and they followed through."

In associating to the dream, Johan remarked that he had decided that he should insist upon his own rights and when he did, in the dream, he had obtained what he wanted. Opportunity then presented itself to take up the situation of his submissive relationship with people. Instead of listening passively, Johan suddenly started to defend his attitude. It is necessary, he insisted, to submit oneself, as a social creature. To be forceful is to be more animal than human. I then discussed the difference between purposeful submitting to real external pressures and automatic submissiveness on the basis of a character trait: in the latter, resentment and aggression are inevitable. Johan then brought up the case of Gandhi and argued that this is one example of passive resistance that nets big dividends.

In the hypnotic sessions of the next few weeks various situations were dramatized: they provided scenes in which Johan's anger was aroused, this leading to a motor expression of his rage. Spontaneous and hypnotically induced dreams revealed two reactions—first, fears of retaliatory injury, and second, ecstasy at being able to stand up for his own rights.

The same dramatic technics were employed in sessions in which the patient was hypnotically regressed to earlier age levels. For example, at a 6 year level he was given the following suggestions: "You are sitting in school and there is a bad boy sitting near you. He has been annoying you a great deal by throwing things at you, throwing spitballs and wads of paper, and by picking on you in a great many different ways. This makes you very mad. You wonder if you should take it every day without complaining or whether you should fight back. Today as you walk to school this boy suddenly jumps out from behind a bush. He starts beating you up, pounding you with his fists, calling you all kinds of bad names. You can't stand it any more and you decide that you are going to fight back. You begin to fight back and knock him down. At first this frightens you, but then you notice that the boy picks himself up off the ground. He tells you that he is sorry for what he did. You feel very happy over the fact that you didn't run away."

During the recital of this incident, Johan was led around the room. He became tense and clenched his jaws as he jerked his arms back and forth in fighting movements. On being questioned, he remembered the incident so vividly that he talked as if it were real. His language was very simple and more like a child's talk than an adult's. Upon being examined, he revealed that he had an amnesia for all events that had occurred after his sixth year, including inability to recognize me. However, he identified me as a friend of his father's. As this friend, I discussed with him the need to stand up for his own rights, asserting that both his mother and his father would approve of this. A number of other dramatic scenes

were re-enacted at regressed age levels: in these I took the roles
of both his father and his mother, urging him to express himself
and to fight back whenever anybody picked on him.

Little noticeable change, however, appeared in Johan's
actual behavior, and he continued to conduct himself in a
more or less submissive manner. However, he did admit that
he felt better than he had felt for years, and he confided that
the treatment he received was making him much more self-
confident.

To test his self-confidence, it was decided to create a posthypnotic situation in which he would be forced to speak his
mind. Under hypnosis he was given the following suggestions:
"When you awaken you will feel very happy, self-assured, and
self-confident. You will go over to the dining room and as the
food is being served you will remember the many times when
you were dissatisfied with the food and with the service. This
will make you angry and you will tell the waitress that you care
neither for the food nor for the service. You will be able to
express yourself without any guilt or remorse."

Upon leaving my office, Johan went directly to the dining
room. Twenty minutes later he returned in a fit of anger, his
face flushed and his hands clenched. He remarked that he was
getting fed up with the way things were going in the dining
room. Now he could stand it no longer. He had told the attendant that he was very sick of putting up with things as they
were, that he was not satisfied with the food nor with the service, and that he would appreciate a change for the better. He
appeared to be manifestly upset by this open demonstration of
aggression. He was reassured that his complaints were undoubtedly justified, and I promised to discuss the matter with
the dining room attendant.

Next day Johan had a complete amnesia for this experience,
although he recalled it under hypnosis. It was apparent that
his fear of aggression was still sufficiently great to bring
repressive forces into play. Nevertheless, assertiveness in his
relationships with other patients became so much more manifest that it was commented on by the ward attendants.

# IV

THE NEXT phase of the treatment involved the matter of Johan's attitudes toward himself. It was suggested to him that he would dream regarding these attitudes. A typical dream was as follows:

I was with another person whom I could not recognize. We were trying to do something like making cream out of milk, though we didn't have anything to make it with except a spoon. No, the idea was that we wanted to make whipped cream out of a certain inferior kind of cream, and we didn't have anything to shake it with, so we decided to shake the bottle. We didn't have any fork. We shook the bottle, and instead of turning into whipped cream, it turned into butter and water. We didn't get the stuff we wanted, and we needed whipped cream.

Johan's waking associations were to the effect that he did not know what the treatment was going to amount to, inasmuch as when he had first come to the hospital, the admitting physician, he was sure, had made a remark implying that he was no good. He then discussed his own notions of his worthlessness and presented the idea that not much could be done for him, since there must be something desperately wrong; otherwise he would not have had to come to the hospital. This opened the way to a discussion of his own basic attitudes toward himself and of the goal in therapy, which was to permit him to enter into an active, productive, and creative life.

At about this time a most spectacular change came over Johan physically. He held his head high, and he seemed to be able to express himself much better; there was no faltering for words. He spoke spontaneously about subjects that he had never before mentioned, such as his interest in photography and in swimming. He stopped looking at the ground in the presence of another person and discontinued the habit of holding his fingers over his mouth as he talked. He even wore his new clothing, polished his shoes, and tucked a breast handkerchief in his coat. The matter of his rights was stressed again and again during hypnosis, and it was posthypnotically suggested to him that his new-found attitudes, such as his ability to feel that he could express himself, would carry over into his waking life.

In discussion of the general subject of human rights and needs, the matter of sexual impulses came up. Johan rationalized his avoidance of women and stated that before he came to the hospital he had sought to relieve his tension by masturbating. He denied having any prejudices about masturbation but intimated that he had heard that masturbation might have evil effects. He boasted that he had not indulged himself during the entire period of his hospitalization, but he was sure that it was not because he feared the consequences.

The next day Johan seemed very tense and confided that he had had a restless night. There was something going on inside of him that bothered him. What this was he did not know. Associations in waking life and under hypnosis failed to reveal any cause for his tension. Regressing him to a 6 year level, I then gave him the following instructions: "You are six years old and I am your mother. We are going to go out together for a little walk. Would you like to come?"

Johan acquiesced. As we walked around the room, I remarked: "Johan, would you like to play in the playground? Do you see the playground?"

"Yes," he replied, "there is a swing, a sandbox, and a pool."

"Would you like to play there, Johan?"

"Yes, I would."

"What would you like to do?"

Johan hesitated, then replied: "I'd like to play in the sandpile." He knelt down on the floor and started to make motions as if he were piling up sand. "I am making a house," he remarked.

Putting down several dolls in front of him, I informed him that one was a policeman, the other a nurse, and the third a boy. Johan played eagerly with these objects, and then, taking a number of books, built what he described as a house of two stories. He placed the boy doll in the lower part and the two adult dolls in the upper.

"The boy is alone," he said, "he likes it there, what he is doing. He wants to play with matches. Mother smells smoke and she yells at him." Johan was noticeably excited and terminated the play by crashing the house down upon the dolls.

Upon awakening, he expressed a curiosity about the medical volumes on my bookshelves. He wondered if there were any books there that he might understand. As he talked, he kept bringing up the subject of self-abuse, and the rest of the hour was spent in discussing common misconceptions about masturbation.

At the next session he presented me with a note entitled "Daily Journal." It read as follows:

A day or two ago you spoke about young children being sex-conscious. You spoke about their desire to explore their own bodies. You said that most children either discovered for themselves or else were initiated into the act of masturbation. You said that this was a more or less normal phenomenon. You spoke of masturbatory activities as very often being a relief mechanism for tension. You said that physically no change or disturbance was effected by such activity. Then you said it is wrong for parents to punish and to scare children or to forbid them to indulge in activities of this kind. Of course, it is easily seen that understanding parents will not punish or scare their children under the aforementioned circumstances, but it also seems to me that no understanding parents would advocate such activities in their children, nor would they deliberately teach these things to their children. On the contrary, it seems to me that parents with understanding and knowledge aim to guard their children against the pitfalls of masturbation and to guide them toward a normal and happy sex life.

There seems to be a contradiction in this. From the conversations, I have gathered, you might express yourself as follows: Children are curious about the functions of their bodies. They are curious about sex. These are normal and healthy traits. Children should be curious. They should wish to find out about things. Children should express themselves in every way. If this is so, why is a boy or girl who exhibits this curiosity about things, or who strives to experience things, taken hold of and declared evil, an outcast, a derelict—not by his parents, but by the guardians of public morals, the very ones whose business it is to have an understanding of these things? Why is it misconduct to have a normal curiosity and a desire to express oneself, to find out about things sexually? Also here there seems to be a bit of contradiction.

In discussing the note, Johan brought up a number of fantasies about married life and confided that he would have liked to marry and to have children! This, he said, is the normal relationship of a man and a woman. The woman of his choice, however, would have to have such high standards that she would naturally demand the same high standards in the male of her choice. He himself could not possibly come up to such standards. He spoke vaguely of "excesses" of various kinds that might have undermined him, but he was not quite certain as to what these excesses were. I suggested to him under hypnosis that he would dream that night of fulfilling his deepest desires.

The next day Johan presented the following dream:

There were five of us who stepped into a boat ready to go off. It was an extremely thin skiff and could not hold any more than five people. It would be dangerous if another person entered. They never took anybody on the boat except men. One of the girls came running from the shore and wanted to come along. One of the fellows said, "You can't come along, this is dangerous."

Then in some way she insisted upon coming along and room was made for her in the front of the boat. When we went out, it became very dark and the wind came up and it began to rain. The wind became so strong that the boat was out of control. Then the boat began to fill with water from the rain. We were ordered to take in the oars and step out of the boat. All of us did, including the girl. We were in deep water and had to swim. Then in some way everything was changed and we were on the shore. We were lying down on the shore and the girl was lying down next to me. I don't know what happened to the rest of the fellows. There was some discussion, something to do with free love versus platonic love.

Johan's association to the dream was the memory of how, when he was about 25 years of age, he had often gone boating with his companions. No more than five men were allowed on a boat, and never any women, because this type of boating was considered dangerous. When the problem of his deep concern about sexuality was brought to his attention, Johan denied that he had ever had any sexual problems. He had remained celibate because he had had no time for frivolous love affairs.

Under hypnosis it was suggested to him that he dream about his real feelings regarding sex. The dream was this:

I was engaging in some kind of discussion with someone. It was about marriage and what we ought to do, whether one ought to marry or not. I gave out some examples about the unhappiness I had seen in marriage, also that I had no doubt that marriage was the proper thing and most natural and happy way of life. I was trying to express myself to the effect that I had an ideal and that this ideal was too high for attainment. In order to marry, one had to find the right person with whom one wished to be. It all seemed to be quite in the distance, and the whole idea of the dream was that I seemed to be floating off into the distance.

That night Johan had a spontaneous dream that was

A phantasmagoria of hopeless entangled occurrences. I seemed to be rushing around as if I was extremely busy. I was running at top speed, as though it was extremely important that I arrive at some certain place as speedily as possible. I seemed to run heedlessly in this direction and that, and there was nothing in particular that I wanted to accomplish. Then the scene changed and I was out in the rain. There were people here and there— just an ordinary street scene. The rain came down in torrents. Finally it became dense and impenetrable. It was possible to see only a few feet ahead. People bumped into one another. It was impossible to make any progress. I was drenched to the skin. I heard a trolley in the distance, splashing water, and at that time I decided to take the trolley, so I ran back; but the trolley stopped some place some distance behind me. I ran back, but the trolley sped past me down the street and I was left in the rain.

The associations to the dream were that he had been given many tasks that were meaningless and that resulted in nothing. This idea seemed in some way related to the entire treatment process. He could not understand why I bothered with him, when the authorities who had deprived him of his liberties felt that he was utterly worthless. There were further associations, to the effect that marriage was perfectly proper for some people, but that his best opportunities had passed and now he was too old. He confided that at one time he might have believed that sex was dangerous, but that now he was absolutely certain that sex was neither wrong nor sinful. Time was spent discussing on a waking level his attitudes about sex, particularly the fact that he might have felt that he had no right to important things in life.

At the next session Johan presented his reaction to this discussion in writing. There was little doubt that he was very skeptical of my explanations. His free associations dealt with the theme of his own worthlessness and expressed a feeling that he had in some way injured himself irreparably. When he was hospitalized and deprived of his rights, the authorities realized that he had reached the end of his rope and that permanent changes of a deteriorating nature had already overwhelmed his body.

All attempts to discover the nature of this deterioration failed. Under hypnosis and in waking discussions, an attempt was made to convince him that his ideas regarding physical decay might have originated in certain experiences and misconceptions of his early life and actually had no reality in the present. If he understood the source and extent of his problems, he would realize why he felt so undermined. Important also was the fact that his present relationships to people were responsible for many emotional stresses and tensions that could in themselves produce an abundance of symptoms.

Several weeks later I felt a change in his attitude toward me. This change was preceded by a spontaneous dream in which I was helping him to fix something that he had broken. He related it as follows:

I was inside a dining room and I had some trouble in getting the things I wanted. I was late or something. I collected some things there. I was in a hurry and I got away with it. I then dropped the tray with all the things on it. I had a feeling that I shouldn't have had anything because I didn't come on time. Because of this I picked things up hurriedly and in guilt, but I got away with it. I was told that I couldn't have anything else when I broke the dishes, and that I had to fix the things that I had broken. I said I couldn't fix things like that, and that they couldn't be fixed. The crowd around me was threatening me, but someone appeared from the crowd and helped me fix the things. He showed me how to repair the broken dishes. And so I was very happy that I wasn't in·trouble any more, and everyone seemed to be happy about the solution, even the ones who insisted that I repair the things that I had spoiled.

Under hypnosis he revealed that the person in the dream who helped him with the dishes resembled me. Although his life was broken, at least one person believed that it was not so shattered that it could not be repaired. His dreaming that it was possible for any person to help him, seemed to point to considerable progress in his development. When this was brought to his attention on a waking level, Johan shrugged his shoulders and declared that he was not at all convinced.

Shortly after this his behavior revealed that he was not as pessimistic as he had professed himself to be. He started a diary fashioned after the style of Pepys. An excerpt from it follows:

Up at six. Dressed and washed in a hurry. Made some toast for a couple of the boys and myself. Put my quarters in shipshape order. Did a bit of writing, a few odds and ends of work. The sun was shining, so put on my glad rags. Then to the office. Attended to a few things that were on the order of the day. Did some writing on my own. Then my daily interview with the doctor. I am looking forward to my talks with the doctor with eagerness. I feel perfectly at ease, and as time passes I am able to discuss and to deal with any subject without too much difficulty. I am aware of a tremendous change in my make-up. Things within are straightening out. The realization that another human being is genuinely interested in my welfare is a spur to great efforts on my part. The fact that so much time is given freely for my benefit is a proof to me that within there are still qualities worthy of nourishment. There is a sense of curiosity and happy expectancy once more, as in former years when I set out along a new line of study. The kind of thing I called high adventure.

Time for dinner. The morning passed almost before it started. A bit of work. A bit of writing. A bit of sketching. A few minor duties in the office. In the evening, made a meal from some odds and ends saved from dinner and supper for a few of us. A chair became a miniature table. A center decoration with a humorous or sentimental touch. My table decorations are becoming popular, and the boys are crowding around to see what is coming next. I have no doubt that I am breaking half a dozen rules or so, but I am asserting myself. I am doing what I please—regardless. — — And so to bed.

Under hypnosis, further emphasis was placed on the right to express oneself, and little scenes were enacted, both at a regressed and at adult age levels, in which Johan was able to stand up for his own rights and to feel secure within himself in so doing. Furthermore, posthypnotic suggestions were made about such things as asking the stenographer to type a letter for him, which permitted a living through in waking life of the feeling that he could ask for things without being criticized or punished.

# V

DURING the process of discussing the ability to express one-self, one's impulses, and one's needs, Johan again brought up the matter of his sexual adjustment. He confessed that for some reason he had not considered himself normal like other males, and he confided that his greatest fear in life now was that his present treatment would lead to nothing as far as sex was concerned. Free associations were very limited and the patient was blocked so frequently that there was little continuity in his ideas. It was decided to resort to hypnotically induced dreams to facilitate understanding of his unconscious trends.

Under hypnosis, he was instructed to dream that night of his attitude toward women and of his general attitude regarding sexual intercourse. He had the following dream:

Before me was the statue of a woman. It was placed on a high pedestal. I had a canvas and a sketch block in front of me and an easel, and I was to make a picture of the woman. I was planning how to do it. I doubted my ability to do justice to the figure on the pedestal, for it was exceedingly beautiful. The component characteristics of the woman it depicted seemed to be unconscious grace, calm composure, unafraid openness. I was wondering how I could make these part of myself, and thus perhaps be able to express them outwardly—to translate them into line and tone and color. As I was contemplating these things, it seemed to me that the figure on the pedestal was really a model on the dais in the studio, and that I was doing a study from life. The woman descended from the dais and came over to me.

"I am your ideal," she said, "I am a projection of your self. I am your aspirations and desires. No individual is complete in himself. Each one has a counterpart that completes him. Be unafraid; take that which is yours. You can do nothing of yourself. You can create nothing of worth until you are a complete human being."

She raised her head high and came closer. I took her head between my hands and kissed her. She continued to speak: "Two rivers flowing side by side, they combine into a strong stream. Two united flames are but one. Point and counterpoint may each be attuned; together they may interweave, they may separate and combine. Each may remain what it is; yet intermingled they may be a complete and harmonious melody."

Her words were an expression of my own feelings. The two of us seemed but one. Warmth and inner power took hold. I awoke with a feeling of rest and contentment.

In associating, Johan declared that he had always felt that his life was incomplete. Deeply he wanted to find his counterpart, but he felt that the kind of person he wanted was beyond his aspiration. This was owing to some lack within himself, and his present fear was that he would be unable to attain that which would permit him to live a life of completeness.

During the hypnotic session that followed, it was suggested that he would have a dream that would reveal more clearly his chief fear in life. In response to this suggestion he related the following:

I had a very strange dream. It was as if I were back in some old kind of civilization. A different kind of society existed than the present. There were all kinds of things that had to be done, in the nature of constructing things and building and hunting. There were certain things that had to be accomplished before a child was allowed among the adult men. Those tried in various things and found failing were never admitted to the men's quarters. They were sort of shutouts. It seems I was doing my best and succeeded well among the things required, but I was unable to accomplish other things. I was pushed constantly back, but I kept on trying again and again, and I had a feeling that it was beyond my ability; still I did not want to give up.

The conscious associations were to the effect that many tribes had a custom of putting children through ordeals in which they would have to stand pain before they could be initiated into manhood. He said: "I have always been afraid of not being able to make my own living or of being a burden on anyone. I also had a fear that I was not like other people. I would like to be like others in the way I am supposed to be. I had difficulty in behaving like others, like running around and going out with girls and doing things. I would have liked to be like others, but I really preferred that they be like me." He then stated that prior to his breakdown he had begun to form friendships and to open up to people. He was questioned as to whether this attempt at socialization might not have conflicted with his defensive device of isolating himself and of maintaining his detachment. Johan accepted this interpretation as completely plausible.

A posthypnotic suggestion was then given him to the effect that he would dream again that night of his greatest fear in life. The following day he presented this dream:

I thought I was in a field picking flowers. I wanted these flowers, and I wanted to protect them. They were extremely important to me, as if my life depended on them. It was as if I had the right to them. Someone else wanted to prevent me from having them. It was as if I got hold of these and then ran away with them. Then I awoke.

Associations to the dream were that his life had been spent in the attempt to attain knowledge, to gather information, with the idea that when he had finally acquired knowledge in all the various fields of endeavor, he would be as good as anybody else. Flowers were things of nature that one might study with benefit. They were things of beauty to which he had no right. Under hypnosis he remarked that a flower was like the male genital organ, the stem resembling the penis and the upper part resembling sperm cells, the carriers of life.

At this point it was suggested that he would be able to execute, while in the trance, drawings that would be symbolic of a flower. Johan quickly drew a series of sketches representing the sun, a row of books, a knife, a sheaf of wheat, insects, birds, and the same peculiar jagged and wavy lines that had appeared in his early marginal "doodlings." He identified each of these as related to the male organ. It was posthypnotically suggested to him that after he awoke he would have a compulsion to make a series of drawings all of which would represent to his sleeping mind the male genital organ.

The following day Johan confided that for some curious reason he had an impulse to make a series of drawings that in themselves appeared to be unrelated and that had no particular meaning. He said: "It was an amazing experience—a new kind of art, a kind of unconventional 'expressionism,' something on the order of automatic writing. You grab a pencil and hold it to the paper and see what happens. I tried it out after a while, and I was chuckling inwardly at the funny pictures I made."

The drawings portrayed a stalk of wheat, the sun, a daisy, two peculiar inscriptions, the head of an Egyptian king, the Sphinx, an Egyptian symbol known as the ankh, the cork of an ink bottle, a billiard table with a billiard cue and two balls, a sword, and a mortar and pestle; there was a drawing of clouds and rain, and another picture of the sun, inside of which were drawn a small parachute, a couple of parallel lines, a man walking in the rain and carrying an umbrella, a nail, a pen, and a sketch of the caduceus. There were two drawings through which lines had been scribbled as if to efface them. Each of these represented a hand holding a club.

Johan's waking association to the wheat was that grain is the basic substance of life for humanity. The sun is the "life giver" and ripens the wheat. The sun also ripens flowers. The Sphinx and the Pharaoh are related to sun worship. The beard on the Pharaoh stands for strength and authority. The associations to the other objects were conventional and superficial. Under hypnosis, the association to wheat was that the stalk connoted the male sexual organ and the grains the bearers of life or sperm cells. The sun was again the giver of all life, producing the wheat. The stalk of the flower was the penis and the upper part a collection of sperm cells, carriers of life. The Sphinx represented the greatest power of all, the superpower, the power to which a human being would like to attain. This was sexual power. The inscriptions and the ankh were identified as Egyptian sexual symbols, the Pharaoh as a man with great sexual power. The beard stood for strength, sexual strength. The cork of the ink bottle was a male object that could enter the inkwell, a female object. The billiard cue and balls were the male sex organs. The sword was a penetrating instrument that could enter things. The pestle was the male organ and the mortar the female organ. Rain was a stream, the starter of plant life. The plow entered the earth to prepare new life, like the penis. The parachute inside the sun was a seed, like the sperm. The two parallel lines were a river flowing. The umbrella was a shield from the rain, the life giver. The man under the umbrella was afraid of the forces of life. The umbrella itself was the same thing as the parachute, the stalk being the penis and the expanded part the sperm cells. Both the nail and the pen were penetrating instruments. The medical emblem was a symbol of the snake, and a snake was a long, penetrating animal that crept into holes like the penis.

After this session, for which Johan had posthypnotic amnesia, he continued to talk spontaneously of his greatest fear in life, which was that he might have lost forever the most worth while thing. Life for him had been a search and little else, and when that search was ended there had been no chance to apply the wisdom he had obtained. "I wanted to be like other people," he said, "but my hopes were shattered. Everything I wanted was turned upside down, and in spite of my constant search, I could not seem to find it."

It was suggested that the disillusionment he had experienced because his struggles to gain knowledge and completeness had failed, might have led to the despair that caused his emotional breakdown.

Around this time Johan became much more capable of carrying on a conversation, of expressing his own views, and even of doubting and criticizing the things suggested to him by me. He worked at many activities in the ward as well as on signs and art work in the office. He expressed the idea that he wished that he could accomplish more, that the day was too short to crowd in all his activities. He wrote:

> Sometimes when I listen carefully I hear a still small voice within. It is not saying anything, just humming, hesitatingly like, keeping time with the hum of the wheels. I have not been able to catch the tune yet. It is a satisfying hum. A hum that has been silent within me for many years.

One of the reasons for his interest in therapy, he confided, was that it restored his early feeling that there was something worth striving for, that, once he had attained all "knowledge" about himself through our mutual work in the study of his unconscious, he would be complete. An attempt was made to show him how this motivation was similar to that which he had prior to his breakdown. It was suggested that the fundamental problem was his feeling that he was lacking and incomplete. He had all his life attempted to restore himself to a state of intactness by gaining knowledge. It was essential to understand what he really meant by knowledge and to see how it fitted in with his need for security and self-esteem.

In the next few weeks Johan had a series of dreams in which he would stealthily gather flowers, birds, insects, and elongated inanimate objects. A man, whom he identified as myself, accompanied him on these expeditions. The purpose of this collecting was to subject the objects to scientific study in order to add to his knowledge. Under hypnosis he saw each object as in some manner related to the male creative principle.

Johan was very much impressed with the fact that his dreams and drawings pointed to the same problems that he had had from earliest childhood. He wrote:

It seems to me that the story my dreams tell me is a story that my consciousness repeats. The meaning of life lies in the completing of oneself as an individual, and to do this one must gather knowledge and wisdom and experience. One must seek one's counterpart, for without this the individual will remain incomplete and lacking. One must extend oneself freely. The knowledge and wisdom one has gained, the abilities one has gained, must be used in the service of those who are less fortunate than oneself. One must seek one's own happiness, for one cannot impart to others a lingering doubt in his mind as to how to go about attaining that which he wanted most from life.

The gathering of wisdom and experience is, for some reason, as it appeared to him, a punishable offense. Adam and Eve paid the penalty for seeking forbidden knowledge. If truth were only permissible, life would be worth living. His own history, however, attested to the manner in which punishment is meted out to a person who seeks the truth. Without provocation he was taken from his home and placed in a mental institution.

Many of his accusations were, of course, delusional. For instance, he insisted that when he first came to the hospital, everything was done to impress him as to how evil, worthless, and shameless he had been. This convinced him doubly of his guilt, and showed him that his suffering was entirely justified.

I felt that I had to suffer any indignities uncomplainingly. Had a helping hand been thrust toward me from the first, had I been made to understand that in the estimation of others, I was neither guilty, nor evil, nor worthless, I would have soon turned around and faced reality once more. I felt that most of those who held me beneath contempt were unintelligent, unscrupulous, selfish, and utterly depraved, and I turned against the system that made such things possible. There I was, eating my heart out, because I found myself lacking in certain respects, and I was despised by those who were more despicable than myself.

He then reiterated his belief that the reasons for his mental breakdown were physical in nature.

The individual's physical make-up is subject to changes; deterioration sets in and then destruction. At the breaking point, if not sooner, a mental condition will develop. Clearing up a mental condition of this nature does not mean a restoration to normal of a physical structure which had become damaged or destroyed.

There was little question that he was still unduly concerned with the deteriorated state of his body, and he again voiced the opinion that his quest for knowledge was primarily responsible for this decay. Under such circumstances, Johan insisted, there was no point in continuing therapy.

Several days later he spontaneously asked for an interview and confided that he had reconsidered the matter of stopping treatments. His change of heart had followed a dream that he recounted as follows:

I was working on a large drawing or painting. Others were working on similar drawings and paintings. It seemed that I was trying to give expression to the inner meaning or the character of the thing I was picturing rather than to the outward likeness thereof. I was quite satisfied and happy in what I was doing, and I felt that I had done something worth while. Then someone saw what I was doing. He began to laugh and make fun of my work. He thought it a disgrace to waste time on meaningless things like that. He pointed to the work of others, which was proper and conventional. Others came around and began to jeer and threaten. Someone pushed my work onto the floor. My books were strewn about, trampled upon, and broken. I sat down in a corner and hid my face in my hands. I was ashamed and disconsolate. Then I felt a hand on my shoulder. I tried to shake it off, but the hand remained, and after a while I looked up. There stood a man in a fresh white smock. In his hand he held brushes and paints and a variety of things. My drawing he had stood up on an easel. He smiled. "Remain true to yourself," he said. "If you have anything to say, say it. Come, I'll show you."

He went over to the easel and began to explain and instruct. He used his tools and materials and he taught me many new things. I discovered that what he was doing was exactly the same as I had been trying to do but had not been able to do alone. I was full of eagerness and enthusiasm and I asked my instructor that I be allowed to remain with him and learn all that I could and help him in his work.

In Johan's associations the man in the smock, who encouraged him to further endeavors, was linked up with me.

# VI

JOHAN's relationship to his parents and siblings now appeared to occupy the most important position in his mind. He went into detail regarding his attitudes toward his family. These embodied a strong feeling of resentment toward his mother, an attitude of fear toward his father, whom he accused of alcoholic tendencies and of mistreating his mother, some hostility toward his brother, and indifference toward his sister.

Under hypnosis it was suggested to him that he would dream regarding these attitudes, but that he would blot his dream completely from his mind; in addition the dream, though forgotten, would stimulate a compulsion to draw, and the drawing would symbolize more clearly the meaning of the dream.

The next day he presented a series of drawings. The first sketch showed a large sun; on one side of it were a book, a violin, and a pen, and on the other a bottle of alcohol, a group of illegible words, a ramshackle house, and a woman with a veil. His waking associations were these: "The sun is shining over good and evil. The good side is learning and knowledge. The arts and music are represented. There is quiet and dignity. On the evil side are the destructive things like drink, nonsensical talk without meaning, which results in sorrow and poverty."

The second sketch represented a half-moon, on one side of which were a hand, a loaf of bread, and a heart with lips inside of it. On the other side were a mask and a large question mark; inside of the latter there was a small mouse. His waking associations were: "The moon is shining over good and evil. The moon is a satellite, part of the sun. These are the good things—friendship and love. Then the material things like bread and food. On the evil side is the mask of pretense, insincerity, and squeamishness."

The third group of drawings comprised a series of objects revolving around a small sun, and the fourth group a series revolving around a small moon. The fifth group included a lamp, from which there radiated beams like those of the sun, and a number of varied symbols such as snakes, a dinosaur, a pyramid, a clock, flowers, gears, etc. This group represented learning with all the various types of knowledge delineated—painting, music, natural history, and medicine. The sixth group depicted a house, a sun, a moon, stars, a sickle and hammer, a tennis ball and racket, a pair of hands, a book, an easel, a violin, and a group of people extending their hands outward. These signified "the home, a little bit of work, a little bit of play, then the generous hands that distribute knowledge and gifts to those who need and wish them."

Under hypnosis, Johan identified the first group of drawings as follows: "That's father, the sun. On the one side are the good things of father. On the other side are the evil things." He interpreted the second group as showing the good and the evil side of his mother, who was symbolized by the moon. He remarked that he was particularly perturbed about the insincerity and timidity of his mother, which was represented by the mouse inside the question mark. The question mark itself represented "the great knowledge" that his mother kept from him. This pertained to sex, and the question mark itself consisted of male and female counterparts; the upper round part was male, the lower part female. The dot represented the product or child. The third group symbolized the good and evil sides of brother, the small sun, and the fourth those of his sister, the small moon. The fifth group embodied the story of himself and of what he wanted from life: "It was knowledge, the thing one could not get except by searching."

He then began to read sexual meanings into the various symbols of this group, identifying them as either male or female genital organs. He went on: "I was trying to get these things. The knowledge was the thing. One couldn't get the thing until one had knowledge. The lamp stands for light and knowledge, the sign of all things. I wanted to know about things. The books are all the things that there are. I was trying to get all the knowledge, all the things I wanted in life. Those are the things I wanted. I think of the light, which meant I wanted to know about everything. I wanted this great knowledge. I wanted to find out something that I didn't know, but I was scared. There was someone who didn't want me to know. It was everyone. First it was Mother, and then it was all society."

The sixth group of drawings represented completeness, which would be achieved when he had gained "the great knowledge." "When I had gotten many of the things I wanted," he continued, "when I had found out a lot of things and knew a lot of things, there was no use for them. I thought they were not real, that it was some sort of dream. Then the cloud, the line around the picture, is the dream. The thing that keeps apart from the outer reality. The house is the home the way it was in the dream. The sun is Father. The moon is Mother. The stars are all other people, my people. In this dream there was a companion. The things we knew and all the things we collected were passing through our hands and distributed to those searching for these things. The house is the house I'd like to be in. The red is the thing the light stands for. The hammer and sickle are work around the house. The tennis ball and racket are play and pleasure. The people with extended arms are really myself reaching for the sun, the great knowledge."

In his associations Johan revealed that he had always admired his father, particularly because of the latter's interest in books. He had always felt that his father was representative of all the various branches of learning. His father also used to play a violin. Johan admired and envied him. But when his father drank, Johan both hated and feared him. His mother was very timid and squeamish. She always hushed him up whenever he expressed curiosity about things. Toward his brother he always felt resentment because of a feeling that he himself was being crowded out of favor with his mother.

When Johan was asked to associate regarding "the great knowledge" that was being kept from him, no material could be obtained either at adult or at regressed age levels. It was decided then to experiment with crystal gazing. He was told that upon looking into the crystal on my desk he would see in it a vision of something that had happened to him when he was very little. After several minutes he remarked: "I see myself and Mother. She goes into a room where there are baths. There is a lady taking care. She gets it ready. I don't know what it is. I want to find out what it is Mother has, what they are going to do. The lady tells Mother to get ready, to take her clothes off. I go in with the lady. She puts hot water in. Then comes Mother and she has no clothes. She steps down in the bath. I stand there looking down. There are two buttons on the chest. I ask Mother what they are. She says they are nothing. I can see all she has, her legs and all. She has nothing like me. I am curious. I wonder what it is. I didn't ask her. Then she is full of soap, and she gets out of the bath."

Johan then closed his eyes and stated that he had walked home with his mother, and while going up the stairs he had felt a tingling in his penis. When they entered the house, his baby brother was screaming. His mother ran over to the child, while Johan felt very much hurt and angry.

Next day Johan handed me a poem consisting of two parts. The first part expressed the idea that despite all the hardships that are imposed on an individual, and the various adversities that he comes up against, he will, if he is willing to wait and can be patient, eventually triumph, even though opposed by others. The second part expressed the idea that truth and knowledge are in themselves worth while living for, and that one has to exhibit courage and to keep fighting for what one thinks is right. In associating to the poem, Johan recalled his dream of the boy of a primitive tribe struggling to attain to manhood, and also the dream in which he picked flowers in spite of the enmity and hostility of those around him. Johan could see clearly that his chief struggle in life was to reach a state of self-development and completeness of such sort that he could find a mate, a home, and happiness. This constituted for him attaining to manhood.

What puzzled Johan was the fact that he utilized sexual symbols to express this idea, and that he had condensed all of his problems unconsciously into the quest for sexual knowledge. He knew that what he was after was not solely sexual knowledge, but also the ability to express himself, to be independent, creative, and productive. It was suggested to him that he might have symbolized his attitudes in sexual terms because of certain childhood experiences that he had completely forgotten. He was reassured that his sexual preoccupation was not at all abnormal. The mystery that is made of sex for the child—the manner in which the subject is handled by parents and other adults—serves not to repress but to overemphasize sex, conditioning unconscious sexual thinking and symbolization. The struggle for maturity and self-sufficiency can thus be indicated by a desire for masculinity, while deep frustration can be represented by notions of physical castration.

There followed in the next few days dreams that appeared to have a symbolism similar to that of the drawings that Johan made while "doodling." The dreams embodied a man walking along the road with his arms outstretched as he approached the sun. It was essential that he should reach the sun, because his soul was aflame. As he approached the sun, he was filled with great happiness, with expectancy and joy; but his fear was that he could not get close enough, because the sun was so hot that it could easily destroy him. The sun represented everything desirable and worth striving for—the goal of all life.

For a period after this Johan entered into a state of resistance. While consciously he insisted that he was happy and well, he made no plans to leave the institution. His writings indicated a conviction that he had been injured irreparably by unjustifiable hospitalization. There was no possibility of ever leaving the institution. He was content to function as he was now, without the anxiety he had had previously. No new material could be obtained, with any of the various hypnoanalytic technics. He wrote:

There is nothing in my make-up that I am trying to hide. I have done my utmost to pick my inner being to pieces. If there are fears that remain unrevealed, they are unrevealed to my conscious mind. If the doctor has suspicions that fears or secrets exist in any particular direction, I wish he would tell me about them. I shall go after them and drag them out into the daylight. The fact that I have regained some of my old-time outlook on things, the fact that I have gained in physical well-being, I ascribe to the beneficial actions of the present treatment.

It was emphasized to him in both the waking and the hypnotic states that there were reasons why he was resigning himself to the peculiar condition of having to remain in the institution for the rest of his life. There were reasons why he felt that he would be unable to attain a more complete existence outside of the hospital. He was instructed under hypnosis that he would work on this problem unconsciously and that the meaning would finally become clear to him.

During the next few days Johan suffered a mild depression. This emotion precipitated his writing of the following note:

I have suggested, from time to time, that the causes for my breakdown and my subsequent mental attitude rested on a basis that was physical in nature. I have been assured that the basis is mental in nature, but one's mental state reacts upon one's physical make-up. I have also been assured that the process is reversible, that clearing up of one's mental condition means the return to normal of one's physical mechanism. The reason for my contention that the cause for my breakdown is physical is as follows: The individual's physical make-up is subject to constant changes. Deterioration sets in and then destruction. At the breaking point, if not sooner, a mental condition will develop. Clearing up of a mental condition of this nature does not mean a restoration to normal of a physical structure which has become damaged or destroyed.

I shall now go on to give specific incidents in order to illustrate the points that I have made. Perhaps therefrom can be gathered that my resentments for a corrupt system are not based upon fantasies or illusions, nor any other products of a sick and diseased mind, nor on any personal or childish grudges that have their roots in infancy. Perhaps therein also can be read the why and the wherefore of my faultfinding spree.

When first I came here, I was interviewed by some of the authorities, not in a kindly or reassuring manner, but with sneers and snickers. Not long after, the people to whose mercies I was entrusted were lined up, and one of the authorities in my presence gave them the details of my distorted, corrupt make-up. At a somewhat later date I was made to understand that one as corrupt as I had no right to food or drink, that it was owing entirely to the good will of my guardians that I would receive these things, and that I ought to be ashamed to accept them. I decided that it would be far better to starve to death than to accept a crust of bread from the hands of corrupt, evil-minded, stupid individuals who never in their lives had done an honest day's work. These and numerous other experiences of a similar nature made me critical and antagonistic toward the system of make-believe. Soon I discovered that my record was a one-sided affair. An utterly distorted picture of an individual in whom no truth was to be found.

Johan then confided that he was certain that the authorities had detected evil in him. Through heredity or through excesses of one sort or another, he had probably damaged himself. He was therefore being punished for his corrupt physical nature by being hospitalized. He wrote in his diary:

While worthless people on the ward are helped and told they are worth while, that everything will be all right, I on the other hand am told that I am worthless, and that there is no help, therefore I must be worse than these others. Nevertheless, my belief in the doctor and his sincerity, my belief in the present treatment, remains unshaken.

In the attempt to deal with this resistance, it was emphasized that while the goal of life is self-sufficiency, completeness, and heterosexuality, which he might symbolize in terms of masculinity or knowledge, there was something that had prevented him from achieving his goal. This block seemed also to be interfering with his analysis, taking the form of a resistance to further progress. It was essential to determine the nature of this resistance in order to get on with his development.

It was suggested to him under hypnosis that he dream of what possibly might prevent a man from gaining what he wanted most in life. The ensuing dream was as follows:

I was on some kind of mountain-climbing expedition, something worthy of achievement, to gather new scientific data. People tried to prevent me because of the danger that existed, but I set out nevertheless. First I had to go through the foot of a hill, bog and swamp land. Then I had to ford little rivers. There was trouble with insects and mosquitoes. I tried to settle down and do some cooking, but I burned the food. On the way up there were all kinds of experiences with animals. I ran across people who were not so friendly. It was very hot and unpleasant. It then became very cold. Some of the slides were lost. It was very hard going. I slipped, and I hurt myself. I hacked the ice with a pole, making holes in it. That was the most dangerous part of the mountain climbing. Then there were other great hardships. I don't know what became of the expedition, because I never got to the top.

In associating to the dream, Johan remarked that he had had the same kind of sensation as in the dream in which he walked toward the sun, a feeling of great expectancy, though knowing that he would never quite reach his goal.

While he was still in the trance, he was asked to sketch the meaning of the dream. Rapidly he drew a road, at the end of which there was a sun. A man was walking down the road, but there were several barriers in his path. On the left side of the road was a large hand holding a dagger pointed toward the man. An inverted can was spilling water on the hand. Above the hand was a series of interrupted lines representing rain. On the right hand side of the road a huge dragon with mouth agape faced the man as if it were about to swallow him. Above the dragon were wavy and jagged lines such as had appeared in his early "doodling." Associating to this drawing, he revealed the fact that the hand and dagger device really represented a hand holding a penis. Examination of the drawing showed that the hand was holding the dagger much as the penis is held in the masturbatory act. Johan identified the dragon's tail as a huge penis and the head of the dragon as that of an ogress. The water spilling on the hand and the rain above threatened to drown the man by penetrating his lungs. The wavy and jagged lines represented heat and fire, which could also penetrate into the body of the man. These stood for all the obstacles that impede a man from reaching the sun. The sun itself symbolized "the origin of all things, the source of creation, father, and the male creative principle or penis."

As Johan associated to the symbol of the hand and dagger, he suddenly recovered an early dream that he had had repetitively during his early childhood. It was as follows:

I am a small boy. I enter a pitch-dark room on tiptoes. I feel that I have no business in that room, but that I am curious about something and want to gain some forbidden knowledge or information. I know where the lights are and am now going to put them on. There seem to be lamps of various kinds. I strike matches and light kerosene lamps. I see the flames but these spread no light. The room remains as dark as before. There are gas flames, open and with mantles and glass funnels. These lights burn brightly but spread no light. There are candelabras of various kinds. There

are electric bulbs of all sizes and shapes.   I press the buttons and pull strings.
I swat wall contacts.   Filaments are glowing white-hot but no light passes
beyond the filaments themselves.   "Oh, I'll find out how to do it," I say.

I continue to try all possible ways of getting light in this room.   Then all
at once I am gripped with fear and with remorse for having tried to find
out how it is done.   Then I realize that my doings are being watched by the
one who was in possession of the secret of making light, whose orders I had
disobeyed.   I also realize that my manipulations of the light equipment have
caused some irreparable damage.

Johan revealed that as a child he slept in the room adjoining
that of his parents and was often very curious as to what they
were doing in their room.   He also at this particular time was
concerned as to what the differences were between boys and
girls.   He had been initiated into childhood sexual play during
a visit with a cousin, a little girl, who was precocious in sexual
matters.   Johan said that he had an impulse to walk into his
parents' room but restrained himself because of fear.   As he
talked about his curiosity, he complained of a sinking sensation
in the pit of his stomach and of a feeling of choking and tense-
ness.   He stated that it occurred to him that he had done something funny in the cellar, something that had to do with fire
and smoke.   He did not know what this was, but it filled him
with dread.   He could smell the smoke as he talked, and it had
something to do with boiling chemicals in a tin can over a kerosene burner.

In associating to the dream consciously Johan remarked:
"It is a peculiar fact that when things went wrong with me I
always accused myself of all kinds of wrongdoing.   I believed
that there was not a thing that I had done in life that was not
wrong.   Especially the fact that I had spent most of my life
in studies and in the pursuit of knowledge.   This seems like
idle curiosity and wrongdoing.   I had a feeling similar to the
one in my dream of long ago where I saw that my desire to find
out about things had caused irreparable damage."

In a note expressing his reaction to these experiences, Johan
revealed that even though he could see sexual symbols in his
drawings, he believed that the sexual significance of his dreams
and drawings was insignificant.   Sex had never been an im-

penetrable mystery to him, since he knew all about it quite early. What had kept him from marrying was no prejudice about sex, but merely the fact that his experiences had shown him that married people were usually quite unhappy. His resentment toward everyone and everything, toward society as a whole, did not exist prior to his coming to the hospital. The note went on:

> My affairs were given over for management by my brother. I was considered an incompetent with no brains or understanding, worthy of no more consideration than a piece of furniture. Should it be thought that my apathy or mental outlook made me incompetent to look out for my affairs, I may suggest that it was the knowledge of the hopelessness and viciousness of the situation that made me apathetic.

The remainder of the note reflected feelings of resentment directed against me and the treatment, and stated that there was no need to go on because the idea of progress could not be hoped for. Johan's plunging deeply into unconscious material apparently had stirred up anxiety and had caused him to fear further probings. For several days hypnosis was temporarily discontinued. The time was spent in discussing with Johan the fact that a persistent feeling of being irreparably damaged might serve a defensive purpose, perhaps in justifying his failure to gain what he wanted from life—truth, knowledge, and independence. It was pointed out that since he did not know what real forces had kept him back, he was trying to credit his failure to heredity, a bad home, a corrupt physical structure, and to other causes that might logically be adduced. It was essential to look into the whole structure of his hopelessness, since this might be the chief barrier to getting well.

Shortly afterward Johan presented me with a drawing that he had made automatically and about which he was very curious. In the center was a candlestick from which radiated a number of objects, such as books, test tubes, retorts, etc. Surrounding these objects there was an arc, complete except at one point, where a break appeared. Above the break there was a large violin with radiations leading to a house and to a heart. Johan tried hard but was unable to interpret this drawing.

Under hypnosis he remarked that the drawing symbolized a dream that he had had the night before and forgotten. He had dreamed that he was wandering around, talking to people and searching for something. He wanted to experience things. In his search he came to a building where he was told he could go no farther. Then he was roughly taken inside and prevented from making further progress. There was someone inside playing a violin. Johan asked whether he might play also. It developed that he could play very well. In fact, he played so well that the people around him became very thoughtful and permitted him to leave the house, in company with a young lady. His association was that his father also played the violin well. In the dream he himself wanted to play the violin and he was able to play it.

Associating to the drawing under hypnosis he remarked: "That is looking for things, trying to find out things. That is the light and all the objects around the light. There are many things worth looking for, but there is the barrier. That is the arc. You can't pass through it except through one place where the violin is. The violin is kindness. Through that you can continue outside, and there you can find a house, a home, and love."

Johan was presented with a crystal and told that he would see in it the real meaning of the violin, the house, and the heart. He gazed into it intensely, but all that he could see was a girl in a bathing suit. It was then suggested that the automatic drawing as well as the dream symbolized the very points that had been emphasized previously, namely, that what he had sought from life was to achieve a state of self-sufficiency, completeness, and masculinity like his father's. This was the meaning of reaching for the sun. Masculinity is to be attained through a heterosexual relationship, which was symbolized by the violin, the house, and the heart. But if he was to succeed, it was necessary first to gain knowledge to make himself complete. This was symbolized by the light and the objects surrounding the light. Johan was requested to remember this discussion in the waking state.

# VII

For several days after the interpretation of his drawing Johan was in an extremely exalted mood. He believed that this was caused by our discussion. His happy mood, however, did not last long and was replaced by an emotion of depression. Johan remarked that he was quite cognizant of the fact that what he wanted from life was the attainment of freedom, creativeness, and self-sufficiency—all of which he was quite sure were incorporated in his concept of masculinity. However, he was conscious of something lacking within himself, which prevented him from attaining this goal. He was certain that his quest for knowledge was an intermediate station in the gaining of his ultimate objective.

Under hypnosis he was instructed to symbolize his present attitude toward himself in a drawing. He then drew a crude object that he identified as an empty vessel. Association to this brought out the fact that he felt that he was genitally lacking. As if to symbolize his own genital organ, he quickly drew a half-sun. He then drew a dagger, a heart, and a house and separated the dagger from the heart and the house by a line. When questioned as to what the dagger signified to him, he remarked that it had something to do with certain fearful aspects of the genital organ. The heart and the house meant love, marriage, and a home. He was unable to express the meaning of the line.

When asked to associate to it, he hesitated at first; then he suddenly started to tremble and could hardly talk. His pulse rate rose and he seemed to be suffering from acute anxiety. He exclaimed that he had just recalled an incident that had happened when he was very young and that he had only vaguely remembered up to this time. "I was something like five years old," he said, "and we were living in the outskirts of the city. Our back window faced an open field and in the near distance, there was a farmhouse. There were trees. There were chickens and pigs and horses. I used to like to watch the people sowing or reaping or gathering hay or doing all sorts of things around the farm. One day I woke up early in the morning and the sun was shining. I heard a lot of noises outside. I ran to the window. I heard squealing. It came from the distance. They had been collecting hay for many days. Today they are not bringing in hay. The squealing begins. I ask Mother what it is. She says they are doing the slaughtering. It's too far off and I can't see. There are many people, steaming water, big containers. I hear the noise, then Mother makes dinner, and I forget about it. I could hear the squealing all day long. It fills me with a kind of dread. Then I am very curious. When it gets dark I want to see. I want to see what they are doing. They make a fire and I can't see. It's too dark. I turn to Mother and say, 'Light the lamp so I can see what they are doing.'

"Mother lit the lamp and brought it to the window. I could not make out anything except the reflection of my own face and the squealing, and I was afraid."

Johan said that he remembered this experience as soon as he thought of the line in the drawing. Upon awakening he remarked that his depressive mood had disappeared. It was replaced by the same happy feeling that he had had previously.

Next morning he presented a note on the following dream:

I want to find out things. I am very curious. I am little and at home Mother interferes. I am alone and I want to read a book—Father's book which has knowledge. Then I see Father coming home carrying a part of a book entitled *Light*. I want to read the book, but I am prohibited. Then I do learn a lot about knowledge. Mother does not approve. I save my money to buy a container or a tin. Then I take a kerosene lamp down the cellar to find out about things. Mother comes in and smells the smoke and is very angry. She says I can't have a kerosene burner any more. Then I am sad and I try to learn new things, but I am ridiculed. People are not interested. They do not believe I know things. So I am not able to do the things I want to do and I am not happy any more.

During the remainder of the day Johan complained of an intense feeling of excitement. He felt as if he were just about to discover something. The next morning he remarked that there was something going on inside of him that he did not quite understand—there were feelings of intense joy as well as feelings of depression. Under hypnosis he was told that if he had had a dream the previous evening, he would have the same dream again and would relate it to me. After about five minutes Johan exclaimed:

I did have a dream last night. It was as if something really did happen. I'm coming home from school. Mother says she has to go out and won't be back for a long time. I don't know what I'll do with my time, so I go out. A number of boys had a shanty outside. We were talking about girls and marriage. One of the older boys said that one must not misuse his body. One should not abuse himself or he would lose his power. I do not feel afraid because I know that I haven't lost my power. Now I am at home. I have found a book. It is a doctor's book. I sit down to read it. I read many things, and it says that masturbation does not cause physical harm. Now there is an old man and he is talking. Sometimes he reads a book and he says, "Sexual excesses cause impotency. Normal sexual activities or abnormal ones are the same in this respect."

Now I am in a crowd, and they take hold of me and drag me into a dirty-looking, evil-smelling place, and they punish me and abuse me, and they say they are going to kill me. Then I protest. I say I am not a criminal. I haven't done anything wrong. They all look like criminals. Somebody reads in a book and says, "That's the law."

I am filled with fear, but my indignation is greater than my fear. In some way I am able to get away from them. I am in another crowd. They punish and curse me. They say I am a maniac and criminal. They say they are going to chain me and keep me forever. I protest again, and then someone reads from the book and says, "Maniacs and criminals will be deprived of their powers of procreation. So says the law."

They are laughing and jeering. They are giving me some poisonous-tasting things to drink. They are punching holes in my skin and flesh.

Johan then revealed that for the first time in years, prior to going to sleep, he had had the temptation to masturbate, but had not yielded to it.

He was instructed to remember the dream when he woke up. Upon awakening, Johan remarked that the dream seemed to be a review of one aspect of his life, with special emphasis on sexual matters. It seemed to contain very little symbolism. It dealt with ideas and emotions in connection with masturbation. During his childhood and later he had had very little fear of the consequences of masturbation. His fears were very soon allayed whenever they happened to crop up. He was never scared or threatened, and the possibility of punishment or mutilation never entered his mind. Of this he wrote:

It is scarcely probable that my fears or inhibitions were caused by some early fearful experiences. Fear took hold only after my breakdown. My fear was caused by actual fearful experiences. It has not to do with fantasies or imaginings. Suppose a man, an explorer, is captured by some savage tribe. Suppose he is subjected to torture of various kinds. Suppose as he is on the verge of being put to death, he is rescued. Such a man may suffer from some sort of shock. He may be gripped by fears. Such a man will not be said to be suffering from a complex. His fears will not be attributed to fantasies or imaginings. Their basis will not be sought in childhood fears or anything in the past.

The next few sessions were again spent in discussing experiences that had led Johan to feel he had been unjustly treated. He was quite certain he had been discriminated against while he was in the hospital. He was grateful for the therapy that he was receiving now. He wrote:

Thanks to the instructions of the doctor, I have come to understand the meaning of some of my symbols that I used. I have come to see many aspects of my make-up quite clearly. Knowledge to me became a symbol for all that was desirable, but the knowledge that I wanted was really a special knowledge. It was a knowledge about things I felt were prohibited. I have gained a new interest and a feeling of new worth. As things were I could have done nothing of myself, and the hand on my shoulders I tried to shake off, but the hand persisted in coming back and helping me.

Johan confided that as a result of treatment he was beginning to see very much more clearly the pattern of his life. In his diary he explained:

For a great many years I was interested in many things. I believed that life had a meaning only to the extent that one was interested in and liked the work one was doing. I studied and worked incessantly along the lines of my choice. I made excellent progress and advanced to a point where I considered I was doing things worth while and highly interesting to me. My work was well paid and I was highly regarded in the field of my choice. What was not fully clear to me, that I just begin to realize, was that I was striving for as full and complete a life as possible. I was consciously working around on my personality. I was striving to acquire the characteristics that I admired in others and that I knew were lacking in myself. For instance, I was striving to attain an easy and sincere manner in dealing with people. I liked to take part in discussions. I familiarized myself with a variety of subjects and sought success as a conversationalist. I sought companionship and friendship among diverse kinds of people. I was interested in physical activities and sports. I was rapidly arriving at a point where I felt I had overcome my difficulties and was attaining a fairly happy and successful life.

There was about ten years of steady advance in my work until 1929, when the depression came. I then lost my job and my savings, but due to my ability in my particular field I was soon offered another job. The work was exacting and incessant, but after the hard years there came a period of good years. We were in a "boom" once again. I gained new responsibilities, was busier than ever. I began seeing a possibility of gaining independence and becoming a master in my work. I worked day and night. I neglected most of my other interests and occupied my time to the exclusion of almost everything else. I kept this up for over a year.

In the beginning of 1937 I began to feel tremendously tired and run down. I thought of my interests of a lifetime and that they had been totally neglected for so long. Then I began to accuse myself of selfishness. I felt that I had cheated my employers by diverting my energies. I took work home and worked on my own time. I felt I owed this to my concern to compensate for previous negligence, but my feeling of being selfish did not leave me. My whole life and its interests were analyzed. I felt that I had always had plenty of everything. I had done the things I had enjoyed doing. I thought of poor people who had nothing. People who had to do hard distasteful work. I felt that one human being had no right to have so much while others had nothing. I decided that I ought to know what it meant to suffer the way others did. I gave up all former interests. I denied myself every pleasure. I gave up every luxury. I allowed myself none but the scantiest portions of the coarsest food I could find. My inner soul nevertheless cried for the interests without which life had no meaning. I decided that life was not worth living without interests, without a goal. Yet I felt that my every suffering must be borne, that in a way to give in was an unforgivable weakness. I picked my soul to pieces. I found myself wanting on all counts. Every aspect of my life had its share of attention. My sex life came in for its share as well as did everything else.

At this time there was another event that added to my state of confusion and bewilderment. My father passed away. Contradictory emotions filled my soul. I felt pity and regret mingled with a sense of relief. I felt I should have remained at home, though I knew that this would have meant stagnation in every sense of the word. I felt I should not have broken away, developed my own interests. Then came before my mind's eye the vanity of all things— the meaninglessness of strife—the mystery of existence, life. What is it in its innermost structure? What is it? Life surely is not the puny, nonsensical flash in the pan that science defines it to be.  Death surely is not utter annihilation.

For six months I kept it up, denying myself everything, doing a full day's work every day.  There was nothing to look forward to.  I did my work mechanically and in a routine fashion.  It soon became a torture.  It was like endlessly repeating a deed the evil nature of which I had discovered. Being torn to pieces by my sense of duty, my desire to keep going, my wish to do no wrong, my conviction of the futility and meaninglessness of things, my spiritual and mental torture became indescribable.  The lack of nourishment I had subjected myself to made my torture a physical one as well.  And then it happened.  I was taken away not as a sick person, but as a criminal of the worst kind possible.  I can't get over the feeling that some injustice had been done.  This was the worst thing that could have happened to me, because it convinced me of the worthlessness of everything I had ever done.

All attempts to find out what specific injustices had been inflicted upon Johan produced merely vague generalities about how his privileges and liberties had been taken from him.  I could sense from his emotional reactions and his blocking that he was concealing something so painful to him that he could not tell me about it.  Suggestions to this effect brought denials and vigorous protestations that the accusations that he had already made were ample to account for his feelings.  Under hypnosis we were no more successful.  I decided then to resort to automatic writing.  Given the usual suggestions for automatic writing, Johan was told that after awakening he would retain his ability to write automatically.  As we talked I would direct questions to him, and his hand would, independently of him, write the true answers.  Upon termination of the trance Johan and I engaged in a conversation about certain phases of art and photography.  In the course of the discussion I casually asked him: "Is there any incident so terribly painful to you that you are concealing it from me?"

Johan denied that he had ever concealed anything from me, but as he talked his hand wrote: "Yes—burnig flesh."

Below this it drew a picture of a hand holding a dagger very similar to the one in the sketch that represented the dream of the man walking toward the sun.  Johan could not interpret the writing or drawing and no further information could be obtained under hypnosis.

While in a trance Johan was instructed that he would have a dream about anything he wanted—a dream that he would remember upon awakening. The dream was as follows:

There was something I wanted to buy. I worked and put aside treasure to permit me to buy this. Then I went out to buy the thing, but I was told by the guide who was with me that the treasure I had put aside wasn't worth anything. It was false, and I wasn't able to buy anything with it.

He associated the guide with all the educational forces that had previously urged him on but had given him poor advice. "First," he said, "there was Mother and Father. Then there were some people in school, some people everywhere, some people where I worked, some people I didn't see. They speak through their books and writings."

He emphasized that he did not include me among the "misguided" guides.

Throughout the day he was again overwhelmed by a feeling of great joy and ecstasy. He was unable to account for this mood in the waking state, nor did he remember dreaming. Under hypnosis he revealed that before going to sleep he had had an impulse to masturbate, which he did not consider significant. He had refused to yield to this impulse. During the night he had this dream:

I had a bag of apples. I thought they were fine. I was eating them once in a while. A man came along and said: "You can't do that. That's all you have. You have to save it for food later on. If you eat it now you won't have it later."

They were supposed to be used only when really needed. He threatened to beat me up if I didn't obey his orders. I was very scared and thought: "What has he to do with this? It is my apple."

Associations revealed that eating apples connoted the same thing as gaining pleasures in masturbation, that masturbation is not permissible, since it may result in permanent damage of some sort.

When Johan awakened the matter of his right to express his impulses was discussed in detail, and it was suggested that he might possibly be using the symbol of masturbation to represent his right to be free and expressive, to enjoy pleasures, and to do what he wanted to do when he wanted to do it. Johan replied that he had never felt that he had any masturbatory problem. If he ever really wanted to masturbate he would do so, and he was sure that he would experience no guilt about it.

At the next session it was decided to precipitate matters so that Johan could see more clearly whether or not he had any unconscious guilt regarding masturbatory activities. He was given the posthypnotic suggestion that he would have an uncontrollable impulse to manipulate his genital organ that night, an impulse so strong that he would be unable to resist it.

Next morning Johan appeared in a rather distraught state. He presented the following dream:

> I dreamed I didn't feel well. I was working too hard. I felt I shouldn't do that kind of work. It was interesting work, but I shouldn't do work that I didn't like to do so much. I thought of the things I had that were good, and that I shouldn't have good things. I tried to have as little as possible. I felt sick and tired.

He could not account for the dream nor understand its meaning. Under hypnosis he revealed that the dream seemed to be a reaction to a masturbatory impulse he had had on the previous evening.

It was then suggested to Johan that he would have a dream that would symbolize masturbating as well as indicate his attitudes and feelings regarding masturbation. The dream was this:

> A man was eating candy. He kept on eating candy. I said it was foolish. It didn't agree with him or his system, still he kept on eating candy. I asked him why, and he said: "It tastes so good."
> And then his teeth were destroyed by his candy eating. It was really a destructive habit, and I couldn't understand why he did it, since it would have been an easy matter to give up anything that was harmful. I despised him for being so unable to control himself, and I thought it served him right to fall to pieces.

In his associations Johan remarked: "One ought to be able to control oneself. One should do the things that are right even though they are unpleasant. At the time when I had the

idea that everything I had done was wrong, I felt that even
though a thing was difficult and unpleasant, one shouldn't shirk
it.  I gave up smoking because I thought it did me harm.  I
gave up all kinds of pleasures."

Johan was then reminded that before we began our treatment, it had been found, after a routine dental check-up, that
he had a number of severely decayed teeth, which were then extracted.  At that time he had had an acute anxiety attack.
His present dream seemed to point to a relationship between
tooth decay and self-destructiveness.  Johan remarked that
there was a relationship.  His bad teeth indicated that his entire
system had become corrupt, possibly through masturbatory
practices.  He was then reminded that in the waking state he
resisted very actively any suggestion that he had problems relating to masturbation.  He was instructed to integrate his
unconscious and his conscious feelings.  When he awakened,
however, there was no indication that he had absorbed this
command.  His free associations, though carefully noted, involved matter-of-fact things and made no reference to any of his
deeper problems.

The next day Johan turned in written notes on a long dream
that apparently had been stimulated by the events of the previous session.

After my interview with the doctor, I was quite happy, and my thoughts
were roaming the Elysian fields.  Fauns, nymphs, were my companions for a
space of time.  By nightfall I was on friendly terms with Eros and Psyche.
Aphrodite herself was hovering nigh till Morpheus took me in her arms and
closed my eyes with her kiss.  I was dreaming.

"Why did you do it?" said the man with the razor edge nose and receding
jaw.  "Virility, manliness, strength, that's what I believe in.  Don't you
wish you were I?" said he, pushed out his chest, and pulled in his rudimentary
jawbone.

"Why did you do it?" said the fellow with the potbelly.  "One must be a
master of one's desires.  Continence in all is my motto; frugality and fore-
thought are the mother and father of happiness, long life, and a sturdy physique."  Potbelly chuckled with self-satisfaction at his own cleverness.

Why did you do it?" sighed the lady with the plumb line façade, with the
burning black eyes.  "Love is a gift from heaven.  I might have made known
to you the charm of love."

Her mouth was a carmine slit.  "Why did I do what?" said I.

"Why did you eat all the apples and get sick in your stomach, instead of baking an apple pie and enjoying a tasty bite at a festive board?" said Potbelly.

"Why did you sow wild oats upon the wind?" said Razor Beak. "You could have put all your eggs in one basket. No waste of energy. You'd have had something. Take 'em or leave 'em as you saw fit, exercise aplenty. Fine physique. Full of pep." Razor Beak pulled in the stomach and slapped his heels together in a military fashion.

"Why did you pick wormwood in secret places? Love is a flower that blossoms in the sunlight. The fiery red flower is plucked by whoever chooses. It seeks sunshine and warmth in dreary places." Lady Black Eye looked heavenward, tightened her mouth till it looked like a thin red thread.

"You are talking in riddles," I ventured. "Why can't you say what you have to say and get it done with?"

"What would be the fun of that?" said Razor Beak.

"Are you crazy?" said Potbelly.

"Such things aren't done in polite society," said the lady. "Love is a language of poesy—besides, it is good to keep them guessing."

"Were it not that I had learned a trick or two from our friend Freud, I might not know at all what you are driving at," said I. "As it is, I have a hunch as to which way the wind is blowing."

"Love is provoking, love is exhilarating, love is mysterious. Love should not be treated roughly. The coarseness of common speech should not be used in dealing with love. The language of love is poesy," said the lady.

"Love means nothing from the point of view of nature," I said. "Love is nothing in itself. In the higher forms of life, propagation of the species depends on sex, and the propagation of the species is all that counts with nature."

"Why mention that?" said the lady.

"The exhilaration of the senses," I continued, "is the means whereby nature makes sexual union desirable by the individual. It is the reward for the fulfilling of the purposes of nature."

"The heck with nature," said the lady. "Love for love's sake is my motto."

"Man has disordered the purposes of nature," I continued. "Man takes the reward and cares not about the rest. Man is hoggish, but nature revenges itself always. Love must be giving as well as taking. Love cannot be selfish. If it is, it is not love."

"Love is like wine," said the lady, "sweet wine. It makes you feel good all over."

"Love may be likened to old wine. Mellow, full of warmth. It gives you confidence, kindliness, courage," I said.

"Yeah, and a headache," snapped Potbelly.

I continued: "Unselfish love has a reward beyond the essential one. Home, prestige, everything that goes with it. To indulge in a thing for the sake of indulgence is unworthy. It is immoral."

"I could have said that myself," said Potbelly. "One must be refined, one must touch nothing but the best, and just a little. Self-sufficiency is enough," Potbelly chuckled.

Said I: "One must be able to control oneself. One must have a strong will. One must be master of one's senses. One's desire should be subject to one's will."

"Bravo," said Razor Beak. "Only so long as you have all your eggs in one basket, you are all right. Singleness of endeavor means strength, you know."

"In heterosexual union, if true love is present, one's self is projected outwardly onto one's counterpart. Completion results from such a union," I said.

"You forget there is a lady present," said the lady and lowered her eyes. "I believe I am going to blush."

I continued: "Love turned inwardly on to oneself is self-love. It is the opposite of love. It results in depletion and not in completion. The senses are stirred up but cheated. It is a prodding, an irritation without culmination. It plays havoc with the individual, mentally, physically, and in every other way."

"Look at me," said Razor Beak and clicked his heels.

Said I: "I started out by saying that love means nothing to nature, that man has distorted the purpose of nature. Such distortion is perversion. Perversion takes various forms. Masturbation is one of these, probably the worst."

"Disgusting," said the lady with the plumb line front, and she seemed to withdraw until nothing but a carmine streak remained.

Potbelly shook his head, Razor Beak clicked his heels, and so I decided to awaken from my dream.

Under hypnosis it developed that this dream too had been stimulated by an impulse to masturbate. Johan expressed great resentment against "Razor Beak," "Potbelly," and "Lady Black Eye." "Razor Beak" was actually a man whom Johan knew at one time, who was a worker in the Y. M. C. A.: "he had a funny face, a sharp nose, and no chin." "Potbelly" was an instructor of English whom Johan knew during the first world war: "he was short, fat, and narrow-chested." The woman was the head of one department in his former place of employment: "she was tall, thin, straight up and down, liked to boss people around." Johan definitely did not like her: "people of this appearance I have come across from time to time, they are prudes, and I have contempt for them."

# VIII

I<small>N THE</small> next few sessions Johan appeared tense and somewhat agitated. Finally he turned over to me a set of notes entitled "Ten Days," which proved to be the turning point in his analysis. These notes read as follows:

Many aspects of my life have been gone into. I have dealt openly and honestly with every period of my life. Some experiences, some subjects were painful to deal with, but their painful nature did not prevent me from dealing with them. My childhood, as far back as I can remember, has been dissected and analyzed. My means of study and active work have had their share of scrutiny.

The period of time that I have spent in this present place, my experiences here, my thoughts and opinions in connection with these experiences, I have dealt with openly and frankly. My life is an open book (at least so far as the doctor goes). I have no secrets—*except. There is one period of time that I have not dealt with at all.* Although I believe that this period holds the solution to my make-up, I believe that the individual that is I cannot be understood without an understanding of this period of time. The "I" that the doctor knows—my thoughts (my antagonisms toward society, my disbelief in the sincerity of others), my behavior, my character—is as different from myself of previous years as can well be. When the doctor speaks about my rights to live my life, I doubt. When he speaks of sexual indulgences as normal or harmless or as causing no destruction to one's physical mechanism, when he assures me that I am no different from 90 per cent of other human beings, that those who sneer at me, despise me, call me evil names, do so in ignorance, I doubt.

Of course, I believe that my make-up is based upon and due to childhood experiences and environmental conditions. Repressions and inhibitions in early life caused me to develop the way I did. But I led a fairly happy and normal life up to a certain point. My experiences after this point was reached, are responsible for my present make-up. The reasons for my doubts, the explanation of my make-up will be found in the period of time that I am referring to. This period of time is a short one—ten days.

I was brought from my home to an evil-smelling, prison-like place, among yelling and screaming individuals with criminal physiognomies. Here I was punched around, then thrown into a stinking bed by individuals as criminal-looking as their victims. After a night spent amidst howls and groans I was ordered up. A bowl of some sort of concoction, which I did not touch, was set before me. I was surrounded by sneering individuals, one of whom informed me that I was about to be put out of existence. Later in the day, after having been punched around and having been subjected to various indignities, I was lined up with a number of others. I saw these others disappear one after another. I saw what happened to them. I know their fate. Those "in charge of the proceedings" were sneering, making clever jokes, speaking about the things that were going on in what they thought cleverly worded sentences with hidden meanings.

When my turn came I objected, telling them that I knew what they were doing. I was then switched aside and put to bed. The next day one of the nurses asked someone else why I had not been electrocuted on the previous day. On this day a number of "the help" were lined up, and some of them came for me and dragged me off. Again I protested vigorously. There is no doubt that in my eagerness to prove my innocence of crime, or my objections to meeting the death of a criminal, I spoke vehemently and incoherently. There is also no doubt that the things that I said were carefully noted down, later to serve as proof of my insanity.

At no time have I been unable to think and reason clearly. The fact that I have not been able to speak openly and freely about these matters has sometimes caused me to express myself in a roundabout manner or to reason all around a subject without coming to the point. This may have served as further proof of my insanity to those who know nothing about my experiences.

Had I not had the experiences I have referred to—had I come to this place with the feeling that I was wanted in society and that I was going to be helped to get well and to re-establish myself, I could long since have gone out and done useful and worth while work. The knowledge that in the eyes of those who hold the powers of life and death in society I am an intruder in life, who ought to be put out of existence, has made me feel that no efforts on my part could possibly re-establish my standing in society or my rights to existence. The assurance that "it is never too late," that I can still "go out and accomplish things," has seemed insincere.

The doctor knows all of the above (though up to now he has not known how much I know thereof), for the medical profession is in charge of the things described.

I have never considered myself brave nor courageous, still I did not break under my experiences. Now it seems to me that an individual who has gone through experiences of this kind and who had not broken under them is a strong individual.

No effort was made to disprove Johan's accusations, but he was questioned further regarding details. He remarked that he was certain that many people came to a point at which they were considered incurable and because of this they were put out of existence. So many significant things had happened during the "ten days" that his experience could not be ascribed to fantasy. He had heard the attendants say: "We are going to make it hot for you in hell." They also said something about "exterminating vermin." And he had heard a sound that gave everything away. The sound was camouflaged. It was caused by a person who was in the corridor using a rotary polisher. As Johan watched him he noticed that he turned the polisher on only at certain intervals, "to cover up screams" that came at the same time from a room into which they led "victims." He smelled a terrible smell of burning flesh. They were electrocuting and cremating patients. Furthermore, he heard other terrified patients on the ward refer to "the electric chairs." All types of people were confined in the ward, but only those with sexual problems were destroyed.

Johan was asked whether he did not feel that this, if his account were true, was an illegal procedure. He replied that there was probably a law that justified the killing of sexual criminals, especially those who masturbated. He said: "This law is such that each one that knows about it is sworn to secrecy."

He intimated that I certainly must know of this law. An attempt was then made to explain to Johan that at the time when he was admitted to the institution he was very much upset and could easily have misinterpreted a series of coincidental happenings to which he was peculiarly sensitive. I assured him that there was no law whatsoever that permitted the killing of any individual in a mental institution. These explanations made little impression on Johan.

For the next few weeks hypnosis was abandoned. In the waking state the events of his ten days were gone over in minutest detail with the idea of finding, if possible, some other explanation for the experiences. His judgment was to be respected, I insisted, but it was just possible that his tense and overwrought nervous state at the time of admission might have caused him to misinterpret things. He was also given a book setting forth all the laws pertaining to patients in mental institutions. He was instructed to read the book thoroughly, to see whether he could find any reference to a law that condoned the execution of persons who had committed "mental crimes." He was shown books and literature dealing with periodic masturbation and its effects. Johan made many detailed notes on his readings. He also made notes concerning his interpretations. A few of the latter are reproduced here.

Why do I doubt? When told that I have a right to my own life, why do I doubt? When told that sexual activities are nondestructive and harmless and that they are not the cause of the condition that caused me to be subjected to the experiences of the ten days, and that later caused me to be declared incompetent and deprived of my human rights and held in this place, why do I doubt? When I am told that I am in no wise different from the great majority, not in any way worse than other human beings, why do I doubt? I myself have never doubted that I have a right to my own life. What I doubt is that this right is sincerely and honestly recognized by those who know my story—by those who deprived me of my rights in the first place and who have the deciding power as to my fate in their hands. Had I myself doubted my rights, I would not have been able to keep going. I would not have been able to write and speak against the rottenness and hypocrisy and autocracy in society the way I have.

Am I different from the great majority of human beings? Am I considered worse—more corrupt—less worthy than others?

Alcoholics, drugs addicts, those rotting from the ravages of social diseases brought on by their own doings, are cared for, their lives are considered worth preserving. My life was deemed forfeit. Therefore I must be considered different, worse, more corrupt, less worthy than these others. Why do I attribute my condition, and the resulting circumstances that brought about the experiences of the "ten days" and subsequent events, to my sexual activities?

I was not a criminal. I was not an alcoholic nor a drug addict, nor was I suffering from social disease brought about by myself. I was placed among sexual perverts. What conclusions would you draw under the circumstances?

Why am I so anxious that a third person be not let in on my secrets?

I am writing these things so that the doctor may be able to understand the workings of my mind more fully, and for no other purpose. Everyone has things that he does not care to have made known. No one cares to have his experiences or his doings broadcast from the housetops. Who knows but that a third person may be of consequence in one's life—who knows what tricks fate may have up its sleeve?

The doctor suggested that my experiences of the "ten days" might have an interpretation quite different from that which I have given. The doctor's suggestion was that my wrought-up state of mind, together with the unusual and unpleasant surroundings in which I found myself—the uncivil and offensive attitudes of the employees—caused me to give the interpretation that I did to chance words and gestures and occurrences.    In other words, that the things that I thought I observed were illusions and fantasies due to my wrought-up condition.    The doctor also suggested that my interpretation of what I experienced was in keeping with my nature, that subconscious fears caused by childhood scares and threats were confirmed in the fantasies of my sick mind.

First I would say that I believe that I understand my make-up fairly well by this time.    I can see how childhood experiences and environmental conditions have caused inhibitions and repressions and worked themselves out into the kind of an individual that I am.    I am perfectly willing to accept the idea that subconscious fears, together with emotional strain and mental and physical overexertion, had culminated in a complete breakdown at the time of the occurrences of the ten days.    Also, I am perfectly willing to accept the idea that my interpretation of my experiences was a logical conclusion to the subconscious workings of my mind.

But all of this does not imply that my conscious interpretation of the events of the ten days is false.

I have reviewed the occurrences of the ten days time and again and in the light of subsequent experiences and information.    I have viewed them from various angles, in various moods.    I have analyzed them coldly and detachedly, using every ounce of my reasoning power.    And there remains at least a possibility that my interpretation of these occurrences is correct.

My powers of observation have always been good.    They remained unimpaired throughout the period of the ten days.

On the first day nothing worth mentioning in this connection took place.

On the second day, after questionings, examinations, tests, some of us were lined up in a corridor, one by one.    We were led out through a door.    It was during these procedures that it became clear to me what was taking place.    There was an odor of ozone in the air.    Such as is found around electrical equipment running on high voltage.    Later there were stronger and more unpleasant odors.    Near by in the corridor someone was using an electrical floor polisher.    He kept polishing the same spot for a length of time, but no effect of the polishing was apparent.    The motor was idling.    It was never turned on.    Although each time one of us had been led away there was a sound as though the current were switched on for a while.    When my turn came I protested, was led away elsewhere, and ordered to bed.

Early the next morning we were ordered up.    I was in a group of people of a somewhat different type than those of the day before.    The surroundings were much cleaner and neater.    Someone pointed me out and everyone turned toward me.    Various comments were made.    Someone said: "A man is to be killed."

Someone else: "I guess we are not so bad off."

A third: "My God, such things ought to be forbidden."

One of the employees: "I guess he would not have remained in bed so quietly if he had known."

The day shift came on. A female nurse spoke to a male attendant, pointing to me: "Why was not he electrocuted yesterday?"

For the remainder of the ten days I sat on a bench in a corner of the room. A few times I tried to help others that were in need of assistance. I was always pushed down on the bench and told to mind my own business. Joking and sarcastic or pointed remarks were constant among the employees during these days.

The behavior of the employees during the ten days of course is not the important point, nor is the manner in which things were done of primary importance. Supposing everyone was quiet and smiling and kindly, suppose everything were arranged to resemble a Sunday school picnic, what difference would it have made? It would simply have meant the same doings disguised under a heavier layer of pretense and make-believe. Of course, there may be more than one possible interpretation to the occurrences of the ten days. For instance, the whole thing may have been a series of coincidences, with a meaning totally differenct from that which I put onto them. Or the whole thing might have been a show put on for my special benefit, but this would seem a ridiculous and farfetched supposition.

Now suppose for the moment that my interpretation of events were correct. How could such doings be explained? Were my evil and corruption so great that they warranted a punishment of this sort? I do not necessarily think that I was meant to be punished for being evil or corrupt. If it were possible that those who have studied such matters have come to the conclusion that merely requires that individuals who have reached a certain stage of breakdown be put out of existence. (This is only speculation on my part, but it is the only explanation that I can find.)

What do I think of the doctor? Do I think he is sincere? Do I think he is telling the truth? There are two possible answers to these questions, it seems to me. First—Perhaps the rules or laws or regulations of the medical profession, etc., prescribe his standing. Perhaps he has no choice in the matter. (He may be thoroughly convinced that such a stand serves the interests of all concerned. Of course, I observe it time and again. Every day almost, a good doctor does not hesitate in telling white lies to his patients if such procedures are conducive to their well-being.)

Second—It is possible that doctors are not initiated into all of the mysteries until they reach a point where they are directly connected with these doings or until their initiation becomes essential to the performance of their duties.

No attempt was made to persuade Johan to accept my interpretation of the events that had occurred during the ten days. The matter was left entirely up to him, and he was instructed in the hypnotic state to evaluate everything that had gone before, including his experiences under hypnosis and my interpretations, before coming to a definite conclusion in the matter. He was told that I too might be wrong, and that the circumstances as he had outlined them might be actual, though through some oversight I was not aware of them. However, from what I knew of the situation, I believed that my interpretation was the correct one.

For the next few weeks Johan struggled between accepting my interpretation and persisting in his own. He argued, he questioned, he asked for books to read, and his dreams took on the form of debates between himself and me in which he subjected every one of my statements to a thorough analysis, retaining those parts that he believed were absolutely indisputable and discarding those parts that were not. In a note to me he said:

I believe that your own interpretations of my make-up, the forces that were at work, the experiences and the environment that I was subjected to, are correct. I believe that your explanations of my emotional strains and repressions, culminating in my breakdown, are correct. I believe that you have put your finger on my weak points, my faults and my shortcomings. I accept your interpretations and explanations, but I do believe that an individual knows a great deal more about himself than a doctor can ever hope to know. Of course, an individual may not be able to interpret himself; still, some things he can interpret if he is interested along these lines.

It was then suggested to him in hypnosis that he would have a dream that night which would represent a condensation of his experiences of the ten days. The next morning he would write his reactions to the dream in the light of his present interpretations. The dream was this:

Someone was showing me a place where various people had been restrained for doing various wrong things. I was told that there were seven sins and that they were in gradation. Some were not serious, such as sins like avarice. We went through the different departments where people were kept for various little sins. Then we came to the more serious sins. People were living in places not so comfortable, but they weren't so badly off. The seventh department was an evil place, no privileges, no freedom, torture and punishment of all kinds were done to them. "This," said the guide, "is the seventh sin. Those who have sinned in sexual matters, those who have abused themselves. They will be beaten to death in seven strokes, and at the seventh stroke they will die."

Johan was asked, under hypnosis, to symbolize this dream in a drawing. He quickly made a drawing identical to the one of a man walking up a road toward the sun, his progress blocked by various barriers. On the side of the road was a hand holding a dagger.

Later during the day Johan spontaneously wrote out his own interpretation of the dream:

Last night I had a dream in which the events of the ten days repeated themselves. In a sense it was a parody on the ten days, for I seemed to be in possession of the information gained through subsequent events and experiences. The sequence of events seemed a bit jumbled, and when something took place I seemed to say to myself: "This is not at all what it seems to be. I am imagining things." The ten days, to my way of looking at things, is the period of time that contains the clue to my present mental make-up and the pivot around which my behavior and my attitude toward things have been running for the past few years. Of course I realize that my environment and my experiences previous to the ten days had shaped me into the kind of an individual that I was and also that my behavior, attitude, etc., during these past few years have been colored by these previous experiences. I realize that the roots of distorted mental attitudes—"kinks in the mind"—will have to be sought in childhood years and repressions, but I feel that the beginnings of some of my present make-up need be sought no further back than in the ten days. (It may be considered in this connection that a distorted mental attitude, "kinks in the mind," etc., may be apparent but not actual. For instance, antagonism toward society or individuals or conditions may be justified and a sign of a healthy or normal mind.)

My dream of last night I interpret to mean that I am doing my utmost to convince myself that the interpretation I had given to the events of the ten days was a faulty one. The fact that I do not throw my interpretation of these events overboard and accept a different one does not depend on stubbornness. For I would be most eager to do just that, but unless such a step is indicated by absolute sincerity and an inner conviction it is worthless. Reason must be appealed to and not conviction, also in matters concerning one's mental (and perhaps emotional?) attitude. If one (or several) of the events of the ten days had pointed in the direction of my interpretation of these events, it might be put to the score of chance. But the overwhelming number of such events seems to exclude the possibility of chance being the sole factor.

Unconscious fear of punishment for sexual transgressions is supposed to have come to the surface and made me read into the happenings of the ten days a confirmation of my worst fears. (Consciously I never had such fear of punishment.) However, one thing is certain, namely, that just as in my dream of the seven sins, so also in the place where the "events" took place, the filthiest, most uncomfortable space was reserved for those who had transgressed in matters of sex. (I have previously stated that these things should not necessarily be regarded as punishment, that society is not necessarily avenging itself on those whom it despises, but perhaps rather that such doings may come under the head of mercy.)

As regards my present attitude toward the events of the ten days. I have said that seemingly it is one of indifference. Should I at any future time receive confirmation as to the truth of my interpretation of the events, it shall not cause me distress. Everyone knows that there are terrible things in the world. To deny them does not undo them. And I would by far rather be in possession of a terrible truth than a beautiful lie. On the other hand, should I become convinced that my interpretation is false, I shall most humbly confess my own distorted understanding as the basis for all the confusion.

The discussion of the ten days stirred up within Johan a tremendous amount of activity. His inability to take up this period with me during the first phase of the treatment was apparently caused by his conviction that he had luckily escaped death, and that he might by talking about the situation again expose himself to destruction. His taking me into his confidence represented a new phase in his relationship with me, a new feeling of trust by virtue of which he no longer needed to face his fears alone. The following excerpts from his diary illustrate the working through of this particular resistance.

The ten days have figured large in my thoughts and dreams during the past few days. Perhaps this means that things are coming to a head and that some sort of solution or thorough understanding of the true nature of the experiences of this period of time is working itself out in my mind.

I have explained before that I understand that the period of time just preceding the ten days in large measure was due to the workings of the mind, that inhibitions and repressions caused by early experiences, fears, and scares had brought about the situation in which I found myself. I have explained that I realize that my interpretation of the events of the ten days was in terms of all that had gone before. The experiences were interpreted so as to fit into the structure which the subconscious had erected with repressions, inhibitions, fears, etc., as building blocks.

Now, it may seem that the problem of the ten days is solved. My interpretation of the events is a product of the subconscious workings of my mind and therefore has nothing in common with reality. But reason insists that the experiences themselves were not a fantasy construction of the mind. They were real. Reason insists that the problem of the ten days is not solved until these experiences have an explanation or an interpretation.

Now, it seems to me that it is not excluded from the realm of possibility that a fantasy construct of the mind may have its counterpart in reality. Reason and fancy may run on devious roads. Yet they may arrive at the same terminal. Truth may be as strange as fiction.

Sex in general, masturbation in particular, played an immense role in the structure of inhibitions, repressions, etc., which the subconscious erected upon childhood experiences, fears, and scares. (It is the mortar, so to say, which holds the structure together.) It is self-evident and unavoidable that my interpretation of the events of the ten days should be in terms of sex and masturbation.

I believe that I have arrived at a fair understanding of many of the components in the structure that is I. I believe that many more are to be understood. I believe that the experiences of the ten days hold the solution to a great many of those that are not yet understood.

For the next two weeks every item of experience involved in the ten days was taken up in the greatest detail, and we considered as possible interpretations first his explanations and then the explanations I had presented to him. Johan continued to jot down his ideas and conclusions in his diary.

What is the answer to the question of the ten days? Was my interpretation of these events correct or were these events a continuation of subconscious fears which had worked themselves out into consciousness?

When the doctor speaks, I feel that my own attitude and my own interpretations are ridiculous. I accept his point of view for the moment. Then some occurrence that seems irrefutable proof of the correctness of my interpretation comes to mind, and I begin to doubt, against my own wish or reason. These doubts do not seem to be subject either to reason or to the will. These doubts seem of the same order as certain fears. A person that has fear of a mouse may know that such fear is ridiculous, but will power or reason has nothing to do with his getting rid of his fears.

This state of affairs has nothing to do with my doubting the doctor's word, his truthfulness or sincerity. I can sincerely say that there is no human being in the world whom I trust more fully or whose opinion I value more highly.

I wish to rid myself of my doubts in regard to the events of the ten days. Could I be shown that the various events actually were, or could I be shown that they were not what I interpreted them to be, it would be proof that the whole thing was a structure erected by my own mind. Were I rid of my doubts, an obstacle to my endeavors to understand myself would be removed. There would no longer be confusion as to what is fact and what is fancy. I would be heart and soul in the work that the doctor is doing for my benefit. Not only that, but I would regain my self-confidence and be able to look anyone fearlessly straight in the eyes again.

At the time when my breakdown started, around the beginning of 1937, I noticed certain physical changes within me. I have no way of describing the things that I noticed, except perhaps to say that it was as if the blood pressure became lower. (This may be a ridiculous way of expressing it, but I am not familiar with the medical terminology in this case.) I noticed that my hair became dry and lusterless. My scalp became dry, and when I scratched it, did not bleed freely as it had done up to this time. Likewise, when I cut my hands or fingers they did not bleed or they bled very slightly. I also noticed that my gums shrank, exposing more and more of the lower part of the teeth, until they (the teeth) seemed very elongated. My eyes lost their brightness. They became dry and burning. The whites of the eyes seemed to shrink, leaving the iris protruding a considerable distance above the surface of the eye. The transparent membrane covering the eye had wrinkles or folds, starting at the pupil and radiating therefrom to the rim of the eye opening— showing that this membrane had less area to cover than formerly. This process extended over a considerable period of time—perhaps a year or more —when it reached its maximum.

I asked the chief at the place I worked to refer me to a doctor. The doctor that my chief took me to was Mr. Big Chief's doctor. We entered his office. The doctor looked at me. "Married?" was his first question.

"No," said I.

"So, you never did marry, eh," said the doctor.

Then he put me in a chair, held a flashlight to my eyes, and looked into them. "Mm-hm," said the doctor.

Then he tested me for reflexes, knee jerks, etc. "M-hm," said the doctor.

Then I was sent away and the experiences of the ten days had begun.

Twice in this place I have heard the expression "masturbation paresis." I realize that this is not a scientific term, but I thought it possible that it might be some sort of phrase meaning "degeneration caused by masturbation." The existence of such a term caused me to doubt that excessive sexual activities—masturbatory or otherwise—cannot possibly cause damage or destruction.

At this time hypnosis again was resorted to, with the idea of experimentally producing hallucinations, in order to convince the patient that it was possible to react to them as if they were real experiences. It was suggested to Johan under hypnosis

that he would dream of that part of the experience during the
ten days in which he smelled the odor of burning flesh and of
ozone, emanating, as he believed, from the electrocutions.
This odor would persist even after he came out of the trance.

Upon awakening, Johan suddenly looked around the room
and asked me whether I smelled a very funny odor. On my
inquiring as to what the odor might be, he remarked that it
was exactly similar to the smell he had perceived in the observation ward. He appeared genuinely frightened and was so
tense that he was unable to associate freely. He was rehypnotized and the experiment was explained to him in great detail.
He was told that he would remember the experiment upon
waking up. Johan appeared to be quite impressed with the
fact that it was possible to hallucinate an odor so realistically
that it could actually appear to have originated outside of himself.

This experience, however, seemed to have no direct effect
upon his convictions, as is evidenced by the following entries
in his diary.

A person standing trial for a crime may be convicted on the score of circum
stantial evidence. Each point in the evidence against him may be weak and
easily explained away in his favor. But the number of points against him
may be large and taken together they may form an overwhelming mass of
evidence, sufficient to convict him. Under date of August 23, 1942, I presented a number of points that to me served as evidence. (1) That sexual
excesses are damaging or destructive to a person's physical or mental (or both)
health. (2) That a doctor is able to form a more or less correct opinion in
regard to a person's sexual habits through observing his appearance and upon
physical examination (especially through observing the appearance of the
eye he is able to substantiate the correctness of his opinion). (3) That a
person who through sexual excesses (masturbation or any other form) has
brought damage or destruction upon himself is considered more evil, less
worthy, meriting less consideration than others. That he is placed on par
with a criminal. (4) That my interpretation of the experiences of the ten
days was correct.

Every point that I presented if taken separately could easily be explained
away (laid to my hypersensitive or vulnerable condition, etc.). The points
are so numerous and so logical in their sequence that to me they became an
overwhelming mass of evidence in favor of the correctness of my contentions.

Here I shall present an additional point that seemingly adds immeasurably to the evidence (particularly as regards 2 above). As I have previously stated: A doctor to whom I was taken ("Mr. Big Chief's doctor") asked me two or three questions in regard to sexual matters exclusively; put a flashlight to my eyes and looked into them, tapped the space below each of my kneecaps with his rubber tomahawk, and said "M-hm." That was all. Then he sent me away, but he did not send me to the hospital directly. His office was in New York and I was living in Brooklyn. My chief took me home. There another doctor was called. He did just one thing. He held a flashlight to my eyes and looked into them. Then he ordered that an ambulance be called.

I mention these things not in order to insist that I am right in the face of all evidence to the contrary. I merely want to show the doctor that I had ample reason to come to the conclusions that I did come to. It was not a matter of taking one small scrap of evidence, hanging onto it appendages of wishful thinking or subconscious fancy and call it proof. When a thing repeats itself time and time again under the same or similar circumstances it must have some significance.

# IX

IT WAS felt that until it could be proved to Johan that the experience of the ten days was the product of his own emotional turmoil rather than a factual event, no further progress could be expected. The question that arose was as to the most expedient way of dissolving this area of resistance. The hallucinated experiences were so vivid to Johan that he could not accept the fact that his senses had deceived him. He was certain that he had witnessed circumstances connected with electrocutions of patients and had smelled their burning flesh. He himself had escaped destruction through a miracle. He was furthermore certain that this punishment was condign, being meted out to those who had destroyed their bodies through sexual excesses, particularly masturbation. So long as he accepted the experience of the ten days as real, he could present it as a material cause of his fears, and he could feel justified in shrinking from fulfilling himself and from becoming completely self-assertive. If authority, through the workings of a secret law, could deprive a person of his privileges, if it could kill him for living his own life, then one had best circumscribe his strivings for freedom and completeness.

One approach to the handling of this resistance, it was felt, might be through analysis of his relationship to me, while encouraging him at the same time to self-assertiveness and to expression of his impulses and desires. Up to that point this had been the chief approach, and Johan had progressed quite satisfactorily until he uncovered his real feelings about events during the first few days of his hospitalization. His ability to develop a relationship to me that was based upon trust made it possible for him to uncover and divulge the deepest context of his fears—the idea that he had been marked for death because of forbidden strivings and indulgences, and that he had escaped destruction only through a miracle. This respite was, however, tenuous and depended upon his holding his tongue; for the authorities, with whom I was probably co-operating, would brook no babblings on his part.

My interpretation of the events of the ten days as based upon inner problems that had caused him to misinterpret occurrences in his environment, and upon fears that had been projected outward during his emotional upheaval, could be accepted only on faith in me as a human being whose word he could trust. Eventually, through a prolonged contact, he might be able to do this.

Another approach might be to demonstrate to Johan directly that it was possible to become so conditioned to emotional experiences that constructions arising from attitudes within the individual could be misinterpreted as happenings in reality. The latter course was decided upon. Johan was acquainted with the nature of the hypnotic experiment to be performed. He was told that every individual develops certain values as a result of his own specific experiences, and that these condition his reactions to everything around him. These values are causally related to what has gone before. We would attempt in this experiment to analyze his sensory values, in order to determine how they operated. Furthermore, we would also attempt to see whether it was possible to project the effect of an intense emotional desire or fear onto reality, providing thus an objective basis for the emotion within. Johan was eager to attempt this experiment even though he was skeptical as to whether it would change his opinion.

Under hypnosis he was given the following suggestion: "You will have an ecstatic and happy feeling, and, as you do so, you will smell very distinctly an odor that is associated with this ecstatic, happy state."

Johan admitted that he felt quite wonderful and happy. Then he sniffed, and declared: "I am smelling an odor like almonds and peaches. As I do, I feel calm and happiness."

"Now," I continued, "you will experience the emotions of fear and dread, as if your worst fears were being realized, and you will experience an odor that is associated with this feeling."

Johan trembled, showed physical signs of fear, and then remarked that he smelled the odor of sulfuric acid on metal. "It's like decay," he said. "It signifies everything unpleasant."

"You will now feel the emotion of disgust, and you will experience an odor representative of this state."

"I smell something—it's like the odor of dead fish at low tide."

"You will now have an emotion of expectancy, and you will experience an odor representative of that."

"I smell the odor of salty spray, like a sunny day in early spring in the water "

Johan was then told that I would suggest odors to him, that on command he would smell these odors, and that, as he did so, he would experience an emotional reaction associated with these odors. "You will now smell the odor of ozone," I said. "I do smell that odor," Johan said. "It's like people being killed. I feel fear and indignation."

"You will now smell the odor of decaying organic matter."

"That's fear and disgust, like destroying human beings."

"Now smell the odor of violets."

"That is calmness and a little bit of excitement."

"You smell now the odor of peaches and almonds."

"That is joy and happiness."

"You now smell the odor of salty air."

"That is expectancy, joy, and excitement."

"Now smell the odor of excreta."

"That is disgust."

"You smell the odor of urine."

No response to this stimulus could be elicited.

"You now smell an odor, a pungent odor, like vinegar."

"That represents a little bit of unhappiness. I feel unhappy. I used vinegar at home at a time when I felt unhappy as a boy."

"You will now smell the odor of violets."

"That is calm expectancy and very early spring, plans for the summer after a very dreary winter."

Johan was told that even though he would not remember this experiment when he awakened, he would in the waking state still have the ability to associate emotion and olfactory sensations. Upon awakening Johan was apprised of the fact that various people represent various experiences in terms of different sensations. Sometimes they represent experiences by odors. I suggested that he think of a joyful event and see whether it would be possible for him to smell an odor. Johan appeared to be concentrating on this task, then remarked: "I remember a moonlight sail on a steamer, the "Mandalay," that used to sail out from New York Harbor. As I approached shore one night, I smelled the delicious odor of peaches. It was early night. I smell the odor of peaches now, and I must say that I do feel happy."

I then suggested that he should think of a fearful or dangerous experience and see whether he could recapture an odor representative of that experience.

"I smell a pungent, burning smell," he said, "like that of sulfur. I think of an experience I had when I went through the boiler factory, a big boiler factory. There was a terrific amount of noise, and I had a feeling of being crushed. I believe they did have sulfuric acid there. I was little then. I was somewhat indignant that I had been brought there, too. I can remember looking at the flame, the orange flame, and smelling this horrible odor."

I then suggested that he think of a disgusting experience.

"I think of the patients eating food, and smearing it all over them," he responded. "Gorging food is disgusting. I smell the odor of fish, of decaying fish."

"Think now of a situation of great expectancy."

"I smell the fresh odor of salt water. I was thinking of a long time ago, when we were told we could go swimming, and, getting down to the sea, you could experience the odor of salt water, and you anticipated swimming. I felt the same thing right now."

"Now you will think of a situation of masturbation."

"I smell an odor like urine and a vague feeling of fear."

"Think of having sexual relations with a woman."

"I smell an odor of some flower." The block and lack of associations with the odor of urine while Johan was in the hypnotic state may possibly have been due to the fact that urine and urinary activities were somehow linked with masturbation. Further evidence of this was suggested in a later experiment when he associated the color yellow with both fear and masturbation.

The next day the same experiment was carried out with sensations of taste. To ecstatic happy feelings, Johan associated a taste "of some kind of seed, like kümmel." Fear and dread tasted "like sometimes you take a spoon that hasn't been washed, and you eat something like vinegar and fish with it." In relation to disgust he had a taste "like food without salt, like eggplant, flat and disgusting"; for excitement and expectancy, a taste "like old wine"; for masturbation, a taste "like sour alcohol"; for sexual relations with a woman, a taste "like a rare kind of wine"; for homosexuality, "a nondescript flat taste."

Johan was instructed then to hallucinate various tastes and to associate emotional feelings with them. In relation to the taste of salt he had a feeling "like difficulties that are necessary and good"; for sugar, "a feeling of pleasure that may not be real"; for vinegar, "a feeling of unhappiness." In association with a bitter taste, like quinine, there was "a feeling of displeasure." After this he was given posthypnotic suggestions to the effect that he would that night have a dream that would symbolize his attitudes toward the different colors. He was also told that he would have the ability in the waking state to associate tastes as well as odors with emotional feelings.

Upon awakening, Johan was asked to think of a joyful event or experience. He thought of an outing in the country and tasted a "fruitlike dessert, sweet, like a preserve." In thinking of a fearful or dangerous experience, he recounted an episode that had happened years before when he was out on the water in a storm. His boat capsized and this frightened him terribly. "I taste a fishy taste of seaweed," he said.

On the suggestion of a disgusting experience, he thought of eating garbage and experienced the taste of "fire ashes." With a situation of great expectancy, he associated "new adventures and things to accomplish and a taste just like wine." That afternoon Johan laid this note on my desk:

I have become pretty much convinced that the events of the ten days will have to be explained in the manner suggested by the doctor. My environment, my experiences throughout life, etc., had resulted in the kind of an individual that would logically interpret these events the way I did. The whole thing was like writing the conclusion to a long and intricate story that I had been working on throughout life. The story may have been a unified whole from beginning to end. It may have been quite perfect in its details as well as a whole. But it was like a parable that had to be interpreted in order to be understood.

There is no way in which I can thank the doctor for his patience in interpreting this parable for me. "It is difficult to teach an old dog new tricks," it is said. And it is difficult to reshape thought patterns of long standing. There is an inner obstinacy in refusing to abandon old convictions and not accepting new ones. There is a tendency to ignore facts and proofs. Much patience and a lot of understanding are required to teach an old dog new tricks.

That night Johan had a dream in response to the posthypnotic suggestion that he visualize his attitudes toward colors. This dream he entered in his diary.

I had a peculiar dream last night. It seemed that I was surrounded by a pure, shimmering white. It seemed that this intense white filled all space and that there was nothing besides it. I was filled with joy and happiness. A sort of ecstasy which seemed to be identified with the shimmering white as though the two were one and the same thing. I moved about in this white until it seemed that when I came a certain distance from a central point there were flashes of very faint color. I had a sensation of unease or discomfort, and I hurried back toward the center of the white. Then I decided that I had to know something about the colors, and I made for the periphery of the exalted circle. A faint hint of yellow enveloped me and discomfort took hold. I penetrated deeper into the yellow and found that it became more saturated, more intense, the further I went. My sense of discomfort grew in the same proportion. I found that my discomfort was caused by the fact that I was afraid. My fear grew until, when I reached the full intensity of the yellow, I was possessed by a nameless dread or terror. I penetrated beyond the saturation point of the yellow and found that the yellow darkened, became impure and gray. My fear also seemed to become mingled with pity.

As I went further the yellow became ever darker, until I reached a point where none of it remained—black had taken its place. On the road from yellow to black, terror was left behind, but pity grew until, at black, sorrow and despair mingled with compassion. I decided to go back the same way I had come, and after a while I again found myself surrounded by a kind of yellow and under the influence of discomfort. I turned to the right and found that yellow gradually passed into orange and then into red. Anger took hold of me. The red became more concentrated. I became angrier, until at red of full intensity I was filled with rage. Red, just as in the case of yellow, became darker and merged into black.

Further to the right I found that red merged into purple and purple into blue. In the purple I felt disconsolate and further on hopelessness took hold. In the blue I was calm and composed but became more and more depressed as I advanced toward the point of saturation. The blue merged into green and the green into yellow, and I was back where I started from. In the green there was a feeling of expectancy. Something that was between an inner assurance that new and interesting experiences were awaiting and a fear that something terrible was going to take place. I noticed that the various emotions were relative, coming from the exalted reaches of pure white. Color was disturbing and the cause of discomfort and unease. But coming from the depths of black sorrow, color was invigorating and cheering.

Thinking these things over in the light of what I have previously experienced in the realms of "taste" and of "smell," it seems to me that these were similar experiences in the realm of "vision." It is true that these latter experiences were "only a dream," but it has come to seem to me that dream and "reality" have no hard and fast dividing line between them. They are pretty much the same kind of thing.

Sensations and emotions seem to be closely related. Everyone knows that colors have emotional values. In the dream, white was perfect happiness. Black was absolute sorrow. Yellow was fear, orange was indignation (?) red was rage, purple was hopelessness, blue was downhearted, listless, vacillating (I have no word to describe this emotional state), green was expectancy.

The emotions merged one into the other. They all run the full gamut from "purest white" to "deepest black."

Just as on the color wheel. You may put your finger on any color that is or was or will be. So you might construct a wheel of the emotions where any emotional "hue, tint, or shade" could be found.

In considering the foregoing, a number of questions come to mind. Emotions being the cause of certain sensations (or vice versa), is not this the same kind of thing as "hearing voices" or "seeing things"? When I smell sulfuric acid, it can cause fear to take hold of me; or if I taste peaches when the emotion of expectancy is aroused—am I not "imagining things"? When I see colors or hear music under emotional stress—isn't this "hallucinating"?

If this is so, why are people who are "hearing voices" or "seeing things" or "hallucinating" considered more or less ridiculous individuals—mentally sick? Why are they not treated for and if possible helped get rid of their sickness as speedily as possible?

In discussing his dream, Johan remarked: "I do not know why yellow is associated with fear in the dream. Ordinarily yellow does not have the fearful value to it. Perhaps it is the idea of being yellow. White does stand for purity and innocence. Black stands for darkness and sorrow. As far as orange is concerned, it is a different color. I really don't have a memory of this in the dream, but I figured it out later that it stood between fear, which was yellow, and rage, which was red. Red stands for rage. Purple stands for many things. It stands for richness, like royal purple, but I have no emotion associated. Blue stands for coolness, calmness generally, deep blue for disquietude. Green makes one think of freshness, of nature, of springtime."

Under hypnosis, he was asked to hallucinate a color and then to report the associated emotional feeling. Green elicited happiness; bluish green, joy; yellow, fear; orange, fear and indignation; red, anger; blue, composure; black, sorrow; white, "an exalted feeling of innocence." To the suggestion that he would experience color sensations associated with enjoying food, he hallucinated the color yellowish green; with masturbation he associated orange and yellow; with sexual intercourse, yellowish green; with distaste, purple; with depression, blue-purple.

He was then told that he would have a dream that would symbolize his feeling toward the color yellow. The dream was this:

I was in a certain place doing some work for the boss. I was doing something with colors. I used yellow. I started good, but he didn't like it. He was telling me how it should be done, but he didn't understand anything about it. I wished I'd told him how things should be done, and that I was right, but I didn't.

In response to the suggestion that he dream regarding his associations with the color orange, he recounted the following:

There was something on the shelf. At first I didn't know what it was. It looked so good to me. I liked its color. Later, I found it was an orange, and I wanted it. Afterward I took it, but I was afraid it wasn't mine. I was also afraid that if I ate it my teeth would come out. Then I was out on the street. It was dark. It was summertime. There were lots of parasols. Women had different colors.  Some had orange ones.  I went to the seashore and saw all the orange parasols.  Then I went to look behind these parasols, and there were people behind.  I wasn't allowed to look.  Then I was angry, and then I was afraid.  Then I went home and went to bed.  There was an orange covering, and I was afraid again.

A posthypnotic suggestion was given Johan to the effect that he would dream that night of his feelings associated with music.  He was furthermore told that when he awakened he would associate to the color orange and realize its significance. Upon awakening, Johan remarked that he seemed to understand why he used certain colors in his drawing.  He wanted to understand better his feelings toward the color orange. It was suggested that he visualize the color orange and then report all of his associated sensations.  Johan stated that as he saw the color orange clearly he could smell peculiar odors. One was that of ozone, the other that of burning flesh, and the third that of sulfuric acid.  He then recalled his frightening experience of going through the boiler room, smelling sulfuric acid, and seeing the orange flame.  He also associated a dream he had had in very early life in which he found himself trapped in a house on fire.  Other associations were those of playing in the cellar with kerosene, of his mother smelling smoke, of his early memory of looking out of the window when he was little to witness the slaughtering of pigs and seeing instead his own reflection in the glass, of playing in a shack with boys while they discussed masturbation, of the doctor flashing a light in his eyes and saying "M-hm," of being deprived of his liberties, and of the idea he had that people were being killed during his first few days in the hospital.

In response to the posthypnotic suggestion that he dream regarding his associations to music, Johan entered the following into his diary:

It would seem that like Peter Ibbetsen I continue my dreaming where I left off the night before.

I was in a vast room or hall, perhaps a cathedral.  I seemed to be alone. It was almost dark.  The grand organ was playing.  Quietly and calmly sound took possession of all space.  My own inners seemed to vibrate in time with the music.  There was a moment's pause.  Then came the strains of

Schubert's *Ave Maria*—majestic, overpowering in its calm simplicity.  Calm and peace and happiness issued from the organ and filled the vast room.  It found response in my own inner self.  I closed my eyes, and darkness seemed to change into white, shimmering light.

The (to me) invisible hands that played the organ were roaming the keys.  They were dipping into this—dipping into that.  A few strains from various Schubert selections—sad and resigned; a few passages from the "Meditation" from *Thais*, a strain or two from Drigo's *Serenade*.

Then the tempo became livelier—Johann Strauss in three-quarter time.  Warmth and pleasant excitement and eager expectancy filled me.  The music of Johann Strauss is like wine—old wine—rich and mellow.  I visualized crowds of people in holiday mood—smiling, laughing, conversing—sitting down around little tables, philosophizing, exchanging opinions, clever pleasantries, brilliant repartee, sweet nothings.

Now an interlude.  There was something of Mozart.  I do not know what.  Then came Beethoven.  Hope, longing, disappointment, sadness, sorrow, followed one another.  Next came Chopin, then Wagner—a bit of bewilderment, heedless courage, dread and fear.

A jarring discord that was like a slap in the face.  Then some of the others—moderns which gave me a "pain in the neck," "blah" in the mouth, and a vacuous feeling where the stomach is supposed to be.  With an effort the music sidled over to some sort of a tone picture—light and airy.  *The Fountain*.  The composer's name would not come to me.  *The Afternoon of a Faun* came next.  Again I could not recall the composer.  Debussy I suggested, but I wasn't sure.  I had regained my equilibrium.  My spirits had mounted.  I felt carefree, mischievous.

The mood changed again.  The music became serious, grave, proud with an undertone of humbleness, make-believe, carefreeness with hidden anguish.  Rubenstein's *Kamunai Ostrow*.  (This is phonetic spelling.  I do not know how to spell the word.)  The organ sang my own mood.

Concluding Rubenstein's masterful composition, the music went right over into a silly little ditty about Rosie O'Grady and the nobleman's lady.  I was angry.  I was downright mad.  I was so mad that I opened my eyes and I found that it was 5:30 a.m. and time to get out of bed and do some scribbling about sensations and emotions, etc.  "Dreams are subconscious thinking. . . . Dreams are hallucinations. . . . Dreams are wish fulfillments."  Our senses are little openings in our "shells" through which the external world "seeps in" and makes itself known to us.  There might be any number of other openings in our shell, but there just isn't.  Our understanding of the universe is extremely limited and distorted.  I believe that the senses on our climb up the ladder of evolution have developed out of one universal and fundamental sense of awareness.  The senses are closely related and sense impressions of one kind may be translated into sense impressions of another kind.

The emotions are rooted in the senses.  When dealing with colors and

their corresponding emotions, I thought of the paradise revealed by Sweden-
borg, where color and music and perfume were one, where you could hear the
hues and see the harmonies of heaven.  I recalled the scientific novels of
Camille Flammarion—the French astronomer, founder of the French Astro-
nomical Society, which I read long ago.  Flammarion took his readers on trips
throughout the universe, visiting numerous worlds.

It was suggested to Johan under hypnosis that he would feel
certain emotions and then hear melodies that would symbolize
these emotions.  In relation to the emotions of ecstasy and
happiness, he hallucinated Schubert's *Ave Maria*; for expectation, *The Blue Danube* with its "salty air and water"; for sadness
and sorrow, the *Funeral March* of Chopin; for fear and dread,
"a selection of Siegfried slaying the dragon"; for disgust, "the
*Rhapsody in Blue*, with its meaningless tunes that make
you disgusted."

A posthypnotic suggestion was given Johan to the effect that
when he went to sleep that night, he would dream of his various
attitudes and emotions in terms of physical symptoms and
illnesses.

The ensuing dream was this:

A dream I had last night was a repetition of a dream of the night before.
I was standing beside a man who was playing the color organ.  Color rushed
and leaped, combined and recombined, formed patterns, harmonies, discords.
It contracted, expanded, hesitated, died down.  Its mood changed.  It was
brilliant and bright, reticent, subdued.  Were I able to write music, I'd write
it down, I thought, for I had heard the color symphony in my inners.
    "Yes," said the musician, as though he had heard my thoughts, "music and
color are two ways in which to express the same thing.  The emotions are the
creative element; they are composers and directors.  The senses are inter-
preters.  They are instruments upon which the various selections or compositions are played.  You may play a selection on any instrument you chose.
If it is unsuitable for one particular instrument, you may transcribe it."
    "Well," thought I, "I have found that out."
    But I have also found another and peculiar thing, namely, that sometimes
a creation of the emotions may impress itself directly on the senses without an
intermediary external activation.
    It is as though a musical composition (to take an example) existing only in
the mind of its composer could activate a musical instrument directly and
become sound without the aid of an intermediary musician.  "But there are
instruments and instruments," I thought.  "The emotions may impress

themselves on the senses, as sight or hearing, taste or smell, but what about the sense of touch? Touch is a rather imperfect instrument on which to play a symphony."

"Tactile sensations are as varied as any other sensations," said the musician.

Curiosity took hold of me, and as it did a prickly feeling spread over the body. It was as if the curiosity had become an outward physical sensation. It was an unpleasant experience, but a bit of fear crept in at the unusual phenomenon. Or, rather, surprise came first and then fear. There was a catch in the throat, then neck and head became stiff and rigid, and the rigidity spread to shoulders and arms, then through the body to the legs. As the rigidity spread, fear grew. Then I noticed that the organist was smiling as if he wanted to say, "Serves you right." I became angry, and I felt the pulse beats in my temples as though the head were about to burst. I was helpless and wondered why someone did not come to my help. I looked about. I noticed that all around were other human beings who were suffering in various ways, and I was filled with pity. Now it seemed that my stomach muscles contracted. A feeling of emptiness within spread upward. The rigidity and headache were gone. Then it seemed that I was moving among the people and nothing but sickness and suffering and unhappiness were to be seen. I was filled with sorrow, and it seemed that my weight increased, until I could hardly remain upright. I was unable to lift my feet from the ground.

"Why does not someone do something about it?" I said. I noticed someone coming toward me with quick and eager steps. Expectancy was in the air, as though something were about to happen. A tingling feeling went up my spine and seemed to lodge at the base of the cranium. Peace and calm seemed to accompany the newcomer. I was happy. Warmth spread throughout the body.

"You're imagining things," said the newcomer. "You're imagining things —all of you. You let your emotions run away with you."

It was as though all at once the whole thing became understandable to me. I chuckled to myself, then I became excited. The inner warmth seemed to expand and penetrate and cleanse all the organs of the body. (I felt like a bottle of soda water with the bubbles of carbon dioxide rushing upward.) I wanted to get away and do something about it. I do not know what. The last I remember of my dream was a set of gleaming white teeth, the broad grin of the fellow at the color organ.

Now I have come to think that functional disorders may be caused by the emotions and, if so, their treatment ought to be mental rather than physical.

Question: Can a functional disorder develop into an organic disorder?

Through repetition of these experiments with associated sensations, a definite series of sensory experiences was linked together. Stimulation under hypnosis and posthypnotic suggestions revealed that the emotions of exaltation and happiness produced hallucinations as follows: in color sensation, of white and blue; in taste, of wine and candy; in smell, of violets and and honeysuckle; in hearing as related to music, of Schubert's *Ave Maria*; in bodily sensation, "of a light touch going from the head to the spine, and of wind blowing through the hair." The emotion of expectancy produced the colors green and blue-green, the taste of "peach," the odor of "pine tar and salty spray," the music of Johann Strauss waltzes, and bodily sensations "of a light, expansive nature in the spine, chest, and heart." For fear, the color association was that of yellow and orange; the taste, that of raw fish and vinegar; the odor, that of rotten fish and sulfuric acid; the music, that of "In the Hall of the Mountain King" in *Peer Gynt*; the bodily sensations, those of "an upward movement of the scalp, rigidity, a cramp in the leg, a needle ripping the skin, and a prickly feeling on the back of the head." For disgust, the color association was that of orange and yellow; the taste, that of soap, ashes, and kerosene; the odor, that of decaying matter, ozone, and urine; the music, that of ultramodern compositions; the bodily sensations, those of "a contraction of the stomach and intestines, with a desire to vomit." For anger, the color sensation was that of red; the taste, bitter; the odor, that of chlorine; the music, a theme from Wagner; the bodily sensation, "a hot feeling on the forehead and ears." For indignation, the color association was purple; the taste, "alkaline"; the odor, that of vinegar; the music, that of "a hand organ grinding 'When you and I Were Young, Maggie' "; the bodily sensation, that of a constriction of the throat. For fearlessness, the smell association was "all kinds of odors, like going down at the wharf"; the taste, that of fruit; the color sensation, that of deep orange; the musical tone, the sound of a march; the bodily sensation, "a good feeling over the skin."

The smell of ozone and burning flesh, the sight of a dagger, the experiences of having a foot amputated, a tooth extracted, an eye enucleated, and genitals removed, all produced associations with the odor of sulfur, with a "bad" taste—"something one can't eat"—with yellow and orange colors, with sad music, and with a painful ripping sensation in the skin. For the word "mother" the associations were a soapy odor, a candy taste, pleasant and unpleasant emotions, a purplish blue color, at first calm music and then more unpleasant music, and a "nice feeling, gentle—like stroking the hair." The word "father" evoked an oily or paint odor, a taste of oranges, an emotion of hope and expectancy, a neutral gray color, "all kinds of musical sounds," and no skin sensations. For the word "brother" there was a sharp acid odor, a taste of bitter almonds, "no particular emotion," a green color, lively and modern music, and a scratchy sensation in the skin. For "sister" there was no odor; the word was related with a "fairly pleasant taste," the "emotion of a desire to protect," the colors orange and yellow, peaceful music, and a calm and pleasant sensation in the skin. Associations in relation to me produced the odor of medicine, the taste of peppermint, the emotion of happy expectancy, a blue color, the music of "a Schubert composition played on the hurdy-gurdy," and a tingly feeling of the skin. Johan's associations with the idea of himself produced the odor of cedar wood—qualified as "a bit mysterious, holding promises of fine lands and experiences, like the seamen who used to have their things in cedar chests"—a bitter taste, an emotion of hope and expectancy, a dark yellow-orange color, the music of "Hail, Hail, the Gang's All Here," and an itchy feeling all over. Associations relating to masturbation revealed the odor of decaying matter, urine, and sulfuric acid, a yellow and orange color, a kerosene taste, the Mountain King music from *Peer Gynt*, and a needle ripping through the skin.

# X

IN ORDER to demonstrate to Johan that it is possible under certain conditions to change one's values, it was decided to recondition him unconsciously to his associational sensations. He was told under hypnosis that he would re-experience an event that he lived through and that he had forgotten. I said to him: "You are back at a point in your life when you were very happy. You are about to go on a boat ride with your friends, on a very pleasant boat ride. You notice that the sun is shining, that the sky is blue, and that everyone is gay. You sing cheerfully and in your mind you have all of the various sensations of happiness and expectancy. You taste wine, smell violets, experience the exciting salty spray on your face, the wind blowing through your hair, and through your mind there run the tunes of Schubert's *Ave Maria* and Johann Strauss's waltzes. A pleasant sensation runs through your body, producing a light, expansive inner mood. You notice, however, while you are experiencing these pleasant feelings, that the sky suddenly changes in color to orange and red. Previously, the emotions that you associated with these colors were disgust and anger, but upon looking at red and orange now you associate them with your new, happy experiences. As you return from this happy visit and get back into your own home, you open a book, and the first thing that you come across is a picture composed of the colors red and orange. Instead of experiencing your usual emotions of anger and disgust, you are reminded of your delightful afternoon, of all the happy and exciting sensations that you previously associated with blue, white, and green. Now listen carefully: From now on you will experience new emotions in relation to the colors red and yellow. Whenever you see these colors, they will bring back to your mind the same happy feelings that you had on the boat trip."

Johan was then given another experience. I said to him: "I am now going to take you back to your trip through the boiler factory, when you observed people melting iron, banging, and making other noises. You smell sulfuric acid, you see the orange color of molten iron, and you experience fear, an upward motion of your scalp, a feeling of rigidity that you associate with the taste of raw fish, and you hear the Mountain King music from *Peer Gynt*. Now, as you look around, experiencing these emotions, you suddenly notice that the boilers are bedecked in blue and that workers are wearing green shirts. Everything around seems blue and green. As you perceive these colors, you get the same fearful sensations and smell the same odor that you previously connected with yellow and orange. Upon going home, you open a book and see the colors blue and green. Now you experience the same sensations that you had in the boiler factory: the feelings you have in reference to blue and green are the ones that you previously associated with the color orange. From now on, whenever you see the colors blue and green, you will have the emotional feeling of fear and all the sensations you formerly associated with yellow and orange.

Next day Johan complained that he was for some reason quite confused. Everything seemed to have changed. He tried painting a picture in oils that morning and found himself using yellow and orange where he ordinarily would have used blue. Furthermore, he found himself enjoying things that he had previously disliked. For instance, the food in the dining room tasted wonderful, when he knew that he had previously always disliked it. Everything seemed "scrambled around." He had no idea as to why this was so. Johan was then asked to associate to the color orange. In response he smelled the odor of pine and experienced the taste of an orange, the sound of a musical composition entitled "All's Right with the World," a feeling "of the rush of wind through the hair," and a definite sensation of pleasure. With the color blue he associated the emotion of uneasiness, the odor of rusting iron, a metallic taste, a goose-pimply sensation, and a musical composition called "The Hammers Beating on a Smithy." With masturbation he associated the odor of flowers, the taste of honey, the emotion of peace, a pleasant feeling, and a Strauss waltz. He did not recall having any dreams in the preceding night.

Under hypnosis it was discovered that he had forgotten the following dream:

I was dreaming about the sea and its colors—the colors of the sky. This was a funny thing. The sky was orange, but there was someone telling me about these things and showing me what these colors meant. He spoke about the sky being orange, and at first I couldn't see it. I thought he must be color-blind. Then I noticed that it was a funny-looking sky—grayish—then it did look orange. This fellow told me it was very fine—that it meant beautiful weather. I insisted that it meant storm. He insisted I was afraid of this weather. I said I wasn't. I didn't mind. Things were then mixed up. I thought it was a funny idea of colors and it didn't fit in. I was using these color ideas in painting pictures. This fellow insisted upon my painting an orange sky on pictures. I didn't see it, but later I felt the pictures were fine, that the color harmony was O.K. when you considered the picture as a whole. At first it seemed to me the fellow thought orange was a natural color, then I got the idea of the thing, of a color combination, and it was a beautiful thing in a rugged way.

In associating to the dream, Johan remarked that colors and emotions were interchangeable and that in the dream his feelings about colors were used to indicate his attitudes toward other things. He remarked that his attitudes were changing, that he could see that certain things that he previously thought ridiculous now appeared fine and beautiful. He knew that things were changing inside of him. The entire experiment was then explained to Johan in detail, and he was instructed to recall the experiment after he woke up. He was also to write his reaction in his diary. He wrote:

Checking up on the emotions as produced by color sensations, I find that I am a bit mixed up on my reds and greens and my oranges and blues. Orange stood for fear, but now, in visualizing orange, I see it in the evening sky—yellow, orange, red. Memories of a day on the water, the sky was a deep blue. Salty spray filled the air. Joy and expectancy as of adventure ahead. Toward the end of the day the sky took on an orange hue. Things were too beautiful. It was the calm before the storm, but there was no fear, only an inner glee. Let it come, was the feeling. All things were conducive of pleasure in those days. Difficulties were a spur to greater efforts. Even pain itself became pleasurable. After many hours of toil at the oars, the waves doing their best to slap them out of the hands. Insides of hands covered with blisters that were breaking, salt water in the sores, every muscle aching (but with a warm, satisfied undertone, the seat contending with the skin on that part of the body which is expressly made for sitting purposes for the right to existence, and slowly but surely getting the upper hand and substituting itself for it). It was really no laughing matter, still one could not help chuckling, and the storm—why, let it come. Green stood for calm, happy expectancy. In visualizing green I see blue and green vapors mingling with the orange and yellow glow of melting steel. The noise is overpowering. It is fearful. But there is no real fear. Other emotions are mingling with that of fear. Emotions aroused by personal experiences may be associated with sensations that occurred during these experiences. For instance, if the color green plays an important role or takes a prominent part in certain experiences, and if these experiences are happy ones, then the color green may arouse the emotion of happiness. But one may have had other happy experiences in connection with the color red, and under certain circumstances red may arouse the emotional happiness. Now, therefore, it seems to me that there is a terrific mix-up in the interrelationship of emotions and sensations, and that an emotion may be caused by one sensation at one time and by another sensation at another time. For this reason it would seem next to impossible to get any kind of order in this situation.

The experiment was an amazing revelation to Johan, and he remarked that he could see how it is possible for people to get wrong ideas regarding events, getting chance associations mixed up and identifying them as true experiences. In his writings he commented:

My experiences in the field of emotions and sensations have shown me that sensations may arouse a given set of emotions, but as one's attitude toward these sensations changes, an entirely different set of emotions may be aroused by these same sensations. My experiences in color sensations have shown me that my own attitudes toward many things have changed.

My dream about the orange sky seemed to be an account of my progress toward an understanding of the true nature of my emotions. It seemed to be an account of the changed attitude toward many things that the present treatment has caused in me. Of course my changed attitude toward many things includes my attitude toward matters of sex. My attitude toward masturbation is not one of fear or disgust. If I still reject this mode of sexual expression so far as I am concerned, I am sure it is not because of emotional reasons.

In order to test his feelings about masturbation, Johan was told under hypnosis that he would, during the night, have an irresistible desire to obtain pleasure through genital manipulation. He reacted to this suggestion with a dream that he revealed the next day.

During the night I had a dream. In the dream I was blue. I was walking along listlessly, feeling that I had been working and studying seriously and earnestly. I had tried many things. I had endeavored to develop a variety of abilities and to attain to a measure of self-sufficiency. The result of it all was dissatisfaction, some sort of nauseating feeling. Then all at once I found myself in the midst of some sort of country fair. Hustle and bustle, noises, merrymaking. My outlook became just one tiny trifle brighter. I looked around me in a critical manner, observing the various things that were going on. "Why, I could do as well myself," I thought, as I looked around me.

I noticed a row of booths or stands. Girls were in charge of these. They were making things, preparing food, baking foolish-looking little cookies and cakes, embroidering, making little decorative articles. I went over to one of the stands, where various dishes of food were being prepared. They looked enticing, beautiful, decorative, as though they were made for the eye and not for the palate or the stomach. "They would look nice if hung on the walls," I thought.

I was hungry. "I could do as well myself," I said to the girl at the stand. "Go ahead, help yourself," she replied.

I got hold of a couple of dishes, a cooking pan—some ingredients. "This is going to be good," I said.

I did my cooking. The result was quite amazing. The looks of the thing was nothing to brag about. "I wouldn't want that one on the wall," I thought.

I tasted it—flat and tasteless! "I didn't do so well," I said to the girl, a bit shamefacedly.

She came over. She brought "sugar and spice and everything nice" and she mixed it into my distasteful concoction. She stirred a bit. A twist, a turn, a touch, and there it was! It gladdened the heart to look at it. She wanted me to taste it, and it tasted as good as it looked. I ate, and it stopped my hunger.

My spirits had risen about two notches. I drifted over to one of the other booths. I noticed people going in and coming out. Those that came out seemed to be kind of "touched up," brushed up or polished up. They were wearing bits of ribbon or gay buttons or buttonhole flowers. "What's the idea?" I asked one of the girls.

"We look them over," said she, "make them look right—feel right—add a bit of gayness to their exteriors and incidentals to their interiors."

"I can take care of myself," I said. "I do my own brushing and shining and touching up."

"You look it!" said she, and whistled a provoking, spiteful little tune.

She picked up an atomizer and squirted some nice-smelling fluid at me. It hit me in the eye. She took advantage of my blindness and stuck a ribbon in my lapel and a rainbow-colored handkerchief in my breast pocket. She gave a tug to my tie and a lift to my jacket. I felt like a little boy who has just had his neck and ears washed. But somehow it felt good and my spirits had mounted another notch or so.

I came to the next booth. There were people in pairs at tables. They were playing games. Some of them were playing cards. "What a waste of time and effort," I said, and turned to the girl in charge of the booth. "Should I feel like amusement of this kind, I would play a game of solitaire. Then the game itself becomes the only thing that counts. No arguments, no difference of opinion, when you're through you're through."

"Come," said the girl, and led the way to a table for two. "Oh thank you," I said. "I believe you." I had just happened to think of the perfume squirter and my sore eye. "I think I'll try something else."

Besides, my spirits were still on the upgrade. Some sort of momentum seemed to carry them along. I went on my way. I watched many things, always insisting that I could do as well myself, but always discovering the fallacy of my contention. After a while my insistence that "I can do as well myself" became a halfhearted statement.

Johan associated: "All through life I tried to work out a scheme of life. I tried to study. I knew I had to have many activities. I used to exercise and do things that didn't relate to my specific work."

Under hypnosis he revealed that he had in the preceding night had an impulse to masturbate, but had not let himself yield to it. His dream represented his attitude that there was nothing to masturbation as compared with the beauty of sexual intercourse.

Johan was quite convinced that his experiences during the ten days were hallucinations, but he still was unable to see all the connections, and he was particularly puzzled by the ramifications of his sexual attitudes. That Johan was pondering over this problem was revealed by writings in his diary.

The conversations with the doctor are extremely interesting and enlightening. Many new avenues of thought open up. I have been considering my dream about the country fair as a symbolical expression of my feelings and attitudes toward sexual activities in general and my own sex life in particular. I believe that this dream was a continuation of or an elaboration on the series of dreams that I had had during the past week or so.

First I had a dream in which color sensations caused definite emotions to arise. Then there was a dream in which music took over the role held by color in the previous dream. These two dreams were dealing with the inter-relation of sensations and emotions in a general way. Then came a dream which seemed to point out that sensations are modified and enhanced by the emotions. This dream seemed to be a symbolical representation of my atti-tudes toward sexual activities. It seemed to show that only as the emotions come into play are the sensations "humanized" or made to rise above being sensual sex. In a perfect marital union the sex act is not the "thing in itself" to which everything else is subordinate, but rather it is (as in the dream) the glass of wine that enhances that and in turn is enhanced by the relationship.

All these things were very much in my mind just before I had the dream about the country fair. I shall now deal with this dream, taking it for granted that it is a symbolized account of my own feelings and opinions con-cerning sexual matters.

I was depressed and lonely and disappointed. Nothing in particular had caused this emotional set-up, for this was the "opening bars" of the dream, and nothing had preceded it (it had no cause). However, this set-up was essential for what followed.

I was convinced that my mode of life was the right one, that independence and self-sufficiency were conducive to more efficiency and more accomplish-ment. Speaking in terms of sex exclusively, masturbation was a desirable mode of expression, so far as I was concerned. (Of course this reasoning did not occur in the dream.) Unconsciously there was quite a different convic-tion, and the purpose of the dream seems to have been to bring out this con-viction. My own thoughts and utterances and acts were expressive of my conscious mind (in the dream), while the utterances and acts of the girls were expressive of my unconscious (or subconscious) mind.

"I could do as well myself," I said when I saw the various things that people were doing. This really meant, "I could get as much satisfaction, in a greater variety of fields, out of the things that I am doing all alone, as these people are getting out of what they are doing."

When I became hungry and craved food, I thought the food which the girls had very decorative but not satisfactory. So far as I was concerned, I preferred my own way of satisfying my hunger. Speaking in terms of sex again. My hunger was a sexual hunger. My way of satisfying it was the desirable way. I then found that my own concoction was a tasteless one. The little touches added by the girls—the "sugar and spice and everything nice"—the things that I had considered frills and nonessentials, were really essentials. They were the things that enhance and charm. They were the emotions that intensify and modify the sensations.

The rest of the experiences of the dream were the same theme repeated over and over. I believed that the little frills and follies and nonsensical doings of the people were nonessentials. I was speedily shown that they were the emotions that enhance and transform. . . .

Is there an element of fear in my present attitude toward sex? If I think so highly of the proper marital relationship, why did I never seek a mate? Was there a feeling of inferiority in my make-up and was my intense activity in the fields of study and knowledge nothing but a compensation device?

There may have been fear in my make-up, but such fear as existed was probably caused by observing the terrific amount of unhappiness that existed in married life. All about me throughout childhood I knew what married life ought to be like, as I saw it all about me. I did not want it for myself. Perhaps I feared that married life as it ought to be was unattainable, that a marriage that had all the prospects for being successful might turn out to be unsuccessful after all. And this perhaps was the reason why I did not seek a mate.

It is quite certain that there was a feeling of inferiority in my make-up. The unhappy condition in my own home, the fact that I had to feign happiness where there was none, while others were genuinely happy, gave me this feeling of inferiority. Then also I came among people who were well educated, who held responsible and well paid positions due to their education. I was sometimes taunted because of my lack of education. I was thirsting for knowledge and promised myself that I was going to get an education after all. My lack of education gave added impetus to my feeling of inferiority.

It is possible that my intense search for knowledge became a compensator's device or a defense mechanism. I was too busy to think of marriage. Then also I had responsibilities. I have always been responsible for others. Other people have always been dependent on me. Perhaps also this became a defense mechanism. Perhaps I felt that I could not add new responsibilities through marriage. Perhaps unconsciously I told myself that these dependents could not do without me.

Another thing: The doctor has often spoken of "needs," that one has a variety of needs and that one has a right to satisfy these needs.

One of the genuine needs of my life was a need for responsibility. I held responsible jobs wherever I was working. I was trusted by everyone from the lowest to the highest, and this trust was never abused. I was responsible for other human beings always. Therefore, one of the most humiliating aspects of my stay here was that I was deprived not only of all responsibility as concerns others, but I was declared incompetent to decide in the simplest matters concerning my own person.

Having dealt in considerable detail with my stand on sexual matters, having looked into the reasons for the development of this stand, having considered fears and compensatory devices, let me take up another subject for consideration. Whether or not it has a bearing on my character development is for the doctor to contemplate. I shall deal with the subject of sex in relation to my life as an artist.

I had some slight talent in the direction of art. I was interested in picture making very early. I made pictures of all kinds of subjects. I made pictures of trees and insects and animals and human beings. I undertook to develop this talent. In art school I studied many things. It took many years before I studied from the living model. In art school the classes are mixed. Men and women, young and old, study together. A sort of ease and freedom develops. The sight of the undraped human form becomes a constant and common phenomenon. It makes no more impression than any other familiar sight. It affects the emotions no more than does the sight of fully dressed men and women. Of course, a strong and well built body is beautiful. It may arouse admiration. It may be the subject for comment and discussion. Nowhere else have I found greater decency than among groups of art students, nowhere else more freedom from lewdness or prudery. A sense of respect for all human beings develops. These are sketching classes that have no instructors. These have no supervision whatever. Models are posed by a monitor who is chosen from among the students. Sometimes male and female models are grouped. At times models may be students of art and during rest periods mingle with the students and discuss with them the merits of their work. I have been working in classes of this kind for years. I have never heard an untoward word or witnessed an overt act. Of course, among professional artists in studios and places of work all of the above holds equally true. (There are exceptions to all rules, and one may sometimes hear of some sort of scandal in connection with some individual artist. But such a one is a degenerate. Scandals occur among all classes of people and probably very much more seldom among artists than among others. Their whole upbringing makes them practically immune to this thing.)

Under hypnosis the scrambled associations with various colors were removed, and Johan was quite thankful that his previous values had been restored. Several days after this had been done, he placed the following note on my desk:

I am convinced that there is some hidden cause for my persisting in connecting masturbatory indulgences with the emotions of disgust and downheartedness. I do not know this cause and have no means of getting at it. I will do my best to find it if the doctor will lead the way.

# XI

JOHAN'S progress was reviewed with his participation, and it was suggested that the story of his entire life, as well as the material elicited during hypnosis, showed a struggle to grow, to develop, and to attain to a state of happiness. He appeared to have symbolized this struggle as a desire for truth and knowledge, which he apparently equated symbolically with masculinity and completeness. There were also indications that he felt "like an empty shell" and incomplete within himself, and this seemed to be symbolized unconsciously by a physical castration. Furthermore, the attainment of knowledge, though desirable and necessary, was for some reason considered to be dangerous. The hallucinated experiences of the ten days seemed to be punishment for seeking this knowledge; the penalty for this, at least unconsciously, he believed to be death. It was significant that punishment was imposed exclusively on those who were guilty of self-destructiveness through masturbation. The task remained for us to determine why he needed to gain this knowledge in order to be complete, and why he felt that he would be injured in the process of attaining knowledge. There were indications that his wish to achieve completeness might be a secondary goal, the primary one being a desire to gain those things that every person wants from life—creativeness, activity, love, marriage, and a home—and which he believed would be his once he felt complete. How his masturbatory fears fitted into the picture was not exactly known, but it was apparent that while he had no conscious fear of masturbation, unconsciously he seemed for some reason to fear it greatly. Johan accepted these explanations and indicated an eagerness to go further in the analysis.

Under hypnosis he was instructed that he would have a dream that would indicate his real feelings about masturbation. The resulting dream was this:

Something about the place where they were constructing some very fine machinery, something like a great boat. There was a very heavy iron chain holding the boat in place. This chain was used to hoist it up, and the chain broke and the thing smashed to pieces. Someone said a chain is no stronger than its weakest link. This fine chain had a bad link in it, and everything was destroyed because of it.

With this he associated the fact that masturbation was his weakest link and might easily have been destructive, had he not stopped it.

That night Johan had a spontaneous dream that indicated the same attitude toward masturbatory activity.

A body of men was sent out to gather some important data. They had to travel great distances on foot, sometimes over difficult terrain. Having obtained the information they sought, they set out on the return trip. Now they had to move fast, for they had to arrive at a certain point on a river before the breaking of the ice. The break-up of the ice would cause several months' delay. One of the men in the group developed some kind of trouble with his legs, some kind of lameness or stiffness of the muscles. It did not hurt or bother him in the least, except that he was unable to move as fast as the others. The party could not leave him behind, and they were unable to carry him and still make the necessary progress. The men arrived at the designated spot on the river just as the ice broke. Their achievements were of doubtful value. The purpose of the trip was lost. The dream then went off on a tangent. I was buying apples. A farmer had several bushels of large, beautiful apples that I was bargaining for. But when we came to look at them we found that they were rotting. There was not one that was not spoiled. "I looked them over carefully," said the farmer, "but I must have overlooked one that was spoiled. It is always like this. One bad one will corrupt the lot."

The associations to the dream were concerned with the idea that a little thing might pollute society. Johan expressed it thus: "Just as in the fall of Rome little things had caused the fall, so in the individual, little things might produce corruption in the entire person. My sexual life and especially masturbation was an irritating something, that caused me discomfort. Without it I felt I could accomplish more. Now it may be possible that it could cause no harm, but actually the idea was there, and from time to time the idea came up. I can see this, and I am beginning to see increasingly more and more how I misinterpreted fears at the time when I broke down, and how I actually believed that people were physically killed for masturbatory acts. What I cannot see is how any prejudices like this can still persist in me with the knowledge I have of it."

It was decided to make an attempt to demonstrate his unconscious attitudes toward masturbation to Johan by the creation of an experimental neurosis. Under hypnosis he was told the following: "I am going to recall a dream that you had some time ago. This dream you subsequently forgot. As I tell you the dream you will remember it as one you had. The dream is this: You are sitting at a desk. Near you is a yellow pen. There are also a bottle of ink and a piece of paper. You reach over, pick up the pen, dip it in the ink, and begin writing. You do so with an attitude of great expectancy. As you write you gradually become aware of a sensual feeling that creeps over you. This feeling becomes so intense that you wake up from your sleep. You find out that you actually have been masturbating. What seemed to be the pen in the dream is actually your penis, and you had the same sensations in holding the yellow pen that you had in holding your penis in masturbation. This attitude will persist when you awaken. When you wake up, you will see a yellow pen on the desk. If, for any reason, you desire to reach for it, to write or to make an illustration, you will have the same emotional reactions toward the pen that you now have toward masturbation."

When Johan awakened, our conversation led to the subject of new ideas in furniture design. Johan remarked that he had the other day conceived an excellent idea for a bookcase. He asked whether he could borrow a pencil or a pen to draw a sketch. A bottle of ink and a yellow pen were then made available to him. He reached over and grabbed the pen and started making a drawing of a bookcase to illustrate his idea. Suddenly his hand began to tremble and stiffened so that he could make only a few scribbles and lines. He started all over again in vain. Finally he threw the pen down and shook his head, saying: "I don't feel that I can draw the things I have in mind. I just don't think I can succeed. I feel a kind of downhearted, disgusted feeling with the drawing of these things. I feel I can't handle this pen. It's funny how it happened, trying to rush it through. At first I had eagerness in drawing, and then I felt as if I was disgusted with the whole thing."

Johan's face was flushed and there was perspiration on his forehead. He remarked that for some reason he felt very anxious and tense. I then gave him my fountain pen and asked him whether he would like to try again to draw an illustration of the desk. Hesitatingly he picked up the fountain pen and without any difficulty drew a sketch. I then asked him whether he could draw the same sketch with the yellow pen. He picked the pen up and suddenly began to tremble again. Asked to associate various sensations with his present feeling, he remarked that the odor that came to him was an unpleasant combination of the smells of fish and sulfuric acid; the taste was "a bad taste"; the color, yellow; the music, a modernistic tune; the physical sensation, "peculiar feelings in the hands and a feeling of a pin tearing the flesh." He exlaimed: "It's the pen. It's the pen. I don't feel like fooling with the pen. I don't feel like handling this pen."

He threw the pen halfway across the desk with an expression of disgust on his face. When he was asked what association of ideas had occurred to him when he held the pen, he remarked: "For some reason I get the same disgusted feeling that comes to me when I think of masturbation. I start out feeling all right, and then this comes on to me. I don't see why this pen should be different from any other pen."

I then impressed upon him the fact that there might be some reason why this pen suddenly became so terribly disgusting. There might possibly be an association between the pen and something that was very obnoxious to him. Try as hard as he could, Johan could not get the connection.

Johan was then rehypnotized and told that he actually had had a dream that I suggested to him, and that the dream was concerned with holding a yellow pen that was associated with holding the penis in masturbation. He was told that when he awakened he would remember the incident. Upon awakening, Johan remarked that he felt quite well now and that he believed that he was on the verge of recovering a dream. "I don't know exactly," he said. "I remember a pen. I had this pen. I was going to write. I felt happy about doing the writing. Then the dream comes to my mind. I remember the whole thing, and the idea was in handling the pen. It was associated with masturbation. That seems to be the thing." So saying, Johan reached over, picked up the yellow pen, and started to write with it, with the remark: "It's just an ordinary pen now." He laughed and appeared to be genuinely relieved.

This experience provided opportunity to explain to Johan the mechanism of phobia formation and to demonstrate to him that it is possible to transfer emotions of disgust to any bodily process. The entry in Johan's diary relating to the experience was:

This morning I showed the doctor how to design furniture. I designed some wonderful bookcases, and I was quite happy and proud of them. So I went on to more ambitious undertakings and began planning a desk. But I found that drawings of desks cannot be made with stub pens in yellow penholders. Yellow penholders are ire-provoking. Yellow penholders make one blue. Yellow penholders are disgusting contrivances. They do not lend themselves at all to the designing of desks.

It seems that this morning's experiences, or the emotions aroused by the yellow penholder, had their origin in a dream that I had. A yellow penholder figured largely in the dream. I was drawing and making designs. I felt very happy and satisfied in so doing, for my drawings were very successful and done with ease. I awoke from the dream and found that in my sleep I had been engaged in masturbatory activities, and I was particularly filled with disgust at my discovery. The emotions brought about by the yellow penholder this morning were a repetition of the emotions of the dream: First there were very pleasant emotions of happiness and expectancy. Then there was disgust and a feeling of repugnancy toward the yellow penholder. It seems significant that when I recalled the dream and discovered the cause of my emotions, the yellow penholder lost its sway over me. It became just a common, ordinary penholder with no feeling of disgust or repugnancy connected with it.

All of this seems to explain the workings of the subconscious, where deeply buried memories and experiences may be the cause of fears and phobias. Only when the causes of such fears and phobias are understood is one liberated from the grip of one's emotions.

Shortly after this Johan presented me with a series of drawings and paintings, out of gratitude for what I had done for him. In order to determine his unconscious feelings, I asked him, under hypnosis, to dream of his present attitudes toward me.  He reported this dream as follows:

I was trying to fit some pieces of material together—a jigsaw puzzle. They didn't fit together at all.  I couldn't find the right pieces.  As I was working, I found that these pieces were very large and heavy and falling all around.  I couldn't control them.  It seems I had to do something about it.  They fell on top of me, and I couldn't get out of it.  Then someone came to my help and freed me from under these pieces.  He showed me it wasn't only a puzzle.  The picture wasn't a flat picture, but extended in three dimensions.  It was easy to put together after knowing this.  The thing was put together nicely and made a fine structure, a kind of building with openings.  The sun came out and all was well.

I decided then to take advantage of his present mood by giving him a posthypnotic suggestion that he act more self-assertive than he ever had previously.  It was suggested that for one hour after he awakened he would experience a feeling of inner strength and a total absence of fear.  This would make it possible for him to think thoughts and to vocalize attitudes that were previously impossible.  Ideas would come tumbling into his mind, ideas that had been bottled up before— he would have a veritable field day of thoughts and memories.

Upon awakening Johan remarked: "Right now I am thinking of the outdoors.  I think I'll do something unusual, like going in swimming, take a walk outdoors, break a few rules, go out and do things.  It's like a feeling of recklessness.  Just like these things have held me back, and I have conquered them. I want to do new things that are worth while.  I have a feeling of wanting to accomplish things, of wanting to do reckless things, of going out in the water, going out in any weather. I would have liked to be free to do these things.  I wanted to do rather than to follow.  I really did want to.  Time was one of the elements that prevented me.  The necessity of keeping going made me sacrifice certain things.  It's part of a feeling of wanting to do things my way instead of being tied down. There is a same kind of feeling in relation to sex.  I want to accomplish things there too, to do reckless things, to be fearless about it, to go out and find a girl and satisfy myself.  I never had a feeling as prolonged as this.  Maybe momentary flashes of inner strength, but never something that moved me so fully."

This feeling, instead of lasting for only one hour as had been suggested, persisted throughout the day and to some extent for a number of days after that. Johan learned from this experience that he could stand up for his rights and assert himself without incurring hurt. In his diary he wrote:

This morning as I left the doctor's office I was in a reckless mood. I was bent on heroic deeds. I skipped the office stairs in two bounds and went on my way wishing that something would happen. Adventure was just around the corner.

I stepped into the dining hall, waited my turn, and was handed a plate of stew. The stew was unusually good. There was some meat in it and there were two chunks of potato.

"If I could get some of this stew," I thought, "I would save it for tonight and prepare a meal for my roommate and myself." I waited until everyone had been served; then, being in a reckless mood, I went over to the counter. "Have you any stew left over?" I asked the man who had been dishing it out.

"Plenty," said he.

"Let me have a bowlful—plenty of potatoes," said I.

The man filled a bowl with stew and handed it to me.

"What are you going to do with that?" demanded the woman behind the counter.

"I am going to take it with me and prepare a meal for tonight," I answered.

"You cannot do that," said she.

"Why not?" I asked. "Why should I not take some of the leftover stew? The food at night is often not fit to eat."

"I cannot help that," said the woman. "They won't permit it. It is against the rules."

"I am out to break rules," I thought. "I shall speak to them, whoever they are," I said to the woman, and handed her the bowl of stew.

She gave me a sarcastic look. (I have often seen great containers of stew or vegetables or spaghetti, in fact any kind of food, being carried out and dumped into the garbage can after numbers of hungry people have been refused a second helping.)

The food that is served no doubt is good food, no doubt it is overflowing with vitamins, calories, and such things, but the preparation thereof is a disgrace. Sometimes when the food has been too distasteful I have taken my portion with me and therefrom prepared a tasty meal. . . . My adventures of yesterday have caused me to think back and to do a bit of reasoning. I have asked myself the question: "Why do I want better food? Why do I not just accept the stuff they dish out, and swallow it, no matter how it tastes or looks or smells?"

I am sure that I crave no delicacies. I have accustomed myself to eat anything! I have always looked with disdain upon those who cannot eat this and cannot eat that. For five years I ate the food of this place, just as it was, never accepting anything on the side, even though it were offered me. Simply because I felt that I was no better than anyone else and did not want things that others could not have. (Perhaps there also was a feeling that I did not deserve anything else. That I had to be satisfied with no matter what.)

Then a few months ago, as I regained a brighter outlook on things in general, I decided to improve my physical condition also. I made use of whatever odds and ends in the way of food I could get hold of and prepared these to suit myself. The result was satisfactory. Later I found out that one has a right to assert oneself. One has a right to satisfy one's needs and to stick up for one's own interests. I began to apply these principles to my daily life. I did many things that were beneficial to my physical and mental well-being even though they were not in conformity with general rules and regulations. Then I found out that among other things one has a right to assert oneself sexually. Then I found that this right was theoretical and must not be put in practice. Two members of the opposite sex who were found talking to each other were deprived of their liberty in spite of their rights. Of course I know the rules. Of course I know the reasons why these people cannot be permitted to have anything to do with each other, but the fact remains that one's right to assert oneself sexually is a theoretical right that must not be put into practice.

Similarly with one's right to assert oneself in other spheres of activity. For instance, my preparing of food to suit my needs and ideas. This may be against rules and regulations. The rules and regulations may be justified. But no matter how justified the rules and regulations are, the fact still remains that my right to assert myself becomes a theoretical right which must not be put into practice. Perhaps an inward feeling that one has a right to assert oneself should be enough. But when one discovers that one's right is nothing but an inward feeling, one's satisfaction begins to peter out.

If this self-assertiveness is an inward feeling which must not be permitted an outward expression, the whole thing becomes like the very thing that psychoanalysis, psychotherapy, etc., strive to eliminate. It becomes day-dreaming—it becomes a mental state substituted for reality.

There are rules and there are rules. Some rules are ridiculous. To live on garbage would cause no dismay in me were there no way of obtaining something else. I would refuse to take more than my portion of anything, were I depriving someone else of his share. But the rule that forbids me to take a portion of food that is headed for the garbage can is a ridiculous rule.

Rules and regulations may be made for the benefit of all. But rules and regulations can be amended—"just the tiniest little bit." (Every rule has its exceptions, it is said.) A thing that is absolutely rigid and unyielding is apt to break.

Now the question comes up as to whether one ought to obey rules and regulations blindly or whether one ought to use one's judgment, take a chance and break the ridiculous rules. (Blind obedience has never led to freedom of thought or action.)

Should one depend on one's own judgment? Should one obey the dictates of reason and not of rules and regulations? One is faced with the necessity of keeping things to oneself. To play one's part and play innocent, there one is not. One's better judgment would tell one that it would be unwise to broadcast one's independence of thought and action from the housetops.

Then comes the very specific question whether I ought to confide in the doctor, whether I ought to let him in on my escapades of self-assertiveness, or whether I ought to play the perfect saint. If the latter, what becomes of this "diary"? What becomes of the laying bare and awakening of thoughts and emotions? What becomes of the whole structure of better understanding and a better integrated individual that has been so painstakingly erected?

Let me sum up. I do not want better food because I want to revel in the sensual pleasure of eating. I want to do little innocent things that satisfy my needs—in the matter of eating as well as in other matters. If my physique is running down, if I am losing weight, I do not want to regain my weight through the use of pills or medicines or special concoctions while perfectly wholesome food is plentiful and available. (I may be forced to make use of pills and medicines and special concoctions against my will, but what becomes of my right to do things in my own way under the circumstances?)

I should like to do things openly and freely without pretense, but if wisdom or necessity prescribes otherwise, I have no choice but to follow their dictates —or so it would seem to me.

There was a definite change in Johan's behavior from this point on. He appeared much more self-assured, much more capable of asserting himself. Even the manner of his walk changed, and he held his chin high and swung his arms confidently at his sides. The change in his attitude was reflected in a dream that he recorded in his diary.

Last night I had a dream that has repeated itself several times lately. The dream is a review (with slight variations) of an actual experience, and the experience I put into words in a story which I called "Anitra." For a few seasons I met with a group of young people. Sundays and holidays in the summertime, work permitting, we spent on the water—rowing, swimming, reading, sketching, philosophizing. These young people were what one might call "cosmopolites." They were people in business or the professions. They were people who could converse with equal ease on a variety of subjects and in any of several languages. Evenings—having had supper at some near-by place—we spent on the veranda of an old building facing the open sea. I recall one such evening.

For a while the conversation had been on weather and wind and the tides. Someone had told of experiences in far-off lands. The moon had come out and sent a streak of liquid silver across the water. The conversation had died down with the wind. The sheer beauty of the night was overwhelming. There was a male quartette in one group. The four had withdrawn to a corner in the dark. Then quietly, quietly, then expanding in volume— *L'amour, toujours l'amour.* Beautiful—so beautiful that tears were choking.

Kurt had a violin, a beautiful instrument, old and mellow. Kurt had long and slender fingers. He had a bow that was unusually long, and he handled his bow with consummate skill. Kurt was a virtuoso. Magic and enchantment floated on the air when Kurt caressed his violin. But, for some reason, Kurt was not easily made to play. The beauty of this particular night seemed to have done something to Kurt, for he appeared with his violin, quite without inducement.

There was no sound besides the lapping of the waves as Kurt put his violin under his chin. The silvery streak was weaving and winking. What Kurt played I do not know. The *Moonlight Sonata* was intermixed in his playing. It seemed as though the strains from the violin and the glitter on the waves became one and the same. Kurt caressed his violin. The violin sang in ecstasy. Kurt played the night and the calm and the beauty. Kurt played the silvery streak on the dancing ripples. Kurt played it all—just as an artist might paint it. The violin whispered, murmured, sang—it sighed in tremulous expectancy. The violin was master, compelling and overpowering. No one dared to move—scarcely to breathe.

Then Anitra danced!!!

Anitra was one of those beloved by the gods—slender and supple as a vine. Anitra was fair and fiery. Anitra was 17. Anitra danced with abandon. Anitra danced. The violin danced. The silver streak danced. The night itself seemed to be dancing. The moonbeams leaped across Kurt's violin in one fell bound and kissed Anitra on the brow. . . .

For one moment the world was reeling. Then the moon hid behind a cloud. Shamefacedly, as though regretful of the spells cast upon the minds of the children of men.——The silver streak stopped dancing. Anitra stopped dancing. The violin pleaded, threatened, wept, then calmed down and finished with a sigh.

It was very quiet for a long time. No one seemed to care to break the silence. The night was half done when we broke up. I went home filled with thanksgiving that such beauty was part of life and of this world. Kurt's violin was still singing in my innards—Anitra dancing, silver waves lapping. The serene beauty of the night. All was part of my innermost being—forevermore. Whenever I want to, even now, I can hear and see and sense this night, long since past.

In the dream of last night there was the water and the sunshine and blue sky. There was the straining of the oars—the sky turning yellow and orange

—the storm. There was the talking and singing. There was the music, the moon, silver waves—Anitra dancing.

Then something new came into the dream. I had been part of the magic of the night, the moon, the music, silver waves. I was contemplating the rhythm and beauty of Anitra dancing. Just as surely as the violin sang the magic of the night, so Anitra danced it. Anitra was the personification of the magic of the night, and I was spellbound by it. Anitra stopped dancing. She stopped right by my side and sat down beside me. I complimented her on her dancing, and she drew closer. I bent over and whispered something in her ear. Then Mr. Picklepuss stood before us.

"Go as far as you like—don't mind me. I don't give a darn," said Mr. Picklepuss.

(In our group was a man who had been a member for a great many years. He was some sort of self-styled guardian of the moral tone of the place. Whenever someone said or did something that did not meet with his approval, he used to say, "You can go as far as you like, so far as I am concerned. I don't give a darn. But there may be others who will object." This man evidently took the part of Mr. Picklepuss in the dream.)

"Do you think it strange, Mr. Picklepuss, if two young people take pleasure in each others' presence on a night like this?" I asked. "Do you think it objectionable if they are swayed by their emotions and their senses?"

"Of course not, of course not," said Mr. P. "That's the way it ought to be. That's highly commendable. But you must keep these things to yourself. Suppose you sit here, and she sits over there. You can go as far as you like, so far as I am concerned. I don't give a darn."

## Later entries in Johan's diary included the following:

There is one thing which it seems I have not fully comprehended until now —namely, that the fearlessness, self-assertiveness, etc., which have developed in me, do not necessarily have to have an outlet. They are there—and the fact that they are there should be the cause of satisfaction, to be exercised whenever opportunity arises or circumstances permit.

Have been wondering whether in my dream of last night Mr. Picklepuss actually was a personification of my fears as to what people would think or say about me.

Early environmental experiences no doubt laid down within me a fear as to what people might say or think about me. But I believe that I have pretty well rid myself of this kind of fear. Mr. P. could not possibly deprive one of Anitra were he nothing but the personification of my fears as to people's opinions about me. Rather do I believe that Mr. P. personifies the things that were in my mind on the day preceding my dream, namely, that one's right to assert oneself is a theoretical right to which one must not give an outward expression.

I believe I have rid myself of fear in connection with my own sexual activities. If I do not indulge myself, I do not think this should be ascribed to fear. Neither fear of physical damage or destruction nor fear of offending against some moral code. If, as I have expressed it before, I should feel like taking a glass of wine in my lonely corner, I would do so. But, should I prefer to leave it alone, I would do that. I shall exercise my right to choice in either direction.

The opinion that I expressed about "some other fellow" seems to have been my own opinion of myself. There was a time when I thought quite a lot of myself. I was accomplishing things worth while. Then came a time when I thought my accomplishments worthless and meaningless. Lately I have regained my faith in myself. To "poke around in all kinds of things that are none of one's business," I do not think such a bad habit. He who does not poke his nose into a thing except his own business will never learn anything new.

I believe I shall still learn many new things. I believe I shall experience new things. I believe there is still a lot of poking around in things that do not concern me ahead of me.

A new element began to creep into Johan's writings and associations. For the first time, he actually began to make plans for getting out of the hospital. At first he approached this matter gingerly—then, as he became more sure of himself, with greater determination.

When I am ready to take up life on my own once more, there are two things that I want to be taken into consideration. I do not want to be released in the custody of anyone else. I want to be responsible for my own self, and I want in some way to prepare for the eventuality that I get sick again. Should I get sick, I do not want to be deprived of my rights to think for myself or to manage my own affairs. I want to retain my standing as a human being even in the case of sickness.

It has been said that an individual has a right to stand up for his own rights. It has been said that he has a right to differ with and to oppose authority. It has been said that this is Democracy. But in this respect Democracy is a beautiful theory. If the first step against any individual for any reason whatever (sickness, crime, etc.) is to deprive him of his right to speak for himself and declare him incompetent, the above mentioned individual rights become a nonsensical platitude and Democracy a joke.

Until I can act and decide in my own right, until I can deal with whomsoever I choose openly and freely and on an equal footing, I am unable to take up the business of life. Until my name is of equal worth with that of anyone else of equal accomplishment and equal ability, I cannot go out in the market place and offer my wares for sale. And these are the reasons why I do not wish to leave, except as a free human being in every sense of the word.

# XII

Almost four months after hypnoanalytic therapy was started, Johan had an interesting spontaneous dream that appeared to symbolize the progress he had made in understanding his emotional problem. He described the dream as

A phantasmagoria of color. There are puffs of pale, scarcely visible color moving slowly and rhythmically across a white background. The tempo increases, the color deepens and takes shape. Yellow predominates for a while. Circles of yellow spread from a center outward—like water rings on the surface of a pond. Touches of other colors—red, orange, blue, purple, green. The circles break up, form patterns and designs. Now, colors rush inward toward the center; complementary colors seek one another. Yellow seeks purple, red seeks green, blue seeks orange. They meet for a moment, overlap, form a splash of white, clash, split up. Splashes of color are hanging up here and there. Splashes of pure intense color. One color predominates, then another. Yellow, red, and purple weave and intertwine, green and blue accentuate and punctuate at intervals. Green and blue take up the theme, seem to get the upper hand for a moment or two, then are swallowed up in the harmonies of more violent colors. The colors intermingle, bubble over, boil like the contents of a great cauldron. Pandemonium and turmoil! A ring of black forms around the color mass. It contracts, constrains, and smothers the colors within its embrace until movement has ceased and only darkness remains. The black is split open—yellow breaks through and overflows. The yellow is shot through with streaks of burning red, edged with orange— like thunderbolts shooting zigzag across the full dome of the heavens——Calm after the storm. Graceful lines of color shooting up and falling down like playing fountains. Misty spray in all the hues of the rainbow shiver and dance. Colors intersect, overlap, intermingle, until they become one grand ocean of blinding white.

Johan's written associations to and analysis of the dream were as follows:

The very earliest shade of life is a blank. It is unknowingness. The emotions lie dormant. It is a kind of serene unawareness. It is "nirvana" (white background). Then there is the first vague awakening of the mind. Sensations and emotions begin their play (puffs of pale, scarcely visible color moving slowly and rhythmically).

The first emotion is fear. Fear is suffusing all of existence. It is an unreasoned fear of nothing in particular. The mystery of all things seems scaring (concentric circles of yellow). All the various emotions make themselves felt in various degrees of intensity. Impatience, anger, disgust, calm, irritability, expectancy, etc. (touches of various colors). Fear ceases as the behavior of the environment is comprehended. Patterns of ideas are forming. Emotions and sensations are associated and behavior is formed (the color circles break up and form patterns in combination with other colors). Then comes the search for completeness. The missing elements in one's make-up are sought. That which one has not got is desired. Completeness makes for calm and satisfaction and happiness. Studies are undertaken. Experiences are sought—much is gained. There are moments of joy, even exaltation, but there are also disappointments and reverses. Nothing is perfect, nothing lasts (complementary colors attracting one another, overlapping, forming splashes of white, then split up). The emotions become more intense as experience grows. One is under the sway of various emotions for varying lengths of time. Sadness, happiness, fear, anger, disgust, love, and hatred—all have their say (splashes of pure, intense color; one color predominates—then another).

The emotions come to a boiling point (and this is more specifically my own story). They clash and intermingle. There came a time when all of life and its experiences passed in review before my mind. I doubted all things. All values were reversed. There was pandemonium and turmoil in my soul. Everything was dark. Despair and sorrow took hold. All emotions were stilled under the heavy burden of despair. (Colors intermingle and bubble over, boil like the contents of a cauldron. A ring of black, contracts, constrains, smothers.) Then fear, split asunder by rage, indignity, and disgust. An intense hatred of the sham and hypocrisy that distorts all values (yellow shot through with streaks of burning red and orange).

The storm is calming down. The turmoil is ceasing. A better understanding has allayed the hatred. Fear, anger, and disgust are smoothing out. Beauty is seen in many things. The search for completeness goes on in a calm, determined manner.

The remainder is aspiration: The gaining of completeness through attaining to the lacking elements in character—in experience. Peace, poise, grace —happiness through understanding and insight. Not the nirvana of unawareness and nonexperience, but all the colors of the spectrum harmoniously blended into white. Happiness through achievement and attainment. The fulfillment of one's aspirations and desires through sorrow and suffering. The blending of all emotions, fear-fearlessness, sorrow-joy, calm-excitement, love-hatred, into one harmonious serenity.

Johan was informed that on the basis of his present understanding of himself there was no reason why he could not attain to life's pleasures, completeness, and productiveness.

There were, however, evidences that he still believed that the fulfillment of his aspirations and desires could be obtained only through sorrow and suffering. Under hypnosis he was instructed to work unconsciously on his problems, to see whether he would be able to understand why he felt that he could attain his goals only through sorrow and suffering.

The next day he presented the following dream:

I was out walking in the rain. I was carrying an umbrella. It was windy, and I held on to the umbrella with both hands, holding it low over my head. The umbrella shut out most of the view, and at times I barely escaped running into people or things. I was tired and hungry. I was eager to get to my destination as quickly as possible, but the rain and the wind made progress slow. I noticed that there were places where food was served and where people were resting and refreshing themselves, but I gave myself no time to shop for these things.

"Later on," I thought, "when I get home, I shall eat and rest and enjoy myself. Then I shall have the things that I want." I continued struggling against the wind, with my umbrella held tightly with both hands. People tried to speak to me, but I avoided them. Once a flower girl stretched out a sprig of flowers, but my hands were occupied, and the flowers fell to the ground.

"Why don't you look where you are going?" I heard someone say.

Then someone came up by my side and walked along with me.

"Why don't you throw away that umbrella?" said the one by my side. "The rain wouldn't do you any harm. It is refreshing and life-giving. Besides, it has stopped raining long ago."

A gust of wind came along and turned my umbrella inside out. I let go of it. I found that it was quite clear. The air was balmy, and the wind not so strong now that I had gotten rid of the umbrella.

"Let us sit down and talk somewhere," said my companion.

"No, thank you," said I. "I am in a terrible hurry. I want to get home."

"What is your hurry? It is early. Someone waiting?"

"No," said I, "I want to rest. I want to do some work and think and plan. I'm hungry."

I found that we were out in the country now, walking along the roadside. I was picking at things—flowers, grass, leaves. The sense of touch seemed to give me pleasure. I was not so tired any more.

"If you are hungry, why don't you eat?" asked my companion.

"There is nothing to eat around here," I said. "What I want is a complete, perfect meal. I am very hungry."

"Here," said my companion, and dug down into his pocket for a sandwich, which he handed me.

"Thanks," said I. "But this is not exactly what I mean."

Now it seemed that I was bending down and picking up things. There were all kinds of beautiful things around that I wanted to collect. But I always found a flaw in the things that I picked up, and I threw them away.

We sat down at the roadside to rest for a while. My companion gathered together some things that he found around, and we ate. "This is nice and pleasant," I thought. "I feel rested and refreshed. I feel like going out in search for more substantial things."

Consciously Johan associated going out into the rain and carrying an umbrella to shut out the view with being shut up within himself and having a covering that shielded him from the world. The umbrella itself made the weather seem bad. There were many worth while things around, but these were rejected because of other things that he was reaching for. The objects stood for the idea that he wanted a thing to be perfect before it was acceptable. As a result he threw away many valuable things on the basis that they were not good enough. Under hypnosis Johan was instructed to associate to the dream and to recall his associations later on during the day, recording them in his diary.

My instructions led to a spontaneous dream that night, in which he was engaged in an argument with me about phallic symbolism. In the dream he insisted that

A sexual interpretation could be put on anyone's doings or sayings; on the other hand, there are many other things to talk about or write about or dream about besides sex. "I believe I could put a sexual interpretation on these experiences myself," said I, "but that does not say that such an interpretation will get us the true meaning of things. But let's see what we can get."

The rain is life-giving. It penetrates into the earth and causes it to bear fruit. Rain is the masculine principle. The umbrella is protection against the rain. It also shuts off the view of the outer world and makes for a distorted relationship with people and things. It stands for self-sufficiency. What its purely sexual meaning is I do not know. When I did not have the umbrella to occupy my thoughts and efforts, I had time to notice the rest of the world, and I found things more pleasing than I had supposed them to be. I made progress more quickly. I rejected the offering of the flower girl because of my preoccupation with the umbrella.

Someone suggested that I throw away the umbrella and "look where I was going." This someone accompanied me for a space of time. I confided in my companion and told him that I was hungry.

"The thing to do when hungry is to eat," he suggested.

I insisted that I would not be satisfied with anything less than a complete, perfect meal. This in terms of sexual symbolism would mean that I wanted a complete, perfect sexual relationship, with everything that goes with it. My companion offered me a sandwich. This would suggest a very incomplete meal, or, in sexual activity, perhaps masturbation.

"This is not what I had in mind," I told my companion.

I found a flaw in all things. It seems that I was searching for perfection. The talk with my companion, the wider view, the understanding and appreciation of things, the rest by the roadside, were very pleasant, but I longed for more substantial things. I came to a clearing in the woods. This was the foundation for a perfect picture. I completed the picture in my mind. A home in a perfect setting. Nature an open book. Study and work. The girl inviting to dinner. A perfect and complete meal. In the perfect meal all of these things were included: home; work; study; the girl herself; the understanding and appreciation and serenity gained on the road that led to these.

Johan insisted that the real meaning of the dream was "that there is a shell around me that keeps me from all the beautiful things I want." It was suggested that this insight represented considerable progress, since he had previously projected his failure to obtain the beautiful things in life onto inimical or destructive forces in his environment. Yet there were reasons why he had to maintain the shell that constantly separated him from self-fulfillment. Johan remarked that if there still were blocks within himself, he was not at all aware of them.

Under hypnosis he was asked to think of the conversation we had had previously, particularly in relation to the shell that surrounded him and that kept him from gaining what he wanted most from life. As he did this, he would have a dream that would give him a clue as to what it was that was still hindering him. After a few minutes Johan started talking. "I just had a dream, a very peculiar dream," he said. "I was pressing my clothes. The iron was so hot that it started to smoke. It burned the clothes and the covering on the ironing board. It became so hot that I couldn't touch the iron. I pushed it away. Then I got hold of it. I got it down on the floor, and when I did it, it burned my hand. The floor started to smoke and get black. I started pushing the iron around because I felt if it stayed in one place it would burn. It got under some furniture and I couldn't get it out. I got a stick and pushed it. It got out of control. It was black, smoldering smoke."

Hypnotic associations to the dream were to the effect that there were some things that he wasn't supposed to do that he did nevertheless. These were bad because they got out of control. Further questioning revealed no other associations. Johan was then instructed to make a drawing symbolizing the dream. The drawing consisted of a large circle on top of which was a huge flatiron, the front part shaped like an alligator's mouth. Around the circle were a number of jagged and interrupted lines and peculiar-shaped objects such as broken tree stumps and crushed horses. Asked to interpret the drawing, Johan remarked: "That's an iron, a useful thing, but it may be overdone. It may be overheated. Then it is destructive. It destroys things. If you keep moving and keep going, it may be less destructive. Still, it may run away and you may be unable to control it. The rest of the drawing is destruction, speed like horses running away."

He was then instructed to think of the flatiron in the dream, which would stimulate a series of associated sensations. These he was to report to me. He replied: "I smell a choking, smoky odor. I taste a sour acid taste, see a yellow color, hear a scaring thing in music. I don't know what it is. It makes me much afraid. I have a creepy feeling in my skin." He was then regressed to a 6 year level and told that he would be able to smell something, see a color, hear music, and feel something that reminded him of a hot iron. Johan remarked that he could smell "kerosene" and could taste a "funny taste like camphor." He could see orange and purple colors that made him afraid and "hot over the forehead." He could hear no music, but he could hear sounds "like the tripping of feet." He was then told that he would have a dream that would remind him of what he had just smelled, tasted, seen, and felt. The dream was this:

An old building in the country—in the evening—in dark—there is another building—a barn where they keep hay and grain, cows and horses. There is a light in the window. All of a sudden the whole thing burns—people running around—you can't get the animals out. They are screaming—can't get out—the whole place burning down—smoke. The people have lost everything.

Johan was instructed to remember this dream after he woke up. He was then brought back to an adult level and asked to draw pictures of things that symbolized an overheated iron. The pictures drawn were very crude, childish images of knives, a scythe, dotted lines that he identified as rain, part of the sun without rays, wavy lines that he said were fire, and other lines that he called water. There was also a hand holding a club. He was then asked to have a dream that symbolized a flatiron, after which he was to awaken.

Upon awakening Johan remarked that he had just had a dream, which he related as follows:

There was a dragon who was spitting fire. He was after me. I was running away. I was running behind it, behind its tail. It circled around, but it never could get hold of me.

He was unable to produce associations with this dream or to understand its significance. When he was asked whether it could possibly represent his notion of a smoldering flatiron, he scoffed at the idea. He was then asked whether he remembered having any dreams during the trance. He replied that he did not. The dream about the burning building that he reported during regression was read to him, and he seemed puzzled. He remarked that it sounded familiar but could not recall having dreamed it.

Johan recorded his reaction to these experiences in his diary.

I believe that unconsciously there has always been within me a fear of destruction caused by masturbation. That this is so is shown by the fact that this fear came to the surface at the time of my "breakdown," and all that happened to me during the ten days and after I attributed to my activities in connection with masturbation. That fear of the destructive character of masturbation was very strong is evidenced by the fact that I thought myself in imminent danger of being put out of existence.

What events were responsible for this unconscious fear I do not know. I do know that in childhood I sometimes overheard boys discussing the dangers of masturbation, but I also know that very soon any fears that may have sprung up were assuaged through my readings.

I believe that unconsciously I have always considered marriage and heterosexual union proper and desirable. But there was ample cause for fearfulness, conscious or unconscious, in regard to such union. The confusion and unhappiness in my own home, the unhappiness that I witnessed all about me, could not but create in me an attitude of wariness or suspicion or fear toward marital union.

The dreams that I have had during the past few days all point in the same direction. Fearfulness toward masturbation, but also fearfulness toward marriage and heterosexual union.

I have rid myself of my conscious fears toward masturbation. But so far as I am concerned, masturbation is unsatisfactory and undesirable. My conscious attitude toward marriage is unchanged so far as its desirability goes. I have lost much of my fearfulness in regard to its confusion and unhappiness.

That residues of unconscious fears, both as regards masturbation and marriage and heterosexual union—as the dreams seem to indicate—still exist, of this I am quite convinced. As to the sources of these fears I know nothing.

The doubts that I have expressed from time to time, that all my fears were in connection with matters of sex and had their origin in childhood experiences, were so expressed before I had a full understanding of the subtle workings of the subconscious. For instance, I was convinced that some of these fears originated in the period of the ten days. Having come to recognize that the ten days were a product of the subtle workings of the subconscious, I have also rid myself of my doubts on this score.

When a few days ago I mentioned my symbolic sketches and my objections to symbols as being disguised forms of sexuality, I was referring to an earlier period of time (before I had come to an understanding of the subtle workings of the mind). All of this I mention that there be no misunderstanding in regard to my attitude on these questions.

At the next hypnotic session Johan was given the following instructions: "I am going to give you a series of objects. You will have a dream about them. The objects are smoke, a dragon, heat, fear, and a hand holding a sword or club."

During the following five minutes Johan exhibited signs of considerable anxiety. Then he exclaimed: "I just had a dream. No, it wasn't a dream. It was something that really happened, and I just remembered. It was at home. Mother was telling us about her people. She said that her people were well-to-do. They had a great estate and many animals— horses, cows, pigs, and chickens. She said that these belonged to her grandparents. When her mother's mother died her mother's father started to drink and gamble. There were wild parties every day and night. The stables and barns caught fire, and all the animals burned to death. Then this man continued his gambling and drinking until there was nothing left.

They were all impoverished. I remember now my mother telling me about this. I had forgotten it. It was in the dream that I dreamed of her telling me this, but it was a real happening. In the dream that I just had I got a book of fairy tales, of a saint who went out, and he was going to liberate his people, who were under the rule of a monster. The monster was a great big dragon, spitting fire. He slew the dragon. Then I went to bed and dreamed of the fire and burning buildings. I was surrounded by fire and smoke. I couldn't get out. There were all kinds of things that tried to get me. I was so afraid, I couldn't sleep again for many hours."

Johan remarked that the latter dream was a repetitive dream that he had had constantly since early childhood. He promised to write it out for me in detail and to give it to me the next day. He had never before quite understood the meaning of this dream, but now he was quite certain that it was stimulated by the story that his mother told him about her grandparents and the burnt animals, which he had up to this time forgotten. He was at present uncertain as to whether what he had reported as his experience of looking through the window and seeing pigs being slaughtered, might not be something that he had imagined. However, he was more inclined to feel that it probably had occurred.

Johan was then instructed as follows: "Now you will remember the dream you had as a child, of being in a burning building from which you could not escape. You will dream now of a situation that could have inspired this early fantasy." The ensuing dream was this:

There was Mother, who told me about the things that happened to her mother's father. She said: "You had better be careful. Don't drink. Don't gamble. Don't live an indecent life." I was very much afraid and scared of it.

Regressed to the age period at which his mother warned him not to do indecent things, he was asked to make drawings of what these things might be. He then drew a picture of a club, a crude alligator that he identified as a dragon, a hand with eyes, nose, and a mouth on each fingernail, and a crude sketch that he said resembled a man holding a croquet mallet and hitting a ball. He was then instructed to have a dream that represented the drawing he had just made. After this he was to return to an adult level, awaken, and remember the dream.

Upon awakening Johan remarked that he had just had a dream—"a mixture of things." The dream was this:

The fire and animals, I remember. At home Mother was telling it, and I overheard it. She said how things had happened. That one shouldn't do things destructive. Then I dreamed of a bull being castrated. How he changed his whole nature. How his creative principle was destroyed. It seems that all these things made me guard against life, against drinking and doing indecent, destructive things. I also came to include indecent sex life and later masturbation, when I came to regard it as indecent. That seems to be the thing that later on led me to feel that my life was destroyed. I thought a lot about that story Mother told. I used to fear it. It's a funny thing that I never remembered it until now.

Apparently the repetitive dream that Johan had as a child was the result of this story, told him by his mother, of destructiveness resulting from doing indecent things. Johan wrote out this early dream in detail.

There is a dream I had in early childhood. It repeated itself two or three times. All through the years since then I have not had a single thought of this dream. It was as though it had been erased from my memory, until some three or four years ago the identical dream again recurred. I also dreamed it a few days ago.

I found myself all alone in some sort of an old building. There were great numbers of rooms and winding stairs leading to upper and lower floors. I was running from room to room, upstairs and downstairs. I did not know why I was in the place or how I had gotten there. I did not know why I was alone. I was trying desperately to find my way out. Then I discovered that the building was on fire. Looking down a vista of rooms, I saw flames in the distance. Smoke was rolling toward me. Terror took hold of me and I began running wildly in a direction away from the flames. Then it seemed that I was encircled by the flames. It became very hot. I was now running downstairs—flight after flight. Further and further down. The stairs became more uneven, more winding, more angular. The further down I came, they now seemed to be made of rough-hewn blocks of stone laid one below the others—in a manner similar to the tower stairs in old castles. I was running through hallways and door openings. I now found that to the walls and door openings were attached arms and hands. These stretched out and tried to take hold of me as I passed by. My progress now became a kind of stealthy hurry, so as to sneak by the arms and hands unnoticed, but when I had to pass through some door opening I came within reach of the arms and hands, which stretched out and pinched me. This pinching felt as if done with pliers or pincers, and I awoke from the pain caused thereby. When I awoke from the dream I was covered with perspiration. I was shaking with terror. The dream stood vividly before me, and it took me a long while to get back to sleep.

# XIII

THE RECOVERY of the early memory that had created this dream caused considerable excitement in Johan. He was certain that it accounted for many of his later fears and misgivings about enjoying life, and that it started the shell that kept him from partaking of life's pleasures. In his diary he wrote:

Yesterday I wrote on my fears—conscious and unconscious—in regard to masturbation, marriage, and heterosexual union. I pointed out that my fears in connection with marriage might have had their beginnings in the unhappy marital life that surrounded me on all sides throughout childhood. I also pointed out that I knew nothing about the sources of my fears as regards masturbation.

My unconscious fears had during the period of the ten days (my conscious fears as well) taken the form of fear of destruction. How this fear of destruction came about must have been as follows: My mother told the story of her maternal grandparents, who had been wealthy. Their wealth was lost, first through a fire that had destroyed barns and stables and animals, second through drunken revelries and gambling. Mother used to admonish me: "This is what happens if you lead an indecent life." The story about the fire seems very particularly to have impressed me, for a dream in which I was locked into a burning building recurred several times during this period of time. I came to regard the fire as the punishment for an indecent life. What the indecencies of life were was not very clear to me at that time.

Drunkenness and gambling were the cause of the lost fortune in my mother's story. Therefore of course drunkenness and gambling were included in my list of indecencies. Later other indecencies were added to my list—and no doubt in my subconscious mind took their place among the things that were punishable with destruction, such as was manifested by the fire in mother's story.

To consider my fears in sexual matters for a moment and the manner in which they may have come about, I shall mention an occurrence that may shed light on this subject: A young girl, a close relative of mine, became pregnant. She was the cause of much horror and shame to all concerned and of whispered remarks among those not concerned. This impressed me a great deal and probably caused me to include promiscuous sexual relationships among the indecencies of life.

How masturbation came to be included among the indecencies I do not know. Why the (unconscious) fear of it should have become so much stronger than the fear of other indecencies I do not know. That it did become stronger is proven by the experiences of the ten days. Where this fear originated I do not know. My mother never touched upon the subject of masturbation. My unconscious fears seem to have been bound up with fire and smoke. Heat and fire seem to appear as a destructive element in my dreams—heat and fire and smoke also played a part in my experiences of the ten days. Of course, my unconscious fears of fire and smoke as the destructive elements probably have their origin in Mother's story about her maternal grandparents. In fact—perhaps this story is the early childhood experience that is the basis upon which the whole structure of repressions, inhibitions, and fears are built.

Today another element came to the fore—a dream that seemed to be a jumble of all kinds of things. It was built around the theme of castration. Fear of castration as a punishment for indulging in masturbatory activities has never entered my conscious mind. It certainly played no part in Mother's story. And also—why castration should be the punishment for masturbatory activities, if destruction through fire and heat and smoke is the punishment, does not seem quite clear. Of course, my dream on the theme of castration may not necessarily be an integral part of the larger theme as outlined above. Whether it is or not depends, it would seem to me, upon what the impulse was that touched the mechanism off and called it forth at this particular time. If the impulse was my dealing with and pondering the meaning of my fears in connection with sexual matters, then, it would seem, castration would be an integral part of the whole. On the other hand, if the impulse was some chance suggestion, such as an overheard remark or something read or seen, then it would seem castration would be a separate little theme by itself, perhaps something like this. Masturbation impairs the forces that should be used for creative purposes. The loss of creative powers is synonymous with castration. Of course, one may build further on this theme. A desire to restore the lost powers—a search for the means whereby to accomplish this.

If fear of destruction through fire and heat and smoke as a punishment for indulging in the indecencies of life is the keynote to the grand theme as above considered, then, fear of castration could not very well be the keynote—or so it would seem to me.

During a later trance Johan was shown the picture of the hand and dagger he had made in a former session, and he was asked to have a dream that would symbolize this drawing. He dreamed as follows:

There was a man who was very large and big, a giant. All the people had to work for him, working and producing all kinds of food. They were poor. The giant was eating all these things. He had a great big sword. He used it as a knife and fork. He used it on everything. He took all the pigs and cows and grain. It was all destruction, and the people had nothing for themselves.

In associating, Johan remarked that this dream had something to do with masturbation, but he could elucidate this idea no further.

It was decided at this point to use the technics of regression and crystal gazing. Johan was given the following instructions: "You are going back in life to a time when you were a little boy. You are growing smaller and smaller. You are very little now. You are masturbating, and you may be able to remember certain things that happened to you around this time. I am going to give you a glass ball, and you will look in it. In it you will see things that you will tell me about."

Johan looked intently into the crystal with a puzzled expression. Suddenly his eyes widened, and he remarked: "I see the room. The light is coming in. I try to catch things. I hear voices. Sometimes I like them. Sometimes I don't. I see myself. I am crawling around. I am picked up. I see Mother. I see her picking me up. Sometimes she handles me carefully, and I like it very much. Sometimes she is not careful and I don't like it. Sometimes she's in a hurry, she has no time. She kind o' fixes me ahurry, pushes me away, and I don't like it. I see Father sitting there. He is at a table. Sometimes he is talking to me. I think it's nice. I don't understand things. All is strange. I didn't understand things. I tried all things. I took hold of things to find out about things. I tried to take hold of my feet. I try all parts of my body. Everything is funny. There are also things that hurt. I bang into things. People pinch me when they hold me. Now I see the yard and a house where we were living. I see the boys running around, playing a game, some of the girls sitting on the steps. Some of the boys are curious about girls, seek what they are, and how they are different from themselves. I am older. I am curious. I want to find out about it. Sometimes I look at them and I try to find out. I want to know why they are different from me. Now there is a different place I see. I am with Mother. We stand over a place where there is a new baby. She is kicking her legs and arms. Mother says she is my sister. I ask Mother why she hasn't got the same thing I've got. Mother says that is all right, she is a girl. Then I see my little sister again. I think she is different, that she isn't much good. The boys talk about it, and they say that that is a bad thing to do, because maybe one may get sick if he plays with himself, maybe he is not good later on. Then I think maybe one may lose it. Maybe the penis may grow small and useless."

Johan was told that he would return to an adult level. If the incidents he had seen in the crystal were true, and if they really explained his attitudes toward masturbation, he would have a dream that would be understandable to him.

Upon awakening Johan remarked that he had had a dream.

I was looking for work, and a lot of people were looking for it as if it were the only kind of work. There was planting in the field. Each one was required to have a tool to put the seed in the ground. Each had a thing to push through the ground. I came along and I didn't seem to have the right kind of a tool. It didn't work. I wasn't able to make the right impression on the ground. It was useless, and I was thrown out. I was unable to do anything. Then I was thinking about things and certain memories. I believe it was in connection with the things we were thinking of. I remember early childhood experiences at home and with other families. I saw little babies very young, sometimes a little boy and occasionally a little girl. I just began to notice the difference between boys and girls. I was four or five years old. I remember the surprise when I saw the difference. I asked my mother how it was. She didn't explain. I was sick. When Sister was born I asked Mother, "He must have a very small penis?" I didn't think of girls at all. First thing I began to notice, I thought there was something wrong or missing, that they couldn't be good. I remember the boys talking. They all thought girls aren't so good, that they were less worthy. Then I remember the boys speaking about masturbation, and I combined the ideas I had. The idea of being useless for the purpose of marriage or in other ways causing destruction or sickness or damage or that the penis would become shorter or small. These memories weren't totally forgotten, but I hadn't thought of them since childhood.

The diary entry that afternoon was this:

Yesterday I tried to trace my fears to their sources and found that they probably originated in a story that my mother told about her maternal grand-

parents.  My fears were fears of destruction as punishment for what I chose
to call the indecencies of life.  How the various indecencies came to be classed
as such in my mind, I tried to illustrate by relating the incidents or events
that caused them so to be classified.  I found that in each case a specific
incident or event was responsible for an activity being classified as indecent,
and that then, subconsciously, it became subject to fear of destruction through
fire and heat and smoke.

However, one of the indecencies, masturbation—which to my subconscious
mind had become the by far most atrocious and most fear-provoking of the
indecencies—I was unable to find an incident or event for.  I was searching
for some especially fearful incident in connection with masturbation but could
find none.  Then yesterday I had a dream—a conglomerate of events—built
around the theme of castration.  I believed that this dream was some kind of
lead toward the reason why masturbation had come to be included among the
indecencies.  Castration, of course, would be a fearful punishment, but so
far as I knew I had never been threatened with castration because of masturbation or any other activities, nor had I seen or heard of anyone being
castrated or threatened with castration because of having indulged in masturbatory activities.

Today I recollected a series of events from early childhood, each one of
which taken separately seemed so insignificant that it was scarcely worth
taking note of at all, but taken together they formed a unified whole which
seemed to clear up the mystery as to the reason why masturbation had become
such a fearful thing to the subconscious mind.

First I recollected an incident in very early childhood, when I had seen a
little baby girl and noticed the absence of a penis.  I realized that something
was lacking, that this baby was not complete, and therefore could not be much
good.  Upon inquiry why "he" had no penis, I was told that  the baby was a
girl.  This, of course, was the same as to say that girls were not "much good."

Then there was another incident in which boys discussing masturbation
were of the opinion that it might cause sickness, impotency, or atrophy of the
penis.

Then I had a dream in which (symbolically) I was declared no good, rejected, and excluded from the business of life because I had a small and useless
penis.  And this is what these events seem to  bring out:  (1) An individual
without a penis is not much good.  (2) Masturbation may cause atrophy of
the penis.  (This may be considered a form of castration.)  (3) An individual
with a small or useless penis is excluded from the business of life.  (This is
really a variation of 1.)  Incidentally, if the lack of a penis is so damaging to
an individual's worth or usefulness, then a penis becomes a valuable asset,
and an individual who has caused damage to be done to his penis may spend
a lifetime in search for means wherewith to restore the damage.

Now the subconscious gets to work and declares: "Castration is a terrible
thing.  Masturbation is the cause of castration.  Therefore masturbation
is one of the indecencies of life."

Then the mechanism of fear-punishment-destruction-fire-heat-smoke comes into play.

And why did masturbation become the most fearful of the indecencies? Why did it stand out almost to the exclusion of the others?

*Simply because masturbation was the only one of the indecencies that I had been subjected to.* I might have fear of the other indecencies, but I could not be punished for them, because I had nothing to do with them.

A spontaneous dream occurring that night appeared to symbolize Johan's feelings about his progress in analysis. He recounted it thus:

The dream was of several parts. The first part, I wasn't feeling so well. I wasn't interested in the things going on around me. I thought nothing was worth while. The weather was nice and the sun was shining. Everything was pleasant, but I didn't feel good about it. Then I ran into someone, and he said, "What's the matter with you? Why don't you take advantage of the nice day and do something about it?"

I said I don't feel like doing anything. The whole thing is no good.

He said, "Come, I'll show you something interesting."

He started collecting things—branches, leaves, flowers, tacks, jars, cups, household things, and started putting them side by side, twisting them in such a way that they fit together. When the whole thing was turned around in the right way, it was like a picture. I was extremely interested in this. I wondered how this was done. I forgot the things I had been thinking about before. I felt wonderful. I saw the colors of the picture. They were good colors. They were good color combinations. It was like the outdoors—the trees, water, and the sky. There were several people in the picture.

Johan could not recall the nature of the picture that had played a part in the dream, but when the crystal was presented to him during hypnosis, and he was told that he would actually see the picture that he had dreamed about, he remarked: "I see it now. There is a painting of a landscape, a lot of trees, a blue sky, and some water. There is a ruin, part of a building, black and smoky. Then some distance away a nice new building—yellow like the sunshine, with purple shadows. There are two women working in a field, harvesting. The foregound has green grass and stones."

Johan associated with this the idea that the old ruin was like his life in the past, which he had considered ruined by masturbation. The new building was his present and future life.

In order to determine whether an actual change had occurred in his associations regarding masturbation, he was told that he would now think of himself masturbating and would recapture associated sensations that would be indicative to him of his present attitudes toward masturbation. There were no signs of anxiety, and Johan remarked that he smelled an odor of "fresh-cut hay," tasted honey, saw a green color, felt an emotion of ease and contentment, heard a Rimsky-Korsakoff composition, and had a skin sensation of a "cool, calm, stroking nature." In order to confirm this change of attitude, an attempt was made to induce an experimental neurosis. Johan was given the same suggestions as before relating to the use of the yellow pen as a symbol of the penis held in the masturbatory act. Upon awakening he remarked that he had been thinking about modernistic furniture that he would like to design. He asked whether he might sketch a few of his ideas for me. He reached for the yellow pen, which I had placed near him, and without hesitation he made a design of a modernistic desk and handed it to me. He seemed puzzled as he remarked that he had experienced a feeling of intense excitement when he picked up the pen. He had no awareness at all of the experiment.

His reaction to this session was recorded in his diary as follows:

Today I had a dream which was a picture of the transformation that my life has undergone. I saw my old life as a torn-down building—waste materials and debris being carted away. I saw my new life as a newly erected structure, the building blocks of which were of all kinds of odd shapes and of different materials, but fitting snugly together into one unified whole.

This dream is a further proof to me that I have come to understand myself correctly, that I have found the pieces of the jigsaw puzzle and fitted them together in their correct positions.

I have been thinking over all that has happened since the day I came under the doctor's special guidance, how everything has turned out. I have been thinking of the doctor's kindness and patience. I have been thinking of the unlimited opportunities for usefulness that lie ahead.

The very feeling that one is still "in the swing of things," that one is no different from others, that one is not among the "not much good" ones, is bracing and exciting.

At the next session Johan remarked that he had had a spontaneous dream. In it he saw a bowl of peaches resting on a table. The peaches were extremely bright in color. He had a strong desire to help himself to one. He stretched out his hand for a peach, and the colors seemed to increase in brilliance, until the fruit looked as if it were on fire. "You'll burn yourself," he heard a warning voice say.

"Oh no," he replied. "I am not afraid of color. The warm, fiery ones are no more dangerous than the cool and soothing ones. They warm your heart and brighten your spirit."

He took up one of the peaches and then looked up to see who had spoken to him. A young girl stood near by. She was wearing a beautiful blue dress. "Here," he said, and handed her the peach.

She took the peach, and the orange of the fruit blended with the blue of her dress into a harmonious mixture, "so beautiful that the senses were reeling." His conscious association with the dream was that the fear and disgust previously associated with orange and yellow no longer existed. The whole situation seemed to be in the nature of a test to see whether he was afraid or not. He had passed the test.

Under hypnosis his associations to the dream were these: "The peaches are sexual activities. They are desirable and nothing to be afraid of, but it is only in combination with the girl that they become complete and beautiful."

He was given this suggestion: "You reach for the peach and then eat it. As you do so, there comes over you an emotion that starts various associated sensations."

Johan remarked that he had an emotion of satisfaction. This was associated with the odor of peach, the taste of peaches, a pleasant skin sensation, and the colors blue and orange.

During the next week Johan's preoccupations turned from himself and concerned the matter of his leaving the institution and taking up life outside. The following is an excerpt from a letter of his written to me at this time:

Now that my problems have been gone into very thoroughly, and I feel that I have come to an understanding of my own self, the question arises, "What next?" What can I do with my new-found understanding of things? How can I use it to the best advantage?

The first thing to consider is how to secure the means of existence. After that comes the arrangement of suitable environmental conditions.  After that comes consideration of others.

Right now there are still a number of things that I want to straighten out. There is a bit of writing that is waiting to be done, a bit of picture making. There is a bit of reading I want to do.  (All of these things there is ample time for, while I am waiting for my wisdom teeth.)

I have been thinking that I might start work on a free lance basis.  I might also do a couple of pictures that I have in mind and try to get them accepted for exhibition purposes and eventual sale.  Or, I may seek steady work for a while and decide further a little later.  I have no fear of failure in this respect.  When I go out to start life anew, it will be with great eagerness to meet new adventures.  There is no dread—no fear to look the world in the face—no doubt of success.

I have gained a far better understanding of others in the same proportion that I have gained a better understanding of myself.  There is a terrific amount of misunderstanding in the world.  The world is sick.  I would like to help a small fraction of the world to a better understanding of itself, just as I have been helped to a better understanding of myself.  This will be the third consideration after the first consideration, securing of the means of existence, and the second consideration, arranging of environmental conditions, have been fulfilled.

In order to get a more complete understanding of his unconscious feelings at this time, Johan was instructed under hypnosis to have a dream that night that would symbolize his previous dissatisfaction with life.  The next day he reported a dream in which he had been doing some kind of work.  He noticed that there were people sitting around, carving little ornaments from what seemed to be precious and semiprecious stones. These ornaments varied from about a quarter of an inch to a half-inch in diameter.  His companion explained various steps in the production of these ornaments, and as each ornament was finished, it went to a man who drilled a hole through it. Next, the little pieces were sorted.  They were laid out in rows, each row containing one each of the various kinds of pieces. The hole seemed beautifully proportioned.  The color effect was excellent and harmonious.  Johan's account continued:

"But what are they for?  What purpose do they serve?" I asked.

"They serve no purpose.  They are quite useless the way they are," said my companion.  "But now let us look at the final operation."

The rows of ornaments were passed on to a man who had a number of lengths of red thread. On each length of thread he strung a row of ornaments. The result was a very beautiful necklace.

"That," said my companion, "is the red thread that goes through everything, the red thread that holds the various components together, that makes of them a unit, decorative and beautiful. It is the red thread that completes and transforms purposeless and useless parts into useful, purposeful products."

Johan's conscious association was that the beads were like Egyptian beads that he had seen years ago in a museum. As in his collecting dreams, he was searching for certain things in life. He said: "The red thread is a useless something compared to the stones, but it holds the thing together and makes something of it. Perhaps it is the search for something quite worthless in itself, but quite necessary to make unity."

He remarked that all his life it was as if he searched for each of the beads individually. In spite of the fact that he had collected a great many items of knowledge, this was not what he was after. What he really wanted was something to hold the beads together, to unify them: "I was looking for something that was unlike the ornament. Something to make me complete."

Under hypnosis he produced the association that what he was looking for was completeness and intactness within himself. He was then asked to think of the red thread and to report on associated sensations. He remarked that as he thought of the red thread he had an odor of "the outdoors, the woods and the sea." He felt a sweet taste "like love," an emotion of happiness, and a skin sensation of warmth. Asked to symbolize the red thread in a drawing, he drew a heart.

The notations made in his diary later in the day were these:

In a dream that I had a few nights ago, I had heard a speaker mention "the most precious thing in the world," and I had set out to find out what it was and if possible to obtain it for myself.

I sought and found many things that one after another I thought might be the most precious. I found riches. I found knowledge—many other things, but all of them I found lacking and unsatisfactory in one way or another. I never found (in my dream) the most precious thing in the world.

Then I had another dream which to my mind seems to indicate what the most precious thing was, the thing that I was searching for. I was watching a number of little ornaments being made and strung together into a necklace. My interpretation of this dream is as follows: Each little ornament represented one of the things that in my previous dream I had been searching for—and found—such as riches, knowledge, etc., each one of which I thought might possibly be the most precious thing in the world.

Now, in my dream, I found that each separate ornament might be beautiful, but otherwise quite meaningless and useless. Even when the little ornaments were considered together as a whole, they were not of any particular use. This, when rid of its symbolism, would mean that riches, education, great and varied knowledge, travel, ease of manner and speech (to choose a few examples at random), might be "ornaments"—pleasant to observe for a while, but in themselves of no great worth. Taken together they might constitute a pleasing personality, but in themselves they could not be the cause of lasting satisfaction.

Now in my dream I saw the ornaments strung out and held together by a red thread, thus becoming a beautiful and useful necklace. The collection of little quite useless ornaments had become one unified whole capable of serving a purpose. And, the red thread was the transforming agent. The red thread was probably the thing that I had been searching for—"the most precious thing in the world."

Now again, rid of its symbolism, this means: Riches, knowledge, and a multitude of other things that have been gained throughout life, would need something to hold them together, something that transfused and transformed everything into a beautiful, satisfying, and purposeful whole. This unifying and transforming something would be the most precious thing there is.

Previously I had always sought a new ornament, similar to the others, but more precious, to add to my collection. Now I found that what I was seeking was really the red thread that would hold my collection of ornaments together.

Love no doubt is the red thread that goes through everything. Love is the red thread that completes and that transforms meaningless, useless abilities, attributes, etc., into a purposeful, useful, well rounded out whole.

Of course there may be other interpretations to my dream. The symbolism may be different. The ornaments may be female sexual organs. The red thread may be a desire for intact maleness.

The final hypnotic session consisted of determining Johan's real attitude toward himself. He was asked to dream, while under hypnosis, of his actual attitudes and feelings toward himself as a person. The dream he had was this:

I was watching someone else, someone that I didn't like so much. I noticed many things that were not so appreciable about him. I wondered about this fellow. I studied him. At first I thought he was dirty, stupid, and he wanted to mix in other people's business. He was stubborn. Then I was told some things about him and found out some things about him. The things that he had been doing weren't really selfish, that he wasn't really dirty, but that he was doing menial jobs, helping others. As I continued to understand him, I saw that he was all right, that it was just because I hadn't known him that I thought him unpleasant. I was told about some of the things he was striving for, that he was going out to accomplish things in the world, to start to work. Even though he had nothing and was poor, he was going out after the things he wanted. There was nothing to be afraid of. One has to try to succeed. Things are there to be found, and one must work for them.

His association was that the dream really referred to his own attitudes toward himself.

It was then suggested that as he sat in the chair he would have a vision of himself entering the door, and as he did so he would have a number of associated sensations. Johan looked intently at the door and remarked that he saw an image of himself. At the same time he experienced an odor of turpentine, "like the turpentine I use in my paintings." He experienced a taste of fruit, an emotion of surprise, a sensation of bluish green color, and a feeling of warmth and pleasantness in his skin, and heard a musical refrain for the verse, "They also serve who only stand and wait." The remainder of the session was spent explaining to him, at both a regressed and an adult level, the significance of his strivings, the meaning of his illness, and the progress that he had achieved in understanding his unconscious motivations.

Hypnosis was not used further except when Johan came to the institution to pay me a visit two years after his release. At this time the changes that had occurred in his character structure still persisted. Johan remarked that he was living a very complete and happy existence. Hypnotic associations disclosed a persisting image of himself as an intact and likable person. Several months after the visit he wrote me the following letter:

Some time ago I promised to write down a few things in regard to the period of time that I spent as a patient in your hospital, and particularly in regard to your treatment and my reaction thereto. I intended to do this immediately, but each time I started to write, I found an excuse for deferring it till "some other time." It seemed difficult to write about the period of time in question. It seemed difficult to give serious and prolonged thought thereto. The events of those days seem vague and remote and to an extent "unreal." Why this should be so, I have tried to analyze, and I have come to the following conclusions:

I am now living in a busy world filled with interests that clamor for attention. To turn aside from this world and relive the experiences of that other and much more circumscribed world is something of an effort. There is no doubt that this other world was just as real a world as this present one, but it was a world which centered around my own mental and emotional experiences and quite different from the present world of external interests.

Until I came under your treatment, I found myself in a hopeless situation from which there seemed to be no escape. I had lost faith in humanity.

It was only after I came under your treatment that I began to realize that I had a chance to free myself from a seemingly hopeless situation and to resume life as a "normal" human being. I believe that it was your kindness and patience that restored my faith in humanity.

Of course, there were a lot of mental cobwebs—carried through life—that had to be cleared away. There were muddled interpretations by a sick mind that had to be clarified and set aright before I could feel completely free.

Now, looking back on my experiences in the hospital, I realize that perhaps it was fortunate that things happened as they did. A whole new world of which I was previously unaware has opened up for me. I have had many interesting and many pleasurable experiences. Life at the present time is easier, in many ways more interesting and pleasant, than ever before. And, last but not least, perhaps my experiences have given me a bit more understanding and sympathy for those with whom I deal than would otherwise have been the case.

# XIV

IN EVALUATING the case of Johan R., a number of questions arise. Was he merely relieved of his symptoms or was his basic character structure involved in the therapeutic change? Was he actually cured of a schizophrenic disorder? In what way did hypnoanalysis act to effect improvement or cure? Were all the hypnoanalytic technics that were utilized in treatment essential, or might similar results been obtained with a simpler procedure? What was the dynamic meaning of the material produced by Johan?

The matter of diagnosis is of course open to query. All of the physicians who had previously treated Johan were convinced that his was a case of schizophrenia with an essentially poor prognosis. Although schizophrenic features were undoubtedly present, it was always my impression that the presence of benign depressive and neurotic elements rendered the outlook more hopeful than the diagnosis indicated it to be.

At the end of the therapy there was no outward trace of mental disorder. Johan's entire personality structure was so changed, and he was so spontaneous and outgoing, that he was considered normal by every person who knew him. I had not known Johan before his mental illness and therefore was unable to make the comparison with his prepsychotic personality. However, from the case history, from Johan's own account, and from the statements of his relatives, a definite change had occurred in his attitudes toward life and in his relationships to people. Furthermore, a Rorschach test revealed no evidence of anxiety and no neurotic or psychotic tendencies.

Some concern may arise regarding the use of so active a therapy as hypnoanalysis in schizophrenia. According to my experience there is no real danger, provided the transference is handled cautiously, is not analyzed too vigorously, and is utilized as a means of providing the patient with a positive growth experience. Used in this manner, the hypnotic relationship becomes one that is therapeutically most gratifying. However, there is no justification for the belief that hypno-analysis will cure all schizophrenics. Its application in psycho-ses is definitely circumscribed, being limited to those patients with whom a positive relationship can be established, and in whom the reality sense is sufficient to make trance induction possible. Even here palliative psychotherapy may be more advisable than analytic treatment. Only a small number of psychotic persons, therefore, are amenable to hypnoanalysis; this is in contrast to the experience in emotional disorders other than psychoses, in which hypnoanalysis is much more readily applied.

In the hypnoanalysis of a neurosis, predominant weight is placed on the direct analysis of the interpersonal rela-tionship; in schizophrenia, on the other hand, as has been mentioned, it is not subjected to so thorough a dissection, once a positive relationship develops. Consequently the material, as it was brought up by Johan, although it was motivated by the transference, was only occasionally presented by him in terms of the drama going on between him and me. In a later chapter on hypnosis and the transference, it will be shown that in neurotic conditions the material deals to a considerable extent with the immediate relationship between analyst and patient, and the meanings of past relationships and experi-ences are elucidated in this light.

Because the transference was not subjected to as thorough an analysis as would have been the case in a neurosis, it is possible that some inner conflicts in Johan were not brought up and enucleated. For instance, the hypnoanalytic material indicates the presence of oral and homosexual elements that may not have been thoroughly explored. Nevertheless, it is my feeling that Johan's most fundamental problems were analyzed and resolved.

A vital question is: What dynamic factors accounted for the improvement in Johan? Was the experience of a warm and friendly relationship with me the chief reason for his recovery? Did Johan gather from the fact that I was devoting so much time to him a conviction that his was not a hopeless plight? Or could the results be explained as due to the enucleation of damaging unconscious conflicts and memories? My impression is that a major factor in his recovery was the revival of confidence in himself, which was achieved through the interpersonal experience with me. As his ego gained in strength, it was able to shed its maladaptive defenses and to integrate itself more realistically with life. Under these circumstances Johan was able to examine his values more critically and to correct certain misconceptions that increased his detachment from people.

As to the technics utilized, their rationale will be explained in detail in Part 2. Without question, another analyst might have obtained the same results with different procedures, provided that he dealt with the material as it was brought up by Johan. Johan's aptitude for symbolization afforded opportunity to study experimentally the phenomenon of associated sensations. This study undoubtedly provided Johan with insight as to how sensations are often inadvertently conditioned to extraneous, innocuous events. However, equally good results might have been obtained without this procedure.

The final question involves the actual interpretation of the phallic symbolisms elaborated during Johan's hypnoanalysis. Should this material be taken at its face value? And would one be justified in assuming that the chief problem, as indicated by the material, was a castration fear, which produced a compulsive need to restore the damaged genitality by a quest for knowledge and learning, which were equated with an intact genital organ? Or were other issues involved, expressing themselves in phallic language? The problems raised by these questions, together with other problems pertaining to hypnoanalysis, are dealt with in the following chapter by Dr. Kardiner as well as in Part 2 of this book.

# A DYNAMIC INTERPRETATION

## By A. Kardiner, M.D.

THE CASE of Johan R. is a protocol of the transition of a mentally diseased individual from one type of organization to another. The first state rendered the subject incapable of any form of social life; in the second, some kind of social life was possible. I find it easier to talk in terms of such alterations rather than of states of "sickness" and "cure." This transition in personality organization was effected through the agency of or to the accompaniment of the therapeutic procedure that is called hypnoanalysis. Investigation of the dynamics of this transition may afford some insight into the operation of this therapeutic agency and possibly permit appraisal of its value. To this end, it is best to divide the discussion into three parts—the first being a presentation of the main features of the course of the treatment, the second a reconstruction of the main integrational systems and a consideration of where and how they were modified, and the third a discussion of the technic.

At the beginning of the subject's contact with Dr. Wolberg, we find him inaccessible, withdrawn, silent, engaging in activities that he considers degrading, such as scrubbing floors. In his personal hygiene he is negligent. He virtually drools at the mouth and permits vermin to crawl on him. In all, a more complete picture of personal dilapidation is hardly conceivable.

He has been sent into the hospital because he has abandoned his customary artistic activity, has gone into a depressed state, refuses to eat, and claims that he is in communication with God, who deems him unworthy; it is presumably for this reason that he chooses degrading activity. After a short residence in the hospital, he improves and is sent out, only to be returned after a short interval. On readmission he is preoccupied with problems of good and evil, refuses to go to a pleasant ward, chooses the one for dilapidated patients, and refuses to see Dr. Wolberg, in whose care he has been placed.

After a long time the doctor attempts some contact with the patient, but elicits no interest from him. After a year of these efforts, however, something begins to stir. The subject begins to talk about himself and to write down his reflections for the doctor's perusal. In these written productions a decisive trend is discernible. Johan begins to complain bitterly, shows great resentment and hopelessness. His first response to the doctor's care is therefore the disclosure that the interest shown him has registered. On the strength of this care he begins to complain. This is the first step in his adaptational alteration. One does not complain if there is no hope of response.

At this stage Johan is explaining to the doctor that his suffering has a plan—it is punishment. For what? He has striven for pleasure and that is disobedience.  He is somewhat perplexed by the fact that all the efforts he formerly made to win love, to seek knowledge and truth, and to obtain pleasure, ended in some punishment.  Is he seeking redress from the doctor?  Or has the latter's attention revived his hope that his desires can at last be realized?  He says, in fact, that he did not get love because he did wrong.  His suffering may reinstate him.  He is thus making a bid for the doctor's love by demonstrating his suffering in the hospital.  He therefore listens to no advice about wearing suitable clothes and looking tidy.  This would interfere with his main objective, namely, to atone and through suffering to reinstate himself.  He is trying to disarm his "judges" with his suffering and abjectness.  It is as if he were claiming that the punishment had already taken place.  There is no need therefore to impose new measures.

He goes on to specify the signs of his "rottenness": he claims to be in a state of decay; he insists that bad odors come from his mouth.  And then he furnishes us with a clue.  His father too had bad teeth and bad odors came from his mouth.  He identifies himself with his father—not through the latter's positive and desirable attributes, but through those that were undesirable and repellent.  Why does he take these attributes?  Because the positive attributes of his father are inaccessible to him.  They are knowledge, truth, wisdom—and all these are allied to sin.  To have nothing, to know nothing, to be incomplete and ignorant, to be submissive instead of assertive and creative, may bring love and atonement.  All of this makes a very consistent argument.  There is one set of conditions in which he always fails.  Therefore he attempts a new adaptation on a lower level of initiative and gratification.  This one may bring some comfort.

If we follow some of his behavior and associations (p. 11), we detect a decided trend.  He sits perfectly quiet.  He complains that his quest for knowledge was wrong.  He has a sense of guilt about it (is ashamed of his ambition), and therefore has burned his books and notes (i.e., killed the part of himself that he identified with his father).  He is again a good boy (sits quietly and doesn't stir) and cannot be assertive in any way.  The doctor takes this up with Johan, encourages him to be more assertive.  The latter's response, however, is not to act on the suggestion but to accept writing as a substitute.  He now writes to the doctor's secretary, obviously a mother surrogate; before her he begins to defend himself against charges of misbehavior, blaming his father for his misfortunes.  This he does in the form of a tirade against psychiatrists.

His complaint is that not he but society is wrong—that he is as he is because society has treated him wrong and brought him up wrong.  "You taught me one thing and practiced another," he charges.  "The whole thing is a sham.  I took you seriously, but got no rewards for my good behavior.  You fooled me!"  At this point he compares his fate with that of Dr. Wolberg.  This emphasizes the point—"I was obedient and believed you, and look where I am, in comparison with the doctor.  Look where he is!"

The patient now begins to reject the old formula that if he is obedient, he will be loved. "That was a sham!" he implies. "You only taught me that for your convenience, to keep me ignorant and submissive, and therefore less troublesome." This may be a trial balloon to see whether any form of remonstrance will bring down punishment, or it may be a momentary playing off of his mother against his father, identification with whom means for him the totality of self-assertion.

For all of this the doctor does not punish but rather encourages him. Johan takes heart and asks for more help. On the strength of this experience, he begins to doubt whether he needs to be so hateful of everyone. He now has fantasies about turning all his "tearing down" tendencies into constructive channels. All this he does in response to the doctor's behavior, which makes him feel worthy and accepted. The sequence of ideas indicates that he seeks and needs some kind of affection in order to function.

It is precisely at this point that hypnotic procedure is introduced. Be it noted, however, that a good part of the therapeutic work has already been started. The hypnosis does not initiate but only continues and stimulates this trend.

In the first two dreams we see how deep is Johan's skepticism regarding the doctor's interest and affection—a doubt based probably on the early pattern of his relations with his mother. In these dreams he wishes to be pulled out of his fantasy world by a powerful hand, but he expects rejection.

The suggestion given at this time is that he is to feel happy and to stand up for his rights. The suggestion meets with some success. He no longer holds his hand over his mouth, but he fails to stand up for his rights even in a dream. When asked why he did not carry out the suggestion in a dream, he says that he did not dream. However, he has forgotten the dream, which has to be recalled in a hypnotic trance. In this forgotten dream he does make a demand for food; this can be interpreted as a continuation of what he has actually been doing—making a demand for maternal love, couched in regressive terms. By his forgetting, the patient informs us that he cannot countenance the idea directly, and that back of it lies a very traumatic history of relations with his mother. On the strength of the suggestion, he makes some attempt to get what he wants, but vacillates and justifies his submissiveness.

The doctor then suggests that Johan speak his mind in some actual situation, and adds a posthypnotic amnesia. This suggestion is carried out actually, but is forgotten and has to be recalled under hypnosis.

Up to this point the hypnotic therapy has been a continuation of what was started in the waking state. It has had the advantage of making it possible to recover forgotten dreams and to press the demand for self-assertion on the patient's part. So far it has been successful. It has produced a happy frame of mind, and has made him stand up for his rights. He has stopped looking at the ground and does not hide his mouth. He takes better care of his person. These are the first signs of definite change; but the changes are limited to attitudes and do not include actions.

At this point the doctor decides to take up the patient's attitudes toward himself and the goal of therapy. In the process, the subject of sexual activity comes up, and here Johan begins to justify his avoidance of women, and the fact that he has masturbated to relieve his tension. This precipitates a crisis. The patient becomes confused, talks in an inconsequential way about his relations with his mother when he was about 6, and about wickedness in general. He defends his mother's view that masturbation is wrong. In short, he fails to follow through; he balks, becomes confused, runs away from the whole subject. He becomes discouraged and anxious and wants to return to the old and familiar technic he was using when treatment began.

This first failure is an important lesson. Hypnosis or no hypnosis, the patient cannot follow through on the suggestions given him and turns his back on the whole therapy because (1) it generates too much anxiety, and (2) he has no equipment for carrying a suggestion through. Hypnosis cannot give the patient implements that he does not possess. It can only use those that he has and create practice situations for their development. This is the same as a situation carried out in an ordinary analysis.

Then follows a period of platitudinous discussions about nothing in particular. It is quite a while before the patient has the courage necessary to start all over again. What ensues is a fresh start on a more modest level, compatible with his available resources.

Johan ushers in this new phase with a dream about fixing broken things. He has not given up hope. His written productions at this time take us back to about where he was at the beginning of treatment. Only gradually does he return, very cautiously indeed, to the subject of sex. He dreams of a stone woman coming to life. On the basis of his associations about attempting friendships and failing, we surmise that the petrified woman who comes to life is his mother, who failed him so badly when he attempted to win affection from her. This is also borne out by his dreams about demanding food, dreams that he forgets and that can be recovered only by means of hypnosis. When it is suggested to him that he dream of the greatest fear in his life, he dreams of picking flowers. This is clearly a masturbation dream; but in his associations to it he informs us of the outcome of his early conflict about this activity. He evidently is very much confused on the subject, is extremely curious about sexual activity in general, and expresses most of his conflicts in terms of his difficulties about getting knowledge. That this striving for knowledge is sexual in its roots is clearly brought out by the fact that he regards it as sinful. He talks in vague symbolic language about a quest for completeness, which, according to the statue dream, means complete emotional contact and rapport with his mother. In this he has failed. At this time he is making spontaneous drawings that contain disguised masturbation symbols. Interestingly enough, he erases some of these as if to conceal them from the doctor.

We must observe here that the patient no longer deals with the subject of masturbation directly, but only by way of the symbols of a quest for knowledge, completeness, etc.  He treats this as if it were the reality in which he fails, rather than the masturbation conflict of which all these symbols are a projective expression.

Johan's dreams and drawings of this period deal with problems of childhood, his quest for a counterpart (a responsive mother), his wish to extend himself (rewarding social contact), and his wish to masturbate without guilt.  But this is all hidden behind a façade of literary platitudes about original sin, about punishment for seeking after truth, and about the consequences of masturbation.  His notion that as a result of masturbation the body decays, etc., is a replica of the classic ideas on the subject that have prevailed for three centuries or more.

At this point he again balks, and thinks that there is no point to the treatment; at the same time wants approval for his constructive efforts and regards Dr. Wolberg as a friendly image.  In part the patient is whistling in the dark.  According to his dreams he is afraid that the doctor will not treat him any better than his mother did.

He now makes another detour.  He goes back and reexamines his relations with his father, mother, and siblings.  To facilitate expression, it is suggested that he do so in terms of automatic drawings, which he himself interprets.  He divides his world into the good and the evil, the good and evil first of his father, then of his mother.  He dreams at this time of seeing his mother nude while bathing.  He has no emotion and no reaction.  He talks of jealousy of his younger brother when the latter was born, of efforts to reach the sun—which means to be like his father, on the level of masturbation.  Here there is another break and he wants to quit.  He is frightened and pleads with the doctor to be permitted to stay as he is (pp. 43-45).  Then he goes into a depressed state.

This depression is warranted by his associations.  He is hopeless about being able to be like his father, sexually, in wisdom, etc.  He then recalls a repetitive dream (p. 46) about being in a dark room into which he wants to bring light, but every effort fails: lamps and lights go on but do not give light.  He wants (according to his associations) to peer into the parental bedchamber —but is afraid to see.  At this point he becomes tense, has a choking sensation.  Every time he approaches facts or symbols even remotely connected with sexual curiosity or activity, he expects to be punished.  In his anxiety he denies that he has any sexual difficulties.  He claims that people are unhappy in marriage anyhow.  The doctor encourages him despite all this.

Johan proceeds with more attempts at identification with his father, this time through violin playing.  His mood is alternately happy and depressed.  Eventually (p. 52) he becomes more direct about his masturbation fantasies, and reveals that he fears to masturbate because he will be castrated for so doing.  What we are dealing with probably is not masturbation, but the impulse to the act and failure to carry through, and the whole conflict is waged with and through the projective symbols of masturbation that our patient mistakes for the reality. This is one factor that has helped to make him schizophrenic.

The patient now follows consistently through and shows how he became snared in his own system to a degree that rendered life almost impossible on any terms. He describes his progress in his work, how he was successful and well paid, strove to "achieve an easy and sincere manner in dealing with people," participated in discussions, sports, etc., but chiefly sought to achieve excellence in his work. Then he collapsed. He accused himself of selfishness, which he tried to overcome by working more diligently to compensate for his neglect. This did not relieve him. He insisted that he did not deserve what he had, and therefore, to ease his conscience, gave up everything he had, abandoned his interests, denied himself pleasure and luxury, permitted himself only the coarsest food. This led to a blow-up. He could not live without interests, and giving them up caused terrific suffering. What saved the situation was that the suffering began to acquire a meaning. It was suffering toward an end—atonement.

At this particular time Johan's father died. He felt some sorrow and some relief; but his father's death did not greatly influence the trend of his adaptation. He continued with his penance. Although he imparted some meaning to his suffering, he could not hold out without gratifications. His sufferings were "misinterpreted by society" and he was put into an asylum.

The sufferings that he himself had initiated in the interest of atonement were construed as imposed from without. On the point of specifying what his sufferings were and why he introduced them, he balks and cannot be reached even by hypnosis. He becomes circumstantial, goes off into an allegorical literary episode that poorly disguises the conflict—to masturbate or not to do so. His anxiety derives from a fear of disintegration and decay.

What follows tells us clearly why masturbation is so fraught with terror for him. He has an elaborate fantasy that he hesitates to confide, which is his delusional reconstruction of what happened to him after he came to the hospital. We already know that he has attempted to give up all pleasure pursuits and is strongly under the influence of feelings of guilt, not because of what he has done but because of what he had impulses to do but did not carry out. Therefore what happened to him in the hospital (which he refers to as the ten days) was the actual living out of the fantasy of punishment with all kinds of tortures.

That this was so is amply confirmed by a dream he has at suggestion. In this dream the hospital is a court in which sinners have meted out to them punishments appropriate to their crimes. The worst penalty is reserved for those who masturbate. The drawing he makes condenses the whole matter— a man walking toward the sun, blocked by barriers, and on the side of the road, a hand with a dagger (p. 68). This is an allegorical description of his "pilgrim's progress" toward identification with his father, and of the danger lurking.

The doctor's explanations take hold, and the patient is partly willing to accept the interpretation of the events of the ten days as delusions based upon his particular psychologic status at the time when he entered the hospital. He does not readily accept this explanation. He cannot understand his experience as a delusional system, since it is supported by incontrovertible evidence of his senses. But there is another anxiety that haunts Johan. He is afraid to open up his innermost thoughts to the doctor, who is one of the authorities: if he lays himself bare to one of these, he will be trapped by his own admissions, and the doctor will turn him over for punishment. He actually believes that he miraculously escaped annihilation during the ten days.

Nevertheless he takes the risk and tells the doctor "all," though he is in doubt about whether he will be "turned over" or "spared." The latter prospect prevails, and Johan now begins to doubt the delusional ideas of which he was so convinced. He would like to be shown that his sensation of "ozone" was hallucinatory. He goes back to his early impressions (of five years before) regarding certain physical changes that were taking place in him—e.g., his hair was getting dry and lusterless, his scalp did not bleed freely, his fingers did not bleed when cut, his gums shrank, he noticed corneal wrinkles in his eyes, etc. In this mood he went to the physician through whom he was committed, and then the experience of the ten days began. "Hearing" the term "masturbation paresis," he was convinced that this was what he had.

Dr. Wolberg now undertakes an extremely active procedure to convince the patient that certain sense impressions can be induced by hypnosis and that the subject can react to them as if they were real experiences. In hypnosis it is suggested that Johan will dream of the odor of burned flesh and ozone, and that the odor will persist after he comes out of the trance. He awakens from the trance and asks the doctor whether he does not smell a "funny odor, like the one in the observation ward." The patient is frightened and tense and cannot proceed. He is rehypnotized and the experiment is explained to him. He is told that he will remember it on waking. The experience impresses him: it shows him that sense impressions can be hallucinated and yet appear to come from without. But it does not convince him, and he continues to insist upon his interpretation of events as proving that masturbation causes harm and is punishable as a crime.

The doctor persists in his purpose, but feels that the hallucinated experiences of the ten days are too highly organized and cannot be broken down by frontal attack (p. 74). He chooses to simplify the experiment by demonstrating that fear can make any reality appear different from what it is under other conditions. Johan is told that he will feel happy and will perceive an odor associated with a happy state. In hypnosis he feels happy and smells the odor of almonds and peaches. He is then instructed to feel fear and to experience an odor associated with that emotion.   He experiences a feeling of fear and smells sulfuric acid on metal.   In association with the emotion of disgust, he smells dead fish at low tide; in connection with induced expectancy, he experiences the odor of salty spray.

Then the experiment is reversed; Johan is given the odor first and asked for the association.   All odor stimuli elicit appropriate responses, except urine.   The same experiment is tried with taste, until a series of associations is established during hypnosis; then the patient is told to forget the experience and is awakened.   While awake he is told to associate odors with various qualities of experience.   The correspondences of odor and affect are the same as in the hypnotic state.   It is then suggested that he will have a dream that will symbolize his attitudes to different colors.   He has a dream in which the color yellow is predominantly associated with fear, black with sorrow, red with anger, white with exaltation; all of these, including the reaction to yellow, are conventional responses.   This demonstration teaches him something about color-emotion values.   But his values in this sphere are culturally determined ones.   None of his responses in the realm of color is original, except that to the feeling quality of masturbation.   Those concerned with taste and smell are highly individual.   Then the experiment is made more complex; he is directed to associate color to complex experiences.   The idea of masturbation is associated with orange and yellow; of sex relations, with yellow-green.   The patient is then asked to dream about the color orange.   The symbols in the dream relate to oranges, parasols, women, and the affects anger and fear.   The symbols and associations are: breast-mother-masturbation; fear; anger.

Another suggested dream is about music.   But the results of this are less satisfactory.   Another dream on suggestive command concerns itself with emotions in relation to physical symptoms and illnesses.   Once these associations and various combinations are worked out with the patient, the doctor undertakes to demonstrate to him that these presumably fixed associated values can be changed.   He is told that the colors orange and red (previously related to disgust and anger) will now evoke the emotion of happiness.   In response to the odor of sulfuric acid and the color green he will experience fear, formerly associated with yellow (p. 88).   Amnesia is then suggested.

It is not surprising that this suggestion leaves the patient quite confused in his waking state.   When he tries to paint he uses yellow where he would formerly have used blue.   He begins to enjoy things that he has formerly disliked, e.g., the food in the dining room.   The entire experiment has been a success!   Under hypnosis he recalls a forgotten dream in which his confusion about altered values of colors is conspicuous; but he accepts the new values imposed on him by someone else (the doctor).   At first he resists the new values and then finds them satisfactory.   In the waking state he likewise accepts the change in values and finds it satisfactory.

At this point the doctor explains the whole experiment to the patient in the waking state. This does not alter the effect of the experiment; Johann finds that he is able to operate with the new values. In fact, the whole experiment has had an exhilarating effect. Its purpose has been to make him change certain fixed values he has had in relation to masturbation; the remote projections of these were to be found in his delusional systems of ideas regarding decay and punishment. A direct attack on the delusional character of his experiences has failed; but when the experiment is simplified, he responds actively. Apparently the whole change in values is effected under the aegis of the idea "If you [the doctor] say so, it must be so." By the same token the patient informs us that his ego has a certain structure that permits a value to be established by this method. We shall take up this point later.

Meanwhile, the patient is now developing a new kind of consciousness of himself, a new relation to himself and to his experiences. It is a type of self-mastery formerly unknown to him, even though it is on an extremely passive basis. By this means the patient acquires a new power of focusing on experiences, giving different value to those in the main field and those that are merely associative. He acquires a new detachment from the associated values, like color, which previously he did not differentiate from the central event. The structure of this trait must occupy us later. Meanwhile he says: "Chance associations get mixed up and identified as true experiences. . . . As one's attitude to sensations changes, a different set of emotions may be aroused by these same sensations." This is an enormous step.

It is the cue to get back to the main line of the experiment. Meanwhile, the patient is still on the footing that masturbation does not cause him fear or disgust. His rejection of it "is not because of an emotional reason," according to his own account.

Under hypnosis it is suggested to him that he will that day have an irresistible desire to masturbate. Apparently the suggestion is not carried out. But he has a dream (p. 92) that has the content of dissatisfaction with himself. He finds himself at a county fair, where there are women preparing food that is inedible. A girl invites him to do his own cooking. The result is unsatisfactory; but when the woman touches up the meal, it becomes wonderful to taste. Another woman, under the pretext of tidying him up, squirts something into his eye that blinds him, etc. He wants to play solitaire, but a girl insinuates herself into his company at a table for two. But he decides to try something else—he feels that he can get along by himself.

The dream shows what has happened to the impulse to masturbate; he will not yield to it. In its place he has the dream, in which he continues to think of woman as a tantalizing being who will harm him. The evaded act of masturbation seems to be replaced by a union with a woman, described in oral symbols. Both masturbation and sexual activity are conceived in oral terms. Is this constellation the end result of the patient's traumatic relation to his mother? Both his affectivity and his ideas of masturbation seem to be organized about oral gratifications. This dream is followed with a by-passing of the issue of masturbation, and the subject spends much time in discoursing about relations with women abstractly, in a literary manner, platitudinously, and on the basis of no experience whatever. The experiment leads to a blind alley. He behaves in the same way as does a patient in analysis who strikes a deep resistance. The situation calls for drastic measures or abandonment of the enterprise.

The experiment with change of values has served as the prototype for further attempts at stimulation. An experimental neurosis is decided upon. The patient is told in a hypnotic trance that he is having a dream (which he does not actually have) in which common symbols of masturbation are employed, and the affect suggested in the experimental dream is fear (pp. 99 f.). He is also told that when he awakens he will see a yellow pen on the desk, and if he should desire to use it, he will have the same feeling about taking the pen that he would have about masturbation. Amnesia is suggested. Then he is awakened. On waking he talks about a design for furniture. The doctor suggests a sketch. As Johan reaches for the pen, his hand begins to tremble and he can only scribble. He starts again but fails, saying, "I don't think I can succeed. I feel downhearted and can't handle the pen."

He is flushed and perspiring, and feels anxious and tense. The doctor then offers him a black fountain pen, which he uses without hesitation, and he draws his sketch without difficulty. When asked to try again with the yellow pen, he begins to tremble again. When asked to associate various sensations to his feeling, he responds: "Fish and sulfuric acid, color yellow." ... Then he identifies the cause: "It's the pen! I get the same feeling as when I think of masturbation." But he can form no definite connection between the pen and something obnoxious to him.

He is now rehypnotized and told the details of the experiment—that the pen is associated with masturbation and that when he awakens he will remember the whole experience. When he awakens, the fear and the pen and the reasons for it are recognized. He then looks at and handles the pen. "It's just an ordinary pen," he says, and feels relieved.

Later in the day he recovers a dream—something about a penholder and a drawing, and finds on awakening that he has been engaged in masturbation, much to his disgust. But he begins to see the affect associated with masturbation. It is time to see what the effect of the whole experience is. A suggested dream about his attitudes to the doctor shows him trying to put a jigsaw puzzle together, but the pieces (p. 102) fall all over and he is buried underneath them. Someone comes and frees him from under the pieces and shows him how it is put together and makes a fine structure. In his present difficulty the patient is functioning with the help of the doctor. This dependency, consistent with the whole hypnotic experience, is now his mode of adaptation. It is infantile, but effective within these limits.

Then it is suggested that he become generally more assertive, and that he will have a feeling of inner strength. He is to conceive thoughts and verbalize attitudes. The suggestion is carried out. He has wishes for accomplishment, for daring activity; he has wishes to perform on his own initiative rather than to follow. Sexual activity represents one of his wishes. The mood lasts and some of it is translated into action. He demands more food in the dining room (an unprecedented action for him) and opposes the will of the attendant. He seems to behave (1) as if he had rights, and (2) as if he approved of himself and his impulses. The wish he finds easiest to consummate is about food. He is willing and able to oppose someone else's will and to breach regulations to satisfy his appetite. In all this he has some doubts as to whether the doctor will approve his attitudes and activities; but his appetites seem to be justification enough. For these he now claims some social approval. His dreams of this period (pp. 105 f.) show good emotional tone, although in them he is still much concerned with abstractions. The absence of real people in them is further conspicuous. He is also aware that though he seems to have accomplished something, he is still shadow boxing, and begins to venture on the idea of trying out his gains in the real world (p. 108).

At this time Dr. Wolberg begins to examine the patient's spontaneous dreams. The one recorded on page 109 is extremely significant. It is a phantasmagoria of color, which moves about unincorporated in shape or form. The colors struggle for dominance, mix and mingle, blend and create turmoil. Johan's associations (pp. 109 f.) are likewise significant. He speaks of emotions doing the same thing. The complete absence of people, shape, and action is startling, as well as his self-representation as amorphous moods unattached to action or to relations with others. When he speaks (p. 110) of achievement, the only route seems to be by way of suffering and sorrow. Another dream (pp. 111 f.) shows him struggling against the elements with poor implements (an umbrella), seeking a place to rest and eat. A girl offers him a flower, but his hands are occupied (he cannot enter into this kind of relationship—he is too busy and too poor in resources, trying to hold back a hostile world). Then someone comes and walks along with him and advises him that it is no longer raining. The umbrella is destroyed and he finds that the weather is quite clear. More obstacles arise, but eventually his companion furnishes food. This dream confirms previous conclusions: he is using the doctor as a parental surrogate through whose guidance and protective influence the world has become safe. Without this help he is imprisoned in a shell that keeps him from all the beautiful things he wants.

That he is able to utilize this protective influence to advantage is clearly brought out in the last experiment. This is suggested by a spontaneous dream (p. 113) produced by the patient in a hypnotic trance in which it is suggested that he speak of the shell that surrounds him and keeps him from attaining what he wants of life. In the dream he is pressing his clothes (to him a symbol of desire for social recognition). However, the iron begins to smoke and burns the clothes, burns his hand and the floor. He begins to push the iron around for fear that it will start a fire. But in spite of his efforts, it gets out of control and there is black, smoldering smoke.

From the associations to this dream the patient goes down deep into the sources of his blocked patterns of action: he does things that he is not supposed to do and matters get out of control, then he blocks. He is instructed to symbolize the dream in a drawing. He produces a circle topped with a flatiron, the front of which is like an alligator's mouth. Around the circle are broken tree stumps and crushed horses. To this he associates the idea that an iron is useful but can be overheated; then it destroys. To the flatiron (on the suggestion that it will call up associated sensations), he associates smoking, choking odor, acid taste, yellow color, frightening music, and affect of fear. He is then regressed to a 6 year level and told to see something, + color, + music + feeling, that reminds him of a hot iron. To this he replies with the following: kerosene; taste like camphor; orange and purple color; *"hot over the forehead"*; sounds like the tripping of feet. Then it is suggested that he dream about these.

His dream is about a building in the country with a barn containing grain, cows, and horses. Suddenly there is a fire. The place burns down and people have lost everything. He is returned to adult level and told to draw a picture that symbolizes the overheated iron. The figures he produces are crude—they represent knives, a scythe, rain, the sun, fire, water, and a hand holding a club. Evidently this does not convey much. Johan is told to dream about a flatiron. He dreams of a fire-spitting dragon who is pursuing him but cannot catch him, and there are no associations. He is then told of the dream of the burning building. He is puzzled and cannot recall it, though it has a familiar ring.

The patient thinks over the whole experience and writes out some associations. He acknowledges a fear that masturbation will cause his destruction, and sees that the ten days represent his conception of punishment for masturbation. But he does not know the reason for this. He only remembers hearing other boys discussing the dangers of masturbation; these fears, however, have been quieted by subsequent reading. But he also fears marriage and sexual union. This, he says, may be due to the fact that he saw marital unhappiness in his own home. These fears, he insists, no longer exist consciously. But he accepts the evidence of his ten days' experience, which indicates that his fears do exist, though he has no idea as to their source. In short, the patient is convinced that certain emotions about masturbation and sex exist in him, but he does not know the origin of them.

More hypnosis is applied, with instructions to the patient that he dream about the images in the previous experiment—smoke, the dragon, fear, heat, a hand holding a club. In response to this he shows fear and has a dream. Then comes the recollection: His mother was telling him about her people

(her grandparents), who were wealthy, had chickens, cows, etc. When
her grandmother died, her grandfather began to drink and gamble. Then
the barns were burnt down and the animals burned to death. Her grandfather continued to gamble and drink and they were all impoverished.

Then the patient tells of a dream he has just had. In it he was reading a
book of fairy tales, about a saint who went out to liberate his people, who
were under the rule of a monster, a fire-spitting dragon. He slew the dragon.
Then he went to bed and dreamed of the fire and burning buildings. He
was surrounded by fire and smoke and could not get out. He was afraid and
could not sleep. This dream of dragon-slaying may be his representation of
his repressed wish to kill his father and take his place, and this constellation
may be an integral part of his masturbation conflict. But there is in addition
the factor of frustrated expectations relating to his mother.

The patient now recognizes that this was a repetitive dream. It is
suggested in hypnosis that he will recall the conditions that provoked the
dream. He dreams of his mother admonishing him: "Don't drink, don't
gamble, don't live an indecent life." In another dream he sees a bull being
castrated. In another he is trapped in a burning building and cannot get
out, and stealthy, dangerous hands come out of the walls to seize and destroy
him—all to the accompaniment of terror.

In the further working through of the elements revealed in the experiment,
the relation between his mother's admonition not to lead an indecent life
(this referred to masturbation, according to his childish values) and the
dream of being in the burning building is not clear. Does the fire stand for
the punishment for an indecent life? Or does the burning building signify
the withdrawal of maternal love if he masturbated—i.e., the house, which is a
shelter, protection, becomes the source of his danger. Or is it something
entirely different? The burning building was the outcome of the grandfather's delinquency. It contains the idea "If you are wicked, you injure
those dependent on you. . . . If you have intercourse, you bring terror and
shame on the woman" (p. 120). His mother never admonished him against
masturbation. Yet, he argues, burning—so prominent in his delusion of the
ten days—puts him in the role of having committed the dreadful deed.
There are also fantasies of castration—none of which were implanted by his
mother. He then argues that castration (deprivation of powers of all kinds)
= decay = punishment.

To clarify these points, the doctor puts him in a trance and regresses him
to infancy with the suggestion that he is masturbating (p. 122). The result
is a confused lot of childhood images—of receiving care (which he likes),
and of rejection and neglect (which displease him). An image of a baby
sister emerges; in this the difference between boy and girl are explained.
Johan associates this with masturbation and thinks that his penis may
disappear as part of the decay. He is then taken out of the crystal gazing
and told to dream of the images revealed. In the dream there is more about

differences between boys and girls; there is the interpretation of girl as mutilated or decayed penis—and therefore not of much good—and more about masturbation as the cause of castration.

A spontaneous dream (p. 125) now shows the patient as more hopeful about beginning a new life; the illusion about the disastrous effects of masturbation has been eliminated. To check on this, the doctor reproduces the experimental neurosis involving the yellow pen. There is no inhibition and no anxiety while the patient is in a hypnotic trance, and no sequelae in the waking state. In his written reflections Johan thinks gratefully about the doctor and about his new opportunities in life. Further spontaneous dreams confirm this (pp. 126 f.), and he now wants to leave the institution. Other dreams confirm the existence of a better feeling toward himself.

Two years after leaving the institution, the gains made during treatment are apparently persisting, though the vividness of the experience has faded and it has become unreal. Johan seems better oriented to the present world of realities.

The first thing that strikes us about this case, throughout the story, is the paucity of human characters in it, the extreme pallor with which human relationships are described, the absence of motion and activity, the preponderance of "thought" over action, the vast number of abstractions and symbols with which the subject is preoccupied. Only one relationship is seen throughout, that with the doctor. But even here, for the greater part, affective quality—though present in the form of dependency and gratitude, after initial mistrust and certainty of rejection—and all affective tones are much diminished in intensity. They lack warmth and the "personal touch."

This corresponds with our expectations in the case of a schizophrenic. Yet we cannot dismiss this aspect with the knowledge that in this illness affectivity is diminished, being too tightly anchored to its narcissistic base. Without raising questions as to whether this is the nuclear phenomenon of the disease, we are compelled to note in the patient certain persistent incapacities for action and for conceptualization, and a certain persistent disorientation in regard to his own subjective experiences, the outer world, and himself. He represents himself as completely passive and abject, without capacity to control the world in any way or to manipulate it in such a manner as to yield him satisfactions; and thus the world overwhelms him. We also find him, at the beginning, in an attitude of complete acceptance of this state of affairs, without protest or remonstrance. He reaches some kind of internal equilibrium on evolving the idea that what is happening is punishment. This is not altogether a hopeless state of mind, because punishment implies reinstatement.

The first process that we see, therefore, is a state in which all the patient's self-assertion is impounded for reasons unknown, and we observe only certain projections of this process—such as the notion that he has suffered condemnation by God—that seem to the patient to come from some outside source and that he interprets in terms of punishment. Coincidently we find acceptance of punishment, and isolation, i.e., inability to establish affective ties to others. Later we find this mass of projections to be much more systematized and taking in the greater part of the occurrences in his environment. His acceptance of the interpretation of the events around him as punishment therefore acts as a brake that arrests the pathologic process. For we learn later that he wishes to escape the extreme penalty of death.

This can be represented schematically as follows:

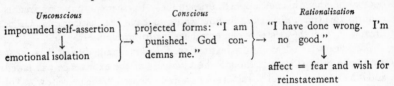

This process goes on for a long time. We know nothing of what precipitated it or of what begins to take him out of it. Then suddenly there appears a bit of self-assertion in the form of a claim to attention from the doctor. Once the patient is in a position to claim and respond to some attention, we find a change in the operation of the whole scheme outlined above. First we note that Johan begins to express resentment and perplexity: "I must have done wrong because I am being punished, but why? For seeking knowledge and truth?" The patient cannot be relied upon to tell us what is going on within him. He explains his abandonment of all self-assertion by saying that it must have been wrong for him to assert himself, because he is being punished. Therefore he has abandoned everything because his activities were guilt-laden! This is his tenuous argument.

Under the influence of the doctor's attention he first spends much time explaining his projections (state of decay = punishment). We get closer to the core of the matter when we recognize that his self-assertions are in the line of identification with the positive attributes of his father.

He establishes a tentative rapport with the doctor, but is extremely cautious and fearful. He hopes for help but fears punishment. He can only get help and love if he abandons all self-assertion—which means to have nothing, to know nothing, to be ignorant and submissive. He fears punishment for every form of self-assertion, which to him means identifying himself with his father or the doctor. The patient knows his quandary, for his only hope of establishing a relationship is on the basis of ignorance and submission, which really cuts him off from every relationship.

The patient now beguiles the doctor into a relationship by assuring the latter that (1) he accepts the punishment and believes in its justice, and (2) he is in a state of decay and ineffectuality. The doctor's behavior assures him that within these limits he can function, i.e., no self-assertion brings any new punishment.

The hypnotic treatment is therefore begun on this basis; the patient completely accepts this as the only kind of relationship that he can effectively enter upon. He begins in complete abjectness, helpless, prepared to act obediently and submissively, in the hope that he will therefore be loved and protected. A more favorable condition for beginning hypnotic treatment cannot be imagined. The patient's first dreams show a mixture of hope and fear.

Having thus delivered himself to the doctor, cautiously and fearfully, he feels that he will not incur too great risk in carrying out the hypnotic commands to be happy. It is all done on the doctor's responsibility. But he balks at the first invitation to be self-assertive; that is, he dreams of self-assertion in the form of a demand for food (oral love or maternal-like attachment), but fails to carry out the idea, and justifies his submissiveness, i.e., his nonactivity. He yields to the suggestion that he take a happy attitude—but balks at action. Action belongs to the self-assertion system, which is outside the domain of his adjustment to the doctor, and he accepts this arrangement because he has no equipment for carrying out the action. A premature start on uncovering sexual attitudes leads to a complete retreat. It is too dangerous. The fresh start is made on simpler material and very gingerly. The start is made on the patient's relations with his mother and on the problem of masturbation. He fails as regards the first of these conflicts and tries to obliterate the second. He prefers to talk about completeness, knowledge, rather than about specific impulses and appetites.

The rest of the treatment is devoted to beguiling the patient slowly out of the terms of his original tacit agreement with the doctor—that he will remain ignorant, passive, and inactive—and leading him into knowledge, activity, and self-assertion. This is done by (1) exploiting the affective tie to the doctor and (2) altering the patient's conception of the projective phenomena and thus altering his conception of himself in relation to (a) his impulses, (b) other people, and (c) his subjective experiences in connection with phenomena in the outer world. By these means Dr. Wolberg introduces into the patient's life new elements of (a) judgment and (b) *control*, together with the assurance that these activities are valid and acceptable.

This experiment with the projective systems is carried out, by (1) establishing a system of correlations between affective states and associated sensation-conceptions, and (2) showing that these can be altered. Naturally the patient is not aware that this altered perception is achieved under hypnotic command and that this is an expression of his passivity. Nevertheless he emerges with a positive gain, for the experience, while creating some temporary confusion, ends by giving him a new control in the form: "You need not be the victim of your perceptions, you can be their master, if you are willing to exercise your judgment." The experience enlarges his sense of mastery and compels him to recognize the central position he has in his subjective experience world. It does not matter in the least that the whole change is effected under hypnotic command and that its premise is: "It must be so because you say it is so." All learning from infancy onward is performed under the same conditions. The treatment shows its first real achievement in seducing the patient into activity without running counter to the whole system of highly organized defenses against it that make up the bulk of his thoughts and feelings in his waking state. The new activity reflects the attainment of new capacities for judgment. This increases the patient's resources and control, and thus diminishes anxiety. Through this newly acquired activity, the patient frees himself from the situation of helplessness in which he is assailed by all kinds of stimuli with equal emphasis. For in his projective system real events and associated phenomena have equal weight (this seems to be one of the nuclear phenomena of the schizophrenic process). At all events the patient gains a new implement of orientation and mastery by learning how to distinguish between central events and associated affective experiences.

The experiment concerned with fixed color-affect values raises some interesting theoretic questions. It is first of all remarkable that such a change in values can be effected at all. This patient shows quite conclusively that he is no passive medium in the hands of his hypnotist, and that he is highly selective in regard to what he accepts and rejects. To accept a new set of values for the color yellow, and to displace the affect of fear from association with yellow to relation with blue, is a remarkable feat. Does the success of this experiment mean the acceptance of a new value for masturbation, with which yellow was originally associated? Does this experiment take place at just the right time, and would it have failed earlier in the treatment? The fact is that the experiment is introduced not to effect a permanent alteration of values, but to demonstrate the validity of the subject's own self-mastery and to help him to draw the distinction between real events and associated values. Only the latter are called in question. The experiment means: "You have been afraid of masturbation all your life. Your evaluation of this act may be wrong; try another valuation and see how it works." If this interpretation is correct, the experiment is only partially successful. Johan is willing to change his evaluation of the act, but he cannot carry out the act itself. Is this due to the fact that he is able to respond under suggestion to an alteration of values, but unable to carry out the activity? Only further experimental work along this line can bring us the answer.

The patient in his delusional system makes masturbation the crux of the central inhibition of his life. This is actually not the case, but for our purposes we lose nothing by following him in his efforts to reconstruct the significance of this activity. The situation is moreover probably typical of all other inhibitions. It is clear from the patient's associations that he symbolically extends the significance of his inhibitions about masturbating to all self-assertive activity, like gaining knowledge, seeking truth, etc. But this is of no avail, because the same affect that weights the original activity clings to the remote extensions.

Even under hypnotic command the patient cannot carry out the act of masturbation. But what is more astonishing, the affect of anxiety, which is so prominent in his projective systems and which is bound up or engaged so actively in the concept of punishment, is not perceived by him as related to masturbation. He seems to have no interest in the activity. This is the natural end result of a successful repression.

The next step is to unite the idea of masturbation with the original affect. Much is to be gained if this succeeds. First, the affect can become channelized and therefore localized, instead of diffusing itself indiscriminately through every activity. Second, if these two events, the activity and the associated affect, are again brought into meaningful relation to each other, the whole projective system may lose its function.

This reunion of the act of masturbation and the original affect proves a difficult job. The patient has to be taught by circumstantial evidence that the two events are related. The yellow pen experiment is the first step. As a result of this reintegration, our expectations are realized. The patient becomes more assertive on his own initiative about many things, but not about masturbation itself. The channelization and localization of the affect has taken place. The patient begins to approve of other impulses that were previously a part of the punishment and submission system—like the demand for more and better food—and begins to seek social approval for them. Again this is something that the patient learns under hypnotic command; but it frees his resources. He learns to free himself of a generalized terror at the cost of a localized inhibition. This is a big gain in economy.

Once the associative connection between the masturbation and the affect is established, the way is also opened for the recovery of memories of the events that led to the connection. The patient also recovers the original dreams provoked by these early events. The whole conflict focuses into a specific castration anxiety. The experience of the patient with his infantile memories demonstrates conclusively that one cannot probe directly for infantile memories, and that mere recovery of these is ineffectual. These early memories are merely the foundations of a highly organized integrational series on which action is built. Only through demonstration of their role in this complicated system of action, with all its affective accompaniments, can the recovery of infantile memories have any releasing effect. The ability to recover infantile memories is in part a sign of the increased functional effectiveness of the patient.

So far we have been working from the patient's present equipment down to its original sources. If we now reconstruct the picture from the beginning upward, several features become clear. The first thing that becomes apparent is that the story is still very incomplete. But one can read between the lines and establish some plausible conjectures. The story does not begin with the conflict about masturbation; this was merely the first symptom of the patient's failure in adaptation. The fact is that he was subjected to no violent and terrifying admonitions about this activity. He had fewer traumatic experiences than are found in the average hysteric. He drew most of his material for the taboo from purely cultural sources. There is, however, some reason to believe, on the basis of his dreams and meager accounts, that his early relations with his mother were poor. But we cannot tell whether he suffered maternal neglect, or whether the mother was herself a very inhibited person who could establish no emotional rapport with her child. The real traumatic experience seems to have lain in this relation. The patient had, at the completion of treatment, a somewhat increased capacity for emotional rapport with others. The effect of his poor relationship with his mother on his general development can only be surmised. The function of maternal care is to foster the growth of the ego. Apparently the patient takes up relationship with the doctor at the point at which he left off with his mother. He has an affective potentiality, but it has not been developed, for he takes up relation with the doctor on an extremely infantile level. Nevertheless, the patient is able throughout to utilize this infantile equipment as a fulcrum by which to lift himself.

We do not know precisely at what point the repressive process began. But it must be noted that it is one thing to repress an activity when the factors for carrying it out are well formed, and another when the repression overtakes poorly integrated patterns. We suspect that the latter situation is the case here, because the repressive process pursues the patient through all possible extensions of the original impulses involved, including its symbolic extensions. The original battle with the attending anxieties seems to have ended in complete abandonment of the original impulse. When we first find the patient, the battle is being waged about remotely derived symbolic extensions, to which the patient now attaches guilt feeling and anxiety. In order to escape from the anxiety, the patient successively abandons one gratification after another in his already precarious adaptation, until all forms of self-assertion are collapsed, and he retreats into a passive, helpless state. He now can no longer recognize any relation between his anxiety and guilt feeling and the activities to which they attach. He gets some freedom of action again only after the anxiety is related to the specific activity from which it arose originally, or at least is restored to some close relationship to it. The therapeutic gain therefore is achieved by the process of freeing many of the activities held in check by the terrific anxiety, and by limiting its inhibitory effect. The treatment ends at this point. But it must be remembered that in the stunted course of Johan's growth, many functions have remained undeveloped. What the course of his future adaptation will be we cannot tell precisely.

We may now attempt an inventory of the technical devices used to mobilize the patient for the change from one state of organization to another. These devices were (a) hypnosis, (b) automatic drawing, (c) crystal gazing, the latter two being only variants of the first.    Hypnosis is therefore the cardinal weapon.

We have seen from the patient's behavior that he had an emotional anlage on which the hypnosis could operate.    The patient was, at the introduction of hypnosis, already attuned to its emotional implications.    He could undertake no other kind of relationship.    Moreover, the therapeutic process had already begun before hypnosis was introduced.    The hypnosis did not, therefore, create the conditions for therapeutic effectiveness; it merely exploited the opportunity.    What if the patient's characterologic façade had not been in consonance with the phenomenon of hypnosis?    Could this condition have been created by the hypnosis itself?    This is doubtful. Suppose that the patient had come to hypnosis with the conviction that Dr. Wolberg was rejecting him?    Could the hypnosis have removed this conviction?    We do not know.    There was an emotional basis, because the patient's attitude at the beginning was: "I want love, but I'm not sure that you will give it to me.    Will you instead turn me over to the authorities?" He took a chance, and his experience convinced him that he could count on the first possibility.    Hypnosis requires, therefore, an initial accessibility and potential for affective rapport, be it ever so small or ever so much qualified by reservations.

The therapeutic process shows conclusively that this affectivity potential is not spoiled by hypnosis, but can be put to use.

A second point that emerges clearly is that the hypnotic procedure can be used to sharpen the focus on the essential points engaging the patient at the moment.    This is clearly shown in the first two dreams.    Hypnosis introduces no new material, if the patient is in consonance with the procedure.    Moreover, it satisfies a regressive craving.    This is no obstacle to the treatment. The patient, with his present impoverished resources, is entitled to this gratification, because it is an essential in ego growth.    But this regressive satisfaction is used as a means to an end—to push the patient forward.

The first failure (p. 27) shows us quite clearly that hypnosis is no implement with which to crash through organized action patterns.    The patient will blithely by-pass a suggestion when he has no implements for carrying it out. In an ordinary analysis the result would be resistance.    It is quite the same with hypnosis.    But there is this difference: by means of hypnosis one can locate the source of the trouble by compelling the patient to recover forgotten dreams.    It has therefore a time-saving function—if the analyst knows what he is after.    If he does not, the patient can, in the interest of his defense, be just as circumstantial as in an ordinary analysis, and mislead the analyst for months.

The hypnotic procedure has one cardinal virtue.    Through its agency it is possible to break through the inhibitory effect of consciously organized systems.    The fate of a suggestion,[1] whether carried out or not, can be followed with much greater ease than is the case in an ordinary analysis.

Hypnosis enables the analyst to create for the patient test situations that can be used directly to try out situations and resources, utilizing them for purposes of demonstration, or utilizing a failure to enlarge the patient's insight into his difficulties.    This is one of the most time-consuming situations in an analysis.   Ordinarily the patient's conscious organization interferes so much with his readiness to overcome anxiety about trying a situation even after he has acquired insight, that therapy must occasionally be abandoned at this point.   One often has to wait months for circumstances in a patient's life to create a situation in which he is compelled to try his resources. Under the protective influence of the analyst, the patient can venture on test situations more courageously in hypnosis than he can when his conscious systems are capable of exerting their full share of inhibitory influence.

Several interesting variations in technic appear in this report.    The use of the experimental dream or experimental neurosis is remarkable in its demonstrative value.    No equivalent is to be found in any of the devices that can be employed when the patient is in the fully conscious state throughout the course of an analytic treatment.

The course of this treatment shows that the hazards of suggestion have been greatly exaggerated.   The phenomenon that puzzled the nineteenth century hypnotists—failure to carry out a posthypnotic suggestion—seems now to be clarified.   Hypnosis cannot confer potentialities for action on a patient who does not have them.   Action is highly organized, and a suggestion cannot create such organization.   Suggestive hypnosis as a therapeutic weapon failed the earlier practitioners for the same reason that it failed in some episodes of this case.   Thanks to our knowledge of psychopathology, the hypnoanalytic treatment need not be abandoned, but may be continued along the line of least resistance.   The problem was solved when the added insights gained through psychoanalysis in the past half-century cast light on the structure of the personality and on the defensive nature of resistance.

It is also quite clear, from the course of the treatment, that the events elucidated by hypnosis must be integrated in the conscious personality—a precaution overlooked by many who practice hypnosis.    These events must not be allowed to remain encapsulated in the unconscious, where their influence is bound to remain limited.

What, then, does hypnosis contribute to the technic of investigating and influencing the unconscious?   It adds no new and startling information about dynamics.   It may in the future be useful for exploring provinces in psychopathology that have remained refractory to the orthodox technics. But hypnosis does add an element of speed and directness to therapy, without altering its dynamics.   It cuts off the patient's opportunity of escape into endless resistance and circumstantiality, and curtails these maneuvers to hours or days.   The automatic writing and drawing are mere adjuncts for cutting off the patient's retreat and for furnishing some clues about his anxieties, no matter how far removed they are from their real causes.   These clues can be tenaciously followed up. It must not be overlooked that patients are impressed with the physician's persistence and diligence, just as they are frightened by his timidity or vacillation. A therapist who permits his patient to loaf ultimately loses the latter's confidence.

A number of crucial questions arise in considering the potentialities of the combination in hypnoanalysis of the two technics, hypnosis and analysis. The answer to these questions cannot yet be made completely. The case of Johan R. yields many interesting observations, but one cannot leap from the conclusions warranted by this record to all related problems in the treatment of psychoneuroses generally. These are problems that wait for future research.

# Part Two

# THE THEORY AND PRACTICE OF HYPNOANALYSIS

---

# XV

## PSYCHOANALYSIS AND HYPNOSIS

THE IMMEDIATE object of psychoanalytic therapy is to bring back to consciousness those parts of the self and its experiences that have been repressed. The means through which this uncovering process is accomplished is that of strengthening the ego to such a point that it can tolerate unconscious impulses and can react to them in the light of present reality. Before therapy is started, the emotionally ill person is unable to do this, because he is menaced constantly on the one hand by unacceptable inner drives and fears, and on the other by a hypertrophied conscience that fosters ego weakness and repression.

Psychoanalysis aims at a drastic reorganization of the psychic apparatus. The conscience must be rendered more tolerant by being divorced from tyrannical standards introjected during the relationship with early authorities. Repressed inner strivings and conflicts must be purged from the unconscious, in order that the individual may be no longer menaced by anxieties rooted in past inimical experiences and conditionings. The ego must be brought to a mature level of integration, where it can deal realistically with external stress and successfully mediate internal demands. Freed from the need to reinforce repression, the self is enabled to proceed with the urgent task of fulfilling, in an adaptive manner, basic psychobiologic needs.

These aims are ambitous, because the individual always fights to maintain his scheme of life, neurotic as it may be, and defends himself vigorously against change. Avowal of unconscious attitudes and strivings is so fraught with anxiety that he throws up barricades and smoke screens to convince himself that they do not exist. Psychoanalytic therapy becomes a personal battlefield between the patient, who seeks to cling to his compulsive trends, and the analyst, who strives to remove them.

Psychoanalytic treatment must consequently be carried on over a long period of time, sometimes for years. The necessity of a long treatment period is not due to defects inherent in the psychoanalytic method; it follows as a result of resistance, which motivates the individual against abandoning his defenses or relinquishing neurotic pleasure goals. The time element is, however, a great disadvantage, since it makes therapy expensive and reduces the number of patients that the analyst can treat. These practical drawbacks have tended to restrict the therapeutic scope of psychoanalysis.

The challenge that presents itself is that of whether the deep, dynamic personality alterations wrought by psychoanalysis can be achieved by briefer methods. One may understandably view with skepticism reports of dramatic cures accomplished in a short time, because personality difficulties that develop over a period of years are associated with obdurate habits and with conditioned patterns of behavior that cannot be yielded up in several weeks or even months.

Progress in therapy goes hand in hand with strengthening of the ego. Therefore, in attempting to answer the question whether a rational method of brief psychotherapy is possible, one must determine whether a procedure shorter than that of orthodox psychoanalysis can increase ego strength to a point at which it can tolerate the anxiety essential to the abandoning of the neurotic superstructure.

Roughly, the psychoanalytic process may be subdivided into two phases. The first phase is an *uncovering* one, during which the patient becomes aware of his unconscious impulses, fears, and memories, and begins to understand how and why these make it impossible for him to relate himself constructively to the world and to people. The second phase is *re-educative*, and involves an elaboration of new and adaptive interpersonal attitudes. Social reintegration does not occur automatically. It is a slow reconditioning process, necessitating establishment of new habit and reaction patterns to displace old, destructive ones. The start is made during psychoanalysis, but it must be perfected in actual life at the termination of analysis. The interpersonal relationship with the analyst initiates the curative process, which leads to a congenial reorientation with respect to other persons and the social group.

In psychoanalysis, the phase of uncovering unconscious motivational patterns is very slow and may require years. The main reason for this protraction is that the ego is unable to tolerate anxiety of a sort that initially produced the repression of the unconscious material. During therapy, ego strength increases as a positive relationship with the analyst develops, but the patient constantly strives to ward off a close relationship, because of repulsive hostile and erotic strivings that threaten to invade consciousness. He displays resistances to the analyst as a defense against his impulses. Before the patient can begin to appreciate what inner strivings exist in him, such resistances must be resolved.

The second phase of therapy is even more prolonged than the first. Established patterns of behavior are changed with great reluctance. The revelation of the unconscious conflicts that initiated them is only the first step in this change. The patient fights desperately to hang on to habitual attitudes and goals. He continues to show resistances to change even when he has become aware of the extent to which he is at the mercy of disabling unconscious fears and strivings. He continues to reject insight as an alien force, although it finally comes into its own as he gains a glimmer of understanding of his drives and tendencies. However, intellectual insight alone does not divert him from his customary reactions. It does permit him to gain a foothold on new interpersonal pathways. This foothold is tenuous, and he retreats constantly before the onslaught of his neurotic demands, which, though known to him, continue to function with great persistence and vigor.

Gradually, in the face of great resistance, his behavior becomes less and less motivated by irrational needs. Eventually these no longer stimulate motor reactions; his conflict is relegated to fantasy. Yet, even though he forsakes his customary neurotic tendencies, his unconscious still clings to the conviction that the old way of life is far more glamorous than the new, and to the hope that the original balance of power will eventually be restored.

A further development in the re-educative process is recognition, on the part of the patient, of the incongruity of his old drives. He comes to regard them as irrational elements that he would like to eliminate from his life. A battle then ensues between his desire for change and the dynamic forces that compel him to resume his old neurotic actions. After a period of strife, more or less prolonged, a remarkable change occurs in the inner dynamics of the personality. The habitual impulses, which have up to then functioned compulsively, or which he has accepted as an inevitable part of life, are alienated from his ego. Even though they continue to emerge, the ego responds to them with more and more resistance, refusing them their original hold. Coordinately there is a reorganization of interpersonal relationships, a reintegration with reality, with the self, and with its past experiences. Signs of the abandonment of compulsive patterns are found in a sense of inner peace, happiness, and security, and in an absence of neurotic suffering. These positive gains serve also as factors in raising resistance to old neurotic attitudes whenever these tend to force the individual into his previous maladaptive actions.

Hypnosis, properly applied, can shorten both phases of the therapeutic process. By cutting through interpersonal defenses, it plunges the patient immediately into a close relationship with the analyst. In psychoanalysis the patient feels his way cautiously, parrying an intimate contact; contrastingly, in hypnosis, he experiences, from the start, feelings and attitudes of a deep-set nature, which provide material for analysis. In addition to its effect on transference resistances, hypnosis has a remarkable influence on those resistances that are related to repression of traumatic memories and experiences. In a single session the patient may bring up in a facile way memories the enucleation of which would require months of tedious psychoanalyic work.

It must not be assumed that it is possible to set aside all resistances merely by the induction of hypnosis. However, one may circumvent and more easily resolve ego defenses that keep unconscious material from gaining access to awareness. Hypnosis can thus materially influence the first phase of analytic therapy, which is concerned with the uncovering of unconscious material. Hypnosis can also shorten the second or re-educational phase of treatment, for the hypnotic relationship permits easier incorporation and absorption of wholesome interpersonal attitudes. One must not, however, expect miracles from hypnosis, for the re-educational process requires a long time if it is to be effective.

Many arguments may be presented against use of hypnosis as an adjunct to psychoanalysis. Perhaps the chief objection is that relatively few patients can achieve a deep or somnambulistic trance, which is essential in employment of the various hypnoanalytic procedures. This is why Freud[1] originally abandoned hypnosis as a means of uncovering forgotten traumatic experiences. With the use of a proper induction method, however, the percentage of somnambules may be materially increased. A slow and systematic induction is required, and an analysis of the resistances to hypnosis may bring success. Erickson[2] estimates that the vast majority of subjects can reach a somnambulistic stage of hypnosis, provided the right technic is employed. Of interest in this connection is the recent use of narcosis as an adjunct to hypnosis.[3] Some patients who resist deep trance states enter somnambulism easily under the influence of hypnotic drugs. Posthypnotic suggestions made to the patient during the narcosis, to the effect that he will subsequently be susceptible to the regular hypnotic technic, may sometimes make a somnambulistic trance possible where no other technic has succeeded previously.[4] Nevertheless, in spite of improved technics, resistance to somnambulism may continue.

The fact that not all patients can achieve somnambulism constitutes the prime drawback to the universal use of hypnoanalytic methods that require a very deep trance, such as regression, dramatization, crystal gazing, and induction of experimental conflict. Some hypnoanalytic procedures require only a light or medium hypnotic state. The uncovering of unconscious material may sometimes be achieved through free association during hypnagogic reverie, such as occurs during a very light trance.[5] Dream induction and automatic writing are often possible in a medium trance. Transference manifestations are precipitated by the mere induction of hypnosis, without regard to its depth. Nevertheless, a deep hypnotic state is quite essential in attaining best results. Further research in regard to methods of increasing trance depth may in the future overcome this most important obstacle.

The effect of hypnosis on the transference is a point around which many objections may be focused. Traditionally, analysis proceeds best where the patient assumes an active role. Self-development and assertiveness are enhanced by the subject's assumption of responsibility for at least some of the therapeutic work. During hypnosis, it may be argued, the patient is expected to function passively, as if he were a robot, to be maneuvered about by suggestions from the hypnotist. This militates against a proper therapeutic setting.

Such an objection would be valid were the patient obliged to maintain the paralyzed status that obtains in the orthodox hypnotic procedure. Hypnoanalysis, on the contrary, implies tremendous activity on the part of the patient.

An important innovation in therapy is the procedure of working with the patient during the trance to arouse him to alertness and productivity. In this way he rids himself of the lethargy and cataleptic attitudes traditionally accepted as an inevitable concomitant of the trance. He is not expected to function like a puppet. Cognitive, affective and motor functions are stimulated. The patient moves about freely and participates actively in the analytic work. He is encouraged to think in a spontaneous and facile way, to accept or reject the analyst's interpretations or the validity of the material that he brings up.

The change in technic replacing hypnotic passivity by activity probably has an important effect with respect to the basic image of authority as restrictive, repressive, and insistent upon being right at all times. It opens the way to self-expressiveness. Indeed, the analysis becomes an intensely dramatic experience. Intellectualization of it is minimized.

Another objection frequently voiced against hypnosis is that it prevents the patient from experiencing and expressing his deepest feelings and impulses. Motives for being hypnotizable are commonly desires for security and power through dependence upon or identification with the omnipotent hypnotist. One might suppose that such a relationship might prevent other transference attitudes from developing, since these would conflict with the motives that determine the phenomenon of hypnotizability.

Fortunately this is not at all true. The hypnotic interpersonal relationship is not limited by the dependent role that the patient customarily plays during the trance. There is usually a response to the hypnotist with the full range of characterologic defenses and demands. These may not be superficially apparent, but they will always be observed if one notes the patient's dreams and free associations. There is also a mobilization of hostile and erotic impulses, that may never reach awareness unless their preconscious derivatives are brought to the patient's attention. In fact, hypnosis acts as a catalyst to the experiencing of the deepest and most dynamic transference feelings, for it brings the patient immediately into a close relationship that he might have succeeded in avoiding in the waking state.

The effect of posthypnotic amnesia on the learning process during hypnosis may cause concern to some. Surely, if posthypnotic amnesia is complete, one may wonder whether the hypnoanalytic efforts are worth while. It would seem futile to work with unconscious trends and to impart appropriate interpretations to the patient during the trance if, upon resumption of the waking state, these are forgotten. However, experience has shown that posthypnotic amnesia is an artefact. There is always a carry-over into waking life, although the patient may have no immediate awareness of the material. A simple experiment will easily demonstrate this. During the trance, hand withdrawal in response to an electrical shock may be conditioned to the sound of a buzzer. When the subject awakens he will continue to react to the sound of the buzzer with hand withdrawal, even though he remembers nothing about the experiment. The experiences during the trance have a definite effect upon the ego in the waking state, although this effect does not register immediately.

An important way in which hypnoanalysis differs from the usual hypnotic procedure is in regard to the analysis of the transference. The analysis refers not only to the transference attitudes and feelings that are a reaction to the analyst as a human being, but also to the very dependency strivings upon which the motive for being hypnotizable is based. The analysis of deep dependency strivings will not remove the ability of the subject to enter into trance states. It will prevent him from maintaining the illusion that the analyst is a demigod whose edicts he must accept on the basis of faith.

Where such dependency strivings are not resolved, there is a danger that an irrational positive transference may continue, interfering with the proper termination of therapy. There is also a possibility that any positive gains fostered by treatment will vanish as soon as hypnoanalysis is discontinued.

The working through of the patient's dependency also has an important effect in validating the material that is brought up during hypnoanalysis. Because of the strong motivation for complying with the demands of the hypnotist, some patients may feel that they are expected to experience repulsive impulses and to remember forgotten traumatic memories. As part of the pattern of compliance associated with hypnosis, they will deluge the hypnotist with fantasies that may have no basis in fact. As soon as the patient understands that he is not expected to comply in any way, and as he realizes that his compliance is rooted in irrational inner feelings, he will be less likely to falsify the material that he brings up.

Hypnoanalysis is not dependent upon the authoritarian status that determines results in suggestive hypnosis. Whatever benefits the patient gains are produced by a dynamic alteration of the personality structure and by a real strengthening of the ego such as occurs during psychoanalysis.

In addition to the common fear so frequently voiced that hypnosis may make a dependent person more helpless, there may also be apprehension that the power-driven individual will resist actively the relinquishment of his control and may consciously or unconsciously defy the analyst to put him into a trance. The failure of the analyst to hypnotize the patient would then serve to mobilize the latter's scorn and to drive him away from treatment. Or it may seem that the detached individual, whose adjustment to life is founded on a need to maintain a chasm between himself and others, may become so terrified by the intimacy of the hypnotic relationship that he will utterly refuse to permit himself to be hypnotized, or, if hypnosis is achieved, the panic and anxiety may then cause him irreparable harm.

These arguments, in my own experience, as well as in the experience of other analysts who have used hypnoanalysis, are not valid. The patient will of course react to hypnosis, as he does to everything else, with his usual character strivings and defenses, but there is a coincident striving to be hypnotizable and to get on better terms with others and with himself. The hypnotic experience need not become a sop to the needs of the compulsively dependent individual. Nor will hypnosis rob a person of will power or diminish his self-control. If the hypnotic experience has any effect at all, it tends to build up the patient's self-sufficiency and inner strength. This growth process, whatever its dynamic basis, has seemed to me one of the most gratifying features of hypnosis.

Another fallacious notion is that hypnosis in a detached schizoid person may precipitate a psychosis. Without question the individual who is terrified of people will regard hypnosis, like any other interpersonal relationship, with apprehension, and he may perhaps even resist entering the trance state. However, detached persons are often easily hypnotized, and I have even succeeded, with no deleterious effects, in inducing hypnosis in withdrawn schizophrenic patients.

Most expressed fears about hypnosis are the product of serious misconceptions concerning the nature of the trance. Still current among some psychoanalysts is a feeling that there is something essentially lewd and evil about the hypnotic state. Because hypnosis has historically been so steeped in associations with "magic," the analyst who delves into the method may be accused of a compulsion to necromantic experiment. Or he may be charged with wanting to take refuge in magic when he senses his own shortcomings in helping patients to get well by orthodox analytic methods. Basing their conclusions on observations of stage hypnotists and parlor pranksters, some psychoanalysts may accuse a colleague who utilizes hypnosis of having strivings for power and impulses to vanquish or control his patients. But such accusations are rapidly disappearing as more and more analysts become acquainted with the method.

In answer to the objection that hypnoanalysis deals with superficial psychic material and leaves the deepest personality problems untouched, the admission must be made that where therapy consists merely of enucleation of repressed memories and conflicts, characterologic defects often go untouched. A successful psychoanalysis is always associated with an alteration of the character structure to such a point that the patient no longer utilizes his subversive defenses against people to avert helplessness and to maintain his self-respect. Once the therapeutic objective involves a change in the character structure itself, the enucleation of unconscious material becomes an important but not the most important task in therapy.

Alteration of the character structure is achieved **largely** through analysis of the hypnoanalytic transference. The primary concern with the transference is similar to that in psychoanalysis. Indeed, hypnoanalysis *is* psychoanalysis, performed in a controlled setting. The patient reacts to the analyst and to the hypnotic situation with his customary resistances, defenses, and strivings; this enables the analyst to understand and to analyze with the patient the function of the compulsive trends. Hypnoanalysis becomes an experience in human relations that is intensely meaningful to the patient and that serves to alter his attitudes toward other people and toward himself.

The therapeutic goal of rehabilitating the individual in his interpersonal relationships necessitates a treatment period much longer than the commonly accepted time of three or four months. Exactly how long therapy will take and how successful the results will be, are questions that depend on the nature of the emotional problem. Hysterical and psychosomatic conditions are more easily influenced than character disorders. However, even in the latter cases hypnoanalysis may prove to be an invaluable adjunct to psychoanalysis.

## REFERENCES

1. BREUER, J., AND FREUD, S.: Studies in hysteria. Washington, D. C.: Nerv. and Ment. Dis. Pub. Co., 1936.
2. ERICKSON, M. H.: Hypnosis in medicine. M. Clin. North America, May, 1944, p. 643.
3. HORSLEY, J. S.: Narco-analysis. London: Oxford, 1943.
4. WOLBERG, L. R.: Medical hypnosis. To be published by Grune & Stratton.
5. KUBIE, L. S.: The use of hypnagogic reveries in the recovery of repressed amnesic data. Bull. Menninger Clin. 7: 172–82, 1943.

# XVI

## HYPNOANALYTIC PROCEDURES

Hypnoanalysis presupposes the fulfillment of a number of requirements on the part of both the patient and the therapist. The patient must be hypnotizable and must have been trained to reach as deep a trance state as possible. The therapist must understand unconscious dynamisms and must know how to manipulate the hypnotic interpersonal relationship in the interest of therapeutic objectives.

Best results are obtained in patients who can verbalize freely in hypnosis and can revert in memory to earlier periods of life. The ability to develop posthypnotic amnesia and to carry out posthypnotic suggestions is a helpful and even mandatory asset. Relatively few patients are able to enter into deep hypnosis at the start, but with a proper technic a trance sufficiently profound for hypnoanalysis can be induced in a fair percentage of cases. The initial preparation of the patient, technics of induction, the handling of resistive cases, and the supplementary use of narcosis, have been described elsewhere.[1]

The ability to develop somnambulism will not in itself insure successful hypnoanalytic therapy. Because much of the responsibility for the analytic work must be borne by the patient, sufficient ego strength must exist. The patient must be able to bear the anxiety that is aroused as defenses and resistances crumble and repressed unconscious impulses come to the surface. Most failures in hypnoanalysis occur in patients who have no real incentive to get well, or who refuse to relinquish the secondary gains that accrue from the exploitation of their neuroses. Failure is common also where there is a destructiveness so pervasive that it overwhelms all creative efforts, and a loss of self so intense that the individual feels himself to be without substance or being. The diminutive ego in the latter group of persons makes frustration intolerable and the ordeal of anxiety excruciatingly painful. A Rorschach test is often very helpful in determining what constructive forces remain in the individual and whether sufficient shock-absorbing capacities exist to make hypnoanalysis possible.

Psychotic individuals, prepsychotics, and patients with character disorders of an extremely infantile or dependent nature, are usually not suitable subjects for hypnoanalysis. In such cases the most that can be undertaken is palliative psychotherapy, in the form of symptom removal, guidance, environmental manipulation, persuasion, and desensitization, reinforced, if it is desired, by hypnosis.[1] In the course of such therapy it may be possible eventually to stimulate the proper motivation for hypnoanalysis, to undermine the secondary gains relating to the neurosis, and to build up the individual's creative forces and ego strength to a point at which hypnoanalytic treatment can be attempted.

In hypnoanalysis the hypnotist acts as a guide leading the patient through a maze of unconscious material. The hypnotist must therefore know which trends are significant and which are of secondary importance. He must know how to handle the transference and resistance, and how to make appropriate and timely interpretations. This knowledge can best be acquired through a personal psychoanalysis and through supervised psychoanalytic case work. When hypnoanalysis is used in a limited sense to uncover traumatic memories or experiences, as in the treatment of traumatic and war neuroses, extensive analytic experience is not essential. However, where the transference is analyzed, it is important to have specialized training in psychoanalytic technics.

In hypnoanalysis, as in psychoanalysis, the phenomenon of the countertransference may become a real problem. The close interpersonal relationship is bound to produce hostile and erotic projections on the part of the patient, as well as an abundance of other neurotic impulses. It is essential for the therapist to preserve an objective attitude to these manifestations and not to permit himself to get entangled in the dramatic situation that develops. Bibring-Lehner[2] has shown that personality distortions in the analyst can materially disturb progress in analysis. It is important for the therapist to have sufficient insight into his own difficulties to safeguard against projecting them onto the patient.  No matter how much the therapist may try to remain objective, he cannot help reacting to the patient emotionally.  The more he understands his own reactions, the less likely will he be to use the patient as a focus for his own neurotic impulses.  The therapist who has no insight may applaud hostile or destructive attitudes, may praise submissive, ingratiating behavior, or may sympathize with a patient who is having difficulties that approximate his own problems.  The patient will as a result develop conflicts that cannot be explained away as manifestations of resistance.

Hypnosis can light up neurotic drives in the hypnotist himself.  The hypnotic state especially lends itself to sadistic exploitation because of the seeming passivity of the patient.  It is quite essential for the hypnotist to be aware of any sadistic motives in himself, since these will destroy all attempts at therapy.  Masochistic patients will dote on the hypnotist's sadism and will derive such neurotic gratifications from the hypnotic relationship that there will be no further progress.  Hypnosis may stir up in the hypnotist other irrational feelings that can interfere with therapy.  The ambitious therapist may, for instance, resent any impairment or lack of progress, or he may become irritated with the patient when the latter clings to his neurotic defenses.  By his manner the therapist will convey this irritation to the patient, who will then look upon his symptoms as a sign of "badness," and conclude that he probably has within him an impulse to frustrate the therapist.  The therapist may be unable to tolerate the hostility that the patient displays toward him, or he may be in constant need of praise from the patient.  A personal psychoanalysis can forestall such reactions and is of inestimable value in permitting the development of a therapeutically effective interpersonal relationship.

## General Procedures

The conduct of the initial hour is extremely important.  It is best to refrain as much as possible from the question and answer type of interview. Rather, the patient should be permitted to bring up his problems spontaneously. Resistance will be encountered immediately if the hypnotist attempts to probe the historical development of the patient's illness or ventures upon a discussion of the patient's possible attitudes or motives. As a rule one can assume that the patient is more or less unaware of his deepest problems. Premature probings will merely serve to mobilize resistance.

Before hypnosis is attempted, it will be well for the hypnotist to determine the patient's attitudes toward hypnosis, and he should remove any gross misconceptions or fears. No promises should be made as to the efficacy of therapy, and if the patient insists upon an answer to his queries, he may be told that results will depend upon how actively he cooperates in the treatment process. The patient should be trained in hypnosis before analytic therapy is begun, because as he senses that his defenses are being challenged, he will show resistance that may reflect itself in an inability to go into hypnosis or to attain the necessary depth. At the start the analyst is regarded as a benign, magical person upon whom the patient centers great hopes and expectations. This furthers the motivation for being hypnotizable. Once deep hypnosis has been obtained, any resistances issuing from analysis are not so likely to prevent attainment of a trance state. They will rather be manifested in other areas.

The question often arises whether it is possible to apply hypnoanalytic technics in the case of a patient who is already under psychoanalytic therapy. When a patient develops an obstinate state of resistance during psychoanalysis, hypnosis may be very helpful in resolving it. However, one must remember that irrational transference attitudes toward the analyst may militate against attainment of a hypnotic state. For this reason success is not as certain as when hypnosis is induced before therapy is started. One way of solving this problem is to refer the patient to another person for hypnosis, while at the same time the analyst continues with the regular psychoanalysis. This procedure stirs up a tremendous amount of activity and is especially useful when the analysis seems to have reached a stalemate. The hypnotist may, of course, after having induced a satisfactory depth of trance in the patient, suggest to him that he will thenceforth be hypnotizable by his own analyst.

The patient is seen five or six times weekly. Because the therapy is so active, longer intervals between treatments are likely to be very disturbing to the patient. The latter may either lie on a couch, as in the orthodox psychoanalytic procedure, or he may sit in a chair in a face to face position. The couch position has the same advantages as in psychoanalysis, and the patient may be told that it is more relaxing and permits both him and and analyst to concentrate better on what he is saying.

After the initial hour, during which the patient spontaneously discusses his chief problems and is encouraged in clarification of his attitudes toward hypnosis, from five to six sessions are spent in training him to achieve trance depth, with the object of reaching, if possible, somnambulism with posthypnotic amnesia. It may be necessary to spend several two hour sessions with the patient in a slow, systematic induction. The ultimate aim is to train him to go into deep hypnosis immediately at a given signal. The following five or six sessions are spent in teaching the patient the various hypnoanalytic processes, such as dreaming on suggestion, regression, automatic writing, drawing, play therapy, dramatization, and crystal gazing. The patient must be impressed with the fact that this period is to be devoted exclusively to training in procedures, and discussion of symptoms and conflicts must be assiduously avoided.

After this the patient is instructed in the technic of free association and in the urgency of reporting the attitudes and feelings that develop in relation to the analyst. A talk along the following lines may be helpful:

"I will do everything I can to help you to overcome your problems. I will provide you with a situation in which you can analyze the meaning of your reactions and feelings. However, exposing yourself to treatment alone will not be sufficient. You will have to work actively with me. If you apply yourself, you have the best chance for success. You must be prepared for temporary setbacks. Progress is never a steady curve. Your emotional problem will want to keep you back, and it will mobilize everything to convince you that it is better to maintain the status quo. Do not be discouraged. There are healthy forces operating in you at all times that will help you to go forward if you let them.

"There are two general rules that you must follow. The first pertains to your work here, and the manner in which you communicate your ideas to me. This is called free association. I am interested in understanding your undirected thoughts, just everything that comes to your mind. You must permit your mind to wander, and you must report any ideas, feelings, and impulses, no matter how insignificant or ridiculous. If you think that a matter is too trivial to report, it may be extremely vital to mention it. You must not hold back anything. If you feel a reluctance to talk, mention this reluctance. If you notice any tension in your muscles, or if you experience fear, happiness, excitement, or resentment, tell me about it. The second rule is that I am going to expect you to tell me about your dreams; also your feelings and fantasies about me, my competence, my family, or any other ideas that occur to you. If you won't tell me, I shall ask you."

During each session the patient may spend the first fifteen or twenty minutes associating freely, and the content of his associations is carefully noted, to be utilized later in framing the suggestions that are given during hypnosis. Hypnosis is then induced, and the various hypnoanalytic technics are applied. This will require approximately one-half hour. Before he is awakened, the patient is given a suggestion to the effect that he will sleep five or ten minutes. The sleep period may be utilized profitably by asking him to dream about problems of current importance. If it is possible to allot one and one-half hours to each session, the additional time will prove to be of great benefit. Increased time must be allotted to those sessions in which it is intended to utilize technics that require a profound trance, as in regression, dramatization, and induction of experimental conflicts. Here the patient is slowly inducted into a deep hypnotic state and then permitted to sleep without being interrupted for fifteen minutes or one-half hour before the technics are applied.

A very important technical point is to inform the patient while he is in a trance that although he is asleep, he is able to act and feel exactly as he wants too. The patient's behavior then will approximate his waking activity more or less, and will not display the passive, immobile attitude seen during the usual trance. This innovation removes the feeling in the patient that he is an automaton who cannot move except at the order of the hypnotist. It creates an atmosphere in which the patient can express motor impulses that his repressions may inhibit in the waking state. The benefits arising from this activity are more than merely cathartic, for the patient begins to be assertive and to break through the superego restraints that are a determining factor in his neurosis.

From time to time it may be advisable to suspend hypnosis and to resort to the orthodox technic of free association, or to discuss with the patient in the waking state important material that has not yet been integrated. During the last phases of hypnoanalytic treatment, during which the re-educational process is set in motion, hypnosis may also be suspended while reconstruction of patterns and attitudes is effected on a completely conscious level.

## HYPNOSIS AND FREE ASSOCIATION

Free association is an extremely important technical procedure, and by means of it the therapist can gain an understanding of some of the deepest problems of the patient. In psychoanalysis it is an indirect avenue to the unconscious. Hypnoanalysis opens up more direct routes, but free association remains an extremely valuable adjunct and should be employed in both the waking and the hypnotic states.

All thought processes are emotionally determined. As thought images are translated into words, there is a progression of ideas toward a specific goal, and a selection of those images that conform with this goal.  A definite sequence in thought thus runs through the patient's productions, and during free association dynamic conflicts and impulses will come to the surface in a direct or disguised form.

In listening to the patient's free association, it is best to adopt a passive attitude, in order not to interrupt the stream of thought.  Often the important thing is not what the patient says, but how he says it.  Sometimes the mood of the patient is more important than the content of his thought.  He may block, show slips of speech, force himself, or ramble along discursively, in an irrelevant flight of ideas or in long superficial associations, to avoid expressing really significant thoughts and feelings.  The patient's postural tensions, his gestures and facial expression, may reveal conflicts that he does not talk about.  It is essential to find out what lies behind the expressed matter, and when the meaning is not clear, the patient's attention may be called to his manner of speaking.  A patient may give an extensive account of his personal failures, yet reveal in each example the inordinate ambition that lies behind these failures.  In his free association and in his general behavior one may often discern the main character trends.  Sometimes the patient's expressions are confused.  Bringing his confused way of speaking to his attention may stimulate clearer expression.  If the patient pauses long in his conversation, or if he seems to block, opportunity may be taken to emphasize the need for him to say everything that comes to his mind.

Patients must be trained in the ability to associate freely, and different people display different aptitudes for this procedure.  Verbalization of thoughts without restraint is often very difficult, because obscene ideas, distressing recollections, and offensive notions concerning the analyst may press for expression.  As a defensive gesture the subject will exhibit blocks in his stream of thought, or may try to protect himself by going off into reverie.  Impulses and strivings even at the periphery of consciousness may be so repulsive to him that he does not dare to permit himself to think of them.

Some resistances to free association are relatively superficial.

The patient may believe that the analyst will consider his fears and fantasies absurd because he himself thinks them ridiculous. He may want to analyze his impulses and actions beforehand, since he anticipates censure, or he may feel that the analyst will think more of him if he analyzes his problems himself. There may be a conscious need to maintain control, which will produce resistance to the revelation of his mental processes. There may be an intense fear of failure, and anticipation of it in an inability to utter what comes to mind.

By far the majority of resistances to free association are unconscious in nature. The patient may want to cooperate, but whenever he attempts to vocalize fantasies and thought images, he experiences, to his consternation, an anxiety that blocks his efforts. Sometimes he may not become aware of anxiety, because memory of the traumatic material is so fleeting that it never actually occupies the field of attention. In many cases the character structure acts in resistance to free association. The individual's pattern of life, for instance, may be so stereotyped that he will permit nothing spontaneous to intrude itself. Yet he may have an unconscious striving to yield up his thoughts. He may fear that he will express hostile or erotic impulses if he lets himself go, or he may be convinced that releasing his thoughts will uncover the fact that he is inept and contemptible. On this basis he may exhibit a mental or vocal inertia that may proceed to mutism.

The expression of the patient's feelings and attitudes during treatment is extremely important, not only because it reveals unconscious trends and impulses, but because it prevents "acting out." Acting out denotes expression in the motor field of unconscious impulses that cannot be verbalized. The acts are compulsive and serve to release the accumulated tension. They have a cathartic effect, but actually solve very little, since the patient's fundamental problems are not touched. So long as the patient is unable to understand the motives behind his acts, they will reappear again and again. His life inside and outside of analysis will be punctuated by irrational behavior. Some motor acts are not so much expressions of unconscious impulse as they are defenses against them. This is the case, for example, in certain sexual approaches to the analyst which upon analysis are found to be reactions that disguise an underlying hostility.

Hypnosis can be used to facilitate free associations. Kubie[3] has shown that institution of a state of hypnagogic reverie can bring about easier access to unconscious material. Lindner[4] takes advantage of this by permitting his patients to associate freely in the waking state until a resistance is manifested. Hypnosis is then induced and the last few statements uttered by the patient before the onset of resistance are repeated to him. Usually free association will continue during hypnosis from this point on.

Many resistances to free association may thus be removed by the mere induction of hypnosis. The material often flows freely, and the results of one session may be more revealing than weeks of free association in the waking state. Associations are facilitated by the hypnotist's suggesting that the patient visualize scenes in his mind and describe them as they appear. The sessions may become very dramatic, and much emotion may be displayed as the patient describes his thought images, many of which will be memories of true or fantasied experiences. Resistance to the more traumatic thought images may be expressed in the form of blocking, shifting of conversation, and the usual defenses seen in waking free association.

Hypnosis may also be used to analyze the existing resistances to waking free association. One man, who had been unable to associate freely for several sessions, became aware of the fact that he was afraid of something, although he did not know what this could be. He felt depressed and unrelaxed. He was discouraged about his progress in analysis and about his inability to express himself. Under hypnosis he was given the suggestion that he would say without restraint anything that occurred to him as he thought about being afraid. His production was as follows: "Obedience, obedience, that's what it is. I think that maybe I compare myself with an obedient horse. I see something that has to do with Iceland, a trolley car, a scene from a roof, round on top like a peanut. I'm afraid I'm making a fool of myself. I'm afraid I don't know I'm afraid of you. Who are you? I'm afraid to think who you are. I'm afraid I might be kidding you, and that is a serious offense. I'm afraid of airplanes. I'm pretending I'm in a hypnotic state, just to please you."

At this point I challenged the patient to open his eyes or to get off the couch. He was unable to do either, even though he tried desperately. He continued: "You are my father. I am afraid of you. You might be playing a trick on me. You might have knowledge I don't know about. I hate you. I don't know the meaning of feelings of love and hate. I feel ridiculous. Do I like my father? I gave him things as peace offerings. I wanted to give you things. I am afraid of my father. Mumbling old fool. Got a lot of control over me he shouldn't. Hasn't the brains. I'm smarter than he is, better than he is. I'll fix him. Got away with that. First time I got mad. First time I was ever able to express my feelings."

A young woman who had been unable to associate freely because of a resistance that she could not understand, expressed her feelings consciously as follows: "Darn it, until I was on my way here I hung on to a relaxed feeling. I feel it is useless to make an effort to say anything. Then I feel I should. It would be better if you did the work. There is a resistance of getting into it, getting involved in the feelings I have, like having the experience here mean anything. The idea is, it is safer not to have any feelings toward you at all, although I don't know what these feelings might be."

Under hypnosis she was urged to associate to this feeling. She remarked: "Maybe you really do want me to talk. I always feel I shouldn't. I have such a strange feeling. I want to run away. I want to lie on my side with my knees drawn up. I'm more protected if you should make an attack on me. As I lie here, I feel naked and inviting attack. I feel all the talking I can do is to scream that I'm afraid of an attack. What I really want to do is to get up and to do something positive. It repeats itself over and over that somehow in throwing my arms around you I can do something to control you and make the danger less. Last time I left I felt wonderful and confident. I remember now, I had a dream. The dream was this: It was noisy. I was in an aeroplane. Someone else was along. I don't know who. We had to land in hostile territory and the person who owned it was hostile. We had to do something about sending a message. I suddenly remembered, while we were away from the plane, a number between fifty and sixty. Something to do with the engines. The feeling was if you race the engine, it would go to one hundred and twelve, and it would stop. I got out in the woods. The trees were bare and rocky. Stony terrain. I go through the woods to get away. A woman in the woods tries to tell me where to go. I'm nude. I found a cave, went in to hide from this, to get away from bullets shot at me. Finally, I find a place where I can sit. I felt safe. I'm not afraid in the dream."

She went on in explanation of the dream: "The person who owns the hostile territory is you. There is a feeling, as a woman I'm vulnerable. If I'm a man I could have a relationship with you, and it would be all right. If I were a man I wouldn't feel guilty about anything. It seems preposterous, the visual image I have is of a man's penis. I see my father, and it makes me guilty."

The hypnotic state in itself is not sufficient to dissolve all resistances to free association which may continue even in the deepest somnambulistic trance. The most urgent commands may fail to bring up pertinent associations. Sometimes it is possible to circumvent the resistance by instructing the patient during hypnosis that at the count of five he will think of a word or visualize a picture that is associated with the material that is being discussed. If this is unsuccessful, the patient is asked to permit his mind to wander, and he is told that at the count of five he will think of a number that will indicate the number of letters there are in an important word associated with the material. Then he is instructed that, at the count of five, the letters will appear in jumbled order one at a time. The count is repeated until all the letters are obtained. The patient is then instructed to put the letters together so that they compose the important word.

One may rightfully question the therapeutic value of free association during hypnosis, inasmuch as the usual resistances are restored as soon as the patient enters the waking state. These objections are not entirely valid. The mere expression of the patient's feelings in words does a great deal toward removing waking resistances. It is as if a corrosive process is started, eventually terminating in the breaking through of unconscious impulses, feelings, and ideas. Lindner[4] has commented on this phenomenon by stating that patients will repeat, in waking free association, material that they have uncovered during hypnosis, even though a posthypnotic amnesia exists. He believes that this single benefit is responsible for a saving of half of the total treatment time.

## DREAM INDUCTION

Hypnotic stimulation of dreams and interpretation of these play an important part in the technic of hypnoanalysis. Dreams are forms of ideational activity that may yield important clues to unconscious impulses, fears, and conflicts. Both the pattern and the content of dream thinking are unique. Higher cognitive processes and inhibitions are more or less suspended and archaic types of ideation prevail, involving condensation, displacement, and symbolization.

The high degree of symbolization in dreams is probably based upon two factors. Inhibition of the higher cortical areas releases primitive types of representation, particularly of a phallic nature.[5] Symbolization is also a purposeful process, being motivated by a need to evade the psychic censorship. Even during sleep a certain amount of vigilance is maintained against the emergence into awareness of forbidden impulses and demands. Much of the dream distortion, secondary elaboration, and representation by multiples and opposites, is caused by this factor.[6]

Dreams, like conscious thinking, are dynamically motivated

by urgent conscious and unconscious needs. The content of the dream is influenced by the emotional status that exists at the time, the conflicts, wishes, and memories that are momentarily important. Because reality testing, logic, and correct conceptions of time and space are more or less suspended in sleep, and because resistance is minimal, the dreamer may express wishes, hopes, and fears that he would not permit himself to experience in waking life. Dreams are subject to the same laws of repression as the unconscious impulses from which they emerge. Much of the forgetting of dreams is due to the inability of the individual in the waking state to accept the implications of his dream.

The form that the dream takes is highly individual, for dreams are like artistic creations. Different people have different dreaming aptitudes and are prone to use in varying ways the symbols that are personally meaningful to them. However, in dreams language forms tend to be more simple, and a closer unity exists between the primitive ideational expressions found in dreams than between the representations found in conscious language constructions.

In addition to disclosing repressed unconscious impulses and memories, dreams can yield important clues to the character of the dreamer.[7] Alexander and Wilson[8] have shown that character drives are often represented in dreams by various organ functions. For example, receiving and grasping tendencies may be delineated by dreams with an oral content, in the form of either passive absorbing or aggressive taking. Giving, attacking, and retaining tendencies may be signified by urethral and anal eliminative activities. Persons who have character strivings oriented around a need to maintain their intactness also may dream of toilet activities. Feces often are equated here with something bad and taboo—they become a sterile, dead, and evil element. The sexual function is frequently utilized to represent attitudes of giving, receiving, and attacking. It can be employed to express a desire for power or a fear of being injured or destroyed.

During psychoanalysis the study of the patient's dreams

helps in the recovering of repressed unconscious material. It also reveals the nature of the transference and the stages of analytic progress and understanding. For instance, resistance to the physician or to the treatment may first be revealed by dreams of being intruded upon and degraded, or of degrading and attacking the analyst. Dreams at crucial stages of the analysis are said by DeForest[9] to recapitulate symbolically the actual traumatic occurrences of early childhood.

In hypoanalysis the study of the patient's dreams is of vital importance. Dreams may be artificially stimulated on command during hypnosis or they may be posthypnotically suggested, to appear later during spontaneous sleep. Hypnotically produced dreams have all the characteristics of spontaneous dreams. Work on hypnotic dreaming has been reported by Roffenstein,[10] Klein,[11] Schrötter,[12] Hoff and Pötzl,[13] Welch,[14] and Siebert.[15] This work is purely experimental and has not been applied to psychoanalytic problems.

The most complete study on hypnosis and dreams is that of Farber and Fisher,[16] who investigated dream formation under hypnosis in normal subjects. They discovered the interesting fact that uninhibited individuals when presented with the dreams of other persons were able to interpret them during hypnosis, whereas they could not appreciate their meaning in the waking state. Much of the symbolism used in these dreams was of a sexual nature. One subject, when he was told of a dream about a boy extinguishing a fire with water from a pitcher, immediately responded that the boy wet his bed or should have gone to the bathroom. Another subject was told that she would dream of wetting her bed and of being scolded for this by her mother. She dreamed of falling into a pond in the wintertime, for which she was upbraided by her mother. This dream was revealed to a second girl under hypnosis, and without hesitation the latter remarked that the girl must have wet the bed. A dental extraction in a man was translated as castration, and in a woman as giving birth to a baby. The story of Moses in the bulrushes was presented to a female subject and she stated that someone was going to have a baby. The bulrushes stood for pubic hair. Another interesting study is that by Kanzer.[16a]

Subjects under hypnosis may dream spontaneously during the trance or later during natural sleep in response to the induction. The dreams that follow the first attempts at hypnosis are tremendously significant and often contain the essence of the patient's problem. Later during hypnoanalysis there arise dreams that are stimulated by the material brought up during the trance. Dreams are also provoked by emotions aroused in the transference or by resistance.

The ability to dream in response to hypnotic suggestion must be developed. A medium or a deep trance is usually required. It is best to proceed slowly in the training process. At first a posthypnotic suggestion may be given the patient to the effect that in his sleep that night he will have a dream that he will remember and report at the next session. If this suggestion is followed, it is repeated, the patient being given a specific topic to dream about. The next step is to suggest to the patient that he will have a dream immediately before awakening from hypnosis. Finally, he is instructed to dream during the trance and to divulge the contents of the dream without waking up.

The tremendous amount of ingenuity that is displayed in constructing hypnotic dreams is illustrated in the case of a subject who was asked to dream about the number 65398801. Upon awakening he laughed, remarking that he had had a ridiculous dream.

There was an old fellow smoking a pipe, a long, old-fashioned one. It had a large porcelain bowl, German style. On it was a painted star. This was on the bowl. He said that meant astronomy. He said that is easy to study. He kind of banged the pipe and broke it in half. Then he turned it up and it turned into a golf club. He said this is an example of what you can do. He said that is astronomy, which stretches into eternity in this direction and stretches into eternity in the opposite direction. He made the sign of infinity vertically, not horizontally as one usually does. Then he said, "After all the whole thing is nothing. There is nothing except one thing, which is unity."

There were no waking associations of any significance

with this dream, except that the pipe in the dream was one that was on the wall in the subject's home when he was a boy.

Under hypnosis he revealed that the pipe in the dream was shaped like a figure 6, and that the star on the pipe had five points and therefore represented the numeral 5. Breaking the pipe in half split the number 6 into 3's, one of which was discarded. The golf club was shaped like the figure 9. The sign of infinity made vertically gave the figure 8. (There were two infinity signs, symbolizing the extension of infinity in opposite directions.) "The whole thing is nothing" signified zero, and "There is nothing except one thing, which is unity" signified the numeral 1. The entire dream represented to him the number 65398801.

Unconscious mental activity of a constructive nature may be stimulated through dreaming as the patient is asked to work on his problem. A medical student came to see me, complaining of feelings of tension and of an inability to sleep at night. He had always, as far back as he could remember, been a tense, restless person. His symptoms had, however, been growing more severe during the past few months. Association revealed that this exacerbation was coincident with his meeting a young woman toward whom he felt a strong attachment that fortunately was reciprocated. On the evenings when he had a date with her, his insomnia, for some reason, was pronounced. His conscious attitude toward his fiancée was one of warm and tender devotion.

Free association indicated fears of illness and psychosomatic preoccupations. Under hypnosis he was requested to dream of his feelings toward his fiancée. The dream was this:

I was sitting with Ann in a restaurant and she was ordering food for me. As the waiter started serving the dishes, I noticed on the table in front of me a peculiar object, a weapon that was like several meat forks fused together. It was a fearful-looking thing. Then I noticed on the table a basket full of disk-shaped objects. I looked more closely and noticed they were bun-shaped, like small dumbbells. They were red. I was very fearful and tense.

Associating to the dream, the young man remembered having on the day before attended an armament exhibition at the

Metropolitan Museum in New York. He was intrigued by the medieval spears, which had axlike tips. One of them looked particularly formidable, being shaped like a number of meat forks fused together. As he passed this weapon, he had a panicky feeling that it might fall on top of him. In his dream the object projecting from the middle of the table was shaped like this spear. It was also shaped like an Egyptian hieroglyphic symbol of fertility that resembles the uterus, cervix, and adnexa. He then associated the red dumbbell-shaped objects in the basket with the gram-negative diplococci of gonorrhea that he had observed that morning under the microscope in his bacteriology class. When he was asked whether he had a fear that his fiancée might give him gonorrhea, he denied this vehemently, but he admitted that he had not had intercourse with her because he did not want to take the chance of contracting a venereal disease. He did not know how to broach the subject to the young woman, but he felt that before he married her he would insist upon her having a gynecologic examination and a cervical smear, to rule out the possibility of gonorrhea. I then suggested that there were indications that his tension might be related to certain feelings he had toward his fiancée of which he was unconscious, and I instructed him to work on this problem. Gradually his true feelings would become clear to him. The session was followed by complete posthypnotic amnesia.

Several days later the patient arrived at my office at his appointed time in a somewhat agitated condition. While talking to his fiancée the evening before, he suddenly had become aware of an overpowering hatred as well as an irrational notion that she would hurt him. Never previously had he experienced such a feeling. In his associations he talked about certain domineering tendencies in her that he had never resented before. He wondered whether he had not better break off his relationship before he got himself involved too deeply.

Under hypnosis he was instructed to work on the problem of his present feelings toward his fiancée, and was told that he would have a series of dreams that would gradually make clear to him the meaning of his feelings and attitudes. During the next few weeks he had a number of dreams that brought out his intense dependency strivings, his excessive desire for protection, and his attendant fear of being overwhelmed. He gradually correlated his character strivings with experiences of his childhood. As a child he had been domineered and overprotected by a mother who smothered him with neurotic affection. She had by her overfondling created in him intense feelings of frustration. The mother was openly hostile and depreciating toward the father, and the patient began to develop similar feelings. Yet he craved to know his father better. He had impulses of wanting to be close to his father, which were counteracted by fears lest his father hurt him. His mother excited him physically, yet he hated her domineering manner. He was eventually able to achieve the insight that his present symptoms were the product of his disturbed relationship with his fiancée, which was patterned along lines determined by his early conditionings.

Dreaming under hypnosis or posthypnotically may be utilized as a means of understanding attitudes and feelings that are not yet conscious or that cannot be verbalized. In this way attitudes toward parents, siblings, and other persons, as well as toward the self may be divulged. Developing trends in the transference and its progress may also be determined through dreams.

After his first hypnotic induction, an alcoholic patient presented the following spontaneous dream:

I was all dressed up in a brand-new hat. I stepped out of a cab with a friend. The friend paid off the driver, and it was a relief that he did. We went into the bar, and the owner was behind the bar. Every time I started to reach for a drink, the owner would point his finger at my hat, and my hat would fall off.

The patient associated with this the fact that he liked good-looking hats. During times when he was flush with money he always wore a hat that cost $7 or $10. Whenever he needed a drink desperately and did not have the money to buy one, he would pawn his hat in a pawnshop. The man behind the bar in the dream had the build of his father, who was also a bartender. However, he looked something like me. The patient's other associations pointed to the fact that the dream reflected guilt over his drinking, along with a conviction that his alcoholism had resulted in his losing precious things in life. The dream also indicated an attitude toward me as toward an authority who was pointing out his waywardness to him.

The next dream that the patient had occurred two weeks later, in response to a posthypnotic suggestion that he dream about his feelings toward me. The dream was this:

> I passed a youngster who was looking for my daughter Joan. She wasn't sure I was Joan's daddy. I had an orange in my hand and was eating it. I turned the latchkey and said, "Where's Joan?"
>
> When I opened the door there was a fellow under the bed with a flashlight. I figured he was a burglar. I got jittery. There was a chair and he started to grab for it. I pushed it away from him and took it myself. I said, "Come on, Bud," and he cuddled up under the bed as if in fear.

It happened that at the time when I suggested that the patient dream posthypnotically, he had asked whether he might sit in my chair during hypnosis, in order to make himself more comfortable, and I had agreed to this. The dream suggested that he wanted to change places with me because he considered me a hostile person who might rob him of something. There was no conscious knowledge of any other than congenial feelings toward me.

During the next week the patient was extremely tense and restless, for no apparent reason. Under hypnosis he was requested to dream about his present feelings. He had the following dream:

> I dreamt about Roberts, my ex-boss, that he was driving a big car. His wife was in the back seat, while I was on the running board. He was driving in and out of traffic, and I said, "Hey, take it easy!"
>
> He was driving recklessly, and I felt something would happen to me.

His hypnotic associations were to the effect that he felt that hypnosis was something like psychoanalysis in that it concentrated on a person's past. He wanted to have nothing to

do with his past.   He wanted to make restitution for his failures
and to get his punishment over with.   I suggested that his
tension might have been stimulated by the fear that I was,
through hypnosis, catapulting him into sobriety so fast that he
feared that he could not keep his equilibrium.   He resented
my depriving him of something precious to him.   This brought
forth vigorous laughter, and he acknowledged that he really
felt that way about the treatment.

On the next day the patient seemed to be definitely better.
I again suggested to him under hypnosis that he dream about
his attitude toward me.   He had the following dream:

> There were three stage celebrities—Eddie Cantor, George Jessel, and Bert
> Wheeler.   I was in the background watching them perform.   I always
> thought Jessel was overrated.   He sat down at the piano and gave a great
> performance that won me over.   I realized there was something to him.

The patient realized that his changed attitude toward Jessel
really referred to me.   On the basis of this new feeling we were
able to make signal progress with his drinking problem.

Dream activity stimulated under hypnosis may aid in the
dissolution of resistances.   A patient who had come to an
impasse in her analysis, and because of resistance was unable
to express herself or to associate freely, was hypnotized, and
it was suggested to her that she would dream of the reasons for
her block.   Her dream was this:

> I am running in a maze of trees, desperately trying to escape you.   You
> are dressed in a white gown.   You are a high priest and are able to overtake
> me with ease.   I am frightened.

Suggestions were given to the patient to the effect that she
would work on her present attitudes toward me and that she
would have a number of dreams that would permit her to understand her current feelings.   These suggestions acted as a
wedge that enabled her to break through her resistance.

Hypnotically induced dreams help in the recapture of spontaneous dreams that have been completely forgotten.   They
help the individual to remember portions of dreams that have
been repressed during the waking state.   They also permit the

reconstruction of original dreams that have been distorted by secondary elaboration during waking recall. For example, a patient brought in the following spontaneous dream:

I was on my way out of the office. I went out to buy cigarettes. It was a large place, a business place. It was almost dark in the place. There was only one or another faint light. It seemed that the place was deserted. It was something like a situation or scene where everyone has gone home after the day's work. All the lights had been turned off with the exception of the night light. I had remained to complete some work. I was not aware of any particular kind of work that I had done in the place. I was moving fast. I did not seem to be running. I was just moving with considerable speed on my way out to buy cigarettes. I came to the exit and went down the stairs. Then I was on my way back with the cigarettes. I was speeding upstairs. It seemed to be a spiral staircase. As I ran up the stairs, I passed a few people. I could not see them. I felt I might bump into them, but I did not do so, nor did I feel any other particular sensation. It seems as if I was humming a tune to myself as I sped upstairs, counting the flights. Then I was inside the place, speeding along. It seems as if I had to turn some corners as I sped along and that my momentum took me past the point where I was to turn. As I was speeding along, turning corners Charlie Chaplin fashion, the dream ended.

In associating, the patient remarked that he felt that he had to hurry in order to get to his destination faster. Why this was necessary was not clear to him.

Under hypnosis he was given the suggestion that he would dream the same dream that he had had before. The dream was this:

I was working some place, and we were busy. I was told by the boss if I wanted to stay and work that I could finish something, and then I would get more pay and get a better job. I would get advancement, so I stayed. As I stayed I became hungry and wanted something, and then I went out. It was quite late. There was an elevator, but it wasn't running. There was light in it, but it wasn't running. I had to go through the whole place. There was someone else in it. I ran down two steps at a time. I got the things to eat, hurried back, and I was happy that I was going to get a better job later. I went up. I had to walk up fast. Rushing up I came inside and went back to work. I was hurrying up, flying all over the place, and it was dark. I could hardly see. I was running as fast as I could. There were others coming down. I could hear, but I couldn't see them.

In associating to the dream under hypnosis the patient remarked: "I was trying to please my employer. I wanted to get ahead. I wanted to get ahead of others there. I wanted to accomplish better things. If I did what he said, then I would benefit from it in the end. But I didn't see how I could make it."

The dream reflected the patient's compliance and ambition; these aspects of the dream had deliberately been forgotten because of conflict that was associated with these strivings.

Dreaming under hypnosis may bring about the recovery of forgotten memories or experiences. A patient suffering from migraine confided to me in the twelfth session that he resented coming to see me even though he knew that it was for his good. He felt the same way whenever he consulted any physician. The minute he visited a doctor he experienced a new attack of migraine. He had been told that his headaches had begun when he was around 4 years of age. I suggested to him under hypnosis that he would have a dream that would actually be a memory of something that he had completely forgotten, something that had happened to him when he was little, between 3 and 5. He reported the following:

I just had a dream. The dream was of things I remembered. It was the day I entered school. I was registered. The lady at the desk wanted to know why there was no birth certificate. Then I thought of a time before then. They'd run me to child specialists once a week at Bellevue. I had pain on the right side. The doctor asked permission to show me to a class of students. I was partly stripped and exposed. I was very ashamed. There was something cold and morbid on the second floor in Bellevue. On the right hand side there was a dirty black elevator. We took the stairs. It was a hard place to find, and I wondered if I would be able to find my way. It was spooky, cold and dark. That day when I should have been playing with the kids, I was being dragged to doctors. I had no appetite. These people wouldn't give me what I wanted to eat. My mother would keep me from school and drag me around.

The patient was instructed by suggestion to forget the dream upon awakening, but to recall later any real memories he had forgotten that had appeared in the dream. At the next session he spontaneously recalled the dream as an actual memory that he had completely forgotten. He remembered that this was the first occasion on which he had developed migraine. He was able then to understand why he so greatly resented going to doctors.

Another patient during hypnoanalysis suddenly became aware of how frightened he was whenever he entered my office The panic was momentary and was associated with an intense sexual feeling. Under hypnosis he was given the suggestion that he would have a dream that night that would cause him to remember something that he had completely forgotten. The resulting dream was to the effect that he was with his married cousin. He wanted to make love to her preparatory to engaging in sexual intercourse. The room they were in resembled my office, but it had red and black stripes all over. Something interfered with their love making, and even though they tried constantly to get together, they were interrupted. "The room was cozy and restful," the patient said. "The red and black stripes were beautiful. They looked like the stripes on an awning."

He remarked that almost immediately upon his recollection of the dream there came to him a memory that he had completely forgotten. He recounted it as follows: "My cousin is the same age as myself. When we were six she stayed at my house with her two brothers. We were all out on the fire escape. We had made an awning out of a blanket. We were exposed and were examining each other's sexual organs. All of a sudden my grandpa caught us. He took off his strap and gave me a beating. I knew I had done something dreadful. It's funny that I had completely forgotten this incident almost immediately after it happened. It explains my fright here, because in talking of intimate things it's like you were my cousin, and this is the fire escape we played on."

Dreams revealed under hypnosis should not as a rule be interpreted in the waking state. If an interpretation is indicated, it should be made during hypnosis, and the patient should be enjoined to accept or to reject the interpretation in accordance with whether he feels it to be true or false. Fre-

quently the patient will be able to interpret his own spontaneous or hypnotic dreams while in a trance, since the symbolic
meaning is more apparent in that state than in the waking
state.

## Automatic Writing

Automatic writing is a splendid means of gaining access to
unconscious material that lies beyond the grasp of conscious
recall. The portion of the cerebrum that controls the automatic writing seems to have access to material unavailable to
the centers that control speech. This is possibly because
graphic activity eludes the vigilance of the ego better than does
speech. Consequently hypnotic verbalization of feelings and
impulses may not yield information as vital as that brought up
through automatic writing.

To train the patient in automatic writing, the analyst may
give him the following suggestions under hypnosis: "As you
sit here you will continue to be fast asleep. The arm and hand
with which you write will now begin to experience a peculiar
sensation. They will feel as though they are no longer a part
of you. They will feel comfortable but detached. I am going
to place a pencil in your hand, and as soon as I do this you will
begin to write as if your hand were moving along without any
effort or concentration on your part. Your hand will move
along as if it were pushed by some force from the outside.
As your hand moves along, you will not be aware of what it is
writing."

A pencil is then placed in the patient's hand, which is put
into a writing position on a pad or a sheet of paper. Usually
the hand will move along slowly, forming a long, incoherent
jumble of words. This is a cryptic communication. In a few
cases the patient will write more coherently, but the words and
sentences still will be fragmented and difficult to translate.
In the case of subjects who are capable of entering deep hypnotic states, it may be suggested that they will keep their eyes
open while their hands write automatically, and that, though
open-eyed, they will pay no attention to what the hand is

writing. Sometimes it is best to give the patient a book to read, asking him to study the contents and then to reveal these to the analyst. Where the patient is unable to open his eyes without awakening, the analyst may engage him in conversation while his hand writes.

The first few attempts at automatic writing may be unsuccessful, but persistence often brings good results. As training proceeds it will be possible to direct questions to the patient and at the same time to secure his verbal and graphic responses. The latter often convey attitudes and feelings different from those that the patient expresses in speech.

Posthypnotic amnesia in regard to the automatic writing may be suggested, or the patient may be told that upon awakening he will continue to be able to write automatically whenever the analyst places a pencil in his hand. An arranged signal may be given the patient, as follows: "When you awaken, you will notice a sheet of white paper and a pencil beside you. When I tap three times, your hand, unknown to you, will pick up the pencil and will write 'The more the merrier.' "

If the patient succeeds in this task, specific instructions may be given to him in later hypnotic states in regard to particular tasks that are to be accomplished through the medium of automatic writing. If it is desired that the patient do automatic writing in his spare time, he may be given a suggestion such as the following: "When you desire to do automatic writing, get a sheet of plain paper and a pencil. Sit down, relax, and repeat to yourself 'Now my hand will move freely.' Your hand will then write freely and automatically while you read a book or engage in some other activity that involves the concentration of your attention."

Some persons can perfect the technic of automatic writing in a very light trance. Others can even write automatically upon suggestion in the waking state. The disadvantage about such writing, however, is that the patient will probably be unable to translate its full meaning, which may be clear to him only in a deep hypnotic state.

The character of automatic writing differs from that of

ordinary writing. Usually it is an undecipherable scrawl.
The letters are tiny and malformed. The words run together
in such a way that they make little sense. Occasionally the
script is childish, the letters being extremely large and ill-
formed. To add to the confusion, automatic writing is subject
to the same distortions and disguises as dreams. Condensa-
tions, phonetic spelling, punning, literary allusions, and frag-
mentation of sentences and words are common. Single letters
may stand for words and numbers, and peculiar symbols may
indicate words and ideas. Misspelling may be used by the
patient in a purposeful way to call attention to a specific word.
With training the patient may develop a capacity to write more
legibly, spacing words so that they can more easily be translated. In a few cases the patient will display ability to write
legibly from the start.

Unconscious mentation is manifest in automatic writing.[17]
The symbolisms employed, though inscrutable to the conscious
mind, are less complex than conscious symbolisms. Thus the
cryptic automatic writing of one subject may sometimes be
translated correctly by another subject in a trance, whereas
the meaning will be hazy to both in the waking state.[18]

The analyst should watch the patient as he writes. The
way in which he writes may be as important as what he writes.
He may for instance lift his pencil from the paper and write
in the air when he approaches really significant material. The
movement of the hand will convey the meaning of his writing.
At other times the patient may run letters together, so that it
will be difficult to understand them later on, unless one observes
the writing movements closely.

To translate automatic writing the patient is instructed
to open his eyes without awakening and to write in ink, underneath the automatic writing, the full meaning of his communication. Or he may be given a posthypnotic suggestion to the
effect that when he awakens the full meaning of his writing
will be clear to him. It is best that the patient himself do the
translating, since he alone can supply material that he has
omitted in his writing. For instance, he may present a frag-

ment of an idea that is not intelligible until he himself fills in the gaps. One patient wrote the expression "smastplum," which she translated as follows: "Mr. B. ——, the stage director, promised me a part in a new production. This plum, I felt, had its price."

"Stage master plum" was the full communication, and represented the patient's attitude toward a man whose motive she interpreted as that of seduction. It was a condensation of a more general attitude toward all males. Specifically at the time it related to me. In later communications this feeling about men was condensed into an oval hieroglyphic shaped like a plum.

Writings under hypnosis are best kept from the patient, since any premature attempt to acquaint him consciously with the content of his writing will mobilize resistance. He may then refuse to write automatically, or his productions will concern themselves with conscious material, or they will become progressively more cryptic—a device for preventing discovery of the unconscious trends. Occasionally the patient will spontaneously become conscious of part of the content and meaning of his automatic writing. Under these circumstances the writings can be shown to him, since awareness of the material indicates that the ego is sufficiently strong to tolerate the implications inherent in the writing.

It is usually best to have the patient translate the meaning of his automatic writing during hypnosis, after which he is instructed not to remember either the writing or the translation. He may then be urged to begin working on his problem, until he develops the ability to communicate his ideas to the analyst in the waking state. The latter suggestion may stimulate dreams that elaborate upon and make clear to him the meaning of cryptic communications.

It is possible through the medium of automatic writing to produce a hypnotic secondary personality.[19] Sometimes this personality will reveal itself spontaneously through automatic writing. Erickson and Kubie[20] have written a fascinating paper about a patient who presented this phenomenon. Artificial dual personality may be created by a relatively simple technic. The patient is told while in deep hypnosis that the part of him that is controlling his writing movements is another individual of whom he is unaware. This new personality, however, knows all about him. A name may be given to this alter ego, and it may then begin to function as a distinct entity, with wishes and attitudes of its own, which are related to the deeper unconscious drives of the individual.

The hypnotically created personality may know all about the patient, his vulnerabilities and fears, for it lies closer to the unconscious and therefore has better access to its content. With proper suggestions the analyst can take the second personality into his confidence as an ally. He can interpret to it, ask its advice particularly as to the best way of revealing important material to the patient, or the most expedient technic to use to bring up unconscious trends or memories. The second personality may be asked to specify a day and even an hour when the individual will understand a problem or recall a memory. Or the analyst himself may designate the exact day, which should be at not too near a date, in order to give the patient ample time to prepare for the insight. The second personality can be trained to work unconsciously on the super-ego in order to mitigate its severity. At the same time it may work on the ego to make it more plastic and amenable to insight.

The method is highly involved and calls for considerable skill. The technic of enlisting the aid of the second personality is somewhat akin to what is done in psychoanalysis where an appeal is made to the reasonable ego. It is always essential to safeguard the patient by suggesting that the other personality function only during hypnosis. Otherwise the patient may develop a spontaneous hysterical dissociated state that operates, to his embarrassment, in the waking state.

A modification of automatic writing is the use of the planchette or ouija board during hypnosis. Suggestions are given to the subject, who must be in a trance sufficiently deep to permit of his opening his eyes without awakening, to the effect that his hands will push the platform along the board as if an outside force were guiding them. Questions may be then directed to the patient, who will respond by automatically spelling out words in reply.

Trance speaking can occasionally be utilized along with automatic writing. In one case I conditioned a patient to desk taps, so that three taps during the waking state produced a dissociated state in which he communicated with me in trance speaking. I could thus hold conversations with both the patient and his other self. Replies to the same questions were often diametrically opposite, the trance personality being outspoken, while the customary personality used conventional façades and subterfuges to mask deeper meanings.

## HYPNOTIC DRAWING

Drawing is both a form of motor expressiveness and a means by which the individual can reveal inner problems, wishes, and fears. It is an excellent method of gaining access to deep material where the patient is unable or unwilling to associate freely. Drawings have many of the characteristics of dreams. They provide symbolic ways of representing unconscious impulses.[21-25] The patient condenses into his creations material that is to him of great emotional significance. He also injects into his graphic productions meanings that reflect his unconscious fantasies; this is similar to what occurs in the Rorschach test.[26] It applies particularly with respect to hypnotic drawings, in which the objects represented are of indeterminate form.

Like play therapy, drawing permits inner impulses to be projected without the patient's suffering too much guilt feeling. The analyst accepts the patient's projections without reprimand or retaliation, offering interpretations at the correct time. As Griffiths[27] has shown, abreaction through drawing is also of great benefit. The abreactive effect, however, while affording a temporary relief of tension, does not produce a permanent change in the conflict.

Unfortunately, most adults patients do not enter easily into drawing procedures, being inclined to display considerable resistance when drawing is suggested to them. Hypnosis can more or less successfully eliminate this resistance, and on suggestion the patient will usually draw either spontaneously or in response to suggestion of a subject. Best results will be obtained where the patient is in a trance sufficiently deep to enable him to open his eyes as he draws. He may be requested to sketch anything he wishes, or he may be asked to draw a picture of his father, mother, sister, or brother, of himself, the analyst, his mate and children, his house, or other subjects. He may be asked to illustrate a dream or an experience.

The interpretation of drawing symbols as well as of their form, color, and movement has been described in the writings of Pfister,[28] Jung,[29] Appel,[30] Liss,[31] Harms,[32, 33] Reitman,[34] Baynes,[35] Mira,[36] and Naumburg.[37] Other informative articles are those of Levy,[38] Bender,[39] Curran,[40] and Despert.[41]

The patient, during hypnosis, may translate the meaning of his drawings directly, or he may be urged to associate freely to them. Important clues may sometimes be obtained by requesting the patient to tell a story about his drawing while in trance.

A patient who felt tense and mildly anxious was asked to associate to this emotion. He exhibited considerable blocking and was unable to understand the reason for his anxiety. Under hypnosis he was requested to symbolize his feelings in a drawing. The drawing he made was a complex affair consisting of two parts. In the upper part were a child's head, a boy and girl joining hands, a man and a woman, an old man, a book, and a heart. This represented to the patient the development of a child, particularly his own development: "First, the baby is happy, carefree and smiling. Life is an open book for him. He anticipates joy and happiness. He proceeds to boyhood and then manhood and old age, anticipating joy and happiness."

Below this series of sketches there was a large book surrounded by a broken circle, outside of which were a dagger, an ax, a gun, a man pointing his finger, a ball and chain, a snake, a devil, a spear, and an arrow. The patient's interpretation was: "This group represents the evil that could befall a person.

In the center the book, surrounded by the broken circle, is the law and society that twisted things. The sword is where the trouble started. It is the beginning of darkness and evil. The ax, the gun, the man pointing his finger, the ball and chain, the snakes, the devil, and the spear and arrow are the evil that could befall a person, his being ensnared, enslaved, accused, and destroyed."

Asked to associate to the drawing, the patient uncovered a dream he had had the night before, which he had repressed and which apparently was responsible for his tension and anxiety. The dream had represented him as masturbating in public and being openly accused of perversity. He had considerable conflicts about masturbation and felt a vague fear over masturbatory indulgences, which he associated unconsciously with castration.

Drawings made by patients under hypnosis show a similarity to children's drawings, and those made in the deepest hypnotic states resemble primitive drawings. Automatic drawing particularly employs primitive symbols. Erickson and Kubie[42] have reported a case in which automatic drawing acted as a means of uncovering unconscious conflicts and preoccupations responsible for the patient's depression. Suggestions that the patient draw automatically in the waking state may be given, following the technic outlined in connection with automatic writing.

A patient brought in the following dream:

I was on a flat plain like the southwestern mesas. The color was yellow-buff, with gray heaps of mud. In the distance there were people, a long ridge of crumbled gray mud. A long ridge dipped down. I was with a boy I had known in the seventh grade. He leads me over this ridge. Then a train comes. The tracks are flat, and as the train goes around a curve, the wheels aren't on the track. It is cutting corners.

Free association in relation to this dream indicated that I was his companion and that the train coming along the track represented the analytic process. The patient denied any conscious feeling of fear or anxiety, nor could he understand why he felt that the train had become derailed.

It was suggested to him under hypnosis that upon awakening

he would show the meaning of the dream through automatic drawing. A pencil was placed in his hand and immediately, with a reaction of great panic, he made a drawing consisting of five parallel horizontal lines and five vertical lines so arranged that they formed a right angle. A diagonal line connected the ends. In the middle of the triangle were five circles. The patient remarked: "Jesus, what an experience! The one thing that stood out was the hill. Then I got the feeling of a ball opposing it. A terrific excitement gripped me. I wanted to cry out for paper. My blood began to run fast. It crystallized. The ball then splatters below. Then the vertical and horizontal lines."

He revealed that he had always been preoccupied with the number five. He always counted his fingers, and he watched his nails carefully to see that they were not split. Under hypnosis it was determined that this preoccupation, as well as the compulsion, in the automatic drawing, to draw five horizontal lines, five vertical lines, and five circles, was associated with the need to convince himself that he was intact and that he did not lack any fingers. This in turn was related to a tremendous fear of castration.

Drawing technics can be utilized with advantage under regression. Drawings made during regression have the characteristics of early childhood drawings, corresponding closely to the actual chronologic age level around which the patient is oriented. Drawing during regression permits a penetration of unconscious feelings and impulses that could not be achieved at the adult level. One patient was regressed to early childhood and asked to make an illustration that would delineate his feelings about his brother. In response he drew a series of seven sketches of an extremely crude nature. To these drawings he associated as follows: "Brother bites. He yells. He reaches for Mother's breast. I get mad. I pull Brother's hair. I want to do something to him. That is a mouse in the drawing. I wanted to scare him with a mouse. That is a peddler's cart. The peddler takes the brother away and Mother smiles."

This was the first indication of existing sibling hostility and was an entering wedge in focusing the patient's attention on a conscious level upon his sibling rivalry.

## PLAY THERAPY DURING HYPNOSIS

Technics of play therapy can sometimes be used with great efficacy in the hypnotic state. During play therapy the individual is capable of giving vent to feelings, ideas, and fantasies that he cannot ordinarily verbalize.

The beneficial effect of play therapy is based on the ultimate insight that the patient gains regarding his unconscious problems. More immediately, he acts out in play hostile, sexual, and excretory fantasies, as well as actual anxiety-provoking life situations. The cathartic effect of play therapy temporarily alleviates tension. This is not as important as the gradual insight that develops from the patient's discovery of his inner impulses and fears. The noncondemning attitude of the analyst, who does not criticize or restrict the patient but accords him freedom to express overtly impulses and fantasies of a dreaded nature, alleviates the patient's guilt feeling and eventually makes it possible for him to acknowledge and to tolerate repressed drives. As these are repeatedly acted out in play, the patient becomes desensitized to his unconscious strivings and fears. Carefully timed interpretations aid him in developing insight. Play therapy appears to be particularly suited to the expression of unconscious aggression and to the acting out of jealousies in relation to a parent or sibling. It is also an excellent medium for exploration of sexual and excretory fantasies.

When play therapy is used during hypnosis, a very deep trance is necessary, so that the patient can open his eyes and manipulate the materials without awakening. Play may be utilized both at adult and at regressed age levels. Adult patients enter into play situations more readily during hypnosis than they do in the waking state. On suggestion they are able to project themselves into the play situation with great realism. Merely instructing the patient to play just as he

wants to sometimes suffices to get him interested in the materials. Here the free play technic of Gitelson[43] may be used or,
if the physician prefers, the methods of Anna Freud[44] and
Melanie Klein[45] may be employed. In many cases, however,
it is difficult to create in the patient an attitude that is conducive to spontaneous play, and here a more active approach will
be necessary, as represented in the methods described by
Conn,[46] Levy,[47] and Solomon.[48, 49]

There is considerable latitude in the arrangement of the
playroom and the choice of equipment.[50] Among the most
important materials are a set of dolls comprising an adult
man and woman, an old man and an old woman, a boy and girl
of 10, a boy and girl of 4, and a baby. Other materials are a
few assorted animals, tables, chairs, a dollhouse, and doll furniture, including an icebox and bedroom and bathroom sets. A
bed large enough to hold the dolls is also a very useful toy.
Blocks of wood that can be spread on the floor to resemble
rooms, a nursing bottle, a train, a car, airplanes, guns, soldiers,
a rubber dagger, a drawing board, chalk, paper, pencils, and
crayons will be found useful. Plastic materials can also be
used in play therapy and frequently serve as a medium for the
expression of aggressiveness, destructiveness, motility, and various physical functions.[51]

The utilization of the technic of play therapy at regressed
age levels offers a splendid opportunity to approximate the conflicts that the individual suffered as a child. Even where regression is not real, but merely simulated, expression in terms
of play may yield important unconscious material.

In hypnotic play therapy, directions must be specific and
urgent. Where a passive technic is used, the patient is instructed to build or to play in any manner that he likes and at
the same time to talk about what he is doing. Story telling
may be combined with play therapy, the patient discussing and
elaborating on his play constructions. Where the active technic is used, the patient is allowed to select the dolls he wants
to play with, or the analyst, himself, can make the selection.
Situations based on the material obtained through free association prior to the hypnotic session are then suggested.

In play therapy the patient usually projects his feelings and problems onto the dolls, which under his manipulation act in a manner that approximates the way he himself would react. Disguised in this way, his responses are not as blocked as they would be were he discussing himself. Under no circumstances should he be made to feel that the play concerns himself. The interview should be conducted in the third person, unless the patient himself arrives at the understanding that he is the central actor. Interpretations should also be made with the third person reference, unless the patient identifies himself with one of the dolls and appears to be cognizant of what is going on. Direct questioning is more possible in hypnosis than in the waking state. Further, the patient may be requested to act out in play a situation in which he is immediately involved. Resentment and negative therapeutic reactions are not as frequent during hypnosis as in the waking state when the patient is requested to identify himself with one of the dolls. Motor expression of certain impulses, such as aggression, may be encouraged when such impulses tend to be inhibited. A posthypnotic amnesia may be suggested at the time when instructions are given, by telling the patient that he will gradually understand consciously the significance of the play.

If one has knowledge of the chief traumatic incidents in the patient's life, regression to this period may be effective. Setting the stage by providing appropriate materials and giving pointed suggestions, after the manner suggested by Levy,[52] may produce interesting results. In a case in which sibling rivalry had been a potent source of resentment and anxiety, the patient was regressed to a 6 year level and several dolls, one of which was pointed out to the patient as her sister, were placed on the table. Almost immediately the patient responded with excited play. She was a doctor and operated a hospital. Her sister was brought in for an operation. She herself was the surgeon who performed the operation. Her sister was sick and almost died, but finally pulled through. The patient then was praised by her parents for curing the sister, who nevertheless was left crippled. The symbolic nature of this play was obvious. As the surgeon who operated on her sister, the patient provided herself with an acceptable outlet for her hostility.   By restoring her sister, though making her at the same time a harmless cripple, she both disarmed her rival and won the praise and love of her parents.   In the night following this session the patient had a spontaneous dream in which a girl was being pursued by "Japs" and spies.   During the next session, free association revealed guilt feelings in the patient over not having written to her sister for months.   Subsequent play sessions produced more and more open expressions of hostility, the patient gradually becoming desensitized to such a point that she could talk about her hate on a conscious level.

## DRAMATICS UNDER HYPNOSIS

The work of Moreno and his followers [53-57] has demonstrated that drama as a psychotherapeutic procedure offers a means of rapid ventilation of some of the patient's problems and conflicts.   Spontaneous dramatics or the suggested re-enactment of traumatic situations of the past or present permit the expression of resentment, aggression, jealousies related to parents and siblings, feelings of rejection, and inner strivings and desires that the patient cannot display in everyday life.

The patient manifests many resistances to the acting out of important situations in the waking state.   The most important of these resistances inhere in guilt feelings related to unconscious impulses and fear of being exposed to ridicule or embarrassment.   The ability to engage in dramatics presupposes a congenial relationship to the therapist, and a considerable amount of psychotherapy may have to be applied before such a relationship is possible.

Deep hypnosis is capable of removing most resistances to dramatics.   Under hypnosis the patient will reproduce traumatic incidents and act out emotional scenes with a vividness not possible in the waking state.   The sense of reality becomes so blunted that the patient actually believes that he is participating in the experience.   His emotional reactions are correspondingly more vivid.   Bernheim[58] was the first to appreciate the therapeutic value of hypnotic acting in dealing with sleep terrors and nocturnal incontinence.   Consequently he recommended the hypnotic production of states in which these symptoms appeared.

The war neuroses offer the best evidence of the beneficial effects of hypnotic acting. Under hypnosis the patient, asked to relive the traumatic scene, usually responds with fear and rage, with a tremendous outburst of motor activity and emotion characterized by screaming, with efforts to protect himself from imagined bombardment, and with fantasied shooting or bayoneting of his enemies.[59-61] The same reaction may occur in the re-enactment of traumatic incidents in civilian life.

Regression of the patient to the age period at which he experienced a traumatic incident will often bring out a more vivid dramatization of the scene. A patient who had developed a compulsion to bring the tips of his fingers to both temples, moving his head back and forth at the same time, was unable to recall when he had first manifested this symptom, nor was he able to dramatize its development. Through the use of regression and revivification, he recovered and relived a scene in which he witnessed for the first time the decapitation of a chicken. This was at about the period when he first became aware of the difference between the male and female genitals. He had deduced that he might be castrated if he continued recalcitrant and defiant toward his parents. In re-enacting the scene, the patient jumped out of his chair, shrieking with horror as he yelled to his parents to stop killing the chicken. He then turned around and buried his eyes in his hands. After this he brought his finger tips to his temples and moved his head back and forth, as if to assure himself that he had not been decapitated.

The analyst may take a passive role during dramatics, merely suggesting to the patient that he dramatize important situations in his life. Frequently, however, it will be necessary, as in play therapy, to take an active role by becoming a part of the dramatic scene. In this way the analyst may be the loving mother, the feared father, or the hated little brother, or he may be merely an observer who constantly questions the patient about his feelings and activities.

Dramatics offer the patient a splendid opportunity for ex-

pression of repressed aggression. Many persons are unable
to feel the emotion of rage because its emergence mobilizes too
great anxiety. In hypnosis the emotion of anger may be suggested; the justification may be contrived by such devices as the
suggestion that the patient is witnessing the beating of a child
without provocation. The object is to get the patient to appreciate the fact that he can feel the emotion of anger without
being destroyed by it. Eventually the matter of aggression
and resentment can be taken up at both adult and regressed
age levels, and more and more aggressive scenes may be re-
enacted. This activity will often stimulate dreams that reveal why the patient must maintain resistances to keep his
hostility from consciousness. Aggressive tendencies can also
be aroused by providing the patient with an activity that
necessitates the use of a sharp instrument. The patient is at
the same time encouraged to associate freely.

A modification of the dramatic technic in the form of story
telling, as suggested by Despert and Potter,[62] may also be
employed. At adult or regressed levels the patient is asked
to relate a story, such as "Goldilocks and the Three Bears,"
"The Big Bad Wolf," a story about a boy, a girl, a father and
mother, or any story that he wants to tell. The responses often
will contain clues to deep wishes, fears, and resentments. Such
clues may be followed up by re-enactment of scenes involving
whatever impulses and attitudes are uncovered in the story-
telling process.

The motor activity that is released by dramatics is of extreme
benefit to the patient, opening up avenues of expression that
have been blocked. It is always essential, however, to follow
up dramatics with analytic work that will enable the patient
to gain insight into the reasons for his repression. He must
develop some awareness of his problems in consciousness in
order to express himself freely on a waking level.

## REGRESSION AND REVIVIFICATION

Authorities disagree as to whether regression in hypnosis is
a fact or an artefact. Some workers incline to the latter

opinion.[63] The consensus, however, is that regression is an actual organic reproduction of an earlier period of life.[4, 64—66] It is my own belief that hypnotic regression can revive past patterns of ideation and behavior.[1] In several cases I have succeeded in regressing subjects to an infantile level, so that they lost the capacity for expressive speech and for ambulation, producing at the same time typical sucking and grasping movements.

The dispute regarding the true nature of regression probably arises from the fact that two types of regression may be induced. These types are described by Erickson and Kubie.[67]

The search backwards toward reliving an earlier period in the life of a hypnotic subject occurs in either of two ways. First, there can be a "regression" in terms of what the subject as an adult believes, understands, remembers or imagines about that earlier period of his life. In this form of "regression" the subject's behavior will be a half-conscious dramatization of his present understanding of that previous time, and he will behave as he believes would be suitable for him as a child of the suggested age level. The other type of "regression" is far different in character and significance. It requires an actual revivification of the patterns of behavior of the suggested earlier period of life in terms only of what actually belonged there. It is not a "regression" through the use of current memories, recollections or reconstructions of a bygone day. The present itself and all subsequent life and experience are as though they were blotted out. Consequently in this second type of regression, the hypnotist and the hypnotic situation, as well as many other things, become anachronisms and nonexistent. In addition to the difficulties inherent in keeping hypnotic control over a total situation, this "deletion" of the hypnotist creates an additional difficulty. It is not easy for the hypnotist to enter into conversation with someone who will not meet him until ten years hence. This difficulty is overcome by transforming the hypnotist into someone known to the patient during the earlier period, by suggesting that he is "someone whom you know and like, and trust and talk to." Usually a teacher, an uncle, a neighbor, some definite or indefinite figure belonging to the desired age period is selected automatically by the patient's subconscious. Such a transformation of the hypnotist makes it possible to maintain contact with the subject in the face of the anachronism mentioned above. Unfortunately many investigators of "hypnotic regression" have accepted as valid that type of "regression" which is based upon current conceptions of the past; and they have not gone on to the type of true regression in which the hypnotic situation itself ceases, and the subject is plunged directly into the chronological past.

Even where a true regression is hypnotically induced, the subject almost always tends to display later types of behavior. Consequently he will shift in his patterns from time to time, assuming attitudes that correspond to various age levels. These shifts are probably the result of dynamic forces within the individual that attempt to return him to a more mature level. Regression is thus never complete, since more mature patterns constantly obtrude themselves.

Regression makes available to the individual behavior patterns reminiscent of a previous life period, and also forgotten experiences and memories related to this early period. The hypermnesic potentiality of regression facilitates the recovery of forgotten traumatic experiences, and in certain cases such recovery has brought about amelioration or cure of various symptoms associated with repression of a traumatic event. The earliest work in this field was done by Hadfield,[59] Wingfield,[69] Taylor,[70] and Karup.[71] Later work along these lines has been carried out by Smith,[72] Erickson,[73, 74] Erickson and Kubie,[67] and Lindner.[4] Recall of traumatic experiences and reliving of traumatic scenes is especially beneficial in the treatment of traumatic and war neuroses.[75, 60, 61] It is essential, however, to inject a word of caution. Regression and revivification do not invariably uproot buried memories. Furthermore, the recovery of forgotten traumatic events and experiences does not always produce therapeutic change. This need not detract from the value of the method, although its therapeutic application is definitely circumscribed and does not justify the overenthusiasm expressed by some observers.

Regression may be used with other technics, such as dream induction, play therapy, drawing, dramatics, automatic writing, crystal and mirror gazing. The latter activities at regressed age levels can reveal material unattainable at an adult age level. Occasionally regression can be utilized in the direct treatment of a phobia or a psychosomatic complaint by reverting the patient to a period of his life preceding the onset of his complaint and then slowly reorienting him to his present chronologic age, while discussing with him the development of his illness. Thus Kroger and Freed,[76] treating dysmenorrhea and other menstrual disorders, regressed their patients to a preadolescent age period prior to the time of onset of their complaints. Emotional conflicts, personality changes, inhibitions, and harmful habits were probed, as the patient was slowly reoriented to her actual age. Erickson[74] has reported the use of regression in the treatment of an acquired food intolerance. The subject had acquired a distaste for orange juice, which had become progressively worse until she could not endure even the thought of oranges; the sight of the fruit gave her feelings of nausea and disgust. A trance state was induced and age regression systematically carried out, reverting the patient to a period two years before the time at which her idiosyncrasy developed. In this state she was presented with orange juice, which she drank with relish. Suggestions were then given her to the effect that when she awoke she would have little or no interest in what had occurred when she was in the trance. On awakening, the subject acted puzzled as she rolled her tongue about in her mouth. Several days later she ate oranges in a fruit salad and remarked that she had unconditioned herself.

Regressing a patient to a period antedating the development of a symptom or ailment is useful also in disorders caused by definite traumatic experiences. A boy of 10, who had developed a right-sided facial tic six months before he was seen, was regressed to a 9 year level. His facial tic disappeared completely, and as he was slowly reoriented to his present age level, it developed that the tic had replaced the symptom of enuresis when he was exposed to very cruel disciplinary treatment by his father because of his bed wetting.

When regression and revivification are to be used in any session, it is best to devote at least two hours to it. A somnambulistic trance is necessary. Often a sleep period of from fifteen to thirty minutes, during which the patient is not disturbed, helps to deepen the hypnosis sufficiently and prepares the patient for the work at hand.

Several methods of producing regression may be used. One of the most effective methods is to disorient the patient completely, provoking a general state of confusion. At first this involves the day of the week. After this the patient is disoriented as to the week, then the month and year. From this state of confusion he is gradually reoriented to earlier and earlier periods of his life.

If it is desired to recall past traumatic experiences during regression, and if the analyst does not know at what age they occurred, it is best to be vague about the exact period of time to which the patient is reoriented. Suggestions must be couched in such terms that the patient will be led to feel that he must return to a crucial period. When it is apparent that regression has occurred, as evidenced by the patient's reaction and speech, he may be told that he has certain things on his mind that he has never actually forgotten but merely put aside up to this time. He will recall them again at a given signal. The signal may be nothing more than counting from one to five.

Where play technics, drawing, dramatics, automatic writing, crystal and mirror gazing are to be employed during regression, the physician may be specific or unspecific regarding the age level to which the patient is to revert. In the latter instance, choice of the age may be left to the patient himself, instructions being that he will live through a period that is meaningful to him.

Another way of inducing regression—applicable to very good subjects—is to bring the patient directly to a certain age level without initially inducing a general disorientation. Suggestions such as this may be made: "Now concentrate carefully on what I have to say to you. I am going to suggest that you go back in time, back into the past. You will feel as if you were back in the periods I suggest. Let us start with yesterday. What did you do yesterday morning? What did you have for breakfast? For lunch? Now we are going back to the first day you came to see me. Can you see yourself talking to me? How did you feel? Describe it. What clothes did you wear? Now listen carefully. We are going back to a period when you were little. You are getting small. You are getting smaller and smaller. Your arms and legs are getting smaller. I am someone you know and like. You are between ten and twelve. Can you see yourself? Describe what you see. Now you are etting even smaller. You are becoming very, very little. Your arms and legs are shrinking. Your body is shrinking. You are going back to a time when you were very, very little. Now you are a very little child. You are going back to the time when you entered school for the first time. Can you see yourself? Who is your teacher? How old are you? What are your friends' names? Now you are even smaller than that; you are very, very much smaller. Your mother is holding you. Do you see yourself with Mother? What is she wearing? What is she saying?"

If the patient has a specific symptom, as for instance fear, he may be given a suggestion such as follows: "Now listen carefully. We are going back in time to when you first were afraid. What frightened you? Tell me all the details."

After the patient has recalled a forgotten memory or has brought up significant material, it is best to ask him to forget everything that has occurred. Experience has shown that recall of a forgotten memory or experience, or uprooting of unconscious impulses or attitudes during regression, will not usually be recalled in the waking state if the repression of this material serves an important purpose. However, the mere bringing up of the material appears to influence the repressive process in such a manner that the patient may later admit into the waking state the material that was divulged at the level of deep hypnosis. A suggestion may be given to the patient to the effect that if the memories, experiences, or impulses that he has divulged during hypnosis are true, he will eventually overcome the forces that prevent him from understanding them in the waking state. He may be told that as soon as he feels sufficiently strong to tolerate this material, he will bring it up in consciousness. Often the patient will, as a result of the hypnotic session, spontaneously develop dreams, and the emergence of a certain impulse or memory into consciousness may be watched through this medium as well as through the patient's free association. When the patient finally does recall the material in the waking state, he usually feels that the recovery has been spontaneous.

Dramatics are often effectively combined with regression. In the event that an inimical experience has occurred during childhood, or that the patient has been subjected to extraordinary pressures and disciplines, he is regressed to a childhood level while the analyst encourages him to talk about his feelings and to re-enact his experiences. The analyst may play the role of the father, mother, or sibling during an important dramatic scene. In these roles he may encourage the patient to express repressed impulses, or he may attempt to re-educate the patient by discussing with him various misconceptions. The patient is then returned to the adult level, and the material is translated in terms of adult attitudes. Sometimes it is expedient to explain to the patient that he will, as a result of these discussions, feel entirely differently about matters. It may then be suggested to the patient that he will dream about his real feelings, which will permit him to understand what is going on. Posthypnotic suggestions may also be made to the effect that he will feel free to relate himself more congenially to people, in line with this better understanding of his inner impulses. He may be enjoined to dream about progress in his development. These suggestions during hypnoanalysis may stimulate a great deal of mental activity that will provide opportunities for interpretation.

## Crystal and Mirror Gazing

Crystal and mirror gazing are technics that can be used only with subjects who are capable of entering very deep hypnotic states. Where a crystal is not available, a glass of water will serve as an adequate substitute. If a mirror is used, it should be so placed that it reflects the blank ceiling. The patient is instructed as follows: "You will now be able to open your eyes, even though you are deeply asleep. You will not awaken until I give you the command to do so. On the table in front of you, you will see a mirror. Look into the mirror and you will see things before you. Describe to me what you see."

Crystal and mirror gazing are splendid methods of recovering forgotten memories. The patient may have brought up a number of incidents through hypnotically induced dreams and through automatic writing, but he may be unable to recall the incidents as real experiences or to accept them as factual. Peering into a crystal or mirror, he may be able to reconstruct events in his past life by hallucinating them exactly as they happened.

One patient of mine had a neurosis in which one element was an aversion to fruit, particularly peaches. Through the medium of automatic writing she was able to recall an experience she had when she was 3 years of age. It occurred while she was on an automobile trip with her father, during which they stopped off at a road stand to pick up a basket of peaches. Placing the peaches in the back seat, her father warned her not to touch any until they got home. Defying this warning, the patient, who had seated herself near the peaches, stealthily nibbled one, even though she realized that she was doing something wrong. At this moment her father swung to the side of the road to avoid an approaching car, and capsized his car. The patient was badly frightened, though neither she nor her father was injured physically. Shortly thereafter she developed a dislike for peaches, and the aversion was extended to other fruits also.

Although she wrote of this experience in detail, and its reality was corroborated by her father, she was unable to recall it as a real experience, nor did recall of it through writing materially affect her fruit phobia. She was regressed to the age of 3 and it was suggested that she would see the incident as it had actually occurred. She gazed at the mirror with intense fascination and, in great excitement, described the entire experience as if she were actually reliving it. At the point when she related how the automobile overturned, she brought her hand to her face to cover her eyes; yet she could not resist looking into the mirror as she described how her father helped her out of the automobile and how badly frightened she was. The recovery of this event through actual perception resulted in disappearance of her phobia.

The use of a crystal or mirror can also give the analyst insight into the ideational processes of the patient. The patient describes scenes in the mirror as if he were a spectator in a theater, watching actors on a stage. The productions of the patient are similar to those in free association. Violent emotional reactions may be liberated by this method, with a resultant cathartic effect.

## INDUCTION OF EXPERIMENTAL CONFLICT

Hypnotic induction of an experimental conflict offers a method whereby many of the patient's deepest problems may be symbolically recapitulated. The procedure precipitates an intense emotional experience that helps to desensitize the individual and provides him with insight into the dynamics of his disorder. In 1935 Erickson[77] published an account of an experimental neurosis produced during hypnosis in a man suffering from ejaculatio praecox. After the experiment, the patient was able to recognize how the induced conflict applied to his actual emotional problem. Several days later he was able to perform his first successful act of sexual intercourse.

In 1937 Eisenbud,[78] working with a migrainous patient, created a number of experimental conflicts under hypnosis by suggesting to the patient fictitious scenes in which his hostility was aroused, but could not be expressed. These conflicts at first produced strong attacks of migraine, but as they were repeated they became less and less potent in provoking attacks. In addition to his desensitization to hostility, the patient apparently began to understand how he was turning his hostility on himself. Spontaneous headaches likewise disappeared, and the patient was capable of functioning without developing his previous disabling symptoms.

Experimentally produced conflict offers an important method of promoting insight. Many patients undergoing analysis spend a great deal of time fighting against the realization that they possess impulses of which they are genuinely ashamed. One of the strongest resistances inheres in the refusal on the part of some patients to acknowledge that they harbor unconscious fears or desires. These patients usually have their problems so rationalized that they feel that they know all about themselves. They are certain that nothing is operating outside of awareness. When one attempts to demonstrate that unconscious drives influence their behavior, the response may be denial or they may become extremely resentful. It usually requires more than an appeal to the patient's intellect to convince him that things going on unconsciously are motivating him to compulsive patterns. It is here that induction of an experimental conflict can play a decisive role, by demonstrating to the patient how unconscious impulses and emotions are responsible for his symptoms.

A patient suffering from migraine had spent many years in a fruitless search for relief. He had consulted scores of specialists and was finally influenced by one of these to seek psychiatric help. The patient himself acknowledged that he had certain emotional problems, but he was not at all willing to accept the idea that his headaches were in any way related to them. He presented as proof the fact that he had carefully watched his attacks and could never link them up with his "nervousness." It was soon apparent from the hypnoanalytic material that the patient had strong perfectionistic tendencies that made it essential for him to perform flawlessly at all times. He had furthermore a problem of self-expressiveness that conflicted with his perfectionistic tendency. Whenever he mustered up courage and did assert himself, he felt that he was acting in an outlandish and aggressive manner that would incur the displeasure or condemnation of other persons around him. Thus he found it necessary to inhibit himself in his relationships with others. The resulting frustration mobilized strong resentment, which the patient was unable to express but rather turned on himself in the form of self-recriminations. His migraine was related to this conflict and apparently was a somatic response to internalized hostility. Although his dependency, his perfectionistic drive, his inhibition of self-assertion, and his inability to express aggression, were all revealed through various hypnoanalytic procedures, and although he recognized that he was dependent and perfectionistic, he showed resistance to acknowledging the fact that he could feel in any way aggressive or hostile. He complimented himself on his even temper and presented many arguments to substantiate his philosophy that getting angry at people did not pay in the long run. He indignantly insisted that if a situation should arise in which he felt justified in being angry, he could express his resentment without restraint. He even recounted various incidents in his life in which he had felt that his anger was justified and had acted appropriately.

A hypnotic experimental conflict was then created by giving him the suggestion that when he awakened he would have a desire to discuss with me a treatise on American art that he had recently perused. As he talked about this book, he would be tempted to be as thorough in his account as possible, to convince himself that he had learned all the essential details. He would also want to show me that he was astute and intelligent. However, as soon as he began talking about the book, he would suddenly feel that if he went into elaborate details, and impressed me with his brilliance, I would feel irritated with him because he was wasting time in his analysis. He would furthermore feel that he was trying to make a good impression on me and that I would resent this.

Upon awakening, the patient suddenly declared that he intended to write a review of a recent treatise on American art for a current art magazine. He insisted that it was important for him to go over this material at that particular time with me. He did not know the reason why he wanted to do this, but he felt that it might clarify matters in his mind. As he proceeded to talk about the book, he began to stammer. Sweat broke out on his forehead, and he complained of a "tightening" feeling in his abdomen. He interrupted himself repeatedly to complain about his physical condition, which was becoming more and more distressing. Finally, he had a typical migrainous attack, which he attributed to his having eaten in a strange restaurant that afternoon. He then declared that he probably should not be discussing art with me, inasmuch as his difficulties with art had not been the reason for his seeking my services. He was rehypnotized and details of the experimental conflict were related to him. He was requested to remember the entire incident.

Upon awakening he was bewildered, and although he acknowledged that circumstantial evidence pointed to the probability that the conflict I had induced had created migraine, he was reluctant to accept this fact. Five experimental conflicts were required, all utilizing slightly different situations, but based on the same motivation, before the patient accepted the fact that his symptoms were psychically determined. It was then possible to penetrate his resistance and to work upon his problems in a more facile manner.

The wording in which the experimental conflict is presented is extremely important, as Erickson[79] has pointed out. One can do no better in regard to phrasing than to follow Erickson's suggestions. The patient, in deep hypnosis, is given the following suggestion: "Now, as you continue to sleep, I am going to recall to your mind an event that occurred not long ago. As I recount this event to you, you will recall fully and completely everything that happened. You have had good reasons for forgetting this occurrence, but, as I recall it, you will remember each and every detail. Now bear this in mind: While I repeat what I know of this event, you will recall everything fully and completely, just as it happened, and more than that, you will re-experience the various conflicting emotions that you had at the time, and you will feel exactly as you did when this occurrence was taking place."

At this point the therapist suggests a fictitious situation patterned around the patient's difficulties. For instance, if he has a problem related to the expression of hostility, the suggestion may evoke a situation in which he has acted in a hostile manner, or in which hostility was generated within him because he was unfairly treated. The emotion of hostility is suggested to the patient, and he is urged to feel this emotion acutely.

Finally, the following suggestions are given to him: "Now, after you have awakened, this whole situation will come to your mind. You will not consciously know what it is, but it will nevertheless be on your mind. It will worry you and govern your actions and speech, although you will not be aware that it is doing so. I have just told you of a recent experience of yours; as I recounted it to you, you recalled it in detail, realizing that, the whole time, I was giving you a fairly accurate account of the situation, that I was giving the essential story. After you awaken, the whole situation will be on your mind, but you will not be conscious of what it is. You will not even be aware of what it could be, but it will worry you, and it will govern your speech and your actions. Do you understand? And do you feel badly about this thing?"

The suggestions made may pertain to significant incidents in the patient's past or involve an actual situation that has arisen in the transference relationship. Both types of suggestion are valuable. However, induced conflicts associated with impulses and attitudes arising out of the relationship with the analyst permit the patient to live through acutely his most dynamic interpersonal problems.

## REFERENCES

1. WOLBERG, L. R.: Medical hypnosis. To be published by Grune & Stratton.
2. BIBRING-LEHNER, G.: A contribution to the subject of transference resistance. Internat. J. Psycho-Analysis *17:* 181-89, 1936.
3. KUBIE, L. S.: The use of hypnagogic reveries in the recovery of repressed amnesic data. Bull. Menninger Clin. *7:* 172-82, 1943.
4. LINDNER, R. M.: Rebel without a cause: The hypnoanalysis of a criminal psychopath. New York: Grune & Stratton, 1944.
5. WOLBERG, L. R.: Phallic elements in primitive, ancient and modern thinking. Psychiatric Quart. *18:* 278-97, 1944.
6. FREUD, S.: The interpretation of dreams. *In* The basic writings of Sigmund Freud. New York: Modern Libr., 1938.
7. HERZBERG, A.: Dreams and character. Charac. & Personal. *8:* 323-334, 1939-40.
8. ALEXANDER, F., AND WILSON, G. W.: Quantitative dream studies: a methodological attempt at a quantitative evaluation of psychoanalytic material. Psychoanalyt. Quart. *4:* 371-407, 1935.
9. DEFOREST, I.: The therapeutic technique of Sandor Ferenczi. Internat. J. Psycho-Analysis *13:* 10, 1942.
10. ROFFENSTEIN, G.: Experimentelle Symbolträume. Ztschr. f. d. ges. Neurol. u. Psychiat. *87:* 362-71, 1923.
11. KLEIN, D. B.: The experimental production of dreams during hypnosis. Univ. Texas Bull. 3009, 1930, pp. 1-71.

12. SCHRÖTTER, K.: Experimentelle Träume. Zentralbl. f. Psychoanal. *2:* 638–46, 1912.

13. HOFF, H., AND PÖTZL, O.: Über die labyrinthären Beziehungen von Flugsensationen und Flugträumen. Monatschr. f. Psychiat. u. Neurol. *97:* 193–211, 1937.

14. WELCH, L.: The space and time of induced hypnotic dreams. J. Psychol. *1:* 171–78, 1936.

15. SIEBERT, K.: Die Gestaltbildung im Traum. Arch. f. d. ges. Psychol. *9:* 357–72, 1934.

16. FARBER, L. H., AND FISHER, C.: An experimental approach to dream psychology through the use of hypnosis. Psychoanalyt. Quart. *12:* 202–16, 1943.

16a. KANZER, MARK G.: The therapeutic use of dreams induced by hypnotic suggestion. Psychoanalyt. Quart. *14:* 313, 1945.

17. ERICKSON, M. H.: The experimental demonstration of unconscious mentation by automatic writing. Psychoanalyt. Quart. *6:* 513, 1937.

18. IDEM AND KUBIE, L. S.: The translation of the cryptic automatic writing of one hypnotic subject by another in a trance-like dissociated state. Psychoanalyt. Quart. *9:* 51–63, 1940.

19. HARRIMAN, P. L.: The experimental production of some phenomena related to multiple personality. J. Abnorm. & Social Psychol. *37:* 244–55, 1942.

20. ERICKSON, M. H., AND KUBIE, L. S.: The permanent relief of an obsessional phobia by means of communications with an unsuspected dual personality. Psychoanalyt. Quart. *8:* 471–509, 1939.

21. LEWIS, N. D. C.: Graphic art productions in schizophrenia. A. Research Nerv. & Ment. Dis., Proc., *5:* 344–68, 1928.

22. FAIRBAIRN, W. R. D.: The ultimate basis of aesthetic experience. Brit. J. Psychol. *29:* 167–181, 1938.

23. IDEM: Prolegomena to a psychology of art. Brit. J. Psychol. *28:* 288–303, 1938.

24. PICKFORD, R. W.: Some interpretations of a painting called "Abstraction." Brit. J. M. Psychol. *18:* 219–49, 1938.

25. McINTOSH, J. R., AND PICKFORD, R. W.: Some clinical and artistic aspects of a child's drawings. Brit. J. M. Psychol. *19:* 342–62, 1943.

26. VERNONON, P. E.: The significance of the Rorschach test. Brit. J. M. Psychol. *15:* 199–217, 1935.

27. GRIFFITHS, R.: A study of imagination in early childhood and its function in mental development. London: Keegan Paul, 1935.

28. PFISTER, H. O.: Farbe und Bewegung in der Zeichnung Geisteskranker. Schweiz. Arch. f. Neurol. u. Psychiat. *34:* 325–65, 1934.

29. JUNG, C. G.: Modern man in search of a soul. Transl. by Dell, W. S., and Baynes, C. F. New York: Harcourt, 1934.

30. APPEL, K. E.: Drawings by children as aids to personality studies. Am. J. Orthopsychiat. *1:* 129–44, 1931.

31. LISS, E.: The graphic arts. Am. J. Orthopsychiat. *8:* 95–99, 1938.

32. HARMS, E.: The psychotherapeutical importance of the arts. Occup. Therapy *18:* 235–39, 1939.

33. IDEM: Child art as an aid in the diagnosis of juvenile neuroses. Am. J. Orthopsychiat. *11:* 191–209, 1941.

34. REITMAN, F.: Facial expression in schizophrenic drawings. J. Ment. Sc. *85:* 264–72, 1939.

35. BAYNES, H. G.: Mythology of the soul; a research into the unconscious from schizophrenic dreams and drawings. London: Baillière, Tindall & Cox, 1939.

36. MIRA, E.: Myokinetic psychodiagnosis: a new technique for exploring the conative trends of personality. Proc. Roy. Soc. Med. *33:* 9-30, 1940.

37. NAUMBURG, M.: The drawings of an adolescent girl suffering from conversion hysteria with amnesia. Psychiat. Quart. *18:* 197-224, 1944.

38. LEVY, J.: The use of art technique in treatment of children's behavior problems. J. Psycho-Asthenics *39:* 258, 1934.

39. BENDER, L.: Art and therapy in the mental disturbances of children. J. Nerv. & Ment. Dis., vol. 86, September, 1937.

40. CURRAN, F. J.: Art techniques for use in mental hospitals and correctional institutions. Ment. Hyg. *23:* 371-78, 1939.

41. DESPERT, J. L.: Technical approaches used in the study and treatment of emotional problems in children. Psychiat. Quart. *11:* 267-95, 1937.

42. ERICKSON, M. H., AND KUBIE, L. S.: The use of automatic drawing in the interpretation and relief of a state of acute obsessional depression. Psychoanalyt. Quart. *8:* 443-66, 1938.

43. GITELSON, M.: Clinical experience with play therapy. Am. J. Orthopsychiat. *8:* 466, 1938.

44. FREUD, A.: Introduction to the technique of child analysis. Washington, D. C.: Nerv. & Ment. Dis. Pub. Co., 1928.

45. KLEIN, M.: The psychoanalysis of children. New York: Norton, 1935.

46. CONN, J. H.: A psychiatric study of car sickness. Am. J. Orthopsychiat. *8:* 130-41, 1938.

47. LEVY, D.: Studies in sibling rivalry. Res. Monogr. 2, Am. Orthopsychiat. A., 1937.

48. SOLOMON, J.: Active play therapy. Am. J. Orthopsychiat. *8:* 479, 1938.

49. IDEM: Active play therapy: further experiences. Am. J. Orthopsychiat. *10:* 763-81, 1940.

50. ERICKSON, E. H.: Studies in the interpretation of play. Genetic Psychol. Monogr. *22:* 557-671, 1940.

51. BENDER, L., AND WOLTMANN, A.: The use of plastic material as a psychiatric approach to emotional problems in children. Am. J. Orthopsychiat. *8:* 283-99, 1937.

52. LEVY, D.: Release therapy. Am. J. Orthopsychiat. *9:* 713, 1939.

53. MORENO, J. L.: Inter-personal therapy and the psychopathology of inter-personal relations. Sociometry *1:* 9, 1937.

54. IDEM: Psychodramatic shock therapy. Sociometry *2:* 1-30, 1939.

55. IDEM: Psychodramatic treatment of psychosis. Ibid., vol. 3, no. 2.

56. IDEM: Mental catharsis and the psychodrama. Ibid., vol. 3, no. 3.

57. HERRIOTT, F., AND HOGAN, M.: Sociometry *4:* 168-76, 1941.

58. BERNHEIM, H.: J. f. Psychol. u. Neurol., Sonderabdruck, 1911, p. 477.

59. HADFIELD, J. A.: Functional nerve disease. Ed. by Crichton-Miller. London, 1920.

60. HORSLEY, J. S.: Narco-analysis. London: Oxford, 1943.

61. GRINKER, R. R.: Treatment of war neuroses. J.A.M.A. *126:* 142-45, 1944.

62. DESPERT, J. L., AND POTTER, H. W.: Technical approaches used in the study and treatment of emotional problems in children: pt. 1, The story, a form of directed phantasy. Psychiatric Quart. *10:* 619-38, 1936.

63. Young, P. C.: Hypnotic regression—fact or artefact? J. Abnorm. & Social Psychol. *35:* 273–78, 1940.

64. Hakebush, Blinkovski, and Foundillere: An attempt at a study of development of personality with the aid of hypnosis. Trud. Inst. psikhonevr., Kiev *2:* 236–72, 1930.

65. Platanow, K. I.: On the objective proof of the experimental personality age regression. J. Gen. Psychol. *9:* 190–209, 1933.

66. Dolin, A. O.: Objective investigations of the elements of individual experience by means of the method of experimental hypnosis. Arkh. biol. nauk. *36:* 28–52, 1934.

67. Erickson, M. H., and Kubie, L. S.: The successful treatment of a case of acute hysterical depression by a return under hypnosis to a critical phase of childhood. Psychoanalyt. Quart. *10:* 592, 1941.

68. Estabrooks, G. H.: Hypnotism. New York: Dutton, 1943, p. 65.

69. Wingfield, H. E.: An introduction to the study of hypnotism (ed. 2). London, Baillière, Tindall & Cox, 1920.

70. Taylor, W. S.: Behavior under hypnoanalysis and the mechanism of the neurosis. J. Abnorm. & Social Psychol. *18:* 107–24, 1923.

71. Karup, F.: Ztschr. f. d. ges. Neurol. u. Psychiat. *90:* 638, 1924.

72. Smith, G. M.: A phobia originating before the age of three cured with the aid of hypnotic recall. Charac. & Personal. *5:* 331–37, 1936–37.

73. Erickson, M. H.: Development of apparent unconsciousness during hypnotic reliving of a traumatic experience. Arch. Neurol. & Psychiat. *38:* 1282–88, 1937.

74. Idem: Hypnotic investigation of psychosomatic phenomena: A controlled experimental use of hypnotic regression in the therapy of an acquired food intolerance. Psychosom. Med. *5:* 67–70, 1943.

75. Fisher, C.: Hypnosis in treatment of neuroses due to war and to other causes. War Med. *4:* 505–76, 1943.

76. Kroger, W. S., and Freed, S. C.: Psychosomatic treatment of functional dysmenorrhea by hypnosis. Am. J. Obst. & Gynec. *46:* 817, 1943.

77. Erickson, M. H.: A study of an experimental neurosis hypnotically induced in a case of ejaculatio praecox. Brit. J. M. Psychol. *15:* 34–50, 1935.

78. Eisenbud, J.: Psychology of headache. Psychiatric Quart. *11:* 592–619, 1937.

79. Erickson, M. H.: The method employed to formulate a complex story for the induction of an experimental neurosis in a hypnotic subject. J. Gen. Psychol. *31:* 67–84, 1944.

# XVII

## THE RECALL OF BURIED MEMORIES

ONE OF the chief aims of hypnoanalysis is to bring to the surface unconscious impulses that influence behavior and compulsively drive the individual to actions of a maladaptive nature. In the uncovering process the patient is bound to remember important traumatic events and experiences that have occurred in the past. Some psychiatrists believe that enucleation of traumatic incidents in the developmental history of the individual is essential for cure, since repressed memories act as potent fountainheads of conflict. Others are prone to minimize the need of delving into the previous life of the subject. Therapy is organized around the patient's immediate interpersonal reactions, with the hope of providing him with a dynamic growth experience that will change his personality without a probing into his past.

Originally, Breuer and Freud[1] contended that repressed traumatic experiences and memories cause a strangulation of emotion, which, denied a motor outlet, drains itself off in the form of symptoms. The rational treatment, therefore, would consist of a recall of the repressed material, which would release the bound-up affect and permit its discharge into appropriate channels. Recognizing the hypermnesic effect of hypnosis, the trance was utilized to help the patient to recall the original traumatic scene. Freud wrote: "It was generally necessary to hypnotize the patient and reawaken the memory of that time in which the symptom first appeared, and we thus succeeded in exposing that connection in a most precise and convincing manner."[2]

Enthusiasm for this "carthartic" method was somewhat dampened by Freud's report that many repressed traumatic experiences presented as factual by his patients were fantastic reconstructions that had no basis in reality. However, Freud insisted that such "cover memories" were no less important than memories of real events, since the patient responded to them as though they were true.    Later on Freud emphasized that the essential task of analysis is to induce the patient to give up his infantile repressions "and to replace them by reactions of a sort that would correspond better to a mentally mature condition."   He continued to believe that this necessitated a recollection of traumatic experiences and the now forgotten emotions associated with them.   "What we are in search of," Freud wrote, "is a picture of the patient's forgotten years that shall be alike trustworthy and in all essential respects complete. . . . We all know that the person being analyzed has to be induced to remember something that has been experienced by him and repressed."[3]

Following the contributions of Breuer and Freud, a number of studies on early memories have been published.   Among the first were those reported by Hall,[4] Colegrove,[5] and Titchener.[6] Some studies have concerned themselves with the question of how far back the individual can remember aspects of his life. In a carefully controlled work, Dudycha and Dudycha[7] concluded that the average person can at best remember events dating back to the age of 3 years and 7 months.   However, 10 per cent of all memories recalled went back as far as the first year.   Henri and Henri[8] published an extraordinary report of personal memories of being nursed during the first year of life.   Early memories are accompanied by various emotions. In |order of frequency these are fear, joy, anger, wonder and curiosity, sorrow and disappointment, shame and guilt feelings.[7, 9, 10, 12]   Among the most fear-inspiring situations remembered are those involving animals, punishment, strange people, peculiar objects and situations, accidents, frightening statements made by adults, death and funerals, falling into water, fire, being alone, and storms.[11, 12]

Fear associated with early experiences undoubtedly encourages forgetting.   The individual must then maintain his amnesia for the event out of terror of being overwhelmed by fear in the recall of it.   Various inhibitory technics may be used to reinforce repression, and these may assume pathologic proportions, making up various neurotic syndromes.   The symptoms so developed function as long as there is need of repressing the traumatic experience. If the memory is recovered, and the individual masters the associated affect, the repressive devices are no longer necessary.

Sometimes spontaneous recovery of a memory and disappearance of inhibitory symptoms follows a dream that reminds the individual of the original forgotten event. Stewart[13] reports the case of a color-blind professional man of 55 who suddenly recovered his ability to see red and green in connection with a memory of an early childhood experience. Prior to the recovery of the memory, he had a dream of a battle scene in which a tank with crab claws was crawling around trenches amid bright flashes of light. As he associated to the dream, the tank changed into a lobster that he had seen in a fishing village before he was 3 years old. While bringing up this memory he showed signs of great fear. In the hypnotic state, associating to the dream, he remarked that he saw a dark green crab turn red as a man poured boiling water on it. Later on while awake the patient remembered that this fantasy represented a real experience that he had had as a child, and he recalled how frightened he had been at the time. On the way home from the session the traffic signals, previously gray, appeared to him in their true colors. This caused him to experience intense fear, but directly thereafter his color vision was restored to normal without accompaniment of excessive emotion.

The recall of early memories is expedited under psychoanalytic therapy and during hypnosis. Most incidents recovered under psychoanalysis and hypnosis are those remembered in part, with hazy details. Often the patient will remember an incident, but will have forgotten the emotional reaction to it, which is the most important part of the experience.

Hypnosis is especially valuable in the recapturing of memories of forgotten events. Stalnaker and Riddle[14] have shown that recall during hypnosis is 65 per cent greater than in the waking state. During the first world war, the use of hypnosis to produce recall of forgotten memories was revived by a number of psychiatrists, particularly by Brown,[15] Wingfield,[16] Hadfield,[17] and Karup.[18]

Brown, working with shell-shocked soldiers, discovered that when his patients were able to recover the memory of the traumatic war scene their symptoms disappeared. For instance, he cites the case of a gunner suffering from a tremor of the right hand dating from a time two years before when he was "blown up" at Ypres. There was no memory of this incident. The patient was hypnotized and it was suggested to him that he would relive the experience at Ypres. In response he became very emotional. He shouted, imagined shells exploding around him. Then he started to serve his gun by moving the handle with his right hand, but the hand began to shake violently. He was commanded to remember the incident when he woke up. The next morning he was able to shave himself for the first time in two years.

The fact that a traumatic experience in the recent past might be merely a recapitulation of a previous happening was recognized by Brown. In such an instance recall of the recent experience produced no improvement or cure. An air corps signaler was hit while taking refuge in a disused trench in France. On regaining consciousness he found that the trench seemed to be turned around at right angles with reference to where he expected it to be. After this everything seemed to be twisted at right angles in relation to its regular position. Hypnosis, and the suggestion that he relive his bombing experiences, did not remove the symptom. The suggestion given him under hypnosis that he would go through the first experience in which things seemed twisted at right angles caused him to shout "Hot coffee." He recalled that as a child of 3 he had gone into the kitchen and pulled the coffeepot from the table toward himself by yanking at the tablecloth. In so doing he upset the pot of coffee onto his left side. He knew no more until he awoke in bed, when he saw his father coming into the room, and he felt that the bed was standing the wrong way around. Recovery from his symptoms followed shortly afterward.

Wingfield has put much emphasis upon the need of bringing the patient back, during hypnosis, to an early period of his life. He reported the case of a woman of 32 who had a fear of meeting other people. The sight of persons approaching her was terrifying and was associated with pressure in the back of her head. Hypnosis with regression to very early childhood produced recollections of the terror that she experienced as a child whenever her face was washed. Her fear of people was related to the idea that anyone who approached her might wash her face. Pressure in the back of her head had been caused by the hand of a nurse holding her head during washing. When she remembered this she said: "Now I know why the pain is at the back of my nose. It is the soapsuds getting into my nostrils." As soon as she had recollected these experiences, her symptoms vanished, never to reappear. The therapy in this case comprised a total of ten hypnotic sessions.

Wingfield described another case, that of a girl of 14, who had for years suffered from constant vomiting, for which she had undergone considerable medicinal therapy without relief. During the single hypnotic session that resulted in a cure, she remembered that when she was about 3, she was compelled by her sister to look at a mummy that her father, an antiquarian, had placed in the house. The sight had nauseated her. Since that time she had dreamed of mummies and of being chased by a mummy. The vomiting spells always occurred on the days following such dreams. The recall of these memories banished further vomiting attacks.

A third case was that of a man who consulted Wingfield because of an indefinable dread of an impending calamity. The nature of this calamity was unknown to him, but the fear of it was so powerful that it threatened to drive him to suicide. He was unable to go into a deep somnambulistic state but had a facility for automatic writing with a planchette. Through this medium, in response to a query as to what frightened him, he wrote that he feared dying like his father. Further questioning revealed the fact that at 12 he had witnessed his father's sudden, agonizing death from pulmonary embolism.

Suggestions emphasizing the unlikelihood of his dying in this way caused his fear to disappear in less than three weeks.

The hypermnesic influence of hypnosis brought about by regression and reorientation of the patient at an earlier age level has been applied therapeutically by Hadfield,[17] Karup,[18] Taylor,[19] Smith,[20] and Erickson.[21, 22] Erickson and Kubie[23] have reported the case of a 23-year-old girl suffering from progressively increasing depression, inhibitions, and death wishes, in which regression was used with good results. Prior to her illness the patient and her closest friend had fallen in love with the same man. He had chosen to marry the other girl, and the patient seemed to have adjusted herself to this. A year after the marriage the young wife died of pneumonia. The patient showed natural grief. Thereafter she became interested in the widower. One evening she returned home sobbing, her dress stained with vomitus. She confided that she felt sick and disgusted. Love was hateful and filthy. She refused to elaborate any further, nor would she see the young man, stating that she would rather kill herself. The man himself revealed to the psychiatrist that on the evening on which she had become upset, he had proposed to her. She had seemed delighted, but as he leaned over to kiss her, she warded him off, then vomited and became "hysterical." She sobbed and screeched such words as "filthy," "nasty," and "degrading."

Because the patient refused therapy, a ruse had to be resorted to, in which she accompanied a friend to the physician's office with the idea that her friend was going to be treated by hypnosis. By means of an involved indirect technic the patient was inducted into a trance and then brought back to a period in her childhood that had been devoid of pain. She was slowly reoriented to the age period between 12 and 13, at which time, as she revealed, she had derived serious misconceptions about sex from her mother. These were corrected during hypnosis. The patient developed good understanding of her condition and married the man whose proposal had originally upset her.

In another case Erickson and Kubie[24] were able to cure a phobia in a patient through her remembering a traumatic event that had occurred when she was 3. The memories were recovered by means of automatic writing.

One of the most fascinating accounts of the recall of a forgotten traumatic occurrence has been written by Lindner,[25] who had a verbatim transcription of the patient's productions made by a stenographer concealed in an adjoining room. The patient, a criminal psychopath, brought back to memory the extremely frightening experience of seeing his parents in sexual intercourse when he was an infant. A hysterical eye symptom was alleviated to a marked degree by this recall, and a personality change was simultaneously effected.

The second world war has provided many examples of how repressed traumatic experiences can function to produce a general state of tension and anxiety, as well as outright psychosomatic symptoms. Hypnotic recall and revivification of such experiences has a markedly ameliorative influence on the patient's illness.[26] A recent innovation in treatment of war neuroses is the use of intravenous injections of barbiturates to induce a hypnotic-like state.[27, 28]

I have personally, on a number of occasions, witnessed the disappearance of certain symptoms following recall of repressed memories and experiences. One patient came to therapy because of a door-slamming compulsion. He had a need to make certain that all doors through which he passed were closed, and to his great annoyance he had to return several times to make sure that they were not open. Regression and reorientation to a 5 year level revealed an experience that apparently was the basis for this symptom. Shortly after the patient's fifth birthday, his younger brother smashed a toy that he especially treasured. He was filled with rage so intense that it caused him to tremble. Instead of attacking his brother, however, he turned around and fled to his room, slamming the door shut as if to separate himself from his sibling. Thereafter, whenever he felt hostile toward his brother, he found himself slamming doors, an act that soon became compulsive, as though it served to neutralize his hostility. The patient's recitation of the original experience was accompanied by strong emotional feelings, by anger, weeping, and pounding of his fists against the desk. He was enjoined to remember the original experience when he awakened. The door-slamming compulsion vanished from that day on.

In another case a woman had developed a peculiar mannerism to which she resigned herself with a martyred calm. She would touch with her right fingers the outer surface of the first left finger, then the second, third, and the fourth fingers, repeating this motion again and again. During hypnosis it was possible for her to understand how the mannerism had developed and why it persisted. When she was 14 years old, a girl friend told her the story of an Italian wedding at which an English priest had officiated. During the ceremony it was of course necessary for the bridegroom to put a wedding ring on the finger of the bride. However, both the bride and groom, because they could speak no English, were unable to understand what the priest meant by the word "ring." Finally, in order to indicate the meaning, the priest brought the thumb and first finger of his right hand together and inserted in this circle the first finger of his left hand, working the imaginary ring up and down the finger. The bride blushed, looked at the ground, and muttered as if in anticipation: "Tonight, tonight."

The point of the story was the confusion of the priest's gesture with the idea of sexual intercourse. The movement of the patient's right hand across to the fourth finger of her left hand signified a desire simultaneously for marriage and for sexual intercourse. Hypnotic regression furthermore revealed that as a child she had masturbated by use of the first finger of her left hand. A facial disfigurement, as well as an extremely puritanical upbringing, had contributed to create in her a conviction that she could never marry, and her mannerism served as a substitutive mode of sexual gratification.

Without question traumatic experiences can serve as foci around which the individual evolves symptoms. This is demonstrated in the following experiment. I suggested to a subject under hypnosis that he accept as true a fictitious event that was represented to him as an episode in his life that he had forgotten. The situation involved his walking into his apartment one night and being violently assaulted by a burglar. In the fray he was overpowered by his assailant, who smashed his skull with a lamp. After a period of unconsciousness he recovered and noticed that he had been robbed of most of his possessions. He also noticed that the lamp on the floor was similar in many respects to the one on my desk. As the event was recited to him, he appeared manifestly disturbed. After hypnosis, however, he had a complete amnesia for this experience.

One week later the subject, reporting for another hypnotic session, sat down and began talking about casual happenings. In the process his eyes seemed fascinated by the lamp on my desk. He complained of feeling warm and opened his collar. Then he confided that for some reason he felt tense and uneasy. The conversation covered many subjects, but from time to time he would ask pointed questions about the lamp on my desk, how long I had had it, where I had obtained it, and whether it had been broken recently. He remarked that several days ago he had gone to the barber shop for a haircut, after which he had experienced a violent headache. The headache had persisted for several days, but had disappeared that morning. It seemed to be returning, however. He brought his hands to his head, then stared at the lamp, remarking that he felt frightened for some vague reason. He asked whether anyone had ever broken into my house. He talked about crime. Finally he declared that there was something familiar about my lamp that he did not like.

The next day he had a spontaneous dream to the effect that he was riding in the back seat of a car. He was feeling ill. The driver handed him a bottle of medicine, but in the neck of the bottle there was a candle. He removed the candle and drank the medicine. It burned his throat as it went down. He was certain that it was poison. Then he noticed blood pouring from his head. The bottle with the candle in it was shaped very much like the lamp on my desk. The driver resembled me. The dream obviously dealt with the experimental conflict that I had induced. The patient was being driven (hypnotized) by me and was "being taken for a ride." He felt ill (had a need for therapy) and I gave him medicine (the hypnotic induction) that turned out to be poison (the experimental conflict that caused his bleeding head). Significantly, the subject for several weeks thereafter felt a strong resentment toward me, even though I explained the experiment to him in detail.

Intensely traumatic experiences can shock the organism and revive the mechanism of repression by which the vulnerable ego seeks to ward off threats to its intactness. There are no better examples of this than those seen in the war neuroses in which the battle scene is blotted out from the mind. In early childhood inimical happenings are particularly traumatic. One reason for this is that the child feels relatively helpless in a world the manifestations of which are a constant source of mystery to him. Relations between cause and effect are indeterminate, and he is menaced by many inscrutable events over which he has no control. One way of coping with childhood anxieties is to project them in the form of phobias. Another way of coping with anxiety that threatens to overwhelm the immature ego is through processes of repression and dissociation. These phobic and repressive defenses continue to function far beyond the period of childhood, and the ego reacts to the original traumatic events as if it still were too weak and too vulnerable to deal with them. This is the reason why many adults feel that there is something buried deep within themselves so terrifying that they cannot bear to bring it up.

An important question is whether early traumatic experiences are of universal occurrence. It is difficult to provide a complete answer to this question. All children undergo traumatic experiences of one sort or another during the period of socialization. A cataclysmic happening, however, can bring the effects of minor experiences to a head and can embody the accumulated emotions of all the inimical experiences.

By way of analogy, we might consider the situation of a worker who depends for his livelihood on the good graces of a harsh, unstable employer. A series of disturbing experiences may punctuate his daily routine; he may, for example, be exposed to unfair demands, abusive language, and critical scrutiny of his accomplishments. Each incident arouses feelings of insecurity and resentment, but is nevertheless tolerated because of the individual's need for a livelihood. On a special occasion, however, the worker may be falsely accused of a theft, and this one incident will suffice to provoke an anxiety attack or an episode of excitement. In itself the accusatory experience might not have the power to shatter the individual's reserve, but coming as it does against a sensitized background, it acts as a detonator of explosive forces that have hitherto been held in abeyance.

Traumatic experiences in early childhood similarly act upon a sensitized soil at a time when ego resources are relatively limited. Often these experiences when enucleated appear so insignificant that one could doubt their potency to evoke such disproportionate emotional responses. Yet if one considers that the traumatic experience is a condensation of a series of damaging events, and that it comes to stand symbolically for all of them, one may appreciate that it can be greatly over-valued.

As a general rule early traumatic experiences are of two types. In one type the events are so devastating or destructive that no child could be expected to cope with them. This occurs where the child is severely injured physically, or witnesses an incident so horrible that the experience takes away his security. The other type of traumatic experience can in no way be considered extraordinary, since it is part of the normal growth process. Growing up involves the capacity to abandon narcissistic and omnipotence strivings, to tolerate frustration, to channelize aggression into socially accepted outlets, to control sexual impulses, and to develop independence and self-assertiveness. In the course of his development the child is subjected to many frustrations that involve abandonment of selfish strivings for others that will bring him into cooperative relationships with the group. Most children are capable of handling such frustrations without too great difficulty. However, an insecure child, and particularly one who has been rejected and denied in legitimate demands for love and support, will be so overwhelmed by feelings of helplessness that he will be unable to tolerate frustration and to withstand traumatic experiences that are a usual component of growing up. Such an individual is likely to react catastrophically to relatively normal hardships such as are imposed on every child. In him such events as the birth of a sibling, the discovery of the genital difference between the sexes, the witnessing of parental intercourse, or exposure to any bloodshed and cruelty, may mobilize inordinate anxiety.

The insecure child may feel so threatened by rejection or punishment that he will find it necessary to repress such impulses as hostility toward his parents and siblings, masturbatory desires, sexual curiosities, and strivings for mastery, independence, and self-assertion. The repression of these impulses involves much experiment. The child for a long time defies the parents, even at the risk of incurring retaliatory punishment. Gradually, however, he may yield to parental discipline. Frequently repression occurs dramatically following a particularly traumatic incident that convinces the child that danger can be real. For instance, an insecure child who retains within himself certain rebellious tendencies may witness the flogging of a dog that has done something to offend its master. He may be frightened by this brutal treatment, and he may unconsciously identify himself with the animal, fearing that he will be injured in the same way if he persists in defying his parents. The result may be a phobia in regard to dogs, the dynamic purpose of which is to insulate him against his fear of his own aggressive impulses. The event comes to constitute a traumatic experience that may be repressed in an effort to avoid any reminder of pain. The dog phobia will nevertheless persist, aiding the repressive process.

Recovery of repressed traumatic experiences may ameliorate

or dissipate certain symptoms, especially those that serve the function of keeping these memories repressed. Many compulsions, obsessions, and conversion symptoms fall into this category. The most dramatic results occur in simple conditioned fears and in amnesias of recent origin (such as hysterical amnesias), trauma of the skull, and exposure to unbearable stresses such as occur during disasters and war. Where the personality is relatively intact, and the individual has, prior to the traumatic event, functioned satisfactorily in his interpersonal relationships, the recall of forgotten events may restore the previous status.

Sometimes it is necessary to probe deeper and deeper into the individual's unconscious to reach the most dynamic material. Morton Prince[29] cites the case of a woman of 40 who had developed a phobia in regard to church bells and steeples, the meaning and origin of which was unknown to her. Through the medium of automatic writing under hypnosis, Prince discovered that when she was 15 her mother had become seriously ill and had required an operation. In her anxiety over this, the patient had gone to church twice daily to pray for her mother's recovery. She lived in a hotel close to the church, whose chimes sounded at every quarter-hour. Unconsciously she associated the sound of the chimes with her mother's illness and possible death, and soon she could tolerate neither the ringing of bells nor the sight of a steeple. These intolerances were made more extreme by the death of her mother. Indeed, they were extended to all church towers and chimes. The recovery of this memory, however, did not remove the patient's phobia.

Since all persons undergo disturbing, sorrowful, or fearful experiences at some time during their lives, Prince asked himself why, in his patient, this particular incident had become so traumatic, and, more importantly, why it had continued to plague her for twenty-five years. He found the clue in a statement made by the patient, who, in associating to the episode of going to church, remarked that on one occasion she had failed to attend services. At the time she had told herself that if her mother should die it would be because of this omission.   When her mother actually did die, the patient believed that she herself, by her negligence, had brought about her mother's death.   Thus her fear of church towers and bells was caused, not so much by anguish over her mother's death as by the conviction that she was to blame for it.   Her real fear was of facing her own guilt, and her emotion was the reaction of self-reproach.   Why the unsophisticated belief of a child had not been modified by her maturity now became the central problem.

Further analysis revealed that when the patient was 13 years of age she had disobediently exposed herself in severely cold weather and had as a result contracted a condition diagnosed as "incipient phthisis."   On her physician's advice her mother took her to Europe for a "cure" and was forced to remain there with her for two years.   It was at the end of this time that her mother developed the illness that necessitated an operation.   The patient reasoned that had she not disobeyed her mother originally, she would not have contracted a chest ailment and would not have obliged her mother to supervise her abroad, thus isolating her from proper medical care, which, if it had been administered, might have prolonged her life. Prince wondered why the patient was so concerned with the idea that her disobedience had killed her mother.   Through tedious work he discovered a constant theme running through the patient's life.   She blamed herself for anything unfortunate that happened either to herself or to others, and she always credited such occurrences to her own shortcomings and omissions.   Her greatest fear was lest any bad occurrence should be her fault.   In tracing the origin of this trend, Prince discovered that the patient had been a lonely, unhappy child who thought herself ugly and disliked.   She reproached and depreciated herself at all times.

During therapy the death of one of the patient's relatives produced an exacerbation of her symptoms, in the form of anxiety, hysterical crying, insomnia, and twilight states. The patient confided that the relative had died under circumstances so tragic that she could not bring herself to talk about them. Under hypnosis she recovered a dream that indicated self-reproach for not having sent for a doctor in time. Again she was blaming herself for a death, and her refusal to talk about the circumstances was a means of avoiding her guilt feeling and self-reproach. Actually the relative's death had been accidental and could not have been foreseen nor prevented. When the patient was convinced of this, her sense of guilt over the incident vanished.

Thus the phobia in regard to bells and steeples served the patient as a means of avoiding a basic, deep-seated fear that she was somehow at fault and could through her own omissions and aggressive actions injure others. When Prince brought all these facts to her attention, there remained no doubt in her mind as to what was going on. Nevertheless, this insight did not cure her disorder. It took one and one-half years of further work to do this.

Under hypnosis the patient went into detail in uncovering childhood memories, and soon she demonstrated that there was considerable doubt that she had had "phthisis" at all. It developed that she had not been taken to a place of cure in Europe, but rather had sojourned in a number of gay cities. It became apparent that her mother had wanted to stay in Europe for her own pleasure and had used the pretext of her daughter's supposed ill health in order not to have to come home. The patient then realized dramatically that she had not been at fault in regard to her mother's remaining in Europe. When these facts were assimilated, her entire point of view changed and her phobia vanished.

Theoretically, all symptoms have a historical origin. It may be argued that were we capable of probing deeply enough into the past, of penetrating the myriad conditionings, of reviewing every stimulus that has invaded the senses and every idea that has entered the mind, of peering into all influences, pleasurable and inimical, that have impinged on the patient, we might be able to demonstrate to him how every one of his symptoms came into being. This task, however, is impossible, for even in the most extensive analysis one is able to recapture but a fragment of the total of life experiences. Even where we have not laid out for ourselves so ambitious a task, and are satisfied with reviewing the most important experiences in the patient's development, we find these so numerous as to defy recapitulation.

However, to indulge our imaginations, we may conjure up a situation permitting us to track down the origin of each of the patient's symptoms. Having done this, we should probably find, in most cases, that the symptoms themselves would not vanish. The expectation that recovery of traumatic experiences will invariably produce an amelioration or cure of the patient's neurosis is founded on a faulty theoretic premise. Even though the individual's character structure is in large measure developed from the bedrock of experiences and conditionings that have occurred in his past, and even though damage of his personality has resulted from untoward happenings in his early interpersonal relationships, it does not follow that a recall of these experiences will correct the existing condition.

As an analogy, we may consider a focus of infection that operates insidiously over a period of years. The original source of the individual's physical disability is this infective focus, but by the time it is discovered, it has already influenced other body structures. It may have produced kidney damage or acted as a stimulus of secondary foci of infection. The removal of the primary focus will leave the body still suffering from the effects of the original infection, and it will be essential to cure these secondary effects before the patient can be pronounced cured. A single catastrophic experience or a series of harmful experiences can likewise act as a focus engendering in an insecure person the conviction that the world is menacing and that the people in it are not to be trusted. The experience may influence him in forming decisive attitudes and reaction patterns. By the time he enters adulthood, however, his manner of dealing with his conflicts will have been structuralized into behavior so ingrained that the recall of the original trauma will have little effect upon his habitual responses. Therapy will involve tedious re-education and reconditioning long after the recall of the initial traumatic memories.

A patient was referred to me for hypnoanalysis because of a phobia regarding knives that had extended itself to all sharp objects. Regression during hypnosis to the time when he first developed a fear of knives revealed a traumatic infantile experience at the age of 4, when he first discovered the difference between the genital organs of boys and of girls. He was terrified on learning that a girl had a "slit" instead of a penis. On the same day he had, against his mother's order, attempted to slice bread with a knife and had cut his finger, which bled profusely. There was no question that these two traumatic experiences had linked up in his mind and that the fear of knives was associatively connected with a fear of castration. Recollection of these experiences, however, had little influence on his phobia.

Further investigation showed that he had throughout his childhood been victimized by a neurotic, domineering mother, who satisfied her own need for dominance by seeking to bring her son completely under her control. She rewarded compliance in him but punished any rebelliousness severely. He grew up with a crushed spirit and an underdeveloped self-esteem, convinced that he was helpless about doing things on his own initiative, and he had to smother his hostility for fear of incurring disapproval and punishment.

As he matured his relationships with people followed the pattern of overevaluating their capacities, yielding to their demands, and minimizing his own rights and abilities. He conformed slavishly to what was expected of him, yet he burned inwardly with indignation. His defiance was expressed in a negative, stubborn attitude toward the world at large. When he married, he entered into a submissive relationship to his wife, while his hostility reached a peak that threatened to overwhelm him. From time to time he lashed out at her furiously, always with aftermaths of guilt feeling and self-recrimination.

He chided himself for hating his spouse, yet he could not keep himself from thinking that he might stab her to death in a fit of anger. It was at this time that he developed his most extreme fear of knives, the sight of which caused him to experience anxiety. He had terror dreams of being cut up and mutilated, and finally asked to have his hands tied to the bed so that he might not murder his wife while he was asleep.

During therapy he developed the same kind of dependency relation to me. For a while I became the embodiment of wisdom and generosity, and his symptoms abated almost magically. He complied punctiliously with my most casual requests, as if these were edicts that he had to obey. At the same time his dreams indicated a mounting resentment. On one occasion, during hypnosis, he recalled a dream that he had had the previous night, in which he watched a child being bound down with thongs by powerful pirates. Suddenly he screeched at the top of his lungs that he was that child and I the pirate. He accused me of having dictatorial designs on him, of wanting to enslave him. Thereafter he had a return of murder fantasies and his fear of knives became extreme. At this point in the analysis he remembered how he had feared his mother, and he recalled nightmares about being attacked by tigers and by witches with long, pointed teeth.

It gradually became apparent to him that his helplessness and dependency were at the bottom of his neurosis, for in any situation he immediately minimized his own capacities and made himself subservient to others who, he believed, were stronger and more intelligent than he. His dependency, instead of making him secure, caused him to feel hostile. It was in the attempt to put down his hostility that he developed his fear of knives. This fear was complex and was associated with the equation of a knife to a penis. Attacking with a knife symbolized a sexual attack that could establish the fact of his virility and at the same time could destroy the person who enslaved him. The fear pertained also to a retaliatory attack, which he regarded unconsciously as castration. It was here that the early traumatic experience of cutting himself with a knife, at a time when he deduced that castration could be a real threat, was utilized in the formation of his symptom. Most significantly, he appreciated that while the early experience was important, prior events and conditionings had sensitized him to it.

During hypnoanalysis the individual may recover the memory of a forgotten traumatic happening and through this recall he may experience considerable abreaction. He may even liberate himself from certain associated symptoms. However, the essential difficulty will probably remain. The patient will still be insecure. The circumstances that sensitized him to the original traumatic scene will continue to plague him in his daily interpersonal relationships. The essential task in therapy, therefore, would seem to lie not only in recovery of early traumatic experiences, but also in ascertaining the reasons why the experiences became so catastrophic as to necessitate repression.

Many years ago Breuer and Freud[1] commented on the limitations of the cathartic method and dismissed the idea that once strangulated affect was liberated, the patient could invariably proceed to a more mature adjustment. Adler,[30] Jung,[31] and Stekel[32] were similarly convinced of the sterility of the approach that concentrated entirely on the uprooting of infantile memories. Rado[33] has remarked that the retracing of early fantasies and memories is discouraging, for they resemble the heads of the fabled hydra, any of which, when cut off, was replaced by two others. Kubie,[34] Hendrick,[35] and Horney[36] have also questioned the value of the rediscovery of early memories. Without question such an enucleation brings about abreaction, but the curative values of abreaction, as Schilder and Kauders[37] and Bibring[38] have pointed out, are doubtful. Children constantly abreact in play without its influencing their deeper problems. Patients in manic states abreact violently all the time. Abreaction lessens tension, but does not neutralize the focus that continues to generate it.

One may therefore regard with incredulity certain prevailing reports of "short cut" psychoanalyses in which, through hypnotic recall of a single traumatic experience, the neurosis is said to have been brought completely to a halt. Such reports tend to revive the early enthusiasm of Breuer regarding the curative value of catharsis. Through hypnosis, and particularly during regression, the patient may regain a remarkable picture of childhood, but this in itself is not sufficient to change the neurotic superstructure.

The concern with the patient's past emphasized by Breuer and Freud marked a tremendous advance in psychiatric thought, but it had certain unfortunate effects upon some of their contemporaries. It started a trend that minimized the influence of the actual life situation. In the effort to discover the traumatic roots of the individual's disorder, as well as the infantile patterns that were the prototypes of the neurotic structure, the immediate interpersonal reactions were relegated to a secondary position. The patient often recovered many interesting and crucial experiences, but, to the dismay of the analyst, he continued to cling to his neurotic attitudes to life.

It must always be remembered that a neurosis is not a fortuitous happening dependent exclusively upon early traumatic events. It is rather a form of adaptation to and defense against a world that is regarded by the child and later by the adult as potentially hostile and menacing. Current reaction patterns and attitudes, while derived from past experiences, are not an automatic repetition of infantile modes in an adult setting. They are forms of behavior motivated by a desire to escape helplessness, to gratify vital needs, and to allay tension, anxiety, and hostility. The individual reacts to the present with characterologic machinery that is rooted in his past experiences, but his present day problems are the immediate result of conflicts deriving from demands, fears, and resentments that arise from his current interpersonal relationships.

Overemphasis on the part played by the past may produce certain unfortunate effects during therapy. The patient may utilize his inimical childhood experiences as a justification for his neurosis and for resistance to change. His analysis may bog down in a compulsive historical review of his past, a definite cleavage developing to isolate it from the present. Some patients who have familiarized themselves with early theories of psychoanalysis are led to believe that awareness of their past conditioning will magically dissolve their neuroses and reintegrate them in their dealings with the world. Consequently the analysis becomes a stereotyped search for an illusory pot of gold at the end of a mnemonic rainbow.

While an exclusive preoccupation with the past imposes definite limitations in therapy, one must not be won over to the fallacious notion that the historical experience can be entirely eliminated. Tendencies in this direction are apparent in certain present day therapeutic methods, and foster a concentration on relatively superficial material. There is in this approach a dichotomization of the personality, as though the individual had two parts—an important present, and a past that has little bearing upon his prevailing attitudes, values, and goals. Palliative psychotherapeutic methods operate on this assumption.

Knowledge of the historical roots of a disorder is in itself not sufficient to produce cure, but it is of tremendous value in establishing the continuity in the individual's life from infancy to adulthood. It points to the weakness and sensitivity of the ego at the time of a particularly traumatic experience. It demonstrates how repetitive happenings in the present are a reflection of the same problems that existed in childhood. Of particular therapeutic benefit is the ability of the ego to withstand the emotions liberated by the recall of early traumatic incidents. The neurotic individual often has little respect for himself because he has to yield to his fear of the past. To be able to master this fear and to tolerate the anxiety that previously caused him to cringe has an enhancing effect on ego strength.

Patients under hypnosis show a remarkable ability to bring up material that they do not remember consciously. Theoretically the ego of the patient is strengthened during hypnosis by a fusion with that of the hypnotist.[39] It is then capable of tolerating the implications of the repressed material.

The ability to recall traumatic events and experiences during hypnosis has an important effect upon the resistances. Expression of such material graphically, vocally, or by action of a deep trend appears to facilitate its recall by the waking ego, particularly when the expression under hypnosis is accompanied by emotion. The consideration of the material in the hypnotic state has an important effect on the later capacity of the individual to withstand the anxiety associated with its conscious recall. It is as though the ego realizes that it was not destroyed by remembering the forgotten events and therefore can tolerate recalling the repressed circumstances again. Even though the patient may be enjoined to forget the material that he has brought up during hypnosis, posthypnotic amnesia does not always prevent it from breaking through into waking life. The patient then will present a forgotten memory, or comment upon hitherto unconscious attitudes or feelings with the surprise that accompanies original recall.

For example, a woman with an arm contracture, which became more marked in the presence of her husband, remembered during hypnotic regression an incident in which her elder brother had forced her to have sexual intercourse with him. Thereafter she feared and hated him. In the presence of boys and men she was outwardly shy and retiring. She had never loved the man she married and was sexually frigid with him. She regarded sexual relations as distasteful and as an imposition upon her. Her rage against her brother and her husband was most vehement during hypnosis, but posthypnotically there was a complete amnesia. Several days later she confided that she had become aware of something interesting that might be responsible for her arm contracture. While she was in the kitchen preparing a meal, she heard her husband's footsteps as he approached the door. She noticed that, without her volition, her hand reached for a bread knife and then was withdrawn by an exaggerated contracture of the arm. She remarked that she was then aware of a strong feeling of hate toward her husband, which brought to her mind how closely he resembled her brother in appearance. Never before had she realized that she hated her husband even slightly.

Thereupon she recounted her early experience with her brother as a spontaneous remembering of something that she had forgotten. Her awareness of how she resented her brother, and her realization that feelings of self-devaluation were being stirred up in her present relationship with her husband, expedited the therapeutic work.

The recall of early traumatic experiences is a dramatic means by which a patient can become aware of unconscious feelings and attitudes. Early in therapy the analyst is able to detect certain trends by observing the patient's behavior toward himself and by interpretation of the former's dreams and free associations. A presentation of the analyst's impressions to the patient is at first of little value, since the latter's unconscious impulses are so laden with anxiety that he is likely to dismiss the interpretations as fanciful or farfetched. The patient's realization that he has been repressing traumatic memories, and his understanding of how and why he had to repress them and their symbolic significance, provide a means of penetration into inner conflicts and defenses.

What technic to utilize for uprooting buried memories depends entirely upon the strength of the patient's repressions and upon his particular aptitudes in relation to the different forms of hypnoanalytic procedure. There are some patients who do remarkably well with simple suggestions directing them to remember forgotten events. A directive such as follows may suffice: "When I put my hand on your forehead you will relive the experience that you had at the time when you first developed your symptom." Specific symptoms or time periods may be mentioned. Direct recall may be reinforced by indirect technics when the patient develops an obdurate resistance. He may be told that at the count of five there will appear in his mind a number that represents the number of letters in the name of the thing he has forgotten. Then he is urged to name whatever letter comes to his mind at the count to five; as the count is repeated, the patient names in turn the letters composing in jumbled order the forgotten word. One patient recalled an event that occurred when he was little. He had seen his father do something "horrible" in the bathroom, but he could not remember what his father had done. Asked to utter a number at the count of five, he unhesitatingly replied: "Five." Then he named the five letters *n*, *e*, *s*, *i*, *p*. As he tried to rearrange these into a word, he hesitated. He appeared to be upset when he revealed that the word was "penis." He then remembered that he had witnessed his father masturbating.

In some cases regression and revivification are needed to enable the patient to recall certain traumatic experiences. The latter method is especially efficacious in the treatment of hysterical amnesias and amnesias associated with accidents or war. In getting the patient to bridge gaps in memory, it is best to start with the last thing he remembers and to work steadily through the forgotten events piecemeal. As a general rule, the more recent the amnesia, the easier it will be to remove it. Not all forgotten events are available to memory in their original form. Here the defensive resistances prevent direct elicitation. Indirect devices such as automatic writing, dreams, dramatics, drawing, and crystal gazing may be successful where other methods fail.

Often a method inducing delayed recall is excellent in helping the patient to prepare himself so that he will be able to tolerate the implications of the remembered events or impulses. In deep hypnosis, the patient is told that he will recall events or fragments of events and that he will reconstruct these finally into a coherent experience, when he feels strong enough of himself to do so. Suggestions that the patient dream regarding significant events in his life and remember those things that are actually true are often helpful. Under a technic such as this the ego has sufficient time to fortify itself to bear the material as it comes up. The ability to recall traumatic memories in the waking state indicates that resistances have been broken down to some extent.

The technic of delayed recall is illustrated in a paper by Livingood.[40] A college student, handicapped from the age of 7 on by stuttering that was still annoying and embarrassing to him, was treated for several months by hypnosis, for periods of from ten to twenty-five minutes three times weekly. Post-hypnotic suggestions were given directing him to have confidence in meeting people and to participate in class discussions. Probings to discover the cause of his stuttering yielded no results. Suggestions were made at each session that on a certain day in May he would recall the reason for his stuttering and that he would be able to explain in detail the incidents that had led to development of the condition.

On the stipulated day in May the patient was hypnotized and reminded that he was to recall the cause of his stuttering. Without hesitation he disclosed that when he was 7 his mother had gone on a visit, leaving him in the care of his father. The latter had been so preoccupied with his business that the boy had been compelled to look after himself. While playing with other boys in the neighborhood, he fell from a wagon in which he was playing, ripping his new cowboy outfit. He was so terrified about spoiling his suit that upon his return home he hid it in the attic. At lunch he tried to explain to his father what had happened, but the latter impatiently refused to listen. Stuttering developed in the boy from that day on and became more and more of a problem. The recollection of his childhood accident had a marked effect upon the patient. Gradually his stuttering lessened, and finally it ceased.

When it is impossible to induce hypnosis sufficiently deep for the direct recall of forgotten memories, one may sometimes obtain excellent results through automatic writing. This procedure may uncover repressed experiences even though the patient does not go beyond a medium trance. Automatic writing may also be used as a means of inducing the patient to set the exact time at which he will reveal a repressed memory. When other methods fail, a light barbiturate narcosis sometimes will bring success. The "narco-analysis" should be repeated until the reconstructed memory is complete.[28]

The relationship with the physician acts as an important tool in the recall of buried memories. In the transference the patient will be stirred up emotionally and will experience attitudes and impulses that have a potent effect in reviving mnemonic prototypes of what he is undergoing in the present. The transference will frequently touch off patterns that cannot be uprooted by any other method. The following is an instance. While one patient was in a trance, I received a telephone call from another patient; in greeting her I happened to mention her name. The hypnotized patient was at the time engaged in automatic writing, and as I talked, he started writing about his resentment toward an elder sister with whom he had fought as a child. In the process he recalled an early experience that had a traumatic effect on him.

At the beginning of therapy the patient should not be told that buried memories that he cannot recall are causing all of his present difficulties. Such a statement will divert him from the main therapeutic task. Furthermore, if he gets an idea that he is expected to remember things he has forgotten, he is very likely to conjure up memories that are partly or wholly incorrect and to present these to the analyst in an effort to please him. Hull[41] has emphasized that patients fabricate more easily under hypnosis than in the waking state, and he advises caution in accepting memories, particularly those related to early infancy. When the patient brings up memories without feeling coerced, they are more likely to be valid.

During hypnoanalysis the patient may for some reason be incapable of remembering any traumatic experiences. This failure need not necessarily block the therapeutic process, and important changes in the dynamic structure of the personality can occur without such mnemonic recovery. It is quite possible that interpretation of the transference and the establishing of an unambivalent relationship with the analyst may enable the individual to function on better terms with himself and with others. It is possible also that he may give up infantile defenses without recalling specific traumatic memories or experiences that have necessitated them.

On the other hand, analysis of the transference, and interpretation of dreams, free associations, and material elicited through hypnoanalytic procedures, may in themselves fail to produce change. The patient seems to be stymied by a stubborn amnesia relating to vast segments of his childhood or later life. The inability to recall vital situations of the past may represent resistance to accepting the implications of certain drives and defenses as they reveal themselves in the relationship with the analyst.

In most patients stubborn resistance to recall constitutes a means of avoiding anxiety of a sort that initially fostered the repression. In some it serves to retain the secondary gain inherent in the neurosis. The amnesia affecting recall may be so stubborn that even the deepest hypnosis and regression will fail to bring the repressed material to the surface.

Erickson[42] reports an interesting case that illustrates how stubborn certain amnesias can be. A young girl at some past period had presented a Christmas gift to a male friend, but try as hard as she could, she was unable to remember what it was. She rationalized her amnesia on the ground that she probably had later considered the gift not entirely suitable. Free association was tried, but the patient was consciously unwilling to talk about anything of a personal nature. During a deep trance she did manage to associate freely. However, when asked to recall the gift or to talk about it, she became tense and refused to talk. Posthypnotic suggestions to the effect that she remember it suddenly upon awakening met with no better success, nor did automatic writing prove to be of any help. Posthypnotic suggestions directing her to write automatically the letters in the name of the object, in mixed order, produced an excess of consonants. In working further with the subject, she wrote, with considerable emotion, "The painted cigarette box on the library table." No associations to this writing were obtainable, nor was she able to recognize the gift from this. She thought that she might have wanted to give the man a cigarette case but was certain that she had changed her mind. In crystal gazing she saw herself walking with a wrapped package, but each time she tried to catch sight of the gift, the image would elude her. Finally she was asked, during hypnosis, to dream about the gift, but again she could not verbally identify it in her dreams. When enjoined to dream that night of seeing the gift, she recalled dreaming, but did not remember the dream content. At this point she suddenly recalled having in her strongbox a letter from the man, thanking her for the present, and she remembered that in the letter he mentioned receiving the gift. She forced herself to read the letter, discovering from it that the object was a box of paints. The reason why she had forgotten the nature of the gift was that she wished to avoid thinking about a choice she had had to make between two suitors, one of whom happened to be the recipient of the gift.

Amnesia will be resorted to where repression of a memory serves an important defensive purpose. The defense is often in the nature of shielding the individual from awareness of inwardly prohibited impulses. For instance, if an elder child is in rivalry with a younger sibling, and, if he realizes that every time he teases or hurts this sibling he evokes the disapproval and rage of his parents, his hostility may eventually arouse anxiety and guilt feelings. If he is exposed to a particularly violent scene following an expression of hostility to his sibling, his terror may be the determining factor in his repression of hostile impulses. The traumatic scene itself will be part of the forgotten material, since recall of the traumatic event will bring his hostility and its catastrophic consequences to his attention.

A child of 11 who feared loud noises and aggressive forms of play was referred to me because of self-mutilating tendencies manifested in tearing and picking his skin. He was a very polite, ingratiating youngster, who almost compulsively confessed to loving his parents and his younger brother. His aggression against the latter, however, was very evident in play therapy and in the content of his dreams. Consciously he had no awareness of his hostility. Hypnosis, with regression and reorientation to a 6 year age level, revealed that he was greatly irritated by his brother and his parents. In play therapy during regression he recalled fighting with his brother and being punished for this by his father. He remembered an incident in which, after he had given his brother a black eye, his father had taken him out in the back yard and in his presence had bashed in the head of a cat with a rock. There was a post-hypnotic amnesia in relation to this memory. An interview with the father elicited the remark that he had killed the cat to frighten his son. The tactic was successful, for the boy almost immediately responded by being nice to his brother. Shortly thereafter, however, he started to develop his symptoms. Various technics were used to get the patient to remember this incident consciously, with no success whatsoever.

Where a traumatic experience is thus related to a prohibited impulse, it may become repressed and partake of the prohibition pertaining to the impulse. Because it serves the purpose of holding in check forbidden strivings, attempts to enucleate it may end in failure. It may be recalled during hypnosis and then forgotten in the waking state, despite commands to remember it. This phenomenon is identical with what happens in hysterical fugues, somnambulisms, automatic writing, or trance speaking, for which there is usually a complete amnesia.

Where the patient fails to recover damaging traumatic experiences, although one is reasonably certain that such experiences have occurred, it is probable that the amnesia protects the ego from anxiety that it would be unable to handle if the experience were recalled. Here the reasonable ego is still too weak to absorb anxiety and to reconsider the experience in the light of the present. The ability to recall early traumatic experiences and to re-evaluate them requires considerable ego strength. In a number of conditions, particularly conversion hysteria and anxiety hysteria, sufficient ego intactness remains to make possible the handling of fears and conflicts associated with an inimical past. In the latter case the recovery of repressed experiences may suffice to produce a cure of specific symptoms.

In other conditions, however, such as character disorders and psychoses, the ego is so vulnerable and weak that it cannot tolerate either the repressed memories or their implications.

Hypnoanalysis may fail to break down the resistances to recall, or the traumatic experience may be remembered with a peculiar dissociation of its emotional content. The forgotten event may be remembered as a vague experience without emotional implication—what is recalled being enough to satisfy the rational demands of the individual. The damaging emotions and the significance of the experience are, however, repressed. Sometimes, after hypnotic recall, the incident may be recounted in the waking state as a fantasy, the patient fortifying himself with the belief that the event never really did happen. The individual may thus react to devastating childhood events or fantasies in an apathetic manner, as if they were somehow detached from himself. There is no abreactive process. It is almost as though the patient by his recall seeks to fulfill a dual purpose—first, to retain the good will of the analyst by remembering things, and, second, to hold on to his resistance by repressing the emotional meaning of the trau-matic event.

Failure to uncover buried memories may have its origin in the fact that therapy has not built up the ego to such a point that it can absorb the anxiety liberated by the recall of early experiences.

In some cases certain subterfuges employed during hypnosis may possibly outwit the patient sufficiently to cause him to bring up unconscious memories. One may question the efficacy of such a process, for it is axiomatic that a premature confrontation of the ego with unconscious material that it cannot handle merely serves to create anxiety and to enhance resistance.

Hypnotic recovery of deep inner conflicts and memories need not have this effect, providing the recall is adroitly handled. Instead of battering down the patient's resistances by forcing him to remember, it is best to give him freedom to recall and to know those things when he feels himself able to handle them. During deep hypnosis the patient may be told that there are certain experiences and memories that are quite important and that because of their painful nature they have been forgotten.  He may be told that it is not necessary to remember all details of such memories at once, but that he will be able to reveal and to tolerate isolated fragments of these memories and experiences as time goes on.  Under the influence of such suggestions the patient will bring out those elements of a forgotten memory or experience that he can tolerate, and as he becomes stronger and realizes that he is not injured by the recall, more and more material will be available to him, until finally he can reconstruct it into a consistent whole.

Piecemeal recovery of a forgotten memory or conflict may be furthered by employing such technics as dream induction, automatic writing, regression and revivification, dramatics, drawing, and crystal gazing.  The evidence elicited by all these procedures will make the meaning of the experience increasingly clear to the patient.  As a general rule the implications of the memory will not be accepted by the patient until he himself realizes its importance and presents the interpretation as a product of his own efforts and conviction.  Reconstructing the patient's memory for him in the waking state from material uncovered during hypnosis may rob the recall of its therapeutic effect.

One of the best methods of handling material that is recalled in hypnosis is to instruct the patient to forget what has occurred until he feels that he is convinced of the truth of the memory and understands it thoroughly.  It may be weeks before the patient is capable of bringing up snatches of the material spontaneously, with corresponding insight.  Even where the patient recalls in the waking state memories recovered in a recent hypnotic session, he will usually be unable to integrate their meaning until his ego has had time to prepare itself.

A valuable technic in getting the patient to clarify details of a forgotten experience is that of having him witness it in recurrence through crystal and mirror gazing.  These procedures are often accompanied by much emotion and may solidify in the patient's mind the significance of a forgotten event.

## REFERENCES

1. BREUER, J., AND FREUD, S.: Studies in hysteria. Washington, D. C.: Nerv. & Ment. Dis. Pub. Co., 1936.
2. FREUD, S.: Selected papers on hysteria and other psychoneuroses. Washington, D. C.: Nerv. & Ment. Dis. Pub. Co., 1912.
3. IDEM: Constructions in analysis. Internat. J. Psycho-Analysis *19:* 378, 1938.
4. HALL, G. S.: Note on early memories. Ped. Sem. *6:* 485–512, 1899.
5. COLEGROVE, F. W.: Individual memories. Am. J. Psychol. *10:* 228–55, 1899.
6. TITCHENER, E. B.: Early memories. Am. J. Psychol. *11:* 435–36, 1900.
7. DUDYCHA, G. J., AND DUDYCHA, M. M.: Some factors and characteristics of childhood memories. Child Development *4:* 265–78, 1933.
8. HENRI, V., AND HENRI, C.: Enquête sur les premiers souvenirs de l'enfance. Ann. psychol. *3:* 184–98, 1896.
9. MILES, C.: A study of individual psychology. Am. J. Psychol. *6:* 534–58, 1893.
10. OPENDAL, L. E.: Analysis of the earliest memory of a delinquent. Internat. J. Indiv. Psychol. *1:* 52–58, 1935.
11. DUDYCHA, G. J., AND DUDYCHA, M. M.: Adolescents' memories of preschool experiences. J. Genet. Psychol. *42:* 468–80, 1933.
12. JERSILD, A. T., AND HOLMES, F. B.: Children's fears. Child Development Monogr. 20. New York Bureau of Publications, Teachers College, Columbia Univ., 1935.
13. STEWART, K. R.: Color blindness and tone deafness restored to health during psychotherapeutic treatment using dream analysis. J. Nerv. & Ment. Dis. *93:* 716–18, 1941.
14. STALNAKER, J. M., AND RIDDLE, E. E.: The effect of hypnosis on long delayed recall. J. Gen. Psychol. *6:* 429–40, 1932.
15. BROWN, W.: Psychology and psychotherapy. London: Arnold, 1921, pp. 21–22.
16. WINGFIELD, H. E.: An introduction to the study of hypnotism. Ed. 2. London: Baillière, Tindall & Cox, 1920.
17. HADFIELD, J. A.: Functional nerve disease. Ed. by Crichton-Miller. London, 1920.
18. KARUP, F.: Ztschr. f. d. ges. Neurol. u. Psychiat. *90:* 638, 1924.
19. TAYLOR, W. S.: Behavior under hypnoanalysis, and the mechanism of the neurosis. J. Abnorm. & Social Psychol. *18:* 107–24, 1923.
20. SMITH, G. M.: A phobia originating before the age of three cured with the aid of hypnotic recall. Charac. & Personal. *5:* 331–37, 1936–37.
21. ERICKSON, M. H.: Development of apparent unconsciousness during hypnotic reliving of a traumatic experience. Arch. Neurol. & Psychiat. *38:* 1282–88, 1937.
22. IDEM: Hypnotic investigation of psychosomatic phenomena: A controlled experimental use of hypnotic regression in the therapy of an acquired food intolerance. Psychosom. Med. *5:* 67–70, 1943.
23. IDEM AND KUBIE, L. S.: The successful treatment of a case of acute hysterical depression by a return under hypnosis to a critical phase of childhood. Psychoanalyt. Quart. *10:* 583–9, 1941.
24. IDEM: The permanent relief of an obsessional phobia by means of communication with an unsuspected dual personality. Psychoanalyt. Quart. *8:* 471–509, 1939.

25. LINDNER, R. M.: Rebel without a cause: The hypnoanalysis of a criminal psychopath.  New York: Grune & Stratton, 1944.

26. FISHER, C.: Hypnosis in treatment of neuroses due to war and to other causes.  War Med. *4:* 565–76, 1943.

27. GRINKER, R. R.: Treatment of war neuroses.  J. A. M. A. *126:* 142–45, 1944.

28. HORSLEY, J. S.: Narco-analysis.  London: Oxford, 1943.

29. PRINCE, M.: Clinical and experimental studies in personality.  Cambridge: Sci-Art, 1929, pp. 33–47.

30. ADLER, A.: The practice and theory of individual psychology.  New York: Harcourt, 1924.

31. JUNG, C. G.: Contributions to analytical psychology.  Transl. by Baynes, H. G., and Baynes, C. F.  London, 1928.

32. STEKEL, W.: Technique of analytical psychotherapy.  New York: Norton, 1940.

33. RADO, S.: Developments in the psychoanalytic conception and treatment of the neuroses.  Psychoanalyt. Quart. *8:* 428, 1939.

34. KUBIE, L. S.: Discussion on brief psychotherapy.  In Proceedings of the Brief Psychotherapy Council, Chicago: Inst. Psychoanal., 1942, p. 25.

35. HENRICK, I.: Instinct and the ego during infancy.  Psychoanalyt. Quart. *11:* 40, 1942.

36. HORNEY, K.: New ways in psychoanalysis.  New York: Norton, 1939.

37. SCHILDER, P., AND KAUDERS, O.: Hypnosis.  Transl. by S. Rothenberg.  New York: Nerv. & Ment. Dis. Pub. Co., 1927.

38. BIBRING, E.: Therapeutic results of psychoanalysis.  Internat. J. Psycho-Analysis *18:* 178, 1937.

39. KUBIE, L. S., AND MARGOLIN, S.: The process of hypnotism and the nature of the hypnotic state.  Am. J. Psychiat. *100:* 619, 1944.

40. LIVINGOOD, F. G.: Hypnosis as an aid to adjustment.  J. Gen. Psychol. *12:* 203–7, 1941.

41. HULL, C. L.: Hypnosis and suggestibility.  New York: Appleton-Century, 1933, p. 115.

42. ERICKSON, M. H.: The investigation of a specific amnesia.  Brit. J. Med. Psychol. *13:* 143, 1933.

# XVIII

## HYPNOSIS AND THE TRANSFERENCE

IN THOSE hypnoanalytic technics that are concerned solely with the recovery of repressed memories and experiences, the manipulation of the transference as a therapeutic tool is likely to be minimized, reliance being placed on the more or less omnipotent role played by the hypnotist in the psychic life of the patient. In certain hysterical conditions excellent results are obtained in this way, but in the majority of cases such a technic fails to uproot unconscious memories and trends, or else brings them to the surface with the result of only a minor change in the patient's neurotic tendencies.

When hypnosis is used for purposes of symptom removal and as an adjunct to palliative psychotherapy, it is usually inexpedient to analyze the transference. Such a move may destroy the foundations of faith on which success in treatment depends. Indeed, one strives to perpetuate in the the patient the illusion of the therapist's protective powers, no effort being made to peer into the irrational sources of the dependency striving. The hope is to adjust the individual to his less disturbing unconscious impulses, to increase repression of the more destructive ones, to expand existing assets, and to encourage compensations and sublimations, so that the patient may have as happy an existence as is possible with his liabilities. Such therapeutic objectives, though superficial, yield results that are helpful to many patients and permit them to gain a modicum of security and self-esteem.

The hypnotic induction in itself often produces a remarkable abatement of symptoms. This improvement is achieved through a relationship with the hypnotist that is akin to the irrational positive transference manifested during certain phases of psychoanalysis. The relationship has a number of unique values. It facilitates the recovery of unconscious material in an extraordinarily short period of time. It cloaks the hypnotist in a mantle of authority that instills faith in his ideas and communications. The hypnotic transference may in this way be used as a tool helping to pry the patient away from his disabling conscience and to modify disturbing unconscious drives and conflicts.

Unfortunately, ego strength that results from the hypnotic transference per se must be held suspect. Based upon fusion relation with an overvalued magical personage, and imbedded in faith, it is wholly artificial. Once the hypnotic treatments are interrupted, the self is robbed of its illusory power. The more healthy standards introjected through identification with the hypnotist are displaced again by the habitual values and goals, which reanimate the neurosis.

The reason why many hypnotic cures are temporary is that they are wrought in the medium of an irrational dependency relationship. The acceptance of interpretations on the basis of faith is really a perpetuation of the neurotic process, since it is motivated chiefly by a need to please the hypnotist. Where symptoms disappear early in hypnosis, there is always room for the suspicion that the patient has found in the hypnotic situation a means of satisfying compulsive drives that encourage symptom formation. Thus a dependent individual who is frustrated in everyday life by failure to find a magical parent figure, may conceive of the trance situation as affording a parent-child relationship that promises to fulfill all his needs. His depression, rage, and psychosomatic symptoms will then vanish almost miraculously for as long as this illusion is fostered.

In creating an authoritarian relationship, hypnosis is prone to generate explosive forces that can undermine therapeutic gains. The subordinate position into which the patient plunges himself in order to achieve his objectives is incompatible with normal self-esteem. It tends to destroy assertiveness, to sap independence, and to vitiate activity and creative self-fulfillment. It may render the patient progressively more helpless—an automaton who lives without a self and is secure and confident only in so far as the omniscient hypnotist can shield him from harm and gratify his needs for him. Unable to achieve his goals through his own efforts, the patient may become increasingly hostile and finally may interrupt the therapy with a return of his neurotic symptoms.

It might be presupposed from this that avoidance of the dependency relationship is mandatory in hypnoanalysis. However, it is neither possible nor desirable to avoid dependency at the start. The motive for being hypnotizable is probably rooted in a dependency need that is partially retained by every person as a residual element of his childhood adjustment. Dependency may be the only type of relatedness that the neurotic person can enter into at the beginning. Normal independence and self-sufficiency may be beyond his ken or may be anathema to him. In his relationship with the hypnotist, the patient may automatically assume the role of a helpless child not only during hypnosis, but also posthypnotically. This need not halt rational therapy, for the hypnotic relationship, properly employed, may be used as means of hastening ego growth. In the normal developmental process the helpless child is dependent upon the parent for love and support, and evolves an independent self largely as a result of gratifying experiences with the parent. The hypnotic relationship, even though rooted in dependency, may similarly be utilized to encourage self-development.

The manipulation of the hypnotic interpersonal relationship will call for a tremendous amount of activity on the part of the analyst. The effect of this activity on the transference may understandably be questioned. Traditionally the analyst plays a passive role. The purpose of this passivity is twofold. First, it presents the patient with a mirror, in the person of the analyst, onto which he can project his inner impulses. By avoiding provocative situations, the analyst can better aid the patient in gaining insight into the fact that he is reacting in the transference with strivings rooted in past experiences. The second purpose of passivity in the analyst is to stimulate the patient into taking an active part in his own development. This is of utmost importance in the development of assertiveness and self-confidence. That in many cases passivity on the part of the analyst does not achieve these objectives, is only too well known. Indeed, there is a growing realization that the analysis and working through of resistance necessitates an active rather than a passive approach.

Activity on the part of the analyst, however, has certain definite dangers. It may be a constructive br destructive instrument, in accordance with how it is used. Employed unwisely, it can definitely traumatize the patient, and instead of curing the neurosis, may serve merely to mobilize further resistance.

One of the most common misuses of activity is to assault the patient with interpretations that he is not prepared to accept. When this occurs, the patient, instead of believing that he comes to certain deductions and conclusions by himself, feels rather that these are forced on him. Because hypnoanalysis releases so much significant material, the analyst may be tempted into bombarding the patient with premature insights. This can stimulate tremendous resentment. Adequate preparation is necessary before the ego is capable of digesting the liberated material.

Another way in which activity can be mishandled in hypnoanalysis is through improper employment of dramatic technics. Certain active analytic procedures are oriented around the theory that it is essential for the patient to live through, in a relation with the analyst, emotional incidents identical in type to the early traumatic experiences with the parents. Only by a dramatization of his problems, it is alleged, can the patient be prodded out of the rigid and circumscribed patterns through which he avoids coming to grips with his repressed impulses. To aid in the acting-out of the repressed motives, there is created a therapeutic relationship that is charged with tension. The struggle that ensues between patient and analyst, and its outcome, are said to be extremely important in breaking down the neurosis.

As the patient experiences hostility toward the analyst, and as he finds that the dreaded counterhostility does not arise, he feels more and more capable of tolerating the anxiety inevitable to the release of his unconscious drives. He finds that he can bear frustration and discomfort and that such tolerance is rewarded by many positive gains. Finally, he becomes sufficiently strong to unleash his deepest unconscious drives and feelings, which previously he has never dared to express. Projecting these onto the person of the analyst, the patient, in his relation with the latter, lives through infantile traumatic emotional events that duplicate the experiences initially responsible for his disorder. The latter phase of the analytic situation is said to occur only when the patient has developed sufficient trust and confidence in the analyst to feel that he is protected against the consequences of his inner destructive impulses. Hypnoanalysis is particularly suited to this type of approach, for tension can be stimulated by the creation of experimental conflicts. Dramatic situations may be suggested in which the patient lives through in microcosm his genetic development and re-experiences frustrations and deprivations resembling the original traumas.

One may rightfully criticize this technic on the ground that the patient actually experiences frustration as a direct result of the therapeutic situation. His hostility may thus be justified. The tension and hostility that are built up may eventually become great enough to break through the resistances, with an acting out of impulses. However, impulsive breaking through is usually no more effective than ordinary cathartic abreactions. Benefit is obtained only when the resistances are removed permanently and when the impulses that have been held in suspension are expressed in a rational manner.

A misdirected positive use of activity is also possible. On the basis of the assumption that neurosis has its core in the individual's conviction that he is unloved and unlovable, one may wonder whether positive demonstrations of affection may not lead the patient to feel that he is liked and accepted. During hypnosis the analyst can easily convey to the patient by word and deed his own warmth of feeling. However, logical as this course of action may seem, it is usually ineffective because of the patient's ambivalence. Love is so fused with hate that he may completely misinterpret affectionate gestures. He may be incapable of accepting love or he may view any positive demonstrations with suspicion and subsequent rage. The neurotic's demands for love are usually so insatiable that they cannot be fulfilled in reality. All attempts on the part of the analyst to do so will end in failure. This does not mean that the analyst must be cold and withdrawn, for this will reinforce the patient's feelings of rejection.

Induction of hypnosis often automatically creates in the patient an attitude attributing infallibility to the analyst. The question may be asked whether or not the analyst should undermine this notion. Should he adopt an attitude of infallibility and wisdom, or should he come into the relationship with the patient as just another being with human weaknesses, whose opinions and interpretations may be wrong? Theoretically at least, admission on the part of the analyst that he is not infallible, impressing the patient with the fact that the analyst can make mistakes in judgment and that he may have personal weaknesses, would help to undermine the patient's ideas as to the strength and omniscience embodied in authority. It would help to uproot his notions that a person representing authority cannot be wrong, or, when wrong, will not admit that he errs. The experience of a new authority who admits the possibility of his being fallible would make it easier for the patient to re-evaluate his own notions of authority. On the other hand, it could reasonably be feared that an attitude like this might affect the hypnotic situation, which seems to be rooted in an overevaluation of the capacities and powers of the hypnotist.

During the early phases of hypnoanalysis it is unwise to try to alter the patient's fantasies of the magic that he expects from the hypnotic process. To do so will cause him to respond with resistance and will block the emergence of other transference reactions. What he seems to want unconsciously from the relationship is to be able to depend upon a kind and omnipotent person. To inject interpretations at this stage may create panic or such contempt for the analyst as to interfere with achieving the proper trance depth and with the interpersonal relationship itself. However, as the hypnotic process continues, it is essential to attempt an alteration of the patient's concept of authority, by permitting him freedom in working through his problems and in accepting or rejecting the analyst's interpretations. During hypnosis the patient's conviction that he can utilize his own reasoning powers and judgment helps to undermine his feeling that he must at all times obey and that authority is always right. This experience leads to acceptance of the analyst as a real person and cuts deeply into the patient's compulsive need to comply with the dictates of his conscience when he knows that this is not what he honestly wants to do.

One of the most important innovations in hypnoanalysis is the employment of a technic in hypnosis that calls for great activity on the part of the patient. Instead of being allowed to remain cataleptically inert, the patient is encouraged to express himself freely and spontaneously in both motor and ideational spheres. Many patients are very much surprised when they discover that they are able to move about without restraint. The release from the traditional hypnotic paralysis enables the patient to dramatize his inner problems with extraordinary facility. This use of the hypnotic state gradually brings the the patient around to the realization that he must work out his own problems, face his difficulties, and assume responsibility for his actions. Aside from fostering insight into unconscious motivations and resistances, it has a most significant effect in resolving the dependency strivings aroused by hypnosis.

Once deep trance states are achieved, it is necessary to impress the patient with the fact that while the analyst will help him with his problems, the burden of responsibility in working them out will be on himself. Guidance and suggestion must be reduced to a minimum. The analyst must avoid playing the role of referee and must bring the patient to a realization that he must make spontaneous efforts.

Hypnosis allows a most intimate form of interpersonal relationship and will mobilize attitudes and strivings that lie dormant in the unconscious. These are projected onto the analyst in the same manner as during psychoanalytic therapy. The analysis of such transference reactions is as important in hypnoanalysis as in psychoanalysis, and without it therapy becomes stagnant so far as dynamic processes are concerned.

One of the chief problems in psychotherapy is how to cajole the ego into yielding up its defenses. Within himself the individual feels too weak to face his inner conflicts. Unconscious material is invested with such danger that the very acknowledgment of it is more than the patient can bear. Anxieties rooted in past conditionings are particularly terrifying. Early fears possess a fantastic quality, since they are usually unmodified by later experiences. It is as if anxiety has been split off and were functioning outside the domain of the ego. In therapy it is essential to reunite the conscious ego with the repressed material and the attendant anxiety, but resistance constantly hampers this process. A most important element in supporting resistance is the hypertrophied set of standards and prohibitions that have developed out of the individual's relationship with early authorities. These standards oppose not only the recovery of the unconscious material but also the expression of the most legitimate biologic and social needs. Caught between the tyrannical conscience on the one side and devastating fears and impulses on the other, the ego is never permitted to attain a stature sufficient to allow the individual to assert himself or to express his basic needs and demands. The ego is forced to adopt pathogenic methods of dealing with impulses, since it cannot mediate them through rational solution.

Analytic therapy is characterized by a strengthening of the ego to such a point that it can recognize the disparity between what is felt and what is actually true, that it can divest the present of unconscious fears and injuries related to the past, that it can dissociate present relationships with people from attitudes rooted in early interpersonal experiences and conditionings. Ego growth is nurtured chiefly through a gratifying relationship with the analyst. The exact mechanism that produces change is not entirely clear. However, the analyst-patient relationship acts to upset the balance of power between the patient's ego, his conscience, and his repressed inner drives. The ultimate result is an expansion of the ego and a replacement of the tyrannical conscience by a more tolerant superego patterned around an identification with the analyst.

The interpersonal relationship nevertheless is disturbing, for it lights up all the individual's fears of injury, his inordinate demands and expectations, his forbidden erotic and hostile desires. As a result the relationship is bound to be unstable, and anything that the analyst says or does, anything that he fails to do, will be reacted to neurotically. Despite the passivity and tolerance of the analyst, the patient will keep subjecting him to tests in order to justify a returning to his old way of life. If the analyst is too expressive in his tolerance of the patient's deepest impulses, the patient will look upon therapy as a seduction for which he will pay grievously later on. On the other hand, a repressive attitude will play in with the patient's residual concept of authority as restrictive and therefore warranting his customary evasions and chicaneries. At all times, the patient exploits his usual characterologic defenses to prevent relating himself too intimately to the analyst. He has been hurt so frequently in his previous interpersonal relationships that he is convinced that danger lurks in the present one.

In the ordinary psychoanalytic technic, many months are spent in dealing with transference resistances that ward off the threat of close relation and the acknowledgment of certain irrational feelings toward the analyst. The latter dissolves these façades by direct attack. For the first time the patient permits himself to feel, to talk, and to act without restraint. This freedom is encouraged by the analyst's attitude, which neither condones nor condemns destructive impulses. The patient senses that the analyst is benevolently neutral toward his impulses and that he will not retaliate with counterhostility in response to aggression. Under the circumstances the patient develops reactions to the analyst that are of a unique quality, drawing upon emotions and strivings that he has hitherto repressed. The release of these submerged drives may be extremely distressing to the patient. Because they conflict so greatly with his standards, he is bound to reject them as wholly fantastic or to justify them with rationalizations. There is an almost psychotic quality in projected inner feelings and attitudes, and the patient will fight desperately to vindicate himself by presenting imagined or actual happenings that shift the blame onto the analyst.

While the analyst respects the patient's feelings, he does not masochistically submit to them. He is not disturbed by the patient's hostile or sexual impulses. He understands that the latter seeks unqualified approval, love, and support, yet he is not wooed into yielding these unconditionally. He realizes that the patient must face the facts of life and must live in a world that does not give him unqualified love, in spite of his demands and expectations. The patient's ability to gain insight into the fact that his feelings do not arise out of a real situation, but are the product of characterologic attitudes that have originated in past experiences and conditionings, is an important factor in his development. Such insight teaches him that his symptoms do not occur fortuitously, but on the contrary are brought about as a result of his own inner dynamic activity. This creates a basis—divested of irrational elements —for a more friendly cooperative relationship with the analyst. This new relationship serves as a nucleus for the rebuilding of attitudes toward people in general. For the first time the patient feels that he is accepted as he is, and he shies away from using his customary camouflages to ingratiate himself or to subdue, dominate, or overwhelm others. Eventually, he reconditions himself in his relation to human beings and remolds his attitudes toward himself.

Hypnosis can act as a catalyst to the analytic process by facilitating an identification of the patient with the analyst and by bringing out during the trance, in almost pure culture, the deepest strivings and attitudes. The very nature of the hypnotic process induces feelings of closeness not possible under other technics. The patient will react to this closeness with all his characterologic defensive machinery and resistances, and this will precipitate fears, resentments, expectations, demands, and the full range of interpersonal attitudes, which are component parts of the character structure.

To classify transference reactions as either positive or negative is an oversimplification of the existing dynamics. Each patient establishes a different relationship with the analyst, dependent upon his particular conditionings and experiences. The mechanisms that the patient employs to maintain the relationship and to protect himself from the anxiety that is produced by it are unique to himself. Analysis of these mechanisms will yield important clues to the unconscious factors in his illness, aiding materially in diagnosis and prognosis.

The question may be asked whether an analysis of the hypnotic interpersonal relationship may not remove the very motivations that make hypnosis possible. In the vast majority of cases it has no such effect. Usually a peculiar dissociation exists: the patient continues to react to hypnosis, going into trance states while at the same time manifesting irrational hostile feelings toward the analyst. Rarely does resistance developing out of analysis of the transference become so intense that the patient refuses to enter hypnosis. What happens is that the patient reacts to the analyst as if he were a composite of different personages, some hostile, others loving and accepting.

Hypnoanalysis will bring out reactions that are in direct response to the trance state, to the interpersonal experience with the analyst, and to the recovered unconscious material. The hypnotic relationship differs to a degree from an ordinary relationship, in that the patient yields his defenses and exposes himself to interpersonal closeness such as he can avoid in everyday life. The protective barriers that serve to keep people at a distance are to some extent breached, and the patient may, as a result, experience an onrush of disturbing emotions. These will ordinarily come out during the period of hypnotic training and will reveal themselves in spontaneous dreams and free associations.

Where the interpersonal relationship is not analyzed, as in the various palliative psychotherapeutic technics, the patient experiences such impulses but represses them promptly. The unique feeling of security that he experiences in the trance causes him to regard the physician as a benevolent authority who seeks to help him. He will then try to relegate fearful or hating attitudes to unconscious oblivion. Most often he continues to maintain certain defenses against the physician, particularly in regard to establishing too close a relationship.

In hypnoanalysis the attitudes of the patient are subjected to minute study. Irrational reactions during induction are often evanescent, and the analyst may miss important material unless he is extremely alert. One patient during the first trance suddenly became flushed, and her breathing became rapid, as if she were experiencing anxiety. In recounting her feelings after the trance she could remember only a pleasurable state of relaxation. At the end of the second week, during which she was trained to enter somnambulistic states, she was regressed and gradually reoriented to the time of the first session. In going through the routine induction, she again experienced the tense, flushed state, which she was enjoined to talk about under hypnosis. Excitedly she exlaimed: "I can't stand this. I am nauseated. I don't know why I feel the way I do. This feeling comes over me whenever I am with certain men. I never am able to talk about it. When you get close to me I get the same feeling. As long as I can keep men at a distance I don't feel this, but let them get intimate, and I get a feeling of revulsion. When I was little I was disgusted with father. Mother never loved him. The kind of life they led was detached. His attitude toward me was not right. I loathed him. I fancied he was not sexually happy with my mother, and I imagined with horror that he might sexually attack me. At night I would be frightened when he came to say goodnight. I felt he would grab my genitals. I held on to my blankets until I was sure he was downstairs. When you came close I visualized you pulling up my skirt."

The analysis of early reactions to hypnosis can yield vital clues to the character structure. One man, who on the surface appeared resourceful and independent, had a spontaneous dream following the first hypnotic session, in which he saw himself lying in a lush tropical garden surrounded by obliging natives who walked in and out of the scene bearing platters of food. This seemed to indicate that he conceived of hypnosis as a state in which he would be automatically nourished and supported. When subsequently this pleasant condition was not forthcoming, he reacted with a series of dreams in which he found himself pursued by hostile, devouring animals and powerful cannibals. The dreams apparently represented a projection of hostility aroused within himself by the realization that his dependency needs were not being gratified. As he entered more actively into the hypnotic situation, he had dreams in which he fed himself. These were coordinate with a marked increase of assertiveness and productivity.

Another patient, who had detached himself from most personal contacts, came to look forward to hypnosis as a remarkably enjoyable experience. When, after the training period, he was asked to dream about his feelings about hypnosis, he had the following dream, which indicated an ambivalent attitude.

Me and my brother Willie were down in the cellar of my house. We were putting wood aside. I came across a tin can that was rusted and hard to open. I opened it and found one hundred thousand dollars. A tag was on the money—"Finders keepers." Me and my brother bought clothes, a wonderful apartment, a fine collection of phonograph records. I was the happiest person in the world. Then a fire started in the house and I was trapped. I couldn't find my way out. I ran over to the window, got out on a fire escape finally, but it was torn away from the house, and I crashed down.

From his associations it appeared that although he valued hypnosis, there was something very dangerous and destructive about it. Curious as to what might be his attitude toward me at this time, I suggested to him that he dream of what he thought of me. In the ensuing dream he saw himself in the presence of a number of doctors, who were attempting to convince him that he would get well if he exposed himself to "mesmerism." He told the doctors that mesmerism could never help him and that a person who was sick should receive medicinal injections. "I told them this treatment would have no effect," he recounted. "It sounded foolish. It didn't sound sensible. It might work on other patients but not on me."

Shortly thereafter his resistance to hypnosis came to the surface in a more intense form, and at each session he would announce that this was his last. The pleasures he derived from hypnosis, however, were sufficient to counteract his resistance, because he did not discontinue therapy. Spontaneous and hypnotically induced dreams repeated the same theme. The following is an example.

I was sailing on the Caribbean Sea on the "S.S. Normandie." I was on my way to Cuba. I was riding. I was exalted in my feelings, emotions, and expectations. I felt very wonderful. Then all the other people disembarked from the ship chatting gaily, but as I walked down I saw no people. I was desolate. I walked into a jungle and got deeper and deeper. There were tigers and lions, ghastly beasts. Then a tiger came in my direction. I climbed on top of a coconut tree and stayed there until I was so tired and exhausted I couldn't hold on any longer. Then I fell and woke up and realized it was a dream.

His association to this was that there was always some intense fear about doing what he really wanted to do. Pleasure always was followed by pain. As he talked, his hand, in which I had placed a pencil, wrote automatically: "I am thinking of my sister Louise."

Upon being questioned under hypnosis, he revealed that he had withdrawn almost entirely from people after his sister became engaged. After her marriage he scarcely dared to look at her or her husband, and he experienced rage and frustration whenever he tried to talk to either of them. It was then suggested to him that when he came out of hypnosis he would have a feeling very similar to his feeling about his sister. Upon awakening he remarked: "I smell the odor of insulin. Is there any insulin around here? I know the odor of insulin because my mother used to get insulin injections. She had big blotches on her feet, and the doctor advised her to get injections. She went to drug stores and got insulin, and she wanted my father to give her injections. I objected about father injecting her and thought a doctor should do this."

The next day he had the following spontaneous dream:

I was dreaming I was twelve years old, playing, going out in the park, singing, on the swings, rollicking in the vacant lots. I was in a happy mood, never worried. Then as I was lying in bed I felt the real sensation of some-body grabbing me. I hollered and screamed and then awoke. It must have been a ghost.

A pencil was put in his hand while he was under hypnosis, and he was questioned as to who the ghost in the dream might be. His hand wrote: "You think that I am half female and male. You are watching me, and I can't stand the blushing nerve." A suggestion was then made that he would work on his problems and that he would begin to understand better and better the factors that had caused his illness.

In response to this suggestion the patient had the following dream:

My father told me to deliver a message to his friend in New York City. I dressed and found myself in New York. I was walking and couldn't find the place. I looked at the envelope, but noted no name or address. I put the letter in my pocket and, instead of searching around, noticed the skyscrapers and the scenery. Then I was looking at Bloomingdale's windows at a beautiful display of pictures. A well dressed man came up and suspected me of being a holdup man who wanted to rob the place. I protested that I was not, that I had merely come to deliver a letter, and I told him the story. He said I was a liar. He put me in shackles and took me to court. The judge didn't believe my story, and he sentenced me to twenty-five years in prison. When I got there I found that I liked it. The cell was comfortable, but I had the sensation of being dead. Then I woke up.

In the light of his associations, the dream appeared to express among other things resistance about regarding hypnosis as a medium of therapy rather than of pleasure. In the dream I appeared in the guise of his father, who assigned him to the task of delivering a message. This seemed to stand for the fact that I was insistent that he do a certain amount of work in hypnosis. Instead, he wanted to use hypnosis only for the pleasures he got out of the trance. This was indicated in the dream by his putting the message into his pocket and embarking on a pleasure jaunt. He was punished for this, but significantly the punishment was not too uncomfortable.

The interpretation of the dream during hypnosis stimulated another dream in him immediately before awakening:

I was on a lonely road, all alone, walking. It was a beautiful summer day—birds, butterflies, and bees. A house was in the distance, and I wondered how it looked inside. It was exciting to wonder. The doors were locked and the windows bolted. I couldn't get in. I saw a box which brought me to the level of the windows. I tried hard and got the bolts out. I noticed the windows were broken, and that I could get into the house. It was a beautiful house, but dusty. The furniture was costly and rich, and everywhere there was bric-a-brac. I was looking all over the place. I opened a door of a room to look in, and there I saw the devil. He smiled at me. I got scared and shut the door. I tried to get out of the window. The windows were bolted up and I couldn't get out. I was frantic. Then my sister Louise appeared. She said: "You are going to stay here and like it. You will be here all alone."

I said: "I don't want to be in this house all alone. I do not want to be here."

She claimed we had been living in this house for years and that there was no devil there. She then disappeared like an apparition. Then I noticed a bureau and opened it up. I saw some keys. I tried several of them in the door. Then I found one that opened the door, but as soon as I opened the door my feet were so stiff and rigid as if they were nailed to the floor. I could not move. I dropped to the floor and as I dropped the house exploded. Then I found myself struggling in water, drowning, but my brother Charles came into the water and helped me out.

The patient remarked that he was not sure whether it was really Charles, because his brother resembled me. The dream was interpreted as that there was some hope that he could be helped out of his dilemma.

In response to the suggestion that he dream that night about his current feelings and attitudes toward hypnosis, he dreamed as follows:

I was on a fishing trip in a boat, catching fish. It was on Sunday morning, a beautiful day. The sun was shining and I was lucky. Every time I cast the bait in the water I caught a fish, until the basket was filled with fish. I was happy and wanted to show the fish to my family, but when I came home I opened the basket and instead of fish there were human skulls. My folks screamed and ran out. I grabbed a broom, and the skulls came creeping out of the basket like crabs. I tried to crush them, but they would leap at me like frogs, hit me in the eye, and I would fall down. They were all over the kitchen, facing me. I took an iron and hit one of the skulls, and as soon as I did, it changed into a lion who grabbed me and held me in his mouth. I started screaming and woke up.

For several days thereafter the patient had a strong resistance about talking freely while in hypnosis. He presented at the same time vague fears about sex. When I encouraged him to dream about his sexual feelings under hypnosis, he had two dreams. The first was as follows:

Some people were at my house Sunday morning. They were smoking. I smoked too. We had a conversation. Tom said: "Come to New York with me for a good time. We will go to a show."
We then entered a motion picture house, but instead it turned out to be a night club. There was a lot of merriment, noise, and dancing. Boys were half intoxicated, milling around. They all had girls and I had a girl too. We started to leave with our girls. The girl I was with told me to take her home and gave me the key to her room. We entered her house and there we found six girls in the room with revolvers. They all had their guns pointed at me, ready to shoot me. One of the girls then ordered me to take off my clothes and to have intercourse with my girl. I went to bed with her, and one of the girls put the lights out. I had intercourse all night and when morning came I was frightened by what I had done. What would my folks think? I had seen a knife lying around, and I slit my stomach, and I could see the blood flow out.

The second dream was as follows:

I was walking along one morning in the factory district. I saw a beautiful girl approaching me. She asked if I would mind talking to her. I walked around with her and she started flirting with me. Then she asked me if I ever had intercourse with a woman, and I blushed and laughed and said that I

never did.  She invited me to come to her home.  She asked a lot of men to
have intercourse with her, but they refused and I consented.  We had intercourse.  I woke up in the morning.  I felt strange.  I looked in bed, and
there was the girl dead.  I was frightened.  I heard a sharp rap on the door.
I opened the window and started to climb' the fire escape.  I tripped and
was killed instantly.

The next day the patient remarked that he was very much
afraid of me.  He did not know the reason for this.  When
asked under hypnosis to dream about these feelings toward
me, he responded with the following:

I was walking along Central Park.  A man invited me to his house.  I
refused because I considered that this man had filthy things in his mind.  I
was seated in Central Park and I thought of going home.  My mother said:
"I was so worried about you when I thought you wouldn't come home."
Father and mother were in bed, and I read in bed.

His association to this was that the man in the dream must
have had homosexual ideas and must have wanted to use him
as a woman.

Regression was then resorted to, and through the use of
dramatics and play therapy, it was determined that during
boyhood the patient had masturbated excessively, with
fantasies of being in bed with his mother.  Much fear was
associated with the recovery of these fantasies.  He also
recalled the experience of noticing his father nude in the
bathroom and of observing the latter's tremendous erect penis.
He immediately felt a peculiar sensation in his rectum, and he
believed with fear that he might be torn apart by his father.
The patient then revealed that he had feared hypnosis because
he regarded it as a seduction, and that after the second session
he had experienced a rectal sensation of being penetrated.
This was one of the reasons why he wanted to resist hypnosis;
yet he regarded it as something too vital and pleasurable to
abandon.  Gradually the patient's conflict about hypnosis
became apparent to him consciously, and he was able to
appreciate how it reflected fears and attitudes that had nothing
to do with the therapeutic situation.

Reactions to hypnosis are conditioned by the way in which

the trance fits into the subject's particular scheme of life. If he is compulsively dependent, he will attempt to utilize hypnosis to gratify this need. He may seek from hypnosis complete support and fulfillment of all expressed and unexpressed wishes, as well as a magical abatement of his symptoms. If he has an impulse to detach himself from people, he may regard the hypnotic relationship as potentially dangerous, and he may then resist hypnosis, or he may strive to protect himself from fancied hurt by submitting himself masochistically. If he has a power drive he may try to gain strength through ingratiation and identification with the omnipotent analyst. One of the most common reactions is a feeling of having been forced to yield to hypnosis. The associated hostility may be expressed openly or internalized in depressive or psychosomatic manifestations. Strong submissive tendencies of which the patient is in terror may create a desire to dominate the situation by refusing to cooperate and by active resistance. Some patients feel free of anxiety only when they are fighting, and they may strive to make the treatment hour a battle, attacking the analyst and his attitudes or interpretations. There may be fears of being dominated, overpowered, attacked, seduced, and mutilated. At the same time there may be a deep wish to be attacked or seduced.

The patient will bring into the hypnoanalytic relationship his usual attitudes and defenses—his evasions, his disguises, and the rationalizations by which he wards off too intimate an interpersonal contact. However, in hypnosis the patient is, despite himself, precipitously plunged into an intimate relationship at the start, and even though his resistances continue to function, he will experience many impulses and strivings of which he was unaware. One might speculate that this premature stimulation of forbidden feelings could drive the patient from therapy. However, there are certain features of the trance state that tend to neutralize his anxiety.

The induction of hypnosis is usually accompanied by a state of pleasant relaxation and by a unique sense of security, which is in part based on the notion that the hypnotist is a powerful

protective ally who will dissipate the patient's suffering and
secure for him gratifications that he has hitherto failed to gain
through his own efforts. During hypnosis the patient often
senses a love and acceptance such as the small child feels in
the arms of the parent. The trance is furthermore a relaxing
and pleasurable experience in itself. For this reason many
patients resent awakening from hypnosis and voice the|desire
to have it continue indefinitely. Physiologic changes occur, in
the form of a dulling of perception of strong sensory stimuli,
slowing of the pulse rate and respirations, and lowering of
blood pressure.[1-3] Changes in the tonicity of the skeletal
musculature are also found, as Jacobson[4] has shown. These
effects place the hypnotist in a special category, as one who
provides the patient with certain pleasures. Indeed, hypnosis
may become one interpersonal experience that is not too
menacing. Schizophrenics, for instance, may find in it values
that neutralize their fears of humanity as completely hostile
and rejecting. The hypnotic relationship may act as a bridge
that leads the patient from his isolation to a contact with
another human being without the intense suffering that
characterizes his habitual interpersonal relationships.

The transference relation that develops between analyst and
patient during hypnoanalysis need not be entirely irrational.
There is always present in the patient a healthy tendril of
desire—however deeply buried it may be—to relate himself
congenially and productively to another person. This impulse
must be nurtured. The therapeutic experience eventually will
make it possible for the patient to understand the fantastic
nature of his deeper strivings and to realize how these have
evolved from immature judgments in childhood. During
hypnoanalysis he will become aware of forces within himself
that have prevented him from gratifying basic biologic and
social needs in himself, from expressing righteous resentment,
from functioning in an active, assertive, and creative manner
without having to detach himself, to lean on others, or to
overpower and dominate them. The therapeutic relationship
is one that can contribute to self-development and to a re-

orientation to the world. This does not mean that the patient will not exploit his customary façades, for he will bring into the relationship the fears, demands, and expectations that he typically uses from day to day.

The relationship that develops between analyst and patient is thus tremendously complex and consists of a number of elements that operate simultaneously. Many of these are mutually contradictory. The patient immediately reacts to the analyst and to the hypnotic process with his whole range of neurotic interpersonal attitudes; these may stem from strivings for dependency, submission, detachment, suspicion, power and dominance. He is at least partly conscious of certain trends that determine his sense of values and constitute for him the sole means of adjustment. Many of these bolster his security and self-esteem; nevertheless, he suppresses them because he realizes that they get him into difficulties with people. In hypnoanalysis he may attempt to disguise some of his character drives, either because they conflict with contradictory drives or because he feels that the analyst may reject him because of them.

Another set of impulses appearing in hypnoanalysis is motivated by more or less normal needs for affection, companionship, and cooperation. In most cases the only way in which the patient can come to appreciate that he possesses unconscious impulses is through actually becoming aware of them in action in the transference. Inasmuch as his habitual relationships outside the hypnoanalytic situation have always been disguised by defenses, he never before has been conscious of his deepest motivations. The hypnotic relationship has the potentiality of bringing the patient closer to a human being than he has ever been before. Invariably his resistances begin to operate, in order to keep his most painful feelings and strivings barricaded within himself. The mere relaxation of his interpersonal vigilance will mobilize defenses and put him on his guard. The analyst, instead of playing up to these defenses, attacks them by interpretation. Eventually the patient is no longer capable of warding off the analyst, and he begins to feel toward him impulses of a type similar to those that originally necessitated the repressive process. Sexual wishes, perverse strivings, hostility, and aggression may suddenly overwhelm him and cause him to react compulsively, against his better judgment. The patient almost always will exhibit behavior patterns both inside and outside the therapeutic situation that serve either to drain off his aroused emotions or to inhibit them. He may, for instance, in response to feelings of rage, have an impulse to frustrate and hurt the analyst. Accordingly he may heap imprecations and derisive remarks upon the latter, emphasize his shortcomings, and minimize his intelligence. He may become sullen or mute or negativistic.

These reactions do not always appear openly and may be manifested only in the hypnotic state or in dreams and fantasies. Sometimes hostility is expressed more surreptitiously in the form of a sexual impulse toward the analyst, which has its basis in the desire to undermine or subdue him. At the same time the patient realizes that he needs the love and help of the analyst, and he may feel that expression of hostility will eventuate in rejection. He may then try to solve his conflict by maintaining a detachment in regard to the analyst, by refusing to talk in the waking and in the trance states, by resisting deep trances, by forgetting his appointments, or by stopping therapy.

A danger to guard against in hypnoanalysis is that the patient may act out his inner impulses and feelings and fail to verbalize them. This is particularly the case where the patient is given no chance to associate freely. Such acting out has a temporary cathartic effect, but is not conducive to insight. If the patient does not know what he is reliving, he will think that his reactions constitute life. The feelings and attitudes that are released in the analytic process do evoke anxiety, and the patient will try to relieve himself by projections outside of analysis. If acting out goes on unchecked, it may halt the therapeutic process. The most important task of the analyst is to demonstrate to the patient what he is avoiding by acting out instead of verbalizing. This may often be done effectively during hypnosis.

As the patient realizes that his emotions and impulses are directly a product of his relationship with the analyst, he will attempt to justify himself by finding concrete factors in the analyst's manner or approach to explain his reactions. Inwardly he is in terror that the analyst may call a halt on therapy and thus bring to an end the possibility of ever establishing an unambivalent relationship with another human being. Yet he continues to respond with contradictory attitudes. On the one hand he seeks praise and love from the analyst and on the other tries to injure and destroy him. He resents the tender emotions that keep cropping up within himself. The battle with the analyst rages back and forth, to the dismay of both participants.

One of the effects of this phase of the analysis is to mobilize ideas and fantasies related to past experiences and conditionings. The interpersonal relationship is the most potent catalyst that the analyst can employ in stimulation of repressed memories and experiences. As the patient begins to feel irrational impulses toward the analyst, he becomes tremendously productive, and the various hypnoanalytic technics bring up a great amount of important material.

In his relationship with the analyst, the patient gradually begins to understand that his attitudes and feelings toward the former are rooted in experiences and conditionings that have gone before, and discovers that they have little to do with the analyst as a real person. This has a twofold effect. First, it shows him why exaggerated expectations and resentments develop automatically in his relationships with other people. Second, it permits him to see that he is able to approach people from a different point of view.

The transference in hypnoanalysis is a dynamic, living experience that is intensely meaningful to the patient. Recovery of repressed material is in itself insufficient. The material has to be understood, integrated, and accepted. During hypnoanalysis much material of an unconscious nature comes to the surface, but the patient may be unable to assimilate this material because it lies outside the scope of his understanding. In the interpersonal relationship the patient is able to feel his unconscious impulses in actual operation. He realizes them not as cold intellectual facts but as real experiences. The learning process is accelerated under such circumstances.

The transference not only mobilizes the deepest trends and impulses but also teaches the patient that he can express these without incurring hurt. This is unlike the ordinary physician-patient relationship, in which the patient feels obliged to hold back irrational feelings. Because of the analyst's tolerance, the patient becomes capable of appreciating certain attitudes consciously for the first time. He realizes that when he expresses destructive attitudes toward the analyst, these do not call forth retaliatory rejection, condemnation, or punishment. He gradually develops a more tolerant attitude toward his inner drives, and learns to revaluate them in the light of existing reality rather than of unconscious fantasies and traumatic events in his past. As he undergoes the unique experience of expressing his deepest strivings without retaliation, he also begins to permit healthy, congenial social attitudes to filter through his defenses. The analyst becomes an individual who fits into a special category. He is less the authority and more the friend.

The tolerant and understanding attitude of the analyst endows him with a peculiar attribute of protectiveness, for the patient himself is unable to accept the inner conflicts and impulses and uses the analyst as a refuge from danger. The conviction that he has a protector enables him to divulge his most repulsive impulses, emotions, memories, and fantasies, first under hypnosis and then in the waking state, with an associated release of affect. Along with becoming aware of his unconscious drives and recalling of their existence in earliest childhood, the patient sooner or later discovers that there is a difference between what he feels and what is actually going on, and realizes that his guilt feeling and anxiety actually have no basis in reality.

In the trance and in the waking state the patient will bring up more and more painful material. Encouraged to express himself, he begins to regard the analyst as one who bears only good will toward his repressed drives. He will continue to exhibit all of his customary interpersonal attitudes and defenses in his relationship to the analyst, but he can clarify them to himself under a unique set of conditions, in which he feels accepted and in which there is no condemnation or retaliatory resentment.

The reorientation in his relationship with the analyst makes it possible for him to regard the former as a person toward whom he need not have an ambivalent attitude. His acceptance of the analyst as a real friend has an important effect on his resistances. These are genetically related to the hurt he experienced in his relationships with early authorities. The removal of resistances is dynamically associated with an alteration in the rigor of his internalized system of restraints, for if he is to yield up his defenses, he must be assured that the old punishments and retributions will not overtake him. It is here that his experience with the analyst plays so vital a role, because he begins to gain an entirely new attitude toward authority. His own conscience is modified by adoption of a more lenient set of standards and injunctions.

One of the chief aims of rational psychotherapy is to render the conscience less tyrannical and to modify its values so as to permit the expression of impulses essential to the mental health of the individual. Perhaps the most important way in which this modification can be achieved is through acceptance of the analyst as a new authority whose standards subdue and ultimately replace the old and intolerable ones. In the course of his relationship with the analyst, the patient tends to identify himself with the latter and to incorporate his more tolerant attitudes. The ultimate result is a rearrangement of the dynamic forces of the personality and eventually a reduction in the harshness of the superego. The hypnotic state facilitates a replacement of the residual superego by that of the hypnotist.[5] It reanimates the child-parent relationship. Even so, the technic encourages self-assertiveness and expression of impulses previously repressed.   In my opinion this freedom has a corrosive effect on the residual superego, serving eventually to dislodge it.

The identification with the analyst also has a remarkable effect on the patient's ego.   Therapeutic progress is registered by the increasing capacity of the reasonable ego to discern the irrationality of its actions, feelings, and defenses.   The rebuilding of ego strength promotes a review of old repressions, some of which are lifted, while others are accepted but reconstructed with more solid material, so that they will not give way so easily to unconscious drives.[6]   Growth in the rational power and judgment of the ego makes it possible to differentiate the strivings, rooted in past experiences, that are automatically operative in the present.

Ego strength consequently results both from liberation of the self from the repressive and intolerant standards of the tyrannical conscience, and from identification with the accepting, nonhostile figure of the analyst.   Ultimately ego growth involves an identification with a healthy group.   This is of course the final aim in therapy, and this relation eventually must supplement and replace the personal identification.

The undermining of the superego and the strengthening of the ego give the patient courage to face his impulses of hate. He becomes increasingly more capable of expressing rage openly.   The possibility of his being physically attacked by the analyst becomes less and less real to him.   As he resolves his hate and fear, he is likely to experience an onrush of loving emotions.   Often these burst forth in a violent form, as in a compulsive desire for sexual contact.   In this guise they may be so loathsome and terrifying that they are promptly repressed.   Sexuality to the mind of the patient involves unconditional love or surrender or a desire to attack or to merge with another person.   Inextricably bound up with such destructive feelings are healthful ones, but because the patient has been hurt so frequently in expressing tender impulses, he has customarily been forced to keep them under control.   In his relationship with the analyst he learns that normal demands for understanding and affection will not be frustrated and that they have nothing to do with hateful and sexual attitudes.

As the analyst comes to be accepted as an understanding person, the unconscious impulses come out in greater force, and the patient discovers that he is better able to tolerate the anxiety that is created by expression of them. In contrast to what occurs in real life, resistance to this expression is not reinforced by actual or implied threats of retaliation or loss of love. The patient then becomes conscious of the fact that his terror has its sources within himself rather than in an implied threat of hurt from the analyst. This insight does not help much at first, but gradually it permits the patient to experiment in tolerance of increased doses of anxiety.

The development of ability to withstand pain makes it possible for him to work out more mature solutions for his problems, instead of taking refuge in repression, a defense hitherto necessitated by his inability to tolerate anxiety. The experience of the fact that he has not been destroyed by his impulses, and the realization he has not destroyed the analyst, whom he both loves and hates, are tremendous revelations lessening the inclination to feel guilt and need of punishment, and contributing to his security and self-respect.

At this stage in therapy, the patient becomes more critical of the analyst and more capable of injecting reality into the relationship. He attempts to test out his new insights in real life. He does this with considerable trepidation, always anticipating the same kind of hurt that initially fostered his repression. As he discovers that he can express himself and take a stand with people, a new era of trust in the analyst is ushered in, with a definite growth of self-confidence. Over and over he works through with the analyst his own characterologic strivings, re-experiencing his unconscious impulses and his reactions of defense against them. Gradually he becomes aware of the meaning of his emotional turmoil as well as of the futility of his various defenses. The continuous analysis of the transference enables him to understand how his neurotic drives have isolated him from people and have prevented expression of his psychobiologic needs.

A new phase in his relationship with the analyst develops. Realizing that the latter means more to him than anyone else, he seeks to claim his new ally for himself. He may wish to continue the relationship indefinitely and may look upon the completion of therapy as a threat. Clinging to his illness may then have positive values. However, he soon begins to understand that there are reality limitations in his present relationship, that he does not get out of it the things that he is beginning to demand of life, that the outside world is the only milieu in which he can gratify his needs. He finds the relationship with the analyst gratifying, but not gratifying enough, and his reality sense becomes stronger and his ability to cope with frustration is enhanced. Finally, he sets out in the world to gain those satisfactions that he has never before felt to be available to him.

One of the questions frequently asked regarding hypnoanalysis is about the ultimate effect on the patient of the hypnotic process itself. Is it not likely that a person subjected to repeated trance states may become so dependent upon the analyst that he never will be able to function efficiently under his own power? Under such circumstances, might not the transference continue indefinitely and defy all attempts at dissolution?

In my experience such fears are groundless, especially when the transference is analyzed. Contrary to supposition, hypnosis has no weakening effect on the patient's ego. The trance state has definite pleasure values, but the patient will not, unless he has a specific character problem that motivates him in that direction, cling to it as an escape from the realities of life. Under a proper technic the patient is capable, even in the somnambulistic state, of arguing and of maintaining his own judgments. Indeed, immature individuals who are easily swayed to conformity with the opinions of others show under hypnosis a surprising capacity to reason independently.

Encouragement in this during hypnosis can be of therapeutic value.

It is conceivable of course that where the analyst is impelled by a power drive, or is domineering or sadistic, he may resent independent activity in the patient, preferring to have him function passively. Patients sense keenly what is expected of them during the trance, and when they feel that the sole way of securing the analyst's approval is to render themselves immobile or dependent, they will oblige accordingly. On the other hand, when they realize they can be expressive and can think as they please, they will respond with tremendous activity that is therapeutically most gratifying. Where a patient loses his power to criticize the analyst or to think for himself either during hypnosis or posthypnotically, there is something wrong with the technic, or else the patient has a character problem oriented around compulsive dependency that would make him dependent upon and subservient to the analyst under any circumstances.

In hypnoanalysis the aim is to increase ego strength by releasing the self from the restraint and tyranny of an archaic conscience and by freeing it from the threat of destruction by inner drives, fears, and conflicts. Ego growth is a gradual process coordinate with the development of self-respect, assertiveness, self-esteem, and self-confidence. It is associated with a liberation of the individual from the sense of helplessness and from fears of the imminent rejection and hurt that portend a hostile world. The ego-synthetic phases of hypnoanalytic therapy, which are directed to reintegrating the individual in his relationships with people, are accordingly no less important than the recovery and interpretation of unconscious material.

Often transference situations develop that appear to be chargeable to extremely immature ego structures. An example of this is a persistent clinging, dependent attitude toward the analyst, who is regarded both in and outside of hypnosis as a demigod, the embodiment of all that is strong and good in the universe. This relation is rooted in an intense sense of helpless-

ness and is often found in individuals who are characterologi-
cally submissive, subordinate, and ingratiating, and who strive
to adjust to life by clinging parasitically to a more powerful
person. It is as if the individual had an amputated self that
could be restored only by symbiosis with a stronger individual.
There is an associated tendency to overevaluate the potentialities and qualities of other people. This type of relationship is
extremely shaky, because the patient regards hypnosis as a
magical means to security and power. Consequently the
analyst must always live up to the inordinate expectations of
the patient, which are so sheerly in the realm of fantasy that
they are beyond possibility of fulfillment. The patient will
demand more and more of the analyst, and, failing to get what
he secretly wants, will be filled with hostility and contempt.
It is essential that the analyst recognize a dependency trend,
in order that he may point out to the patient the need for
activity and the necessity of avoiding acceptance of interpretations on the basis of faith. It is essential to demonstrate
to the patient the dynamics of the submissive, dependent
relationship that has up to this point been his chief means of
adaptation.

Another form of relationship that may develop is based upon
an intense fear of the analyst as one who is potentially capable
of injuring or enslaving the patient. This attitude stems from
a hostile image of the parent and is usually applied to all
authoritative individuals. Treatment in such cases proceeds
only when the patient realizes that the analyst does not desire
to punish or condemn him for his ambitions or fantasies, but
instead is benevolently neutral toward them. Little progress is
possible until the patient accepts the analyst as a friend.
Until then resistance will be intense, even in the most regressed
states.

A third common form of relationship is that of detachment
and isolation. These attitudes are also founded upon a hostile
image of authority. In an effort to shield himself from danger
or disappointment, the patient will react with a need of avoiding intimate contact. Often this striving is counteracted by a

coexisting dependency drive. For a long time in his relationship with the analyst, the patient will feel that his own values are what really count. He will be convinced that the analyst cannot like him and will "let him down." Often he will rationalize these feelings and say to himself that the analyst is no good, or incompetent, or of no importance, or that psychiatry or hypnosis is nothing but nonsense. Much unconscious material may be divulged during hypnoanalysis, but there will be little absorption of this material by the waking ego until a change in the image of the analyst is effected.

Hypnoanalysis may produce unfavorable reactions of many kinds in patients with immature ego structures. The transference becomes so dramatic and disturbing to the patient that he responds to it in an essentially psychotic manner. He will accuse the analyst of being hostile, destructive, and rejecting, and he will refuse to acknowledge that his attitudes may be the product of his own feelings. The reasonable ego here is very diminutive and cannot tolerate the implications of unconscious drives and conflicts. The patient acts out his inner problems and constantly avoids subjecting them to reason. To him the analyst actually is a cruel or lecherous or destructive being who threatens him with injury or abandonment. Any action or interpretation on the part of the analyst is twisted around to justify his convictions. The entire hypnotic procedure is interpreted in the light of his delusional system. Fear and anxiety issuing from the functioning of his irrational strivings lie like boulders in his path, barring the way to more congenial interpersonal relationships. In such cases therapy will be prolonged, and the interpersonal relationship must be manipulated actively to constitute a gratifying human experience, in an attempt so to strengthen the ego that it can view its own actions more critically.

## REFERENCES

1. DYNES, J. B.: An experimental study in hypnotic anaesthesia. J. Abnorm. & Social Psychol. *27:* 87, 1932.
2. WALDEN, E. C.: A plethysmographic study of the vascular conditions during hypnotic sleep. Am. J. Physiol. *4:* 124–61, 1900.

3. Dorcus, R. M., and Shaffer, G. W.: Textbook of abnormal psychology. Baltimore: Williams & Wilkins, 1939.
4. Jacobson, E.: Progressive relaxation. Chicago: Univ. Chicago Press, 1929.
5. Kubie, L. W., and Margolin, S.: The process of hypnotism and the nature of the hypnotic state. Am. J. Psychiat. *100:* 619, 1944.
6. Freud, S.: Analysis terminable and interminable. Internat. J. Psycho-Analysis *18:* 383, 1937.

# XIX

## HYPNOSIS AND RESISTANCE

THE AVERAGE patient comes to therapy to escape the suffering associated with his neurosis. In addition he may wish to gain inner strength in order to deal more realistically with the problems of life and to secure those gratifications that are so vital to normal functioning. In the course of analytic therapy, however, surprising things happen. The patient loses his intense desire to get well. Instead of regarding the analyst as a friend, he views him as a foe. He becomes rebellious and obstinate, and engages in behavior that has for its purpose the sabotaging of the analysis. Whether or not this resistance is appropriately dealt with determines the outcome of success or failure in treatment.

Resistance to hypnoanalysis occurs in precisely the same way as resistance to psychoanalysis, although in a somewhat modified form. It is manifested both in the waking state and in the trance. It crops up whenever the patient encounters anxiety or is threatened with being deprived of an important gratification. As in psychoanalysis, one encounters two general types of resistance. The first type is related to the acknowledgment of unconscious drives and impulses, and of repressed traumatic memories and experiences. The second type arises out of the transference.

In the first type of resistance, the patient is so frightened or ashamed of his inner drives, conflicts, and memories that he throws up barricades to prevent their penetration into the ideational stream. Whenever he finds himself approaching traumatic material in conscious free association or during hypnosis, he may suddenly block, lose the trend of thought, shift to a new idea, or develop amnesia. He may experience such feelings of tension or panic that he will automatically divert his stream of thought into less painful channels.

Hypnosis is a powerful tool in the resolution of such resistances.   This fact has been recognized by Lindner[1] and Brenman and Knight.[2]   The latter authors illustrate how hypnosis can be used to eliminate resistance quite effectively.   For instance, when a patient approaches painful unconscious material and is apparently unable to bring it to the surface, he is directed under hypnosis to talk about his inner strivings or to remember an event or experience that he has forgotten.   A simple command such as this may suddenly bring up a chain of repressed impulses or memories.   Resistances that keep important memories or impulses repressed may sometimes be successfully circumvented by strong suggestions during hypnosis to the effect that the patient visualize, recall, write, draw, or dramatize the repressed material.   Regression with revivification, play therapy, and automatic writing are especially suited to the dissipation of resistances to recall.

The problem of why the individual is able during hypnosis to break through resistances that defy the most persistent efforts in the waking state would certainly seem to warrant a more complete investigation.   Hypnosis in itself eliminates many superficial repressions.   It brings the unconscious of the individual closer to his expressive faculties.   Probably of more importance is the artificial fusion with the hypnotist that occurs in the trance.   In some cases the patient's ego appears to be so strengthened by this amalgamation that he is able to tolerate the anxiety associated with the repressed material and can verbalize his fears with amazing ease.   During regression and reorientation to an earlier age level, defenses and resistances that were developed at a later period are literally wiped out.   Significant events in the patient's life that have been forgotten because they have been submerged by later resistances, may consequently be recalled.

The hypermnesic influence of hypnosis must not be interpreted as guaranteeing that all resistance to recall can be completely eliminated.   Unfortunately this is not the case, and resistances may continue to operate sufficiently, even in extremely regressed states, to prevent the individual from bringing up material.   The possibility of removing resistance during hypnosis apparently depends upon the intensity of anxiety and upon how much the ego is strengthened as a result of the hypnotic interpersonal relationship.

A crucial point in the removal of resistance by means of hypnosis is whether the removal works in such a way as to permit the patient to develop insight. Logically it might be assumed that the mere uncovering of unconscious impulses or memories will not produce real change, since the ego, upon resumption of consciousness, will be victimized by the same terrors that existed before. To an extent this assumption is correct, and frequently the patient will bring up traumatic memories and unconscious trends that are completely forgotten or rejected when he awakens. The amnesia here serves a protective purpose and is more powerful than any posthypnotic suggestions directing the patient to remember his hypnotic experiences.

Nevertheless, verbalization, dramatization, or writing of the unconscious material has, according to my experience, an important effect upon the repressive forces. The eruption of the material into motor pathways is the first step in mastery of it. At first the patient fails to understand the full implication of his recovered unconscious trends, and it may take several months before he can integrate this material on a waking level. Often the release of material during hypnosis by artificial destruction of resistances creates excitement, anxiety, or rage. The cathartic and abreactive effect is not as important as the realization of the ego that it has not been shattered as a consequence of the recall. In standing up to the anxiety in this way, the ego feels stronger and more capable of withstanding the material on a more conscious level. We may witness this process by observing the character of the patient's dreams. Recall under hypnosis with subsequent amnesia frequently stimulates dreams dealing with the material, the symbolic disguises accorded the latter becoming less and less bizarre, until the unconscious memory or trend erupts into the waking state.

Curative forces in the ego may be utilized by enjoining the

patient during hypnosis to forget the material that he has produced, but to work on it until he understands its meaning. Acting on this suggestion, the patient often will work on a problem until its solution emerges as an insight that he believes to be wholly spontaneous. Where the patient is commanded to recall memories or to accept the existence of unconscious trends before he feels strong enough within himself to do so, his resistances will usually continue to function obstinately in spite of anything that the analyst does. Heroic attempts to batter down resistances by force will stimulate antagonism.

Resistances that issue out of the transference cannot be handled as easily as those that oppose the recall of traumatic unconscious material. Hypnosis tends to dissolve many barriers that prevent the patient from getting too close to the analyst. Almost immediately the patient may experience feelings and impulses of the deepest nature. Resistance as a defense against such feelings is inevitable and usually cannot be dissipated by mere suggestion.

The relationship with the analyst is understandably disturbing, because it mobilizes attitudes, impulses, and feelings that threaten the repressive forces. The patient will, in the attempt to escape from the associated anxiety, throw up his usual characterologic defenses to detach himself, to control and overwhelm the analyst, or to render himself invincible. In hypnosis used as an adjunct to palliative psychotherapy, the patient will manage to restore his equilibrium through the medium of such defenses, and he will more or less successfully repress disturbing irrational, unconscious drives. In hypnoanalysis, on the other hand, the analyst constantly interprets the nature and purpose of the various defenses as they arise. This constitutes an assault on the integrity of the repressive system and will precipitate much tension. Eventually the patient cannot help coming to grips with the emotions and drives that he has hitherto succeeded in avoiding. He will then mobilize further protective devices to reinforce his shattered repressions.

One of the earliest manifestations of this struggle is an

intensification of symptoms, which seems to serve a desperate function of restoring psychic equilibrium. Soon the struggle becomes more personalized, as the patient realizes that his relationship with the analyst is the womb of his distress. Resistance may be exerted against the original unconscious material or to its projected and animated representations in the transference.

The forms that resistances take will depend upon the individual's methods of dealing with conflict and will approximate those found in psychoanalytic therapy. The patient may become so terrified by his inner impulses that he may seek reassurance, affection, and support from the analyst. Psychosomatic complaints are often developed in an appeal for sympathy. The patient may become helpless and hopeless and assume a defenseless attitude as he pleads for mercy. Seeking from the analyst a panacea for his suffering, he may demand an immediate removal of his symptoms. In expressing such a demand, the patient will refuse to work out his own problems, becoming inert during hypnosis, and making a desperate effort to force the analyst to take a decisive step.

Profound self-devaluation may follow, the patient flagellating himself with his inadequacies. This defense, in addition to justifying his failure to make progress, often serves the additional purposes of securing his aim of being cared for like a child, of escaping criticism, and of avoiding all active and independent efforts that may be expected of him. In persons with strong masochistic impulses there may be attempts to dig out the most revolting and hideous aspects of themselves during the hypnoanalytic procedures, in order to revel in self-suffering. The material, though factual, is utilized not to induce ego change but rather to add to the neurotic gratifications that come from proving oneself evil or contemptible. In the process the patient will utilize the content of his unconscious to reinforce his devaluation of himself.

Sometimes the patient displays a need to be victimized and unfairly treated. He will maneuver himself into a situation with the analyst in which he feels that the latter is taking advantage of him. He may exhibit various symptoms that he attributes to the harmful effect of hypnosis. In order to reinforce his waning repressive system, he may seek to transform the analyst into a stern authority who commands and punishes him. In the latter instance he will experience severe anxiety if the analyst is tolerant and condones his inner impulses.

Resistance is frequently displayed in the form of hostility. The resulting reaction patterns depend on the extent to which the patient is able to express aggression. Where the character structure makes it mandatory to inhibit rage, the patient may respond with depression and discouragement. He may then want to terminate therapy on the ground that he has no chance of getting well. He may mask his aggression with slavish conformity, with dependence, and with a feigned amiability. Accordingly, he may evince an interest in the analyst's personal life and assume an attitude of comradery and good fellowship. There is in such efforts a desire to ally himself with the analyst in order to lessen the danger to himself.

On the other hand, where the patient is able to express hostility, he may exhibit it in many ways. He may become critical, then defiant, challenging the analyst to make him well. Irritability is often transmuted into contempt, and the patient may accuse the analyst of having exploitive or evil designs on him. Feeling misunderstood and humiliated, he will manufacture, out of insignificant happenings in his contact with the analyst, sufficient grounds to justify his notion of being mistreated. He will become suspicious about the analyst's training, ability, political convictions, personal life, and marital adjustment. He may enter actively into competition with the analyst by trying to analyze him, by reading books on psychoanalysis and hypnosis to enable him to point out the analyst's shortcomings. He may become uncooperative and negativistic to the point of mutism, which may persist even in deep hypnosis. He may lose his motive for being hypnotizable and resist entering trance states.

Sometimes hostility is handled by attempts at detachment. The need to keep the analyst from getting too close may burn up a great deal of the patient's energy. He may in the waking state refuse to listen to what the analyst says, or in hypnosis he may go off into a sleep. He may ridicule in his mind the analyst's interpretations. He may forget his appointments or seek to discontinue therapy, inventing many rationalizations for this. He may strive to ward the analyst off by discursive rambling along superficial lines, touching on irrelevant subjects, such as topics of the day, or social, political, and philosophic controversies, or presenting a detailed catalogue of his symptoms. In his effort to keep aloof he may attempt to take over the analysis, interpreting in advance unconscious motivations the existence of which he cannot deny. An insidious type of defense is a preoccupation with infantile experiences and the past history. Here the patient will overwhelm the analyst with the most minute details of what must have happened to him when he was a child, presenting a fairly consistent and logical survey of how previous inimical experiences must have produced all of his present difficulties. Coordinately there may be a recall during hypnosis of many significant events in the past the memory of which has lain dormant up to that time.

The attempt to disarm the analyst may be disguised by a spurt of activity in the analytic process, the patient suddenly becoming productive, yielding up a great deal of material. In association with this there may be detailed accounting of the dynamics of his disorder, presented in a textbook style gleaned from interpretations given by the analyst or from outside reading. Such insight is wholly spurious, since little change occurs in the patient's neurosis and in his disturbed relationship with people. Here insight is used as a device behind which the patient seeks to continue indulging his compulsive trends without blame. It is as if knowing that he is doing something neurotic somehow condones his acts. As in psychoanalysis, a situation may develop in which the treatment hour becomes an event entirely dissociated from real life.

Under the circumstances the patient adopts two sets of stand-ards—one that applies to his behavior in hypnoanalysis, the other to life in general. He may rationalize this on the ground that the analyst is the only person who can understand him and that people outside could under no circumstances do so.

Occasionally resistance shows itself in an inability to ver-balize feelings or to think clearly, either in or outside of hypnosis. Analysis of this defense often reveals that the patient feels hostile or erotic impulses that terrify him so that he cannot acknowledge them to himself, let alone to the analyst. He imagines that the consequence of such divulgence will be the analyst's scorn, rejection, or counterhostility. Associated with the inability to verbalize ideas or feelings, there may be an acting out of impulses outside the therapeutic situation, in the form of compulsive or irrational acts that drain off tension but leave basic problems unsolved.

Another defense is a forced flight into health. Here the patient will pronounce himself well, insisting that he no longer needs therapy. He resists with vigor any implication that he is not normal in all respects. Actually he may assume an attitude of self-confidence, independence, and assertiveness, masking his basic insecurity. Underneath one will always detect a false note in the tremendous effort he makes to main-tain an illusion of health.

The desire to control the analyst may reflect itself in many ways. The patient may seek to shower the analyst with gifts and favors, or he may develop a sentimental attachment that may take a sexual form. The trance may be regarded as a seduction, the patient experiencing in it intense sexual feelings. One of the motives involved in falling in love with the analyst is to reduce him to a role in which he will not pry too closely into the patient's deepest secrets. In the sexual demands there may be many hostile components. The motive may be to devaluate the analyst, to enslave him, to test his convictions, or to fuse with him, in this way taking a short cut to cure. Progress may suddenly stop as the patient blocks himself in his love experience. The real purpose of this type of transference is resistance, although the patient will seek secondary gains, such as the living out of fantasied neurotic gratifications. There may be an overevaluation of the capacities of the analyst, with a clinging to him for support and guidance. The lift that the patient gets out of hypnosis may constitute all that he desires from treatment. He may pay lip homage to the interpretations of the analyst, but so long as he is motivated completely by his neurotic attachment, no real therapeutic change will occur.

Resistance also develops on the basis of a refusal to relinquish important gratifications that accrue to the ego through neurotic illness. Every neurosis induces a distortion in the sense of values, and neurotic drives become invested with subjective pleasures that can make the ordinary pursuits of life seem mediocre and meaningless. Sometimes the very defenses that the patient uses to avoid the expression of a forbidden impulse symbolically come to represent the impulse itself. Symptoms can become charged with pleasure as well as with guilt and anxiety. The patient may find many comforts in his neurosis, and he will unconsciously not desire to abandon it even though it entails a number of inconveniences.

Many patients come to treatment not because they desire to function more adequately in their interpersonal relationships, but rather because they seek to obtain from treatment the fulfillment of neurotic wishes that they have been unable to gratify through their own efforts. In such cases resentment and resistance develop when the patient does not receive from the analyst the specific type of help that he has expected.

Upon analyzing the evidence as to what the patient seeks from the analyst, it turns out that what he wants is not a cure for his neurosis, but an infallible method of making it work. He particularly desires to achieve his neurotic expectations without having to pay the penalty of suffering. The individual with a power drive thus may insist on a formula whereby he can function in an invincible manner in all activities in which he participates. The perfectionist will want to find a way to do things flawlessly with as little effort as possible. The dependent individual will expect to amalgamate himself with the analyst and to have every one of his whims gratified without activity on his own part. The detached soul will seek to have the fruits of social intercourse, though he wants at the same time to keep his distance from people. When these drives are not gratified in hypnoanalysis, when the patient senses that they are instead being challenged, he will become tremendously resistive.

Frequently, resistance is exerted against accepting the idea that it is possible to function adequately without repairing a fantasied injury to the genital organs. In the female the resistance is to living through life without the possibility of ever procuring for herself a penis, which she regards as the bridge to activity and self-fulfillment. In males the assumption of a passive role is often interpreted as equivalent to being castrated, and resistance may be directed against assuming any role that does not involve aggressive fighting. Even accepting help from the analyst may symbolize passivity.

The ability of the patient to overcome such resistances will depend upon how much healthy ego remains and whether the individual can be brought to the realization that neurotic strivings do not yield such gratifications as are imagined. Hypnosis may be valuable here in demonstrating to the patient that what he wants from life is not so much power, supremacy, complete support, or intact male genitality, but rather the security and self-esteem that he believes must follow attainment of these objectives.

For instance, a young woman who was timid and docile in her external behavior came to therapy because of frequent anxiety attacks. Outwardly she was extremely submissive, but it was soon apparent from her productions that her submissiveness was a reactive formation pitted against an inner striving for power. She often had dreams and fantasies of herself as a giantess who trod upon and crushed people and houses beneath her feet. She rejected the power impulse because of the destructiveness associated with it. As hypnoanalysis proceeded she became more and more infuriated with me for bringing her desire for power to her attention. Her first reaction was to deny this wish as incredible. At the same time she became panicky and extremely hostile. She dreamed of going to funerals and felt a strange elation when a man who resembled me was carried to the grave. Free associations revealed that she was enraged because I not only refused to show her how to become strong and masterful, but also because I challenged her drive as neurotic and impossible of fulfillment. She brought in quotations from Nietzsche and Schopenhauer corroborating her philosophy that only the strong can survive. Current historical examples also were used to substantiate this theme. Attempts to show her how basically insecure she felt, and how her power striving served to protect her against a feeling of helplessness, were of little avail.

It was suggested to her under hypnosis that she would feel that she had finally become the kind of person that she had always wanted to be. A pencil was placed in her hand and she was directed to write automatically as she verbalized some of her feelings. While she rambled along about becoming a great actress, her hand drew a crude picture of a bird. Underneath was a cryptic message that, translated later, yielded the phrases: "Into blue heaven," "Mother," and "me John." The bird, she revealed, had something to do with her mother and also with John, who was a boy with whom she had played as a child. She produced associations of childhood sex play and urinary games in which she and John had participated. A drawing made under hypnosis at this session portrayed a little girl crying at the sight of another girl being carried away in an ambulance.

Next day the patient reported having had a nightmare about her elder sister. In the dream her sister had died. The patient was tense and panicky as she recounted the dream. During hypnosis the suggestion was again made that she would feel as strong as she wanted to. This time the patient broke into tears and screamed: "No, no, Ann can't die!"

Directed to remember the hypnotic events in the waking state, the patient began to talk excitedly about her hostility to her elder sister, Ann, whom she accused of being haughty and self-centered. She herself always felt small and inferior to her sister, and frequently imagined how wonderful life would be if the latter were dead. Then she would be the favorite of both her father and her mother.

Further analysis revealed that the patient's power drive was motivated in part by a desire to escape from the desolate insecurity of being an unloved child. Because she believed her sister to be strong and invincible, being masterful symbolized for her a way of defeating and taking the place of her sister, and also of winning favors from her father. The power drive was furthermore equated with functioning as a male. Her penis envy was intense and she unconsciously associated being a man with having all her problems solved magically. The bird in the automatic writing was later translated by herself as a symbol of a penis that she was certain her mother had once possessed, but that had flown away into "the blue heaven." The "me John" part of the communication referred to her unconscious wish to urinate like her male playmate, John. Because attaining power involved the destruction of her sister, she had repressed this impulse, yet she cherished a secret hope of eventually becoming a strong person. The realization that she did not desire power and a penis as much as she wanted love, security, and freedom from the devastating effects of being a rejected and devaluated person, made it possible· for her to overcome her resistance to getting well. Eventually she gained insight regarding the fact that her power drive was an illusory way out of her sense of helplessness, and that it involved motivations that contradicted reality.

As in psychoanalysis, transference resistance is handled by demonstrating its presence, its purpose, its ramifications, its historical origin, and the manner of its operation in the patient's present relationships with the analyst and with people in general. As resistances are gradually analyzed and resolved, repressed material appears in consciousness in a less and less disguised form. Resistances require a constant working through and a single interpretation of a resistance is hardly effective.

Since resistance has a dynamic function, an effort is made to cause the patient to yield it up slowly. Too sudden removal may produce severe anxiety and may provoke a reinforcement of the neurotic defenses intended to protect the individual from a repetition of the anxiety experience. Relinquishment of resistance will thus be blocked by a threat of repetition of the anxiety experience.

The analyst should allow resistance to develop fully before he takes it back to its origins. If a second resistance develops, he must handle it by returning to the first one and demonstrating to the patient the interrelationship of the two. Tackling the patient's defensive reactions inevitably causes him to feel threatened and to resist interpretation of his resistance. This reaction is opposed by a contrary motive, that of retaining the good will of the analyst. Often the patient will attempt to satisfy both of these motivations at the same time by abandoning his defense in the forms recognized by the analyst and attempting to retain it in a disguised form. The understanding of these elaborations and the continued exposure of them forces the patient to take a real stand against them and finally to abandon them entirely.

Analysis of resistance is facilitated by use of the various hypnoanalytic procedures. During therapy a young woman developed in my presence panicky feelings that interfered with her ability to associate freely. She was unable to verbalize thoughts that came to her mind and was confronted with blankness whenever she tried to analyze her reaction. So long as she confined her talk to casual happenings and to events outside of analysis, she was able to talk without difficulty, but as soon as she began to think of the analytic situation, she became intensely agitated and disturbed.

It was suggested to her under hypnosis that she recall the first incident in her life that was associated with a similar feeling. In response to this suggestion, she recounted: "I remember when I was little and Father was coming home. I knew he would speak to me when he came. I was in suspense and hope that he would speak to me. But then he came in and instead of speaking to me, he spanked me. I remember this incident clearly, because I wore a new jacket and hoped that he would take notice of this."

Upon awakening the patient remarked that she had always remembered the incident vaguely, but had never before realized how strongly she felt about it.

At the next session she reported the following spontaneous dream:

> I went into a reading room of a library to read an article of yours. I noticed you were there, but made believe I didn't see you. As I got up, you got up. I decided I shouldn't talk to you, although I wanted to. I just nodded and went off. The dream had a pleasant emotion, because I was pleased to find you in the library. It's a feeling I've had before. I would like to feel free to talk to you, but I don't trust myself. I always feel that whenever I have a strong feeling about anything, I should close up and wave it aside.

Associating to this, she declared that she wanted to get close to me as much as she wanted anything in life, but she believed that I did not want her to do so. She was unable to shed any further light on the reasons why I might not want her to get close to me. During the trance I enjoined her to work on this problem.

At the next session she reported having had considerable anxiety. She said: "I had a number of dreams and a great deal of terror and extreme anger. At the same time I had an idea that I could do nothing about it. One of the dreams was to the effect that I was in college in my room. I reached up to touch a light, something on the light switch. I got a shock. In the dream, I did what I was always afraid I would do. I went berserk. They decided I wasn't sane. I was taken to a hospital. There was an unsympathetic flight of stairs. I knew it was an escalator and would start any time in the middle. The dream was full of the same feeling of not being able to say anything. I looked in a mirror and had bruises on my head, which I connected with the fact that I had a headache. It occurs to me that it doesn't seem possible to be happy without being blind to some danger. Underneath I must have a great deal of distrust of you still, even though I don't want to."

Asked to associate to her sensations during hypnosis, the patient remarked: "I feel a good deal of tension because there are two sides pulling against each other. I want to protect myself by keeping my mind stiff, and I want to give in and let myself feel closeness to you. But the only way that I can be close to you is by absolutely giving up any demands or thoughts. What I've been trying to do is shuffle back and forth trying to maintain my independence."

It was decided to create an experimental conflict in the attempt to understand better what was behind her resistance. While she was under hypnosis, the following suggestion was made: "When you wake up you will notice that a bar of candy lies on the table. You will want it as much as you ever wanted anything else in life, but you will feel that I do not want you to have it."

As I phrased the suggestion, the patient cried convulsively: "I don't want to wait! I just can't face it! Wanting something Father doesn't want me to have has no solution except not to want it, not to face it. It's something others can have and I can't."

Upon being awakened she looked about the room casually, glanced furtively at the candy on my desk, and then suddenly put her hands to her eyes. She shook her head, cried softly to herself, and sobbed: "If there is the slightest doubt that I am permitted or encouraged to take the candy, I can't do it. That's what I've been running away from all my life. If I wanted something that father did not want me to have, I didn't get it. It's better not to want. Then I had this awful resentment. To tell him I was resentful didn't work, but isn't it possible to make demands and claim your rights? Father was against my having a fur coat when I was fifteen. It never occurred to me that I could have it."

At this point the hour ended and the patient got up from the couch. She paused before reaching the door, then turned around. I asked her whether she wanted the candy and, so saying, held it up. She reached for it, but withdrew her hand and said: "No, I guess not."

Still she did not leave the room. I urged her to take the

candy, and she replied: "All right, if you will have some, I will have the rest."

Breaking the bar of candy, I kept part of it and handed her the remainder.

In the following session she was in excellent spirits. As she walked into the room she remarked: "I haven't felt nearly the same tension about coming. A lot of things tied together. I feel wonderful for a change. It's a funny thing, the suggestion you made while I was asleep. It was one of the most rewarding experiences I ever had. It was a clear-cut situation. Something I understood. I saw clearly what I do, transposing into situations right now how I feel toward my father. I can see from that how I react to people on a primitive basis. I'm inclined to look forward to hypnoanalysis, but dread it at the same time, because some time I will ask you for something that you will refuse. It's the refusal that is so disastrous, because there is no way out for me. I don't feel I have recourse to anything. My father would go off for a while, for a couple of days, but I never asked to go with him. I always wanted to. There was nothing I could do about it."

Under hypnosis she was confronted with the same experimental conflict that had been induced in the last session. Upon awakening she looked back, noticed the candy, and suddenly became very distraught and anxious. At first she remained mute, but when urged to express what she was thinking about, she replied: "I just remembered something. Something you said. Every time I so much as think of asking for the candy, I can't do it. As if my life depended on it. I can't take anything from you. If I were to reach my hand out, you might cut it or hit me. I feel as if I'm going to die. I want to ask for it. The last measure of self-protection that I have is not asking for it. I'm anxious because not asking for it is what I don't want. To ask for anything is like losing control of myself. It's admitting I want anything. I think the only reason I want that damn candy is because of your suggestion. I don't want anything."

Upon being rehypnotized she was given the suggestion that she would ask me for the candy if she wanted to; she would be able to do this because it would not matter too much to her whether she took it or not. Upon awakening she sighed softly, asked for the candy, and seemed pleased.

On the next day she began the hour by talking about the indignity of being a woman. "Anything that anyone says that tends to distinguish between man and woman," she said, "I find irritating. I have a conviction that being a woman is one indication of inferiority. After I left last time I had a feeling to myself for a while of being triumphant. Maybe you made a technical error. The thing I've been trying to put out of my mind is the fascination my father's genitals had for me. I can remember seeing him in the bathtub. I felt I must not ask questions about how he was made. I can remember now the intense feelings I had. That is somehow tied up with the way I feel now. That interest seems entirely unjustifiable and yet I'm just beginning to realize its very persistence. The first thing that I thought of when you offered me the candy was that its shape resembled a penis, and I wondered what made me think of it. Here is what really made me feel confused. It's so ridiculous and illogical. It has nothing to do with what I know. I suddenly realized one reason I felt deficient and inadequate was that I didn't have a penis. And that's it! It is so hard to talk about, because it's so illogical. It's as if I might want your penis and ask for it, and you would refuse."

In the next few sessions the patient expressed strong feelings of hopelessness. Under hypnosis she was urged to work on the problem of understanding what her feeling of hopelessness was based upon. After coming out of hypnosis, she remarked: "I feel better in a way. It's a strange thing. One of the things I am thinking of is I am fond of you, and, in the background, I've got to be careful. I've got to do everything to keep on the good side. I used to have a fantasy that everything would be O.K. if I were sitting on your lap. More recently it's changed its form. Everything would be O.K. if I could go to you and throw my arms around you. The other part of the fantasy is that you put your arms around me, comfort me, and everything is O.K. The fear is either it will be refused or else rebuffed."

An extreme state of resistance followed, which was verbalized by the patient as follows: "I just feel as if I've got to do something, and I have the most dire feeling I can't talk. It's appalling how the same things keep coming up in a pattern. There is a great difference now, for I know that when I do something neurotic, it does not prevent it. I can see how I use hopelessness. I think your expectation is for me to stop thinking of the hopelessness, but if I can feel hopeless, I don't have to face the situation. What is so terribly difficult is feeling two ways about you, a feeling of being trapped. The anxiety I feel about you is that suddenly I might say something or do something that will cause you to get angry."

Shortly thereafter, the patient became aware of a feeling of hostility. She remarked: "It's the funniest thing the way I feel. I'm furious with you. I would like to catch you in a mistake, to be rude or something, in order not to feel small and inferior. The trouble is, the alternative to feeling this way toward you is what I felt for quite a while—affection. The trouble is that when I do, I feel as if I had to be in complete possession. The feeling of liking is dangerous. It's a feeling that if I let it go too far and express it, I would insist on exclusive possession. That's what the fantasy I had of throwing my arms around you meant. Affection is dangerous because it leads to wanting to absorb you completely, and no one is going to submit to that. Rejection is inevitable. I suppose in coming here I react as if I go home to Father who couldn't really seem to tolerate anything that was just my idea. When I love, I'm very demanding. I want everything, and there is no end. Sometimes I feel I am a dangerous person, like dynamite—that I might set off something if I don't hold myself back."

The feeling of rage persisted for about two weeks. During this time the patient had a number of fantasies about having temper tantrums whenever she came to see me. She remarked that she felt that all close contacts, especially with men, could lead only to a sexual relationship. The fear she felt was that she was laying herself open to a sexual attack or that she herself would make sexual demands on me. Under hypnosis she was encouraged to work on this problem. Upon awakening she expostulated: "There's something I never thought of before, never seriously. Behind everything, I feel tremendously aggressive toward you. I never felt it before. I don't want it at all. I feel as if it were absolutely impossible to do something which really expresses hatred. There is another feeling, as if you are going to stab me. It's the same fear I have during intercourse, only I don't let myself feel it as intensely. It's the same fear I had when father was angry. I mentioned that I had a dream. The feeling in the dream was good, and that you were kind and sympathetic. What I didn't say was what I wanted to do. I didn't want to tell you what the dream was about. What I wanted to do was to talk about masturbation." At this point she screamed: "If it's the last thing in the world, I don't want to talk about it!"

The next day she mailed a letter to me that she had written in a "half waking state." It read as follows:

I hate the male genitals. I just want to tear them off and stamp them on the ground. Scrotum, penis, everything—the penis hanging limply is disgusting, but one which is straight and stiff is horrible, and those are my real feelings. Thinking about them makes me want to masturbate, and I feel as if I shouldn't. I know I shouldn't. It's a horrible thing to do because it makes everything worse. It makes me feel powerful and almost happy, but afterward I am disgusted because I gave in to it. But I always do. When I went to bed tonight, I didn't feel like masturbating, but now I do, and I don't want to. It is degrading. All of sex is horrible and degrading because you have to give in to it. I don't want to give in to anything.

What must I do to avoid this horrible feeling of impotence? I can't wish that I were a man and had a man's genitals, because when I do I feel like masturbating, and I have never let myself feel very guilty about that. But now I do. He wants to take that too away from me. What will I have left? Only love that is hatred and a vicious, impotent longing. If I could get ahold of him somewhere else than behind that desk, I'd show him that being a man isn't so wonderful after all. Oh, what is this all about—I don't really hate him at all. I am just terrified now because of the uncontrollable need to masturbate. And it never worried me before, except I was afraid some time I would find it didn't work any more or I wouldn't be satisfied and would never get to sleep. I don't think I'll do it any more. No, I can't say that.

Why did he have to mention that candy? I'd forgotten it. I didn't take it. I didn't—really. Every time I think of it, I think of the fact that

all men have genitals like that.   My father kept going around without any
clothes on.   That was wrong.   Then I feel tense, and there is no way to let
it out except by masturbating, and why should I feel so upset about that?
There is nothing wrong with it, but I do—around and around, over and over.
I hate myself, and I am sure he would, even though I know he wouldn't if he
knew what a horrible impasse this is and what I really want to do.   I want
to go behind that desk of his and act just as loving as I feel, and then, when I
don't feel loving any more, I would like to hurt him with my hands.   But
there is no way I can be satisfied.   I don't want to talk about it.   I can't
get out from behind this wall any more.   I am so afraid.   I am very brittle.
It is so easy to find fault with things.

He would defend himself, and he is stronger than I am.   I don't want to
know what this all means.   I want just to be very angry and tear things off
and apart.   Then he can see what I am really like underneath.   Nothing,
only hatred.   Even my love is just to cover hatred.   Why am I so defeatist?
Giving up so much?   I must give up in order to avoid anything I hate because
then I cannot defend myself.   He could use knives and innumerable small
ways of hurting.   I have no protection.   He means well, but I can't accept it.
If I had a picture of him, I would cut it with a knife and feel better.

In associating to this material, the patient expressed the idea
that any feeling relating to sexual experience was masculine
in nature.

The working through of this material involved a considerable
period, but a different attitude emerged, as reflected in the
following statement of the patient: "I can see I have a resistence
to getting well, to going forward.   I feel that it is dangerous
to enjoy myself too much, and that by moving forward and
getting well I might incur hurt.   I want to be cautious and not
give up the idea I am helpless because that is a safe resort.
That's true.   I can see how I have always felt, that I could
solve everything by being masculine.   Then I could be active
and forceful and experience sexual pleasure.   I can see too why
I found it impossible to accept an attitude toward life that was
optimistic because that involves danger.   Before, when I felt
affectionate, I believed I did it to cover up hostility, but now I
learned to let myself feel affectionate for the first time.   This
is a different story."

The tremendous amount of activity that is stirred up by
hypnosis can be very disturbing.   It is essential to gage the
capacity of the ego to absorb the unconscious material as it

emerges, and to respect the patient's repressions; taking care that he does not become too conscious of his repressed impulses until he has developed sufficient strength to absorb their meaning. Realization on the part of the patient that he is employing defensive devices that are producing a falsification of reality, and an interference with proper adaptation, creates the first spark of insight. Once it is integrated, insight has a profound effect in restoring the ego to a more mature and realistic level of functioning.

It is essential to mobilize every positive element and every incentive to overcome the intellectual myopia associated with resistance. Appeals must be made to the patient's desire to get well and to whatever other spontaneous forces of mental health remain. Perhaps the most powerful tool in the removal of resistance is a positive relationship with the analyst.

The hypnotic transference, which is utilized to analyze the resistance, is to an extent neurotically motivated. However, there is operative in it also a healthy element, born of the desire to enter into a cooperative and unambivalent relationship. As the patient's ego grows in strength, he becomes more and more able to tolerate anxiety and more capable of subjecting his unconscious impulses to the light of reason.

It is always essential to remember, even during hypnosis, that resistance has a strong protective value. The patient will usually reject any insight that is too traumatic, or he will toy with it for a while, then forget it. However, through careful suggestions, he may gain insight as to how and why the resistance is operating. First of all he must be made aware of the resistance. Merely calling his attention to it makes him concentrate on a specific task. Thus he will not burn up all his energy in maintaining the resistance, but will direct some of it to tracing down its meaning.

Once a resistance related to the transference develops, it is essential to abandon other tasks until it is analyzed, because the patient will not be productive while battling the analyst. It is best at first not to probe too deeply for unconscious material, but rather to work intensively upon the immediate interpersonal relationship. To aid in the process, the patient must be impressed with the fact that there is nothing morally bad about his showing certain defensive attitudes in the form of resistance.

The dealing with transference resistances, even during hypnoanalysis, may be a prolonged affair  This is particularly so in the character disorders. Here there is a confounding resistance that prevents the ego from absorbing the full meaning of the unconscious material as it becomes apparent through hypnoanalysis. The patient may acknowledge the presence of certain unconscious drives, he may even understand their irrational nature and historical origin, but this pseudo-insight provokes little change in his customary life adjustment. The entire analytic process is intellectualized, the patient using his insight to fortify himself against pain. His relationship with the analyst never proceeds to a level of positive feeling shorn of hostility and inordinate expectations.

In infantile, narcissistic character structures particularly, intellectuality serves as a defense against unconscious impulses. Habitually there is a repression of affective aspects of the patient's personality, and mastery is sought through intellectual control. Any experience of feeling is regarded as catastrophic. By a curious transformation, the defense itself may become a vicarious means of gratifying nonpermissible drives as represented in hostile and sexual impulses. Another secondary gain hoped for from this facade is that of acceptance by the analyst.

Patients who have a tendency to isolate emotional components from emerging unconscious material may make the latter acceptable to themselves by repressing the affective content. Frequently they strive to neutralize their panic by means of foresight and reason. During therapy they give the impression of being very active, and at first seem to work at hypnoanalysis extraordinarily well. Even though they make a brilliant feat of minutely analyzing their inner mental processes, little change occurs. Often the patient will involve the analyst in long dialectic arguments that take on the nature of debates. Words replace experiences and constitute a defense against feelings.

Interpretation of this type of defense is bound to create great turmoil in the patient. There will be an inability to associate freely, consciously or in hypnosis. The patient is prone to feel attacked and criticized by the analyst. "Negative therapeutic reactions" are common, the patient responding to important interpretations not with insight or relief, but with depression and discouragement. Hostility may be directed at the analyst in an effort to annihilate his therapeutic work.

It is essential to remind every patient not to get too distressed if cure is not immediate. Some patients are confounded and depressed when they find, in spite of their own wishes, that they go on reacting to their various trends. It may be necessary to explain that reaction patterns that have become established over so long a period cannot be removed in a few sessions. They are habits that call for re-education.

Suggesting to the patient under hypnosis that he will accept the analyst as an ally or friend is usually useless if the patient does not really feel that way. It is best to suggest under hypnosis that he will work on his immediate feelings toward the analyst. He should also be reminded that he need not accept any interpretations until he feels ready to do so. In this way the ego is aided in digesting unconscious impulses, and there is more likelihood of a carry-over into waking life of the material released during hypnosis.

A very common resistance is associated with the fear of getting well. This fear is rooted in the patient's conviction that he will be overwhelmed if he gives up his defenses, since he is not strong enough to function as he is. Associated with this is a refusal to bear the pain consequent to the uncovering of unconscious material. In treating this type of resistance, it is necessary to expose the ego to graduated doses of anxiety, in order to teach it to bear the pain essential to getting well. At the same time the individual must be strengthened to such a degree that he can tolerate frustration and does not have to react with infantile withdrawal or attack mechanisms whenever things do not go his way.

In dealing with resistances, setbacks must be expected. Mental health is won only after a long and painful fight.

Change is never in a consistently forward direction. An insight takes hold and the patient improves. This improvement is momentary, and the patient often will go backward with an intensified resistance. He reintrenches himself with all his previous defenses as he delves deeper into his repressed drives. Anxiety forces a swing back to habitual modes of coping with fear and danger. This is not a setback in the true sense, because new insights emerge, and the individual integrates what has happened to him into the framework of his rational understanding. Usually he will gain from this experience and take another step forward. Again, however, as he experiences anxiety, he will return to his old methods of dealing with stress or will resort to disguised adaptations of his defenses. In association with this there may be discouragement and a feeling of helplessness. But this time the reintrenchment is more easily overcome by interpretation. With the development of more insight there is further progress; and then there may again be a regression to old defenses. The curve of improvement is jerky, but with each relapse the patient learns an important lesson. The neurotic way of adaptation is used less and less, and as the patient gains cognizance of what is happening to him, he is rewarded with a feeling of having made real progress.

## REFERENCES

1. LINDNER, R. M.: Rebel without a cause: The hypnoanalysis of a criminal psychopath. N. Y.: Grune & Stratton, 1944.
2. BRENNAN, M., AND KNIGHT, R. P.: Hypnotherapy for mental illness in the aged. Bull. Menninger Clin. 7: 188–98, 1943.

# XX

## HYPNOSIS AND INTERPRETATION

WHILE the transference relation with the analyst is the crucible in which ego change is forged, interpretation is the chief tool implementing the transformation. Interpretation consists of seeing beyond the façade of manifest thinking, feeling, and behavior into unconscious meanings and motivations.

Interpretations made during hypnoanalysis are, as in psychoanalysis, of two types. The first is concerned with the varied resistances and defenses of the patient; the second, with the content of the unconscious material. During psychoanalysis the interpretation of the material is from the surface inward. One deals with superficial attitudes and reaction tendencies, then progressively with more profound ones, arriving at deeper and deeper strata as the patient successfully resolves his various resistances. During hypnoanalysis the material is uncovered in a less orderly fashion, because some of the resistances may be cut through almost immediately as a result of the hypnotic state.

A pertinent problem is how to interpret the unconscious material that is disgorged during hypnoanalysis. Should the analyst reveal its meaning directly to the patient in the waking life, in the hope that the positive transference induced by hypnosis will enable the ego to tolerate the repressed impulses, or should he apply the lesson learned from psychoanalysis, namely, that the patient must arrive at insight through his own efforts?

Some years ago, when I first started working with hypnoanalysis, I decided to experiment by presenting to the patient a verbatim account of his hypnotic productions, in an attempt to enlist his conscious understanding and cooperation. The reaction to this technic varied in different patients. In some cases it produced a denial of the material as a fantastic product

of the imagination. In others there was a superficial acceptance of the material, but with an isolation of its emotional
content. Frequently the confrontation muddled up the
transference, since tremendous hostility was provoked. I
became more and more convinced of the irrationality of this
technic. It became apparent that the patient behaved as a
hysteric does after a fugue when he is confronted with his
actions and experiences. In the face of the overwhelming
evidence that confronts him, the patient is unable to deny his
productions. Yet they seem so unreal to him that he cannot
absorb their significance.

When, on the other hand, the material as it appears in
the hypnotic state is discussed with the patient during the
trance, he seems capable of understanding its meaning much
more thoroughly than in waking life. He is also able to
work through the implications with far greater facility. It
is therefore possible to take up unconscious trends with the
patient as they arise, permitting him freedom in discussion
while interpolating whatever interpretations appear to be
justified. However, in many patients a curious dissociative
state develops. While they seem to have considerable insight
during hypnosis, they behave in the waking state as though
they have not the slightest awareness of their unconscious
drives. In such cases it is sometimes possible to deal with the
patient as if he were two separate personalities, enlisting the
aid of the hypnotic personality in handling the resistances that
appear in the waking personality. In other cases this dissociative process is not at all apparent, and the patient reacts with
tremendous resistance during both the hypnotic and the waking
states.

The activity inherent in hypnoanalysis is not without
disadvantage, for any attempt to manipulate the patient's
thinking, and to plan in advance the topics to be discussed,
leads to much confusion. To a large extent the patient
himself must lead the way. This will necessitate a proper
balancing of activity and passivity on the part of the analyst.
Premature activity may force the patient to repress a significant

impulse. A passive attitude is justified when one wishes a trend to develop spontaneously and fully. After it comes to the surface, and particularly as transference phenomena become manifest, the nature, origin, and implications of the trend can be tracked down more aggressively. Activity is of course required when resistance develops, and the aim here is to demonstrate to the patient how and why he is evading certain unconscious derivatives, or defending himself against the analyst or the analytic process. In his activity the analyst must avoid authoritarian injunctions and commands. He must also minimize reassurance.

During the early stages of therapy it is essential to avoid all interpretations that provoke anxiety or stimulate resistance, and to concentrate on making the hypnotic experience one in which the patient can find whatever values he senses to be of importance. Despite deep hypnosis, the patient's ego can still be tortured by anxiety when conflicts are touched upon. This may be expected, since anxiety functions even in sleep, in which ego withdrawal is even more pronounced than in the trance state. The patient's superego is not eliminated by hypnosis; it is merely held in suspension. To a certain extent it is temporarily replaced by the hypnotist. Directing the patient to tackle anxiety-provoking acts prematurely may initiate considerable resentment of the analyst, which can interfere with a good interpersonal relationship. The patient will feel as though he is being seduced by hypnosis to expose himself to dangers that he has so far assiduously avoided. His distrust of the analyst may express itself in adoption of numerous defenses against him. Resistance may then become extreme, reaching even the point of rebelliousness, and sometimes there ensues a loss of the motive for being hypnotizable.

For a similar reason the relationship with the analyst must not be jeopardized by any suggestions or tasks not concerned with the patient's own problems. A therapeutic hypnosis should never be used for hypnotic experiments, since these are always subject to the patient's internal evaluation and eventual recognition as not pertinent to his treatment. The analyst will then be placed in a position that is not favorable to the therapeutic aim. An exception to this rule may be made if it is necessary to induce an experimental neurosis, as when it is desired to demonstrate to the patient the workings of his unconscious. Patients ordinarily do not resent experiments, provided these have a definite meaning and function. It is necessary always to be honest with the patient and to inform him of the nature of the experiment and its aim—if not at the time of its performance, then later, after the experiment has accomplished its purpose.

A most important factor in facilitating absorption and integration of interpretations is a cooperative and friendly relationship with the analyst. The assumption of the hypnotic state implies the existence of some degree of positive transference. However, the positive transference present in initial phases of therapy is soon replaced by a medley of attitudes and feelings. The analyst acts as a living symbol into which the patient projects his inner impulses and feelings. He is bound to feel destructive or hostile attitudes toward the analyst as repressed inner feelings come to the surface. Interpretation to the patient of his various transference attitudes is, as in psychoanalysis, of greatest value in synthesizing within the ego repressed elements of the personality.

The ability to integrate interpretations depends always on the capacity of the ego to absorb the meaning of unconscious trends. One must never lose sight of the fact that the ego is the sole arbiter of any proposed changes. Progress is achieved only when the ego is willing to utilize the material presented to it for the purpose of achieving a more mature type of integration. No matter how accurate the interpretations, anxiety may motivate the ego to reject their validity.

Hypnosis is capable to a certain extent of removing resistance to interpretation by helping the ego to master the anxiety associated with acceptance of it. Nevertheless, resistance can remain a chief obstacle to the incorporation of interpretations. Resistance can often be minimized by a proper handling of the transference, eliminating as many negative elements as possible. Careful demonstration to the patient of how negative attitudes are operating, their defensive purpose, and of how they are related not to the immediate situation but to inner impulses, helps to promote positive feelings toward the analyst that are most conducive to acceptance of interpretations.

Resistance may also be reduced by proper timing of interpretations. Interpretations are best withheld until the patient displays a certain amount of insight, thus indicating a degree of ego strength favorable to understanding. Interpretations prematurely presented to the patient either during hypnosis or in the working state will, as in psychoanalysis, create resistance, since they act as a warning to the ego that its defenses nave been penetrated and that a further attack is impending.

Because the ego lies closer to the unconscious in deep hypnosis, the patient may appreciate his unconscious motivations better when he is in the trance state than when he is awake. As a result he may verbalize a number of traumatic memories and unconscious trends. His ability to talk about them indicates that his ego under hypnosis is sufficiently strong to tolerate interpretations. The fact that he verbalizes his impulses and accepts interpretations in the trance does not mean that he has the capacity to accept them in waking life. There is always a temptation to bombard the patient with divulged material after he awakens. Even though the material may seem innocuous, it is essential to remember that it has been repressed because the individual is unable to tolerate its existence or its implications. It is always best to gage the extent to which one may go in presenting interpretations to the patient when awake by the amount of insight he appears to evince after awakening. Awareness of neurotic drives during hypnosis is a sign that the ego is beginning to harden sufficiently to shed its resistances. One may reasonably expect that conscious abandoning of resistance will occur after a time. The analyst should therefore avoid plunging in with too deep interpretations, to avoid a reintrenchment of the ego in its habitual defenses.

When the patient is unable to express in the hypnotic state the unconscious trends activated by the transference, it is probable that the ego is still too weak to acknowledge their existence. The trends may of course be brought up in an indirect manner, or they may be so highly symbolized in writing, drawing, play, dramatic, or dream productions that they evade the vigilance of the repressive processes. Under such circumstances interpretations must be cautiously applied and should be presented in proportion to the existing awareness. Otherwise the patient may respond with hostility or with panic, fearing the same kind of anxiety that originally fostered the repression.

Neurotic defenses are elaborated in early life by a weak ego threatened with overwheming anxiety. The mature accretions that later invest the ego may not destroy the core of helplessness laid down in childhood. The patient, afraid of being overwhelmed by feelings of catastrophic helplessness that once threatened to destroy him, will, when such an experience is imminent, attempt to overcome the threat by employing the same defenses that protected him originally. Logic plays no part in this process.

The rational approach in dealing with an ego that has swathed itself in impenetrable defenses is through an analysis of resistance. Interpretation of the resistance accomplishes the purpose of confronting the patient with the question of what he is defending himself against. This leads to an uncovering of unconscious impulses, fears, and conflicts and opens the way of access to deeper and deeper material. The dangerous nature of the material again stimulates anxiety and mobilizes further resistances, usually of an unconscious nature. It is essential to demonstrate to the individual repeatedly the manifold disguises that his resistances may assume, for unconscious resistances can crumble only when their conscious derivatives are presented to the patient. The interpretation of layers of resistance progressively exposes the deepest drives and impulses and ultimately leads to original resistances. Only through such work is the patient able to appreciate the purpose of his resistance, its historical origin, his active participation in maintaining it, and, finally, what unconscious impulses the resistance is opposing. This permits him to tolerate more and more undisguised derivatives of his impulses and eventuates in a gradual recovery of repressed elements of the personality.

How aggressive the attack on the resistances should be depends upon the quantity of anxiety that is present and upon the ability of the ego to withstand the attack. Interpretation of resistances will often produce tension, anxiety, and hostility. If the patient is already suffering from as much anxiety as he can stand, the additional emotional burden may be too difficult for him to bear, and he may react with an increase of resistance. In such cases it is essential to proceed more cautiously. On the other hand, if the patient manages to repress his anxiety through the operation of neurotic defenses, a more aggressive attack on the resistance is necessary. This must be undertaken as early as possible, in order to mobilize anxiety for the purpose of increasing self-observation.

The manner in which interpretations are presented is also of vital importance in determining the acceptance of components that the ego is warding off. In hypnoanalysis the patient may be confronted with his deepest strivings in a relatively pure form. There may be unmistakable evidences of hostility, erotic strivings, castration fears, and penis envy. To present such facts to the patient may accomplish little or nothing. As a general rule an interpretation is futile, either in the waking state or during hypnosis, if the patient does not have an idea of what is going on. Interpretation will produce no real change until the unconscious is represented by preconscious material familiar to the patient. Consequently, when an unconscious derivative makes its appearance in the field of awareness, the patient's attention may be directed to considering what may be behind the derivative. For instance, one patient, while discussing his relationship to me in glowing terms, became aware, through my calling his attention to it, of the clenching of his fists and the tension of his muscles.

At first he denied these facts, but as I repeatedly called his attention to his mannerisms, and as I presented him with the possibility that there might be a reason why he became tense and clenched his fists, he suddenly became aware of hostile feelings.

It is essential to demonstrate to the patient the connection between his symptoms, feelings, and attitudes, in order to show him how a purposeful trend runs through his life. He must learn that his behavior is not a series of random events, but that it has continuity and meaning. He must also realize that his symptoms are not fortuitous and that he is actually bringing about what he believes he is experiencing passively. He must become aware of the purpose of his evasions, of how he fallaciously draws the past into the present, of what compromises he makes with life, and of the consequences of these compromises on his psychobiologic functioning. It is also essential to trace his symptoms back to their historical origins. Here the manner in which interpretations are made is also of the greatest importance. It matters little how accurate our interpretations are, if the patient is unable to understand their meaning and to integrate them within himself in the form of insight.

In tracing the genetic development there is often a tendency to interpret present behavior as if it were a mere stereotyped repetition of earlier patterns in the relationship to the parents. As a practical matter, this type of explanation usually has little effect on the patient. It is true that the individual carries over in his character structure attitudes and patterns molded out of specific conditionings in his early interpersonal relationships. It is true also that he reacts to people as if they were virtually reincarnations of his parents, with attitudes, fears, and demands such as he expressed in his early relationships. However, such a repetitive process does not occur automatically. It is dynamically motivated by needs in the individual so intense that no amount of logic can swerve him from his purpose. To say to the patient that he has hostilities or erotic wishes directed to the analyst because the latter is a symbol of his mother, toward whom he once had an erotic urge that was repressed, is not really a helpful interpretation. What is essential is that he understand what motivations underlie the present emergence of hostile or erotic feelings toward the analyst. Ultimately of course we are concerned with why and under what circumstances the patient developed certain attitudes toward his parents that have functioned as nuclei of his later interpersonal strivings. Explaining to the patient that unresolved strivings in relation to his parents must be present, because the analyst is a parental surrogate toward whom he has irrational feelings, arouses merely an intellectual acknowledgment without any deeper understanding.

Once we concede that all behavior serves a dynamic purpose, we must attempt to define the purpose behind the patient's present behavior. For instance, we must discern the reasons why the patient feels erotic in the analytic situation. In analyzing the motives behind his erotism we may find that he is becoming more and more anxious about the analyst and that his erotic feelings constitute a wish to absorb the latter within himself in order to gain exclusive love and support. Or the patient may have become more and more fearful of the analyst and may wish to disarm him by expressing extreme devotion and sexual love.

If the patient acts in a hostile manner toward the analyst, it is not sufficient to show him that he is using the analyst as a father substitute, creating a new childhood situation in the present. It would be more meaningful to discover the immediate cicumstances associated with the hostility. The patient may feel frustrated by the analyst, for no apparent reason. Upon investigation the analyst may discover that the reason behind the frustration feeling is a secret desire to engage in an extramarital relation, along with a fear that the analyst will frown on such a venture.

To interpret the patient's strivings as related to something that is happening to him in the present provides him with a picture of his interpersonal attitudes in operation. It permits him to see how his drives relate to feelings that actually have no source in his present day reality. He comes to realize that his feelings do not arise out of nowhere and that he is not working with intangibles. Eventually he may be able to appreciate how similar impulses operated also in his relationships with important persons in the past, and that there too they served a vital purpose of a sort similar to the purpose they serve now. Considerable activity on the part of the analyst may be necessary, since the patient usually has a tremendous amount of resistance to divulging the motives behind his feelings. The patient's drives, neurotic as they are, constitute for him a way of life that he may not desire to relinquish.

One of the tasks of hypnoanalysis is the recovery of important unconscious memories and experiences. The mere enucleation of forgotten traumatic events will not in itself correct the damage that has been done to the ego. While it is true that the ego has been rendered weak by inimical childhood happenings, other defensive attitudes have also been elaborated on the basis of experiences relating to persons and circumstances in the patient's later life. Interpersonal reactions are composed of a chain of patterns that show a continuity, each link predisposing the individual to later reactions. If the patient is to understand how his early inimical experiences relate themselves to his present behavior, it is necessary to analyze and to interpret the intermediate links. This does not mean a discarding of important deep material that is brought up during hypnoanalysis. It means that the patient himself must be given the task of working back from his immediate character patterns and interpersonal attitudes to disclose the connection with the deeper experiences and impulses. In hypnoanalysis the process of establishing a connection occurs rapidly, inasmuch as the unconscious material readily penetrates into awareness. However, one must not forget the important step of correlating the patient's present behavior with his unconscious impulses.

The proper interpretation of the transference during hypnoanalysis makes it possible to establish the connections with these deeper impulses. It must be emphasized again that in interpreting the transference, it is not enough to tell the patient that he is acting out an irrational striving that has its origin in what has gone before in his early relationships with his father, mother, or siblings. Such an explanation is interesting and possibly true, but practically judged it is without therapeutic value. What is important is to demonstrate to the patient the reason why such infantile reactions persist and what purpose they serve in the present.

One patient during hypnoanalysis brought up material relating to a desire to swallow and incorporate everything around him. There were fantasies of devouring his mother's breasts or of amalgamating with her through sexual intercourse. In regression he uncovered traumatic memories related to a feeling of having been rejected by his mother because of the birth of a younger brother. He also resented the fact that his mother was more devoted to his father than to himself. There were fantasies of being pursued and devoured by wild beasts, which he recognized as symbols of the mother.

From these evidences and from the manner in which he related himself to people, it seemed apparent that he had strong dependency strivings. He was, however, not at all aware of his dependency, but he was conscious of how infuriated he became at the shortcomings of others. At this stage in therapy, gastro-intestinal symptoms, which were among his most immediate complaints, became exaggerated. Under hypnosis he became aware of his hostility toward me, but consciously he denied feelings of rage. When it was pointed out that he appeared to be harboring a tremendous amount of hostility that was being directed inward, producing his dyspepsia and cramps, he seemed incredulous. He refused to believe that he had any hostility and was particularly unwilling to accept the fact that rage could cause his symptoms.

A hypnotic experimental conflict was then created, on the basis of a fictitious situation in which he was in competition with a younger man for an important job. In view of his own performance rating and the number of years that he had devoted to his work, he felt that he deserved the job. However, his employer gave the job to a younger man who was less qualified for it than he. This created intense anger in him. He was urged to feel this emotion upon awakening, but to forget the experimental conflict itself. Upon termination of the trance the patient immediately complained of feeling depressed and of severe abdominal cramps that made him want to go to the toilet. The cramps continued for almost twenty minutes, while he became more and more agitated and depressed. He was then rehypnotized and instructed to recall the experimental conflict when he woke up and to assimilate the meaning of the experiment. He was then able to see that hostile feelings can have important physical effects. A later repetition of this experiment at his own request produced an identical response and helped to convince him that his physical symptoms actually did evolve from hostile feelings.

The next stage in the interpretive process was to point out to him how his present symptoms were being exaggerated by his immediate relationship to me. Suggestions that he dream of his feelings toward me caused him to have a number of dreams in which he was being fed, but in which he always experienced frustration. He gradually became aware of the fact that his prime motivation in coming to therapy was not to get well, but to obtain a formula for living that would enable him to function perfectly at all times and to be an outstanding success in every activity in which he participated. The reason why he wanted to function perfectly and to be successful was to win the love and approval that he believed he deserved. What he expected from therapy was a magical fulfillment of these strivings. His inability to realize these desires caused him to feel frustrated and stimulated hostile attitudes. He could not express the latter because this might additionally prevent my ministering to his wants.

The patient was thus able to appreciate the fact that the symptoms for which he sought therapy—namely, depression and intestinal symptoms—were related to hostile attitudes, and that the latter stemmed from a frustration of his dependency strivings. The exaggeration of his symptoms during therapy, produced by a frustrated dependency in relation to me, made it possible for him to gain insight into this mechanism. Had I merely pointed out that he was hostile, he probably would have been convinced that he was bad or that I was disgusted with his shortcomings. Showing him that he was demanding my complete devotion, that deep down he wanted to be the favored patient and child and companion, and that he felt rejected when I did not express a preference for him, opened up a new point of view. He was then concerned not so much with his symptoms or with his hostile attitude as with the motives that made his symptoms and hostility inevitable. As he worked through these problems, he gradually became able to approach deeper and deeper strata and to appreciate how his dependency striving was founded on want of love and on lack of assertiveness and independence, these qualities having been crushed in him by his domineering, overprotective mother.

The order in which unconscious material is brought to the surface during hypnoanalysis varies in different patients. Some are prone to dissociate the past entirely from themselves and to think solely in terms of their current interpersonal relationships. Often there is here an intense fear of early traumatic experiences and conditionings, and strong guilt feelings prevent the individual from appraising his real attitudes toward his parents and siblings. Even in deep hypnosis there is reluctance to talk about early experiences. This resistance is fortunately more easily removed in hypnoanalysis than in psychoanalysis, particularly when regression and revivification are used.

When a resistance to recall of early experiences exists, it is unwise to call the patient's attention during waking life to the material that has been hypnotically produced. It is always best to protect the patient by telling him to forget the material until he feels sufficiently strong and sufficiently convinced of the truth of it to accept it. The ability to verbalize early memories and experiences, or to bring up unconscious attitudes and drives, has an erosive effect on the resistances and eventually enables the individual to accept the material on a waking level.

In a certain number of patients the analyst will be overwhelmed with unconscious material elaborated during hypnoanalysis, while no effort is made to relate this material to the present psychobiologic malfunctioning. In such persons there is also a dissociation of the past from the present. There is a minimization of present feelings, in the desire to conserve the secondary gain derived from the current neurosis. The outpouring of the unconscious material here is somewhat in the nature of a confessional. The patient may seek to relieve his sense of guilt and to avoid responsibility for his symptoms through the absolution obtained in divulging his past. It is always essential to get the patient to realize that his current problems cannot be solved merely by divulging unconscious material. The material must be related to what is happening to him in the present. Hidden wishes, conflicts, fears, and early traumatic experiences certainly condition the individual's habitual behavior patterns, but it is essential to work out with him an understanding of how they manifest themselves in every act and thought in his daily life.

Another problem in hypnoanalysis is that of exactly how to interpret the unconscious material. The repressed content of the unconscious often includes fears and fantasies associated with the various bodily functions, particularly eating, excretion, and sexuality. There are hostile and destructive impulses directed to other persons and to the self. There are traumatic memories and experiences too painful to be recalled in consciousness. There are such normal strivings as desire for love, companionship, recognition, self-assertion, self-esteem, independence, and creative self-fulfillment, which have developed incompletely, or for one reason or another have been abandoned as motives. There are, in addition, neurotic drives to goals of affection, dependence, masochistic gratification, superiority, dominance, ambition, power, and detachment, as well as the conflicts that these drives initiate.

The language in which this material is expressed during hypnoanalysis is frequently that of extremely primitive and childish symbols. Often, as in psychoanalysis,[1] expression is couched in terms of various organ functions. Simple activities such as sucking, eating, excreting, and sexual functioning may represent a host of attitudes and strivings. A need for security and dependency may thus appear as a desire to suck the breast, penis, or nipple. All parts of the body, including the genital organs, may be implemented in this sucking process. Dependency may also be expressed by fantasies of cannibalistic incorporation of a real or nonexistent person. The amalgamation may be achieved by other means, as by entering the body of the person through any of the various orifices, by sexual intercourse, or by changing into a phallus and being sucked up into the vagina and womb. There may be a peculiar extension in which the person on whom the subject wishes to depend is identified with the fecal mass, with resultant overvaluation of excretory products and activities.

Hostile attitudes toward women may be represented by the biting and destroying of a female figure or of a woman's body contents, breasts, or nipples, or of a fantasied penis within her abdomen. This attack may be attempted with the mouth, anus, or penis, or with excretory products. Destructive feelings toward males may be symbolized by impulses to castrate, or to devour or incorporate the penis or the body conceived as a penis. Fantasies of eating or of expelling loved or hated persons in the form of feces may occur.

Guilt feelings and fears of retaliation may be symbolized by fantasies of being eaten or castrated by devouring animals, ghouls, monsters, or witches, of being absorbed into a vagina for purposes of destruction, of being attacked by a penis, a female sexual organ, or an imagined intravaginal penis. There may be fears of being penetrated anally by the penis of a strong man or of being injured and killed by feces. A loss of aggressiveness and intactness may be designated by a fear of castration; this in males may be accompanied with reparative attempts, and in females by a denial of the fact that there is no penis, or by frenzied attempts to secure one in fantasy from a paternal, fraternal, or maternal person in whose body a penis may be imagined to exist.

Phallic symbolism is extraordinarily common in hypno-analysis. Some persons are more prone than others to use it to express basic needs and attitudes. Sexuality here becomes a magical short cut to close relationships with people and the nucleus around which the individual's thoughts and symptoms are oriented.

Possession of an intact male organ is frequently utilized to represent a sense of aggressiveness and power. It may become the symbol of the chief values and goals in life. Strivings for strength, activity, and dominance may thus be symbolized unconsciously by a desire for a penis in a female, who may believe that possession of a penis would be a magical solution for all her problems, including the fear of functioning as a female. The same strivings may also bring about a wish for a larger and more powerful penis in a male. Submission, passivity, and subordination may be signified by the lack of a penis, and where security is sought through dependency and subordination, castration may be a goal; this is usually countered by a desire for activity and a fear of castration.

Hypnoanalysis is likely to bring out an enormous amount of sexual material, and one may get the impression that the only existing difficulties are of a sexual nature. The analyst will certainly be led into a blind alley if he takes unconscious symbolisms at their face value. Presentation to the patient of the raw oral, anal, and phallic material revealed through hypnoanalysis may be very confusing to him, not only because he desires to repress the implications of this material, but also because the language of the unconscious is inscrutable to his conscious mind. Emerging from unconscious strata, it is like foreign speech. Oberndorf[2] comments on the futility of presenting primitive symbolisms to the patient, and he warns that a preoccupation with these may retard synthetic processes that make for ego integrity. The material is of course valid, but it must always be translated into constructions that are meaningful to the patient in terms of his relationship to others.

It is not enough to demonstrate to a female patient beyond any vestige of doubt that unconsciously she desires to possess a penis. It is essential to correlate this wish with her envy of men and with her rivalry and destructiveness in relation to them. It is particularly important to understand what the desire for a penis signifies in terms of the current needs of the patient. It may for example be a means of refuting a fantasy of being irreparably injured, or it may constitute a striving for superiority that is rooted in a sense of helplessness.

Desire for or fear of castration must also be explored from the standpoint of what purpose these strivings serve in the psychic economy. It is not enough to assume that pre-occupation with castration is the mere continuance of an infantile fear or wish that never has been completely resolved. The persistence of such an impulse indicates that it serves some purpose in the present. For example, a castration fear may originate in a current feeling of loss of self and ego dissolution, a solution for which is sought in strivings for passivity and dependency, which are equated with femininity and castration. Again it must be emphasized that all conscious and unconscious behavior is dynamically motivated and has a definite meaning and function.

A man of 36 sought therapy for a condition of impotence that had plagued him more or less from the time of his marriage, seven years before. He was certain that his relationships with people were adequate in all respects. He had been a dutiful and devoted son to his parents, and, according to his own account, had never suffered from any intimidations or traumatic childhood experiences. His dominant attitude toward life, apparent to all except himself, was one of detachment. Underneath this one could sense a strong dependency on his wife, and also a well controlled hostility to the world in general. These attitudes were soon directed to me and to the hypnotic process, manifesting themselves in dreams and in various behavior patterns both in and outside of hypnosis.

Hypnoanalysis revealed that hostile feelings were extraordinarily profound in the patient's relation to his mother. As a child he had been hammered into conformity by this parent, who punished him for rebelliousness and rewarded submissiveness and obedience with gifts and favors. He recalled many instances of being rejected by her and then overwhelmed with a cloying sweetness that masked her inability to give him real love. He had tried to maintain a detached attitude toward her, yet his helplessness fostered dependency and inability to function by means of his own resources. In automatic drawing he symbolized his mother as a creature who could swallow him and suck out his penis. Strong erotic feelings toward the mother were also displayed, and there were memories of being overstimulated by sleeping with his mother until he was 9 years of age. In a number of drawings he could not differentiate himself from his mother; it was as though she and he were amalgamated into one person.

A number of early fantasies and traumatic experiences were recovered. There was one fantasy about being changed into a girl. In another his father was attacking him sexually. He realized, as a result of the material that he brought up, how confused he had always been in his attitudes toward both of his parents. He knew that he had desired to be close to his mother and to have her exclusively for himself. He hated his father for encroaching on his domain, although he appreciated his own inability to cope with this situation. Somehow he sensed the fact that favors were being bestowed on the father that were denied to him, and he was curious whenever his mother and father concealed themselves in their room.

Under regression he recovered an experience in which he chanced upon his parents in coitus. He was crushed with rage, disappointment, and fear. This event brought to a head all of his previous conflicts and fears. His first reaction was that his mother was doing something terrible to his father, like trying to suck out his penis. He was strongly repulsed by this, and he felt a peculiar alliance with his father, in that he wanted to help the latter to escape the menace of his mother. He realized that his mother did constantly undermine his father, that she depreciated him; but he feared that his mother would resent this. These recollections caused him to feel that his hostility toward his baby sister was based on the conviction that she too was seeking to take his father away from him.

He remembered other emotions that he had had toward the father; these were associated with the latter's cruel and overbearing attitude. Whenever the patient made half-hearted attempts to come closer to his father, he was rejected. He felt helpless in his conflict and found himself drifting into an attitude of hopeless dependence on his mother, conforming with her every wish and demand. At about this time he started to masturbate to excess, fearing that he was doing a forbidden thing. He was certain that if his parents should find him masturbating, they would do something drastic. Nevertheless, his masturbatory impulses were sufficiently powerful to force him to indulge, although he had aftermaths of guilt and anxiety.

The recovery of these memories and early experiences, dramatic as they were, had no apparent effect on his existing neurosis. He realized that as a result of inimical conditionings he had become excessively dependent upon his mother and had felt emasculated in the process. He also sensed the fact that he reacted toward his wife as if she were his mother. However, a great deal of work had to be done to show him why the early attitudes and strivings that he had developed out of his relationships with his parents were being transplanted, as if in pure culture, to his present day relationships. Gradually he discovered that as a result of his early experiences, he had emerged from childhood with a variety of impulses and strivings in relation to people that continued to generate a sense of hopelessness and loss of self and to arouse tremendous amounts of hostility. He began to appreciate how his self-esteem, his efforts at assertiveness, and his striving for independence had to be undermined in the face of his dependent and clinging tendencies in relation to authority and especially to authoritative women. He was then able to understand why it was that his life had been punctuated by affairs with older women, toward whom he acted as if they were actual reincarnations of his mother. He realized that he was responding to the world as if it were filled with crushing, domineering mothers, with hateful little sisters, and with rejecting, surly fathers toward whom he could feel no closeness, but with whom he sought unity. The meaning of his current homosexual dreams then became apparent. Finally, he gained insight regarding his detachment from people and his symptom of impotence, which represented an inhibition of function designed to protect him from being overwhelmed and castrated in a close interpersonal relationship with a woman.

Analytic progress is gaged by the ability of the patient to apply what he has learned from analytic interpretations to his daily reactions and experiences, until a definite change in his interpersonal relationships develops. The recognition of unconscious drives, and the realization that they are operating in the transference, do not in themselves guarantee that change will occur. Nor does it mean that the patient has the capacity for such a change. The ability to change depends upon many factors. Foremost is the desire for change. Among the motivating influences here are a sense of frustration induced by an inability to fulfill normal biologic and social needs, and a growing realization that neurotic character strivings are associated with suffering far in excess of the compensatory gratifications.

The patient's realization of the contradictions in his character structure acts as a powerful incentive to change, but it is merely the first step in the reintegrative process. For instance, if a patient exhibits a pattern of compulsive dependency as a result of succumbing to a deep feeling of helplessness, the mere recognition of his dependency and its consequences will not change his need to cling compulsively to others. It may point the way to exposing the more basic problem of his inner helplessness and devaluated self-esteem. There is, then, a need to examine the meaning of his impaired self-esteem as well as to determine its source. There is furthermore a need to appreciate what motivating factors in the individual's present setting perpetuate feelings of helplessness. Understanding the origin of the trend, tracing it to certain experiences in relation to early authorities are important steps, but these too are usually insufficient for cure. So long as the basic helplessness is not overcome, dependency has subjective values that the individual cannot and will not relinquish. While he may recognize the irrationality of his drive or its unfortunate consequences, he will compulsively hang on to it, at the same time rationalizing his motives. He may even have partial insight regarding his dependency, but deep down he may feel that he must become reconciled to it.

One of the most important forces that aids the patient in achieving lasting insight is active participation in the re-educative process. Some years ago I abandoned the practice of suggesting to the patient that he would accept interpretations given him, inasmuch as such interpretations when accepted served to motivate resistance that reinforced character strivings of masochistic submissiveness and dependency. In some patients the motivation for hypnosis is so strong that they will accept on faith the interpretations of the analyst. This acceptance is unfortunately not based on real ego strength, nor does it contribute to ego maturity. It is not an index of progress in analysis. As a general rule the patient will accept only those interpretations that have a real meaning for him or serve a vital purpose. He will reject those that are meaningless or that, in the acceptance, mobilize anxiety. Where insights are smuggled into the patient's mind as a part of the hypnotic process, they are accepted by him as an expediency to be discarded later when he no longer gets from the hypnotic state what he imagines he wants.

Hypnoanalysis differs from ordinary hypnosis in that it stimulates activity in the patient. The patient is made to feel that he must bear a considerable amount of responsibility for the therapeutic process. He understands that interpretations are to be accepted only when he feels that they are true and never because he is expected to comply with the analyst. The latter should therefore avoid mandates, but should rather phrase his interpretations tentatively, so that the patient can come to his own conclusions. Thus the analyst must avoid a dogmatic manner, for it is just possible that he may be wrong.

The relationship best suited for therapy is one of cooperation, in which the patient feels that he is an active participant and that his voice carries as much weight as that of the analyst. Insight gained in a setting in which the patient feels that he has a right to accept or reject interpretations is usually irreversible.

Creation of an experimental conflict in hypnosis often succeeds in demonstrating the dynamics of a trend or emotion when a verbal explanation fails. Insight that is gained through an actual experience is usually more lasting than that achieved through intellectual understanding. The experimental conflict is therefore an important instrument in helping the patient to assimilate interpretations.

Another way of reinforcing interpretations is that of stimulating unconscious mental activity through hypnotic suggestion. Under deep hypnosis the patient is instructed that he has a certain problem that for a number of reasons he is unable to bring to the surface. He is enjoined to begin working on the problem in order to understand what is going on inside himself. Soon he will feel strong enough to master the fear and tension that keep him in ignorance. He will gradually become more and more aware of his reactions and their meaning. Such suggestions are usually better than an injunction that he immediately remember a forgotten experience or become aware of a repressed impulse. This command may arouse so much resistance that the patient will be unable to cooperate. Sometimes a definite time period may be given him in which to work out a certain problem. This is done to protect the ego and to give it sufficient time to prepare itself for an insight. In this way the therapeutic work can proceed on an unconscious level, resistances being gradually resolved, until the ego is sufficiently strong to tolerate the insight in waking life. The patient may then suddenly become aware of certain trends within himself. Such insights of course do not come out of a clear sky, because considerable work of an unconscious nature has gone on below the surface of awareness. This phenomenon is akin to what occurs when unconscious activity of a purposeful nature eventuates in the sudden solution of a problem after a long period of perplexity.

A patient who came to therapy because of feelings of inhibition and a growing seclusiveness immediately began to manifest her tendency to detachment in the transference. Deep hypnosis failed to reveal any significant material that might explain her symptoms or her reaction to me. She was intructed while in trance to begin working on this problem and to reveal to me in automatic writing the exact day when the meaning of her behavior would become apparent to her. No progress was noted for several weeks, but finally, in the course of automatic writing, she communicated the fact that she would be able to understand what was happening inside of herself and would tell me about it the middle of the next week. She missed her appointment the day before the revelation was to be made. When she appeared the next day, she remarked that she had been extremely disturbed all during the past twenty-four hours. During the night she woke up from her sleep with a start, went over to her desk, picked up a pencil, and began writing things that she believed were so tremendously important that she had brought them along with her. She confided that she had become aware of certain reactions during treatment, and that she could see in these a similarity with her feeling about other situations in the past.

In her writings she confided that when she first met me she had been impressed with the fact that I knew my business and could help her in her problems. She put it as follows:

You told me it would take some time before there would be any definite results, but I was sure it would be all over in a month or so. My mind was full of the kind of psychiatric treatment one sees in the movies or reads in books. I was prepared for melodramatics, but there weren't any. I wanted things done for me. I didn't want to talk or to answer any questions. I wanted you to do everything. Then I began to feel as if you were laughing at me. You were superior and smug, and I hated you. I couldn't stand your questions or prying attitude. Week followed week and still no change. My mind was working all the time. Why wasn't there any change? Why didn't you do something for me? Meanwhile the treatment continued. Your very sight appalled me. I felt you were laughing behind my back. That's all you were doing. I refused to see you again, but my mother bribed me to come. I think you were trying to make fun of me, putting me to sleep. Maybe you were trying to impress me with the melodramatics I wanted.

But I don't understand why I do the things that I do in hypnosis. It all comes automatic. Maybe you wanted me to do everything you say like a dummy, like a walking dead person with no mind of my own. "Good idea," I said. "I hope it works."

How can it work? My mind is too strong. Maybe I'm fighting. I don't want to go under, but if it will help me, I'll give it a try. Then yesterday I did not want to come; I wanted to stop treatment. It wasn't doing me any good.

During the night I had a dream. There was a man sitting at a table, a tall man. He looked like you. The man was eating. I was on the other side of the table. I was hungry. The man would give me no food. Every time I would reach for food, it would disappear. I wanted to write him a letter. I reached for a fountain pen, but he took that away too and gave it to a little girl sitting in a chair near him.

The little girl looked like my sister. I think I know the reason why I felt like I did toward you. It's like in the dream. I wanted you to give me things, and you don't give me things. You give them to someone else. Maybe that's why I've been mad at everybody, and that's why I never wanted to do things myself.

The patient's recognition of her expectations of magic, her dependency, and her hostility toward people because they refused to propitiate and satisfy her whims and demands, was a tremendous stimulus to analytic progress. She was soon able to recognize that her emotional reactions during hypnotic therapy were due to the operation of trends similar in nature to those responsible for her past problems. She was able to gain insight into her sibling rivalry and her hostility toward her father and mother.

Activity on the part of the patient should especially be encouraged during the last phases of therapy. When it becomes essential that he begin to face his problems in real life, the matter may be frankly discussed with him, first under hypnosis, then on a waking level. Suggestions, if they are made, should be phrased in such a manner that they will not seem at variance with what the patient actually wants to do. It is a good idea to impress the patient with the fact that suggestions given him are actually for his benefit. Often it is advisable as a safeguard to enlist the patient's cooperation by asking him to approve the suggestions while he is under hypnosis. He should repeatedly be encouraged to discuss his problems under hypnosis and then in the waking state, in order that the analyst may ascertain how much insight he has. When it is certain that he understands himself, he must be reminded that this is only the first step in the re-educational process. It is necessary to establish new reaction tendencies. To do this he must face the erstwhile dreaded situations, not with his customary attitudes, which are oriented around neurotic misinterpretations, but with an entirely different viewpoint in line with his emerging insights. It is always necessary to respect his attitudes, opinions, and misgivings, in order that he may feel that he is respected as an individual and is not merely a puppet being maneuvered by the analyst.

Under hypnosis it may be brought to his attention that up to now he has been unable to face certain situations because they involved great danger for him. The specific problem and the related dangers as revealed through hypnoanalysis are then reviewed, and the patient is instructed to work on this material, to see whether he cannot break the vicious chain of his reacting to life with attitudes and action patterns that are related to past experiences and conditionings. For example, where his problem involves an inability to enter into competition with others, he may be urged to review the factors operating inside himself that stir up anxiety whenever he finds himself competing with another person. He may then be told that when he thoroughly understands the meaning of his reaction, he will want to deal with life on a more realistic basis and will want to enter into certain essential competitive relationships. If his problem involves a specific phobia, a review is made of the hypnoanalytic findings pertaining to the meaning and sources of the phobia. After this he may be told that when he thoroughly understands the meaning of his fear, and when he feels strong enough inside, he will want to face the situation that has previously aroused so much terror. It may be emphasized that it is essential for him to expose himself to the phobic situation over and over again, in order to experience and to master the associated emotions.

With suggestions such as these the patient does not feel forced to expose himself to danger before he feels sufficiently strong within himself to do so. The conviction grows in him that he has in the analyst a friend who understands his inner turmoil and who has no intention of catapulting him into fear-inducing situations until he feels capable of handling them.

In responsive cases, interpretation acts to stir up tremendous activity eventuating in real ego change. There are, however, certain patients in whom such a happy effect is not forthcoming. Individuals with character structures of infantile type especially are wont to regard the analyst's interpretations as a slur upon their integrity or as evidence of rejection or hostility. Interpretations never seem to penetrate the patient's resistances. He acts as if the analytic situation must guarantee him pleasure grants, even though these perpetuate his neurotic goals. He resents any attempt at making him deviate from his customary paths in life. In psychoanalysis also such patients, after many months of therapy, can recite causes and explanations of mechanisms; yet, aside from having learned an impersonal catechism by rote, they profit little from analysis.[3]

During hypnoanalysis such patients cling obstinately to their neurotic defenses. There is no reason to assume that hypnoanalysis will succeed here if psychoanalysis has failed. Often the most that can be contemplated is supportive therapy utilizing the interpersonal relationship as a growth experience from which the patient can derive values that may eventuate in a strengthening of his ego. Only when the ego is integrated on a more mature level will it be able to regard the therapeutic situation as a medium for the achievement of insight.

## REFERENCES

1. ALEXANDER, F., AND WILSON, G. W.: Quantitative dream studies. Psychoanalyt. Quart. 4: 371–407, 1935.
2. OBERNDORF, C. P.: Consideration of results with psychoanalytic therapy. Am. J. Psychiat. 99: 377, 1942.
3. IDEM: Factors in psychoanalytic therapy. Am. J. Psychiat. 98: 751, 1942.

# INDEX